D1726930

European Yearbook of International Economic Law

EYIEL Monographs - Studies in European and International Economic Law

Volume 32

Series Editor

Marc Bungenberg, Saarbrücken, Germany

Christoph Herrmann, Passau, Germany

Markus Krajewski, Erlangen, Germany

Jörg Philipp Terhechte, Lüneburg, Germany

Andreas R. Ziegler, Lausanne, Switzerland

EYIEL Monographs is a subseries of the European Yearbook of International Economic Law (EYIEL). It contains scholarly works in the fields of European and international economic law, in particular WTO law, international investment law, international monetary law, law of regional economic integration, external trade law of the EU and EU internal market law. The series does not include edited volumes. EYIEL Monographs are peer-reviewed by the series editors and external reviewers.

Patrick Wasilczyk

Fragmentation of International Trade Law Reassessed

Analyzing the Role of PTA-DSMs Based on Their Adjudication of General Exception Clauses

 Springer

Patrick Wasilczyk
Münster, Germany

ISSN 2364-8392   ISSN 2364-8406   (electronic)
European Yearbook of International Economic Law
ISSN 2524-6658   ISSN 2524-6666   (electronic)
EYIEL Monographs - Studies in European and International Economic Law
ISBN 978-3-031-40600-3   ISBN 978-3-031-40601-0   (eBook)
https://doi.org/10.1007/978-3-031-40601-0

This Springer imprint is published by the registered company Springer Nature Switzerland AG
The registered company address is: Gewerbestrasse 11, 6330 Cham, Switzerland

Paper in this product is recyclable.

Meiner Lili

Preface

This book is based on a doctoral thesis which was accepted by the Law Faculty of the University of Münster (Rechtswissenschaftliche Fakultät der Westfälischen Wilhelms-Universität Münster) in the winter term of 2022/2023.

The author has received funding from the Heinrich-Böll Foundation during the writing of the thesis.

Münster, Germany   Patrick Wasilczyk
June 2023

Acknowledgments

Writing a PhD thesis is often compared to embarking on a journey, and now that I have completed mine, I can truly say it was quite an adventure. There were beautiful moments, challenging hills, and rough patches along the way. But I did not have to face it all alone, and for that, I am incredibly grateful.

First and foremost, I want to thank my wife, Lili, for inspiring me to start this PhD journey and for being my unwavering support throughout. You listened to my rants, gave me the best advice, and most importantly, you brought our amazing son Carlo into this adventure. Without you both, none of this would have been worth it.

A big shout-out to my friends Felix Fouchard and Isabel Lischewski, who were not just colleagues but also the most supportive companions one could ask for. And to Mama, Tata, Anita, and Doreen, thank you for being there when I needed you the most.

I owe a special thank you to my supervisor, Dr. Niels Petersen, for giving me the freedom to explore and the support to write my thesis in my own way, no matter how long it took. The time I spent at the Institute for International & Comparative Public Law in Münster was filled with incredible experiences and learning.

I can't forget to mention Brian Cooper, who took the time to read my work meticulously in such a short period. Your feedback was invaluable.

Last but certainly not least, I want to express my deepest gratitude to all my friends and colleagues. Whether we met in Berlin, Hamburg, Münster, Lima, or Washington D.C., thank you for being there, keeping me company, and believing in this project. We shared unforgettable moments that I will always treasure.

This journey would not have been the same without all of you. Thank you from the bottom of my heart.

Contents

Abbreviations

ACE 18	Complementary Agreement of the Southern Common Market (Mercosur) of 1991
AdC	Cartagena Agreement Establishing the Andean Community
ALADI	Latin American Integration Association
BoP	Balance of Payments
CAN	Andean Community
Caricom	Caribbean Community
CJEU	Court of Justice of the European Union
CMC	Council of the Common Market Council (Mercosur)
CMG	Common Market Group of the Southern Common Market (Mercosur)
Comesa	Common Market for Eastern and Southern Africa
EC	European Commission
ECOWAS	Economic Community of West African States
EEA	European Economic Area
EEAA	Agreement on the European Economic Area
EFTA	European Free Trade Association
EMA	European Medicines Agency
ESM	Electronic Supplement Material
EU	European Union
HS	Harmonized Commodity Description and Coding System, also known as the Harmonized System
IATTC	Inter-American Tropical Tuna Commission
JUNAC	Junta del Acuerdo de Cartagena (predecessor of the General Secretariat of the Andean Community)
Junta	Junta del Acuerdo de Cartagena (predecessor of the General Secretariat of the Andean Community)
MEQR	Measures having equivalent effect as quantitative restrictions
MFN	Most Favorite Nation Treatment

NT	National Treatment
PO	Olivos Protocol for Dispute Settlement in the Southern Common Market (Mercosur)
PO Imp	Implementing provisions on the Olivos Protocol for Dispute Settlement in the Southern Common Market (Mercosur)
PTA/PTAs	Preferential Trade Agreement/Preferential Trade Agreements
PTA-DSM/PTA-DSMs	Dispute Settlement Mechanism of a Preferential Trade Agreement/Dispute Settlement Mechanisms of Preferential Trade Agreements
QR	Quantitative restriction
RoPPO	Rules of Procedure for the Request of Advisory Opinions to the Permanent Court of Review by the High Courts of Justice of the Member States to Southern Common Market (Mercosur)
S&D treatment	Special and differential treatment
SGCAN	General Secretariat of the Andean Community
SICA	Central American Integration System
SPS Agreement	WTO Agreement on Sanitary and Phytosanitary Measures
SPSCAN	Registry of Sanitary and Phytosanitary of the Andean Community
TdA	Treaty of Asunción establishing the Southern Common Market (Mercosur)
TdA-TLP	Trade Liberalization Program of the Treaty of Asunción establishing the Southern Common Market (Mercosur)
TdM	Treaty of Montevideo of 1980 establishing the Latin American Integration Association
TEU	Treaty on European Union
TFEU	Treaty on the Functioning of the European Union
TJCAN	Court of Justice of the Andean Community
TPR	Permanent Review Tribunal of the Southern Common Market (Mercosur)
VenCon	Constitution of Venezuela of 1999
WCO	World Customs Organization
WTO Agreement	Marrakesh Agreement Establishing the World Trade Organization

Chapter 1
Introduction

Eine Ideologie ist Ordnung auf Kosten des Weiterdenkens (An ideology is order at the expense of thinking ahead)—Friedrich Dürrenmatt

Do Dispute Settlement Mechanisms (DSMs) in Preferential Trade Agreements (PTAs, hereinafter PTA-DSMs) contribute to the fragmentation of international trade law? This question has been asked many times and many attempts had been made to answer it. The debate has given rise to criticism of PTA-DSMs from academia and civic society alike, for a variety of reasons which are complex and intertwined.

At the outset of this contribution stands the question whether and how PTA-DSMs contribute to the fragmentation of international trade law. This question arises form a twofold observation: On the one hand, the regulation of international trade is governed by the multilateral legal framework of the WTO, and at the same time by multiple PTAs which provide the rules on the process of trade liberalization between PTA partners. On the other hand, both the WTO-DSM as well as multiple autonomous PTA-DSMs can be called upon for the resolution of disputes arising within the context of international trade.

The coexistence of the rules under the legal framework of the WTO and the rules provided by PTAs calls the coherent and consistent regulation of international trade into question. This parallel structure allows for an *identical* regulatory object to be subject to rules under the legal framework of the WTO as well as those existing under the several and respective PTAs. It has been said that the PTA partners set up PTA-DSMs to secure enforcement of PTA rules to preclude the legal enforcement of WTO rules. The circumstance that WTO rules could not be implemented due to the existence of PTA-DSMs has caused them to be characterized as one of the driving forces for the fragmentation of international trade law: PTA-DSM decisions could violate substantive WTO rules, thus contributing to the diversity of regulation of

---

Supplementary Information The online version contains supplementary material available at https://doi.org/10.1007/978-3-031-40601-0_1.

P. Wasilczyk, *Fragmentation of International Trade Law Reassessed*, EYIEL Monographs - Studies in European and International Economic Law 32, https://doi.org/10.1007/978-3-031-40601-0_1

international trade. Consequently, the establishment of PTA-DSMs has been considered an institutional threat to the WTO, a means to evade the obligations arising under the multilateral legal framework of the WTO—the opposite of the *system of international trade law* established thereunder. A potential violation of WTO rules by PTA-DSM decisions has been the determining standard to measure diversity in the regulation of international trade law and thereby fragmentation of international trade law. This concept of diversity of regulation of international trade, which results in understanding fragmentation of international trade law through a WTO-PTA lens, has led to the assessment of PTA-DSM activity and its effect on *identical* regulatory objects. It has resulted in the characterization of PTA-DSMs to deliver decisions that are *incompatible* with WTO rules.

Irrespectively of this understanding, diversity in the regulation of international trade can equally be assessed from a PTA lens only: It becomes possible, firstly, to consider the variety of rules contained in PTAs concerning an *equivalent* regulatory object. Secondly, it allows us to assess PTA-DSM activity and its effect on these *equivalent* regulatory objects. Starting from these considerations, a higher diversity in the regulation of international trade, due to the existence of varying rules concerning *equivalent* regulatory objects calls into question their *systemic operation*. Even from a PTA lens only, this lack of systemic operation of multiple and varying rules on international trade, contained in different PTAs, constitutes a major challenge for these rules to understand them as a *legal system*. Consequently, the inability of multiple rules on international trade to operate systemically constitutes another standard for the measurement of diversity, since the state of regulation of international trade through PTAs can amount to such a high degree of variety that the rules contained in PTAs must be deemed *incommensurable* with one another. Ultimately, this entails a concept of the fragmentation of international trade law, which is distinct from the one developed through the assessment of PTAs and PTA-DSMs through the WTO-PTA lens.

Even under this distinct concept on the fragmentation of international trade law, the establishment and activity of PTA-DSMs can be understood as contributing to the diversity in the regulation of international trade. Whether and how PTA-DSMs deal with allegedly varying rules contained in the respective PTAs by interpreting them for resolving disputes between PTA partners has remained underexplored. On the one hand, it is imaginable that PTA-DSM issue decisions corresponding with the alleged varying rules contained in the respective PTAs. Consequently, PTA-DSMs would issue *incommensurable* decisions concerning *equivalent* regulatory objects. On the other hand, PTA-DSMs may make use of their autonomy and deliver decisions that do not correspond with the allegedly varying rules under the respective PTAs. PTA-DSMs would then issue *commensurable* decisions despite the *incommensurable* PTA rules when dealing with *equivalent* regulatory objects.

The analysis of the role of PTA-DSMs under this distinct concept of fragmentation has become especially important, as most PTAs contain substantively equivalent rules. Under these circumstances, it is imaginable that PTA-DSMs which interpret substantively equivalent and, thus, *commensurable* rules may come to *commensurable* decisions. At the same time, it is equally imaginable that

PTA-DSMs may use their autonomy and come to *incommensurable* decisions despite the *commensurable* rules they interpret. This would indicate an obstacle to the systemic operation of multiple rules on international trade. The outcome pursuant to which PTA-DSMs may indeed use their judicial autonomy to issue *incommensurable* decisions, despite *commensurable* rules being in place, appears plausible considering their characterization as instruments that contribute to the diversity of the regulation of international trade developed under the research assessing them through the WTO-DSM lens.

This work seeks to analyze whether the actual practice of PTA-DSMs has contributed to the fragmentation of international trade law by delivering *incommensurable* results on *equivalent* regulatory objects regarding substantively equivalent and, thus, *commensurable* rules. A comparative *and* empirical approach is taken to measure actual activity of PTA-DSMs concerning the interpretation of substantively equivalent PTA rules on the trade in goods. It encompasses all decisions containing a legal reasoning on the respective General Exception Clauses under the different PTAs. This has been done by coding and comparing the output of active PTA-DSMs. An answer to the question whether PTA-DSMs have indeed issued *incommensurable* decisions is attempted by identifying *recurring case groups* on these rules adjudicated by more than one PTA-DSM. This approach is taken to uncover whether PTA-DSMs have indeed applied different reasonings and interpretations in similar cases, resulting in diverging findings and ultimately contributing to the aforementioned distinct concept of fragmentation of international trade law.

The work is composed of nine chapters: Chapter 2 introduces the debate on the fragmentation of international trade law due to the activity of PTA-DSMs. It begins by considering the dialectic nature of international law oscillating between *formalism* and *pragmatism*. Following that, the two different approaches also applicable to international trade law, the *predominantly formalist* and the *predominantly pragmatic* approach to it, are presented. Given that the *predominantly formalist* and the *predominantly pragmatic* approaches to international trade law provide different understandings of the legal system of international trade law, they have given rise to assessing distinct notions of diversity of regulation of international trade. These distinct notions of diversity have led to different conceptualizations of PTA-DSM activity for the fragmentation of international trade law: In line with the *predominantly formalist* approach, PTA-DSMs have been assessed against the ramifications set out by the legal framework of the WTO to identify their contribution to the diversity of regulation of international trade. Pursuant to the *predominantly pragmatic* approach, light has been shed on PTA-DSM activity beyond the margins set out by the legal framework of the WTO to verify the claim over their potential to create diversity of regulation of international trade. This has led to different considerations of the impact of PTA-DSM activity on the systemic operation of multiple rules on international trade. While, on the one hand, PTA-DSM activity has been characterized as a systemic threat to the WTO under the *predominantly formalist* approach, on the other hand it has been analyzed as a self-standing phenomenon to verify its contribution to the diversity of the regulation of international trade. Chapter 3 provides *pragmatic* reasons for the reassessment of how PTA-DSM activity has been characterized based on the distinct approaches to international trade law: Firstly, the abstract characterization of PTA-DSM activity and its resulting role for creating diversity of regulation of international trade under the *predominantly formalist* approach can be held against their counterintuitively low activeness. Secondly, theoretical frictions concerning the PTA-DSM contribution to the fragmentation of international trade law under the *predominantly formalist* approach can be exposed, given the different conceptual purposes of the legal instruments under WTO and PTAs rules concerning the market access of imported goods within the participating states' economies. Thirdly, analytical blind spots on the assessment of PTA-DSM activity persist under the *predominantly pragmatic* approach to international trade law with this strand of research primarily dealing with commonalities in a setting of divergences, instead of focusing on divergences in a setting of commonalities. Considering the existent shortcomings under both approaches to international trade law to identify the fragmentation of international trade law, in Chap. 4 an alternative methodology is developed to assess PTA-DSM activity concerning their actual contribution to the diversity of regulation of international trade. Under this methodology, the focus lies on the identification of *incommensurable* PTA-DSM decisions and requires their analysis in *recurring case groups* to verify whether their reasoning and the assessment on the legality of the disputed measures has varied. Chapter 5 presents the results on the actual contribution of PTA-DSMs on delivering *incommensurable* decisions concerning substantively equivalent rules in *recurring case groups*. The analysis covers all decisions of PTA-DSMs which have become active in adjudicating General Exception Clauses contained in the respective PTAs, namely those of the European Union (EU), the European Economic Area (EEA), the Andean Community (CAN),[1] and the Southern Common Market (Mercosur).[2] It exposes the absence of *incommensurable* decisions and considers various factors that have contributed to this outcome. Moreover, Chap. 6 concludes on the past, present, and future role of PTA-DSMs for the fragmentation of international trade law. For this purpose, an analysis of the PTA-DSMs' referencing practices in the identified decisions is carried out to confirm the existence of a transjudicial dialogue between them. Chapter 7 contains the general conclusion on PTA-DSM activity for the fragmentation of international trade law. Chapter 8 includes the annex with the data allowing us to draw the conclusions in Chaps. 5 and 6. Chapter 9 contains the bibliography and lists all supplementary materials used throughout this book. The complete novel dataset on all analyzed decisions of the above-mentioned PTA-DSMs is available as electronic supplement material (ESM).[3]

---

[1] Original title: Comunidad Andina.

[2] Original title: Mercado Común del Sur/Mercado Común do Sul.

[3] The ESM is available under: https://doi.org/10.1007/978-3-031-40601-0_1.

Chapter 2
Fragmentation of International Trade Law due to the Activity of PTA-DSMs

The overarching term "Fragmentation of International Trade Law" is very flexible and adaptive, as it provides room for a multitude of concepts and understandings on the precise functioning of law and economics in the context of international trade. The debate has been triggered by an increase of rules in the international context.[1] Consequently, the debate on the fragmentation of international trade law blends into the more general debate on the fragmentation of international law. It is composed of, firstly, a descriptive finding that multiple international rules exist, which, secondly, is subject to normative appreciation.[2] Although the term builds on a clearly distinguishable phenomenon, i.e., the existence of multiple rules in the realm of international trade, it is very difficult to develop an unambiguous definition of the consequences that are addressed by it concerning the subsequent normative appreciation. Therefore, positive as well as negative appraisals of the fragmentation remain possible.[3]

Given this variety in the normative appreciation of fragmentation of international trade law, the term addresses the abstract problems appearing in connection with the normative appreciation of the increase of rules in this field of law. Ultimately, the term refers to the challenges of the systemic understanding of the regulation of international trade. On the one hand, it requires identifying a system of international trade law. On the other hand, it deals with the consequences of the existence of multiple international rules on international trade for the operation as or within the identified *legal system.*

---

[1] For the most prominent record of this debate, cf. Koskenniemi (2007), A/CN.4/L.682, 13 April 2006.

[2] Kreuder-Sonnen and Zürn (2020), p. 242.

[3] For an overview, cf. ibid., pp. 241–243.

The varying normative appreciations of fragmentation of international trade law originate from the different possibilities of defining the system of international trade law, as well as public international law in general.

2.1   International Law Between Pragmatism and Formalism

In his book chapter, entitled "What is international law for?", *Martti Koskenniemi* describes the dialectic nature of international law as one in which "there is a constant push and pull in the professional world between a *culture of instrumentalism* and a *culture of formalism*."[4] By this dynamic, he describes the different possibilities on which international lawyers can place emphasis when describing and analyzing international law, and therefore an international *legal system*. According to *Koskenniemi*, adherents of the culture of instrumentalism define the international legal system by its ability to produce outcomes in the real world, whereas supporters of the culture of formalism define it by the ascription of norms to be *international* and therefore form part of an international legal system.[5] Whereas instrumentalists accept that some international norms need to be disregarded if they are hampering the achievement of the result they are aiming at, formalists want to attain this result only by upholding all international rules, taking into account the laborious processes by the involved states of choosing and crafting them. In the end, he concludes that neither approach to international law can survive without the other. Each of the described *cultures* is not able set the stage for an ultimately politically charged international law, which, due to these shortcomings concerning the normativity of international rules, enables us to create a political community of international lawyers that constitutes the basis for an effective implementation of international law.

Koskenniemi's observations illustrate well the difficulties that arise when dealing with fragmentation of international trade law. Given the decentralized and unhierarchical character of international law,[6] both, an either purely instrumentalist or formalist logic to international trade law, would annihilate the debate about the legal character of rules that pertain to international trade. For instrumentalists, the existence of multiple rules in the realm of international trade is a testimony to their obsolescence. After all, states prove to be able to secure economic outcomes despite—or maybe even because of—the confusion and uncertainties that come with the existence of multiple rules on international trade. For formalists, the existence of multiple rules that share the same rank concerning a specific regulatory object are difficult to reconcile with fundamentals of legal theory on the validity of

---

[4] Koskenniemi (2014), p. 40.

[5] Ibid., pp. 34–40.

[6] Koskenniemi (2007), A/CN.4/L.682, 13 April 2006, pp. 484–486.

rules that coincide with their ability to contain truth conditions.[7] Consequently, they require additional coordination, which is only possible by having recourse to pragmatic considerations "outside" the law.[8]

It is precisely at the "middle ground" between pragmatic and formalist considerations about international trade law where the debate about its fragmentation takes place. Only here, the normative character of multiple rules on international trade at the international level is not rejected. Instead, it is presumed that multiple international rules can only be regarded as law if they *operate* in a systemic manner.[9] This calls for methods to identify their *systemic operation* to uphold the legal character. Therefore, at the outset of the debate on the fragmentation of international trade law stands the need to comprehend the existing multiple rules in the realm of international trade to form a *legal system* in which all these rules retain their normative character.[10] This necessity of multiple rules to build a legal system is based on an understanding of their normativity that is strongly influenced by the *Weberian* description of law in light of rational human behavior: It highlights the need for the *systematization* of law.[11] Consequently, *systematization* of law corresponds best with the rational purpose of law to provide for *a consistent* and *coherent* legal system,[12] which is a prerequisite for its enforcement and the ability to categorize provisions as law because they are understood as true.[13] Connected to this requirement for a legal system also flows the principle of equal regulation in legal systems. From that it follows that, in a legal system, comparable regulatory objects should be regulated equally, unless there is an objective reason which justifies not doing so.[14]

---

[7] On the difficulties and the importance of truth conditions of propositions about the content of law and its importance for its validity, cf. Navarro and Rodríguez (2014), sec. 4.1.

[8] On the potential of law becoming 'out of touch with life' ('lebensfremd'), cf. Petersen (2009), pp. 121–122.

[9] Valcke (2018), p. 168.

[10] On the axio-logical unity of law, cf. Prost (2012), pp. 175–190.

[11] English translation: "an integration of all analytically derived legal propositions in such a way that they constitute a logically clear, internally consistent, and, at least in theory, gapless system of rules, under which, it is implied, all conceivable fact situations must be capable of being logically subsumed lest their order lack an effective guarantee." as provided in Weber et al. (1954), p. 62.

Original wording: "die Inbeziehungsetzung aller durch Analyse gewonnenen Rechtssätze derart, daß sie unter einander ein logisch klares, in sich logisch widerspruchsloses und, vor Allem, prinzipiell lückenloses System von Regeln bilden, welches also beansprucht: daß alle denkbaren Thatbestände unter einer seiner Normen müssen logisch subsumiert werden können, widrigenfalls ihre Ordnung der rechtlichen Garantie entbehre." Weber (2010), p. 303.

[12] Addressing these principles as 'meta-rules of norm-production' Prost (2012), p. 104.

[13] Concerning the use of rationality in different legal doctrinal contexts, see Raiser (2008), p. 854. It plays an important role for the assessment of the legitimacy of a legal order, see Cottier et al. (2011), p. 41. Here, the term is used to describe a condition of a legal system which does not result in contradictory results concerning the regulatory object. This condition is regularly addressed by courts under considerations under "legal certainty", or at a more abstract level the "rule of law", Tamanaha (2004), pp. 66, 131–132.

[14] Petersen (2009), p. 93.

The possibilities of identifying whether multiple rules in the realm of international trade operate systemically can be ascertained depending on the underlying notion of a legal system. Differences in these understandings have led to the *predominantly formalist* and *predominantly pragmatic* approaches to international trade law.[15]

2.1.1 The Predominantly Formalist Approach Towards the System of International Trade Law

The *predominantly formalist* approach to international trade law builds on an understanding of the system of international trade law as a construct that enables accommodating all existing rules in a coherent and consistent manner. Pursuant to this understanding, fragmentation of international trade law addresses the difficulties of *formal coordination* of multiple rules on trade for their systemic operation.

Following this understanding of the system of international trade law, multiple rules on international trade need to be formally coordinated to prevent their fragmentation. Therefore, formal coordination of multiple trade rules constitutes the essence of their systemic operation and ensures their ability to effectuate a certain state on the regulatory objects they address. It is achieved through applying well-established and well-known methodologies already applied in the context of the law of the nation-state, namely the hierarchization of norms. Consequently, each rule in the realm of international trade is formally coordinated by subordinating them under higher-ranking rules.

Superiority of rules of certain sources is decided by pragmatic considerations. Regarding international trade law, these are especially those rules which have the most impact on creating welfare-enhancing economic effects by measuring their efficiency and effectiveness in their enforcement.[16] Accordingly, pursuant to the *predominantly formalist* approach to international trade law, it is the hierarchy of rules which clarifies how they can be enforced, and by which authorities. Ultimately, the hierarchy of rules in international trade law ensures their systemic operation. In this way, superior norms retain their normative character, independently of the existence of other rules in the realm of international trade.

The *predominantly formalist* approach to international trade law endorses a highly purposive and functionalist understanding of the legal system of international

---

[15]Note that the transition between formalism and pragmatism is fluent, each approach always containing elements of the other. It is in this respect that the method of the economic analysis of law which is generally perceived as pragmatic can also be used in a formalist sense, cf. Posner (2004), p. 152.

[16]Cottier et al. (2011), p. 41.

trade law.[17] The hierarchization of the existing multiple rules by means of herme-neutic principles constitutes a pragmatic consideration about the attributes of law that allow it to retain its normative character. Consequently, the *predominantly formalist* approach equates normativity of law with its hierarchical systematization. This has been translated into legal doctrine, which has sought methods to ensure the systematization of rules towards a legal system through hierarchization. Most notably, *Hans Kelsen* assumed the existence of a so-called *basic norm* under which rules would have to subordinate to constitute a legal system, establishing a vertical understanding of law and its enforcement.[18]

The *predominantly formalist* approach towards international trade law entails the most prominent understanding of the system of international trade law, and corre-spondingly its fragmentation. Hereunder pragmatic considerations over the interna-tional architecture of regulation of international trade have led scholars to assume a central role of the rules contained under the legal framework of the WTO. Due to its quasi-universal membership and a theoretically efficient enforcement by means of adjudication,[19] WTO rules have been regarded as superior to any other rules on international trade given the easy access to a strong WTO-DSM and its far-reaching ordering effect on international trade. This understanding ensures that economically reasonable policies can be implemented through a central administration that can be held accountable for their enforcement.[20]

2.1.2 The Predominantly Pragmatic Approach Towards the System of International Trade Law

The *predominantly pragmatic* approach towards the system of international trade law constitutes another possibility of understanding multiple rules in the realm of international trade to amount to a legal system. Following this understanding, multiple rules operate systemically due to their shared characteristics and effects that can be observed on international trade. Consequently, pursuant to the *predom-inantly pragmatic* approach towards the system of international trade law, fragmen-tation of international trade law addresses the difficulties of considering multiple

---

[17] Such an understanding is very close to the conception of domestic law of the classical modernity, see Seinecke (2015), p. 155.

[18] This can either be the assumption of a constitutional order in public international law or, as Kelsen has put it, the existence of a so-called *basic norm*. This can either be the assumption of a constitutional order in public international law, or, as Kelsen has put it the existence of a so-called *basic norm*. In favor of the existence of a basic norm: Kelsen (2003), pp. 410–411; skeptical on the requirement of a basic norm: Hart (2012), pp. 232–237.

[19] E.g., cf. Cottier et al. (2011), pp. 54–56.

[20] Cf. Walker (2008), p. 386. According to Walker's taxonomy, state sovereigntist, global hierar-chical, unipolar, and regional meta-principles would count as vertical meta-principles, with a decreasing emphasis on the dominance of an all-encompassing vertical international structure.

rules to *operate systemically* due to their varying content, interpretation, and application.

Pursuant to this understanding, fragmentation of international trade law is absent if multiple rules on international trade are interpreted and applied uniformly, irrespectively of their institutional origin. Their uniform interpretation and application confirm the rules' systemic operation and, consequently, their legal validity, irrespectively of the adjudicative body reasoning on their content. In this regard, the *predominantly pragmatic* approach towards the system of international trade law presupposes that, instead of formal coordination of multiple rules, an inherent coordination exists which arises from the specific conditions set out by the regulatory object. The attributes of the regulatory object translate into a common intrinsic logic of these rules, which apply irrespectively of their source.

The understanding of a legal system resulting from the *predominantly pragmatic* approach towards the system of international trade law is heavily influenced by an alternative understanding of international law, which allows one to assume different nuances of legal bindingness in international treaties, or the existence of other purposes of treaty provisions, rather than a singular function of ensuring their enforcement through adjudication.[21] It resonates in *Herbert L. A. Hart's* understanding of the systematization of law: In the case of official and judicial harmony, the rule of recognition, applied by the various actors applying the law, serves to confirm that a specific rule belongs to a legal system.[22] Consequently, the understanding of the system of international trade law becomes less dependent on the existence of an enforcement mechanisms and offers space for alternative factors which ensure the implementation of treaty provisions.[23] These approaches stand out, as they do not aim at identifying a hierarchy of rules. Instead, the purpose is to find recurring and, hence, common characteristics among the different rules that address the same regulatory object.[24] They involve methods ranging from the inquiry into the mutual recognition between legal regimes, the rapprochement between legal regimes by means of the development of common standards, the search for common procedural interpretation maxims of legal regimes, and the search for integration by the judiciary, to non-judicial regime interaction such as politization.[25]

---

[21] Ibid., p. 385 who states: "[a]gainst this rapidly shifting backdrop, it becomes apparent why both the descriptive accuracy and the prescriptive authority of the Keynesian-Westphalian frame have come under sustained attack."

[22] Differently, Hart (2012), p. 122, who refers to official and judicial harmony as a precondition for identifying a legal system's rule of recognition containing the criteria for a legal system to be valid. For Hart, contradictions of rules are not *per se* fatal for a legal system. Persistent contradictions of the rule of recognition, however, can lead to the establishment of a different legal system; e.g., Kelsen (2017), p. 143; cf. also Prost (2012), pp. 87–89; on the specifically German influence for this understanding of law, cf. Prost (2012).

[23] Such an understanding is closely related to a postmodern understanding of law, cf. Seinecke (2015), p. 288.

[24] Acharya (2016), p. 703.

[25] Peters (2017) and Walker (2008).

The understanding of a system pursuant to the *predominantly pragmatic* approach towards international trade law has remained vastly underrepresented in the debate about the fragmentation of international trade law, but is gradually gaining more ground.[26] The reasons for its underrepresentation are diverse. One main reason could be that it involves methods which seem descriptive rather than normative[27] and create some uncertainties, which are embedded in the comparison of international law. Most likely, it is the lack of a central body of administration of norms, and a corresponding enforcement of legal obligations, which makes it more difficult to reflect in equal measure on pragmatic considerations of efficiency, effectiveness, and their legitimacy of their implementation, as opposed to the prevalent understanding under the *predominantly formalist* approach towards international trade law.[28]

2.2 Diversity and Fragmentation of International Trade Law

Diversity in the regulation of international trade is the determinant factor enabling the fragmentation of international trade law under both approaches set out above. Depending on the specific understanding of the system of international trade law, *diversity* of multiple rules on international trade calls into question their systemic operation. Given the differences on the concept of the system of international trade law, the notion of *diversity* differs significantly under both approaches. It has resulted in their different measurement.

2.2.1 Diversity in the Context of the Predominantly Formalist Approach Towards International Trade Law

Diversity in the context of the *predominantly formalist* approach towards international trade law is measured by the difference of international rules on trade compared to the rules available under the legal framework of the WTO. Building on the inherently hierarchical understanding of the systemic operation of international trade law, the *predominantly formalist* approach towards international trade law allows only for this one reference to measuring diversity. In this sense, diversity of multiple rules on international trade does not constitute a problem *per se*, as long as their formal coordination is ensured by their subordination under WTO rules. Consequently, identifying diversity of multiple rules in the realm of international

---

[26] Harrison (2014).

[27] Rosenstock et al. (2019), pp. 11–16.

[28] *Supra* Sect. 2.1.1.

trade requires an antagonistic legal exercise: the comparison of a rule on international trade with a corresponding rule available under the legal framework of the WTO.

Measuring the *diversity* of multiple rules on international trade exclusively against the rules originating under the legal framework of the WTO has important implications for the methodological possibilities that apply in this context: The comparison remains limited to the scope of application of the rules under the WTO legal framework. Therefore, any finding of diversity in the context of the *predominantly formalist* approach towards international trade law can only take place regarding the comparison of an *identical* regulatory object that is both addressed under rules originating under the WTO and any other legal source.

2.2.2   Diversity in the Context of the Predominantly Pragmatic Approach Towards International Trade Law

Diversity in the context of the *predominantly pragmatic* approach towards international trade law describes the variety of existing multiple rules in the realm of international trade. A high diversity of these rules constitutes a reason to assume that they do not address a common regulatory object given the absence of their shared common logic.

The lack of a common logic of the multiple rules speaks against the potential of the respective rules to operate systemically regarding the regulatory object. In this context, measuring diversity is a relative exercise, delimited only by the regulatory object commonly addressed by multiple rules. Consequently, the rule contained within the legal framework of the WTO constitutes one of many different available references against which diversity in the regulation of international trade can be measured.

Measuring diversity of multiple rules against each other has important implications on the methodology that can be applied in the context of the *predominantly pragmatic* approach towards international trade law: It takes place based on the identification of rules which apply to an *equivalent* regulatory object that is addressed by *any rule* in the realm of international trade.

2.3   PTAs and PTA-DSMs as Source of Diversity Within the Fragmentation Debate

PTAs constitute a significant regulatory and economic phenomenon. They provide rules for the process of trade liberalization between at least two states. PTA-DSMs serve the resolution of disputes among PTA partners over the application and interpretation of these rules, with the aim of enforcing the legal obligations existing under these agreements. From an economic point of view, PTAs are significant because they encompass a share of world trade of 37.3%, which could increase even to 54.3% if all negotiated PTAs were concluded and enforced.[29]

PTA-DSMs are critically assessed concerning their contribution to diversity in the regulation of international trade. Independently of which notion of the system of international trade law one applies, PTA-DSMs are said to constitute a major source of *diversity* in the realm of international trade. Although the anticipation of diversity is mostly based on PTAs providing rules on trade liberalization next to very similar ones already available under the legal framework of the WTO for the regulation of international trade between WTO Members, PTA-DSMs have been presumed to increase their diversity due to their nature as autonomous judicial bodies.

Depending on the specific notion of international trade law, different features of PTA-DSMs have been identified as contributing to its fragmentation. In the context of the *predominantly formalist* approach towards international trade law, their ability to issue decisions on trade-related disputes among, *inter alia*, WTO Members has led them to being understood as an institutional threat to the WTO-DSM. In the context of the *predominantly pragmatic* approach towards international trade law, the circumstance that PTA-DSMs issue decisions on substantially equivalent legal bases, and their ability to issue different interpretations on them, calls into question the very content of these PTA rules or, respectively, the actual function of PTA-DSMs.

Independently of the *legal overlaps* between the WTO and PTAs, PTA partners can set up varying PTA rules that lead to different degrees of trade liberalization among them, resulting in different *depths* of their liberalization commitments.[30]

---

[29]Note that measuring the total volume of world trade becomes increasingly difficult [United Nations Conference on Trade and Development (2019), pp. 38–39; Bureau et al. (2019), fig. 4.], and estimates vary as to how much of the share of world trade is affected within PTAs. Cf. Organisation for Economic Co-operation and Development (2003), p. 12, estimating that PTAs accounted for 43% of world trade in 2003; and Bureau et al. (2019), fig. 4.

[30]While "north-north" PTAs contain more and more profound provisions which are legally enforceable between PTA partners, the number of such provisions and their depth decreases in "north-south" PTAs, while being the lowest in "south-south" PTAs. However, a general trend for deeper commitments can be witnessed starting in 1995. Cf. Hofmann C et al., *Horizontal depth: a new database on the content of preferential trade agreements*, WPS7981, 22 February 2017, figs 6; 13; 14.

2.3.1   Diversity in the Context of the **Predominantly Formalist** *Approach: PTA-DSMs Issuing Incoherent and Inconsistent Decisions Against the Legal Overlaps with WTO Rules*

Under the *predominantly formalist* approach, PTA-DSMs have been perceived as contributors to diversity in the regulation of international trade, due to their ability to issue decisions on trade-related disputes among, *inter alia*, WTO Members, independent of the WTO-DSM. Ultimately, this has led scholars to assume that PTA-DSMs constitute not only main drivers of the fragmentation of the system of international trade law, but also that they are an institutional threat to the WTO-DSM and the WTO itself.

This characterization of PTA-DSMs is rooted in the design of the WTO rules on PTAs. The WTO Agreement contains several obligations of WTO Members for the establishment and operation of PTAs. Yet, these rules provide substantial interpretative leeway to WTO Members negotiating and implementing these PTAs. This interpretative leeway was argued to be exploited by WTO Members to implement PTAs that run counter to the economic principles encompassed under the legal framework of the WTO. Under the *predominantly formalist* approach, these WTO-incompatible PTA rules constitute the foundation for presuming the fragmentation of international trade law.

In this vein, PTA-DSM are argued, on the one hand, to uphold this fragmentation by reproducing and legitimizing WTO incompatible PTA rules and by providing WTO Members with the opportunity to have their disputes adjudicated by them under these PTA rules. On the other hand, PTA-DSMs are said to contribute to the fragmentation of international trade law, because they could engage in the autonomous interpretation of PTA rules, which are substantially equivalent with WTO rules. This ability of PTA-DSMs to engage in an autonomous interpretation of PTA rules which are substantially equivalent with WTO rules has been said to lead them to issue incoherent and inconsistent decisions compared to the ones reached by the panels and the Appellate Body (AB) under the WTO-DSM.

Given this possibility, it was argued that WTO Members would feel inclined to turn to PTA-DSMs rather than to the WTO-DSM to receive more favorable decisions than they would under the WTO-DSM. Therefore, PTA-DSMs have been identified as a symptom of retraction from the multilateral approach to regulation of international trade and as a countermodel to the adjudication of trade disputes under WTO-DSM, which would incentivize *forum shopping*.

Against this backdrop, several possibilities to limit the impact of PTA-DSM activity were argued to be implemented at the substantive and procedural level. At the substantive level, WTO Members and scholars have unsuccessfully tried to add precision to the provisions on PTAs under the legal framework of the WTO, informed by insights from economic analysis. At the procedural level, several possibilities were argued to maintain the WTO-DSM as a supreme adjudicative body in trade disputes without being explicitly mandated by the legal text of the

Dispute Settlement Understanding (DSU),[31] the practice of the WTO-DSM, or the WTO Members themselves.

2.3.1.1 Diversity of Regulation on International Trade at the Substantive Level of PTA Rules

PTAs have been considered a source and a major cause of diversity in the regulation of international trade at the substantive level of PTA rules. This development has been assumed in light of the ambiguities of the WTO provisions on PTAs, which would not allow a complete subordination of PTA rules under WTO rules. The large-scale existence of PTAs notified to the WTO served as a confirmation of this hypothesis. Against this development, and due to the fact that WTO Members regulated their international trade in PTAs, which also encompassed the portion of trade within the scope of the WTO Agreement, the emerging legal overlaps concerning *identical* regulatory objects of international trade were the main reason to anticipate diversity in the regulation of international trade.

Moreover, international trade that is not encompassed by the scope of the WTO Agreement has been perceived as a field of regulation of international trade in which the future subordination of PTA rules under the WTO rules is extremely difficult to achieve.

2.3.1.1.1 General Legal and Economic Backdrop of PTAs Within the Multilateral Legal Framework of the WTO

PTAs are the legal instruments that WTO Members resort to with the aim of achieving trade liberalization at a higher pace than under the multilateral legal framework of the WTO. From an economic-theory perspective, the conclusion of PTAs between countries can be described primarily as welfare policy. Accordingly, PTAs, like all other economic treaties, constitute an instrument to obtain welfare gains due to the liberalization of trade among PTA partners.[32] Based on the economic model of comparative advantage of the economies of states, PTAs can assist in exploiting a country's existing comparative advantage vis-à-vis another country concerning its most productive industries by lowering existing barriers to international trade with PTA partners above the concessions already made under the legal framework of the WTO. PTAs play an important part for the withdrawal or reduction of fiscal and non-fiscal trade barriers still maintained under the WTO rules. As a

---

[31] Understanding on Rules and Procedures governing the Settlement of Disputes.

[32] See Schwartz and Sykes (1996), p. 35: "The reason is that any tariff reduction, discriminatory or otherwise, will allow lower-cost foreign firms to displace higher-cost domestic producers, saving resources in production and lowering prices to consumers—so-called 'trade creation'. Thus, where the choice is between preferential trade liberalization and no liberalization at all, preferential liberalization can enhance welfare."

consequence, with the implementation of a PTA these trade barriers cannot further mitigate the comparative advantage of one PTA partner's industry vis-à-vis the other PTA partner's industry.[33] The exploitation of the comparative advantage is argued to result in the specialization of an economy of a PTA partner towards its most productive industries. A development, which is beneficial for obtaining welfare gains due to an increased efficiency of these industries and consequently their increased competitiveness.[34] On the other hand, increased specialization of a PTA partner's industry goes hand in hand with a simultaneous diminishing of its less productive industries compared to those of other PTA partners. As labor and capital are being released due to this process, PTA partners incur so-called *adjustment costs* from trade liberalization. Obsolete labor and capital need to be re-invested into the economic life cycle of the concerned PTA partner's economy for trade liberalization to have a welfare-creating effect.[35] Only where investment opportunities for unused labor and capital exist will countries experience welfare gains from trade liberalization. The extent of welfare gains resulting from the conclusion of a PTA is therefore dependent on the ratio of competitiveness gained through the specialization and the incurred *adjustment costs* materializing due to the specialization of their industries. The amount of adjustment costs incurred by countries which engage in PTAs is innately linked to a PTA partner's market size and composition, which determines the potential for the quick tapping of new investment opportunities. Therefore, welfare gains are especially to be expected for those countries that incur lower *adjustment costs* due to specialization and that have already experienced a high level of competitiveness of their industries at the time of the implementation of the PTA.[36] Against this backdrop, economic theory predicts that welfare gains due to the conclusion of PTAs can be achieved, albeit only if a variety of other exogenous factors of the economies concerned equally exist.[37]

The materialization and administration of these *adjustment costs* constitutes the main reason for PTA partners to resort to legal instruments in the form of PTAs which regulate this highly complex and costly process of trade liberalization among them. Under the *predominantly formalist* approach to international trade law, the term "Regional Trade Agreement"[38] has been established as the generic term to refer

---

[33] Viner (1924), pp. 107–108. In line with the principle of economic advantages, each PTA partner's industries will specialize, as the absence of tariff barriers between the PTA partners will allow the means of production to be allocated in the most economical way. Specialization, however, involves shutdowns of inefficient producers and releases capital and labor due to vanishing of these inefficient industries. This effect can be calculated under the term "adjustment costs". Considering adjustment costs, it may be beneficial for PTA partners selectively to liberalize industries within a PTA to bypass any anticipated negative (political) effects entailed by specialization.

[34] Dür and Elsig (2015), p. 201.

[35] de Córdoba et al. (2006), pp. 86–71.

[36] Ibid., pp. 66–67.

[37] Grossman and Horn (2013), pp. 53–54.

[38] WTO Regional Trade Agreements gateway. In: Regional trade agreements. https://www.wto.org/english/tratop_e/region_e/region_e.htm#rules_ita. Accessed 25 August 2023.

to international trade agreements that are concluded in addition to the obligations under the Marrakesh Agreement establishing the World Trade Organization (WTO Agreement).[39] Moreover, considering the various existing WTO provisions on PTAs, a complex nomenclature exists for these agreements depending on the type of trade they cover, the economic status of WTO Members implementing PTAs, and its status of implementation.

Faced with the risk of incurring welfare losses, PTA partners are inclined to set up rules in PTAs which secure the smoothest transition to an effective trade liberalization among them. In this context, the WTO Agreement contains several obligations for WTO Members to design and implement PTAs in a certain manner that ensures the integrity of the pre-existing concessions made under the WTO Agreement.

Specifically, the implementation of PTAs among WTO Members remains generally prohibited unless certain conditions are fulfilled: Pursuant to the most-favorite nation (MFN) principle, WTO Members are obliged to grant the most favorable treatment offered to goods[40] (or services/service suppliers)[41] of any other country to all other WTO Members. Where WTO Members set up PTAs to offer more favorable treatment to their PTA partners than compared to the treatment accorded to non-PTA partners among WTO Members, this constitutes a violation of the MFN principle endorsed by the agreements in Annex I to the WTO Agreement, namely Art. I:1 GATT 1994 and Art. II:1 GATS.[42] Therefore, by definition, PTAs are inherently discriminatory and generally prohibited, as they do extend the favorable treatment accorded to PTA partners to non-PTA partners among the WTO Members.

Nevertheless, under the legal framework of the WTO it is recognized that WTO Members may want to grant each other higher levels of trade concessions than those negotiated under the multilateral approach of the WTO. The circumstance that WTO Members may want to engage in PTAs to be free to engage in an advancement of concessions made under the WTO is explicitly foreseen in the WTO Agreement. For this reason, WTO provisions on PTAs are crafted as justifications to the violation of the MFN principle that comes with the preferential treatment granted under PTAs among them. They legitimize the *a priori* illegal preferential treatment between WTO Members under certain conditions. Depending on whether the trade in goods or in services is affected, Art. XXIV GATT 1994, the Enabling Clause, and Art. V GATS set out different substantive requirements for PTAs for WTO Members to rely on these provisions as a justification. Additionally, all the aforementioned provisions require WTO Members to notify the implementation of such agreements which are complemented by the "Transparency Mechanism for RTAs"[43] (TMRTA).

---

[39] (1994) Marrakesh Agreement Establishing the World Trade Organization.

[40] Cf. Art. I:1 GATT 1994.

[41] Cf. Art. II:1 GATS.

[42] Rigod (2013); Davey in Bagwell and Mavroidis (2011), pp. 235–261.

[43] General Council of the WTO (2006) Transparency Mechanism for Regional Trade Agreements, 18 December 2006. The TMRTA's objective to increase transparency on PTAs is fulfilled by precise instructions for the notification of PTAs to the Committee on Regional Trade Agreements

The review of the different provisions shows that the WTO Members can opt for different degrees of trade liberalization by means of their PTAs among each other. Regarding the trade in goods, under Art. XXIV:4 GATT 1994 two typologies of PTAs are introduced, namely Custom Unions (CUs) and Free Trade Areas (FTAs), which differ regarding the administration[44] of tariffs towards non-PTA partners.

One the one hand, FTAs according to Art. XXIV:8 lit. b) GATT 1994

> shall be understood to mean a group of **two or more customs** territories in which the duties and other **restrictive regulations of commerce** (except, where necessary, those permitted under Articles XI, XII, XIII, XIV, XV and XX) are **eliminated** on **substantially all the trade** between the constituent territories in products originating in such territories. (emphasis added)

On the other hand, in line with Art. XXIV:8 lit a) GATT 1994, and in addition to the requirement to eliminate restrictive regulations of commerce on substantially all the trade, CUs

> shall be understood to mean the **substitution of a single customs territory** for two or more customs territories [...], in which substantially the **same duties and other regulations** of commerce are **applied by each of the members of the union** to the trade of territories **not included** in the union. (emphasis added)

WTO Members have the possibility to rely on reduced requirements which apply to interim agreements (IAs). IAs are PTAs

> leading to the formation

of an FTA or an CU, as contained in Art. XXIV:8 lits. a) and b) GATT 1994 and further specified in Art. XXIV:8 lit. c) GATT 1994.

The Enabling Clause[45] contains provisions on so-called "Special and Differential Treatment" (hereinafter S&D treatment) of developing countries by developed countries. The Enabling Clause was introduced to react to the needs of poorer countries articulated since the 1950s, which demanded the introduction of changes that would allow them to benefit from the participation in world trade as established under the GATT system.[46] S&D treatment of developing countries reflects possibilities to grant poorer WTO Members, the so-called developing-country Members, more opportunities to engage in world trade by reducing the barriers for the entrance of their goods onto the markets of richer WTO Members, the so-called

---

(CRTA) for PTAs notified under Art. XXIV GATT 1994 and Art. V GATS, as well as to the Committee for Trade and Development (CTD) for Agreements notified under Para. 2(c) Enabling Clause. In particular, Art. Para. 7 lit. a) TMRTA regulates that WTO Members must submit detailed information on notified PTAs, which will then be used by the WTO Secretariat to prepare so-called "factual presentations" on these PTAs and which will serve as a basis for the assessment in the committees. In line with Para. 12 TMRTA, these "factual presentations" are circulated among WTO Members and used to prepare (critical) questions for the legal assessment of PTAs in the committees.

[44] Viner (2014), p. 152.

[45] Differential and more favourable treatment reciprocity and fuller participation of developing countries ('Enabling Clause') (Decision of 28 November 1979 (L/4903)), WTO, L/4903 28 November 1979.

[46] Islam and Alam (2009), p. 21.

developed-country Members.[47] These S&D treatment provisions form the legal basis to justify violations[48] of the MFN principle when developed countries confer preferential treatment to developing countries compared to developed countries.

The Enabling Clause makes it possible for developed WTO Members to grant preferential tariff treatment to goods originating from developing countries in accordance with the Generalized System of Preferences (Art. 2 lit. a) Enabling Clause), differential and more favorable treatment concerning non-tariff measures (Art. 2 lit. b) Enabling Clause), and special treatment on the least developed among the developing countries (Art. 2 lit. d) Enabling Clause). Regarding the establishment of PTAs, it contains a provision on regional or global arrangements established amongst less-developed WTO Members for the mutual reduction or elimination of tariffs and nontariff measures, on products imported from one another (Art. 2 lit. c) Enabling Clause). It provides a justification of the violation of the MFN principle due to a PTA between developing WTO Members, in which they engage in the

> **mutual reduction** or **elimination** of **tariffs** and, in accordance with criteria or conditions which may be prescribed by the WTO Members, for the **mutual reduction** or **elimination** of **nontariff measures**, on products imported from one another.

PTAs falling within the scope of Art. 2 lit. c) Enabling Clause are referred to as *Preferential Trade Arrangements* in WTO terminology.[49] Where developing WTO Members make use of the possibility of liberalizing trade only partially, they are referred to as *Partial Scope Agreements* (PSAs).[50]

In the context of the trade in services, Art. V GATS provides for a corresponding justification for the violation of the MFN principle applying by virtue of Art. II GATS. It requires that WTO Members ensure in their PTAs the *absence or elimination of substantially all discrimination*, in the sense of Article XVII GATS, among PTA partners in the sectors covered under subparagraph (a), through:

> (i) elimination of existing discriminatory measures, and/or
>
> (ii) prohibition of new or more discriminatory measures,
>
> either at the **entry into force** of that agreement or on the basis of a **reasonable time-frame**.

Although the provision does not set out a specific terminology for PTAs, as opposed to Art. XXIV GATT 1994, these agreements are referred to as *Economic Integration Agreements* (EIAs)[51] in line with the title of the provision. In parallel to Art. XXIV GATT 1994, PTAs for the trade in services can be implemented on the basis of a

---

[47] Cf. the second recital of the WTO Agreement.

[48] Although the Panel in EC – Tariff Preferences did not consider Art. 2 lit. c) Enabling Clause, it confirmed that "the legal function of the Enabling Clause is to authorize derogation from Article I:1 [GATT 1994]", WTO Panel, *European Communities — Conditions for the Granting of Tariff Preferences to Developing Countries*, WT/DS246/R, Judgment of 1 December 2003, para. 7.38.

[49] WTO Database on Preferential Trade Arrangements. In: WTO—Preferential Trade Arrangements. http://ptadb.wto.org. Accessed 28 August 2023.

[50] WTO (2019) User Guide of the Regional Trade Information System, sec. 1.3.

[51] Ibid., sec. 1.3.

reasonable time frame if they do not immediately comply with the standard of coverage and the degree of liberalization of trade at the outset of their implementation pursuant to Art. V:1 lit. b) (ii) GATS (EIA with time frame). In parallel to the Enabling Clause, according to Art. V:3 GATS, developing WTO Members can equally engage in PTAs for the trade in services and obtain more flexibility regarding the standards set out in Art. V:1 GATS (EIA DC).

The Regional Trade Agreement Information System (RTA IS)[52] provides a database of international agreements which were notified by WTO Members as one of the specific models of PTAs set out under WTO rules. It is assembled and kept up-to-date by the RTA section of the WTO Secretariat.

2.3.1.1.2 Large-Scale Existence of PTAs and the Increase of Rules on International Trade

According to the WTO RTA IS, a total of 335 Regional Trade Agreements have been notified to the WTO between 1948 and 2021.[53] Although they are a phenomenon of the post-WWII era, a sharp rise in the number of agreements notified to the WTO was witnessed particularly from the mid-1990s. This high number of agreements in force constitutes rather a relatively new phenomenon of modern regulation of international trade. According to the RTA IS, there has a been a steady increase of RTAs since the 1990s (from an average annual increase of 15% from 1990–2000), which has slowed down since the mid-2010s (to an average annual increase of 4% from 2010–2019), see Fig. 2.1.

Until today, according to the RTA IS, there are only very few countries left which have completely abstained from concluding any kind of PTA.[54] Yet, WTO Members differ in their openness to engage in PTAs. Accordingly, the EU, the EFTA States, and Chile are the countries or groupings of countries which hold the most membership in PTAs, whereas WTO Members of the Caribbean have the lowest participation in PTAs.[55] From a perspective of the economic status of countries participating in PTAs, until the year 2010, "north-south" PTAs accounted for the majority of concluded PTAs between WTO Members. They are followed by "south-south" PTAs. "North-north" PTAs account for the smallest share of PTAs between WTO Members.[56] This composition is likely to have consolidated. According to *Acharya et al.*, 69% of the PTAs under negotiation in 2010 were to be concluded as "north-

---

[52] WTO Regional Trade Agreements gateway. In: Regional Trade Agreements. https://www.wto.org/english/tratop_e/region_e/region_e.htm#rules_ita. Accessed 30 April 2019; WTO (2019) User Guide of the Regional Trade Information System. Note that the WTO uses the term Regional Trade Agreements to refer to preferential trade agreements.

[53] WTO Secretariat/RTA Section FACTS&FIGURES Regional Trade Agreements, 1 July 2020 to 1 January 2021.

[54] These being Mauritania, South Sudan, and Somalia.

[55] WTO Secretariat/RTA Section FACTS&FIGURES Regional Trade Agreements, 1 July 2020 to 1 January 2021, pt. below.

[56] Acharya et al. (2011), fig. 2.5.

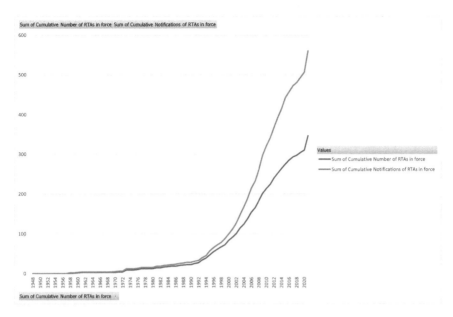

Fig. 2.1   Visualization of the RTA IS data (Source: Data provided by the RTA IS under https://rtais. wto.org/UI/ExportAllRTAList.aspx; visualization by the author)

south" PTAs, followed by 22% "south-south" PTAs and 9% of "north-north" PTAs.[57] Most of the PTAs that have been concluded remain regularly in force on a long-term basis. The status of 18 out of 312 agreements that were notified to the WTO was changed from "in force" to "not in force" from 1948 to 2019. According to the RTA IS, the dynamics allow us to conclude that new PTAs will continue to be concluded at a continuously high rate comparable to the one of the previous years. According to the RTA IS, in the year 2021 a sharp rise of PTAs took place, mainly due to the United Kingdom's (UK) withdrawal from the EU—the so-called Brexit— and the negotiation of PTAs by the UK with important trading partners.

2.3.1.1.3   Ambiguous WTO Provisions on PTAs as the Basic Cause for Assuming Diversity in the Regulation of International Trade

The aforementioned WTO provisions on PTAs contain great ambiguities concerning the *economic content* set up by the legal requirements for PTAs. They constitute the main cause for the anticipated diversity in the regulation of international trade. The broad and general language used in these provisions leaves ample room for their interpretation and allows different degrees of stringency concerning the process of trade liberalization. Due to the complexity of assessing the actual contribution of PTAs to the overall global liberalization of international trade, neither the WTO

---

[57] Ibid., fig. 2.6.

Members themselves nor the decisions of the WTO-DSM have helped to bring further clarity in this regard.

2.3.1.1.3.1   General Requirements for PTAs Under WTO Rules

All provisions acting as justifications for the MFN principle establish certain conditions concerning the legal design of the specific type of PTA envisaged by WTO Members. In this way, the provisions on PTAs follow a common legal pattern across the WTO Agreement, establishing an *internal* and an *external* requirement for PTAs, see Table 2.1.[58] The *internal* requirement contains rules on the legal design and operation of a PTA between the PTA partners. The *external* requirement regulates the trade effects of the respective PTA on non-PTA partners.

Under the *internal* requirement, different elements are prescribed for PTAs which vary according to the type of PTA that WTO Members wish to implement. These elements set out conditions concerning the legal design and functioning of the respective PTA among PTA partners. Four elements can be identified in all the provisions on PTAs, namely the respective PTA's coverage, the points of reference for trade liberalization, and the extent of trade liberalization that must take place based on the designated references and a temporal element, defining the time limit for the accomplishment of trade liberalization. Combined, all four elements establish different degrees of trade liberalization that need to be pursued by PTA partners in order to rely successfully on the justification of the violation of the MFN principle.

The *external* requirement regulates the economic effects of a future or implemented PTA on non-PTA partners among WTO Members. It prohibits certain features in the legal design of a PTA which are understood to have a negative impact on the trade flows of non-PTA partners. As a general principle, the implementation of a PTA must not create greater obstacles to international trade than those that existed before its implementation.

2.3.1.1.3.2   WTO Provisions Providing Economic Guidelines on PTAs

These substantive requirements on PTAs contained in WTO rules can be said to provide economic *guidelines* which need to be reflected in their legal design and implementation, see Fig. 2.2. The legal requirements for PTAs implemented between WTO Members are formulated in a very broad and general manner, which leaves them open to interpretation. It remains unclear how the provisions should be understood precisely regarding the different aspects they cover. This interpretative leeway results in difficulties to ascertain the precise economic content which WTO Members are required to implement. The ambiguities arising hereunder allow WTO Members to maintain different legal understandings of the specific economic requirements for the specific types of PTAs. They constitute the core for assuming diversity in the regulation of international trade under the predominantly formalist approach to international trade law.

---

[58] For the use and understanding of the structure with regard to Art. XXIV GATT, cf. Kim (2018), p. 377.

Table 2.1 Schematic overview of substantive requirements of PTAs under WTO rules

Provision	Art. XXIV GATT 1994	Art. XXIV GATT 1994	Art. 2 lit. c) enabling clause	Art. V GATS	Art. V GATS	Art. V:3 GATS
Name for PTA listed under the RTA IS	CU/FTA	IA	PSA	EIA	EIA with time frame	EIA among developing countries (EIA DC)
Internal requirement						
Concerning the trade in	Goods	Goods	Goods	Services	Services	Services
Coverage of respective PTA	Substantially all the trade	Between partially and substantially all the trade	Partial	Substantial sectoral coverage	Between partial and substantial sectoral coverage	Flexible coverage
Points of reference for trade liberalization	Duties and other restrictive regulations of commerce	Duties and other restrictive regulations of commerce	Tariffs and nontariff measures	Substantially all discrimination	Substantially all discrimination	Discrimination
Extent of trade liberalization based on points of reference	Elimination	Elimination	Reduction or elimination	Absence/elimination	Elimination	Flexible reduction or elimination
Period for the attainment of trade liberalization	Immediate	Over time	Flexible	Immediate, but considering the wider process of economic integration or trade liberalization	Over time	Flexible
External requirement						
Barriers to trade for	Level of duties and other regulations on the	Level of duties and other regulations on	Facilitate and promote trade with DCs and must			

(continued)

Table 2.1 (continued)

Provision	Art. XXIV GATT 1994	Art. XXIV GATT 1994	Art. 2 lit. c) enabling clause	Art. V GATS	Art. V GATS	Art. V:3 GATS
Members outside the PTA	whole must not be higher or more restrictive	the whole must not be higher or more restrictive	not create barriers to or undue difficulties for the trade of any WTO Members	Must not raise the overall level of barriers to trade in services within the respective sectors or subsectors compared to the level applicable prior to such an agreement		

Source: Author

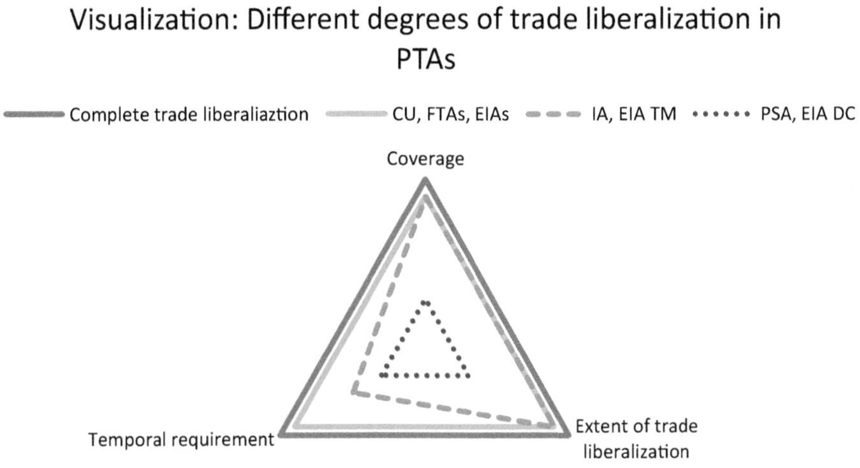

Visualization: Different degrees of trade liberalization in PTAs

▬▬▬ Complete trade liberaliaztion   ▬▬▬ CU, FTAs, EIAs   ▬ ▬ ▬ IA, EIA TM   • • • • • • PSA, EIA DC

Coverage

Temporal requirement

Extent of trade liberalization

Fig. 2.2 Visualization of the different degrees of trade liberalization in PTAs under WTO law (Source: Author)

2.3.1.1.3.2.1 Ambiguities Concerning the Internal Requirement

Regarding the *internal* requirement, the exact coverage of trade that needs to be governed by PTAs remains especially disputed. Similarly, there is no consensus regarding the exact indicators for hindrances in international trade among PTA partners which ensure that the type of trade covered under the PTAs will eventually be liberalized between PTA partners. Moreover, the time frames for the conclusion of trade liberalization in PTAs is equally debated, given that WTO Members argue in favor of flexibility considering the far-reaching impacts this liberalization can have on their economies. The notification and information submitted under the TMRTA so far has remained for information purposes among WTO Members only and was argued as serving merely as a general,[59] non-binding[60] indicator for the average level of trade liberalization taking place in PTAs.

---

[59] According to Para. 2 lit. e) Annex TMRTA, WTO Members are required for PTAs covering the trade in goods to provide statistics on the imports between all PTA partners and on each PTA partner's imports from the rest of the world, broken down by country of origin. According to Art. 3 Annex TMTRA, for PTAs covering the trade in services, WTO Members are required to furnish information concerning the share of gross domestic product accounted for by a service or its production statistics (by services sector/subsector).

The fact that WTO Members are required to provide information on the goods and services that displays the importance of the liberalized economic branches, indicates that WTO Members recognize the welfare-enhancing economic effect of liberalizing their most important economic branches under PTAs. However, pursuant to Arts. 1 and 10 TMTRA, the provisions of the TMTRA cannot be considered as capable of clarifying the existing regulations on PTAs in a manner that would require WTO Members to encompass their most important economic branches by PTAs.

[60] Kim (2018), p. 376, who refers to the transparency mechanism as an instrument to coerce peer pressure on WTO Members.

2.3.1.1.3.2.1.1   First Element: Coverage of Trade Under a PTA

WTO Members are required to cover a certain portion of international trade between them upon the implementation of a PTA. Concerning the trade in goods, Art. XXIV:8 lit. b) GATT 1994 establishes the obligation to cover 'substantially all trade [...] between the constituent territories'[61] for CUs, FTAs, and IAs. This so-called "SAT requirement"[62] remains highly debated among WTO Members. Exact thresholds that would satisfy this criterion are heavily disputed.[63] In the CRTA,[64] an average level of 90% of eliminated tariff lines by means of a PTA was proposed for the trade in goods.[65]

Decisions of the WTO-DSM on this matter did not add precision to this element. The findings in the few cases that involved the legal assessment of PTAs remained general. In the case of *Turkey – Textiles*, which involved the legal assessment of a CU, the AB showed much restraint to engage in economic discussions. Instead, it confirmed some economic observations of a general nature:[66]

> "[...] It is clear, though, that "substantially all the trade" is not the same as **all** the trade, and also that "substantially all the trade" is something considerably more than **merely some** of the trade."[67] (emphasis added)

The understanding of the AB has confirmed that not the entirety of trade between the PTA partners has to be covered by a PTA.[68] Conversely, the content of this provision has become subject to a discussion widely informed by economic theory and aiming at the maximization of welfare effects by PTAs.[69] In this vein, an understanding has developed under which the "SAT requirement" can be understood not only quantitatively, but also qualitatively.

Under the quantitative approach, only the numerical share of liberalized trade in goods based on the overall existing trade of the respective PTA partners would be considered for purposes of assessing the "SAT requirement". Such a calculation would make it easier for PTA partners to select branches of their industries to which the liberalization commitment under a PTA applies. On the other hand, this wide

---

[61] On the institutional and economic importance of the 'substantially all trade' requirement regarding trade diversion, cf. Schwartz and Sykes (1996), pp. 45–50.

[62] Rigod (2013), pp. 427–428.

[63] Viner (2014), p. 63, who proposed a total removal of duties for complete liberalization of trade due to its trade-enhancing—instead of trade-distorting—effect; WTO Appellate Body, *Turkey — Restrictions on Imports of Textile and Clothing Products*, WT/DS34/AB/R, Judgment of 22 October 1999, para. 48.

[64] The Committee on Regional Trade Agreements is responsible for the review of PTAs falling under Art. XXIV GATT 1994 and Art. V GATS, according to Art. 18 TMRTA.

[65] Kim (2018), n. 6.

[66] Ibid., pt. 3.2.

[67] WTO Appellate Body, *Turkey — Restrictions on Imports of Textile and Clothing Products*, WT/DS34/AB/R, Judgment of 22 October 1999, para. 48.

[68] For a historical context of this requirement, cf. Winters (2017).

[69] Cf. *supra* Sect. 2.3.1.1.1.

discretion of PTA partners in selecting the industries in their economies to which the trade liberalization commitment applies was argued to counteract the welfare-enhancing effect resulting from the exploitation of an economy's comparative advantage.[70] It would enable PTA partners to exempt uncompetitive industries from PTA liberalization commitments. As a consequence, uncompetitive industries could continue to remain less productive, given that trade barriers would remain in place even after the implementation of a PTA.

Under the qualitative approach, a selection of industries which is solely based on the net worth of the economic performance of a PTA partner would be inadmissible. Instead, all industries would need to be covered by PTA to a certain degree, e.g., the proposed economic benchmark 90% of tariff lines. This would make the qualitative approach more demanding regarding the liberalization obligation—and consequently have more potential on the creation of *adaptation costs* for both PTA partners' economies, as generally all industries would cease to be protected by the trade barriers existing prior to the implementation of a PTA to a certain degree. In this vein, the qualitative approach to the "SAT requirement" has been argued as securing higher welfare gains.[71] It could be argued that the Fourth Recital of UArt. XXIV GATT 1994 reflects this economic consideration. It states that the

> contribution [to the expansion of world trade] is increased if the elimination between the constituent territories of duties and other restrictive regulations of commerce extends to all trade, and [is] diminished if any **major sector** of trade is excluded. (emphasis added)

The term 'major sector' can be understood qualitatively, as the adjective *major* refers to not only to the size, but also to the economic importance of one sector within the economy of a PTA partner that should be covered under a PTA.

Nevertheless, WTO Members could not agree on a specific benchmark that could be put to the test, e.g., for the resolution of disputes on this matter despite the plethora of economic argumentations on the "SAT requirement".

The debate equally persists concerning the liberalization of trade in services in the context of EIAs.[72] Art. V:1 lit. a) and b) GATS provide that EIAs are required to have 'substantial coverage' (lit. a) 'between or among the parties, in the sectors covered under subparagraph (a)' (lit. b). On the other hand, provisions on PSAs and EIA DCs leave ample discretion to PTA partners concerning the coverage of trade by these PTAs. For EIA DCs, Art. V:3 lit. a) GATS prescribes general *flexibility* for the conditions set out in Art. V:1 GATS, including the coverage of trade by these PTAs. Art. V GATS provides for a combination of a qualitative and quantitative understanding[73] of the criterion on sectoral coverage which applies to EIAs. In its footnote, it states:

---

[70] Mark Manager in Dür and Elsig (2015), p. 201 PTA design, tariffs and intra-industry trade.

[71] Mavroidis (2005), pp. 236–238.

[72] Islam and Alam (2009), pp. 23–26.

[73] Cottier and Foltea (2006), p. 47.

This condition is understood in terms of number of sectors, volume of trade affected and modes of supply. In order to meet this condition, agreements should not provide for the a priori exclusion of any mode of supply.

Likewise, in the case *Canada – Autos,* the panel interpreted the criterion under Art. V:1 GATS in a general manner and held that it prescribes

"a certain 'minimum level of liberalization which such agreements must attain in order to qualify for the exemption from the general MFN obligation of Article II'."[74]

However, it did not further elaborate on precise economic data that would fulfil this standard. Moreover, the same panel stated that EIAs

"typically aim at achieving higher levels of liberalization between or among their parties than that achieved among WTO Members",[75]

which again could only serve as a general principle, but remained far away from an economic benchmark to measure the coverage of PTAs.

In contrast, the provisions under the Enabling Clause on PTAs do not contain any criterion referring to the coverage of trade. This omission serves as an argument for developing-country WTO Members to retain wide discretion on the coverage of trade under the respective PTAs. This corresponds with the economically less demanding approach offered for developing-country WTO Members under the S&D treatment.[76]

2.3.1.1.3.2.1.2 Second Element: Indicators for Hindrances in International Trade Between PTA Partners

Additionally, WTO provisions on PTAs define indicators for hindrances in international trade between PTA partners. They aim at ensuring that the trade covered by PTAs will be effectively liberalized between PTA partners. Depending on whether PTAs cover the trade in goods or services, the relevant provisions set out different requirements.

Concerning the trade in goods, Art. XXIV:8 GATT 1994 defines, for CUs, FTAs, and IAs, duties or other restrictive regulations of trade as references for the measurement trade liberalization in a PTA. The more recent Enabling Clause sets out 'tariffs' and 'non-tariff measures' for PSAs as points of reference. Both references cover fiscal and non-fiscal measures that could hinder free international trade between PTA partners.

Concerning fiscal measures, the term 'duties' refers to tariffs which are applied on goods originating from the respective PTA partner's territory as the first indicator for

---

[74] WTO Panel, *Canada — Certain Measures Affecting the Automotive Industry,* WT/DS139/R WT/DS142/R, Judgment of 11 February 2000, para. 10.271.

[75] Ibid., para. 10.271.

[76] Hamanaka (2012), p. 1240.

hindrances in international trade in goods.[77] The legal test whether or not WTO Members comply with this obligation requires a comparison of tariffs applied on all goods originating from the respective PTA partner's territory before and after the implementation of the PTA. Although seemingly straightforward, it does not necessarily provide for an accurate measurement whether tariffs on goods were in fact cut by PTA partners.[78] As WTO Members remain free to determine their own customs classification, this creates a certain leeway to select or exclude specific types of goods from the disciplines of a PTA.[79] In practice, this flexibility is somewhat constrained given that the majority of WTO Members applies the Harmonized Commodity Description and Coding System (Harmonized System), which contains guidelines on an identical use of tariffs for specific goods. Based on its application, WTO Members express trade liberalization achieved by means of a PTA in the percentage of tariff lines affected by it.[80]

On the non-fiscal side, the economic content of 'other restrictive regulations of commerce' has proven difficult to ascertain. Faced with its interpretation, the panel in *Turkey – Textiles* proposed a very broad understanding covering all measures that have *any impact* on trade but left it equally vague, defining it "as an evolving concept".[81]

Under Art. 2 lit. c) Enabling Clause, two indicators are established equally for fiscal and non-fiscal hindrances for the trade in goods among PTA partners. Yet, a different wording is used, as 'tariffs' and 'non-tariff measures' are defined as the points of reference for the liberalization of trade. Given that tariffs and custom duties are used synonymously, the legal discussion under Art. XXIV:8 GATT 1994 equally applies here. Equally, 'non-tariff measures' and 'other restrictive regulations of commerce' need to be considered as being synonymous.[82] Consequently, the difficulties encountered under Art. XXIV:8 GATT 1994 also reappear in the context of PTAs to which the Enabling Clause applies.

---

[77] See Van den Bossche (2005), pp. 379–389, for the nuances in the use of tariffs and duties. for the nuances in the use of tariffs and duties.

[78] It is possible that PTA partners could eliminate certain tariffs on products which are traded between each other, while at the same subjecting the actual traded products to other tariff lines that remain in place. In a scenario without a PTA, the discipline of Art. II:5, in conjunction with Art. II.1 GATT 1994, can have a limiting effect on WTO Members. Whether Art. II:5 and 1 GATT 1994 prevail in a PTA context under Art. XXIV GATT is questionable.

[79] GATT Panel, *Spain — Tariff Treatment of Unroasted Coffee*, L/5135-28S/102, Judgment of 11 June 1981, para. 4.4.

[80] See, e.g., Committee on Regional Trade Agreements (2019) Factual presentation—Accession of Panama to the Central American Common Market (CACM)—Goods—Report by the Secretariat—Revision, p. 12.

[81] WTO Panel, *Turkey — Restrictions on Imports of Textile and Clothing Products*, WT/DS34/R, Judgment of 31 May 1999, para. 9.120. Moreover, the Panel in this case and other Panels in subsequent cases did not provide guidance on the relationship between the application of trade remedies such as antidumping duties, safeguard measures, and countervailing duties on PTA and non-PTA partners. For a discussion on parallelism see Islam and Alam (2009), pp. 14–18.

[82] Kim (2011), p. 475.

Concerning the trade in services, under Art. V:1 GATS, WTO Members are required to eliminate discrimination between different services in EIAs.[83] 'Discrimination' is set out as the only relevant indicator for hindrances in international trade to measure the liberalization achieved under PTAs covering trade in services. The term needs to be understood in the sense of its use under Art. XVII GATS.[84] Therefore, it requires WTO Members to apply it to the actually covered services in a WTO Members' schedule, since the scope of application of Art. XVII GATS remains limited to the services specified therein. The indicator for hindrances in international trade of 'discrimination' stipulates a clear benchmark from an economic point of view. Nevertheless, it also remains open to interpretation, as it requires a legal assessment on the likeness of services covered under the respective PTAs to ensure whether it is subject to the liberalization obligation established under Art. V:1 GATS.

2.3.1.1.3.2.1.3   Third Element: Extent of Trade Liberalization

The WTO provisions on PTAs require WTO Members to carry out specific actions regarding the indicators for hindrances of the trade among PTA partners. Differences concerning these actions translate into different extents of trade liberalization that need to be aimed at between PTA partners. They vary according to the type of PTA and trade covered thereunder. The extent of trade liberalization of a specific PTA can be analyzed at a quantitative and qualitative level.

At the quantitative level, the extent of trade liberalization refers to the question how much liberalization of trade must take place due to a PTA's implementation. At the qualitative level, the extent of trade liberalization refers to the subsequent question in which manner liberalization of trade must take place in PTAs.

Concerning the trade in goods, under Art. XXIV:8 GATT 1994 PTA partners are required quantitatively within CUs, FTAs, and IAs to 'eliminate duties' and 'other restrictive regulations of commerce'. Qualitatively, this obligation does not provide any information on the specific process of obtaining this result. It has therefore been argued that the liberalization of trade in PTAs requires this process to be reciprocal regarding all PTA partners. The reciprocal liberalization of trade is claimed to align most with key principles of WTO law.[85] It was put forward that the provisions are prescribed to liberalize the trade covered by a PTA between and by all PTA partners.[86] Such a manner of trade liberalization was argued to constitute the foundation of the principle of reciprocity. According to this principle, PTA partners

---

[83] This is most probably due to their low impact on trade in services, Islam and Alam (2009), p. 24.

[84] WTO Panel, *Canada — Certain Measures Affecting the Automotive Industry*, WT/DS139/R WT/DS142/R, Judgment of 11 February 2000, para. 10.269.

[85] Referring to reciprocity as a GATT principle, see Mavroidis (2007), pp. 70–71.

[86] Ibid., p. 64; see likewise GATT Panel, *European Communities — Tariff Treatment on Imports of Citrus Products from Certain Countries in the Mediterranean Region*, L/5776, Judgment of 7 February 1985, para. 4.7. (f).

are required to liberalize their trade equally by the same amount at the same general level, instead of opting for an individual and different level of trade liberalization. This would make the liberalization process in a PTA independent from the efforts for trade liberalization of the individual PTA partners, and as such it was said effectively to prevent unequal trade liberalization.[87] Conversely, effective prevention of unequal trade liberalization in a PTA was argued to be beneficial for achieving welfare-enhancing effects.[88] Connected to the question of reciprocity is the issue of symmetry of trade liberalization in PTAs. Symmetry in trade liberalization describes the equilibrium of tariff and non-tariff concessions made by PTA partners through the implementation of a PTA. Where existent, under the principle of symmetry, PTA partners would be required to make concessions on the same specific parts of trade which are liberalized under a PTA. The principle of symmetry would also have a bearing on the understanding of the "SAT requirement". It would oblige PTA partners to make a comparable selection of trade covered under the respective PTA, resulting in the coverage of the same industry branches. This argument is made regularly regarding the potential welfare-enhancing effects, which depend on the many additional factors such as the size of the economies of PTA partners.[89]

Finally, the duty to liberalize trade in PTAs is not infinite. The provisions on PTAs also foresee exceptions to it, under the condition that specific requirements are fulfilled. Regarding CUs, FTAs, and IAs, Art. XXIV:8 GATT 1994 contains an exception for trade-restrictive measures to be introduced 'where necessary, those permitted' under Arts. XI, XII, XIII, XIV, XV, and XX GATT 1994. Confronted with this provision, the AB in the case *Brazil – Retreaded Tyres* confirmed that a trade-restrictive measure that had been introduced in the context of Art. XX GATT 1994 between PTA partners would not be subject to the obligation to liberalize trade within a PTA:

> "Therefore, if we assume, for the sake of argument, that MERCOSUR is consistent with Article XXIV and that the Import Ban meets the requirements of Article XX, this measure, where necessary, could be exempted by virtue of Article XXIV:8(a) from the obligation to eliminate other restrictive regulations of commerce within a customs union."[90]

Thus, the AB advanced a double hypothesis, namely that the four elements of the internal requirement under Art. XXIV:8 lit. a) GATT 1994 were fulfilled in the given case, for the purpose of establishing yet another hypothesis, i.e., that the exception from trade liberalization in a CU equally applies to trade-restrictive measures introduced in conformity with Art. XX GATT 1994. Although the argument is quite clear about the existence of an exception concerning the duty to liberalize

---

[87] Devuyst and Serdarevic (2007), pp. 29–32.

[88] The issue of "unequal" treaties has been witnessed throughout history. Northrup et al. (2015), pp. 491–499 at p. 493. Cf. also Cattaneo (2009), pp. 47–50, for a critical analysis of the implementation of the reciprocity requirement from a political and historical viewpoint.

[89] Baldwin and Robert-Nicoud (2000).

[90] WTO Appellate Body, *Brazil — Measures Affecting Imports of Retreaded Tyres*, WT/DS332/AB/R, Judgment of 3 December 2007, n. 445.

trade within a CU, it remains obscure regarding its content.[91] The AB in particular did not address the extent of it. Regarding the content of the exception, the trade-restrictive measures within a PTA would have to fulfil the requirements of being *necessary* and *permitted* under Arts. XI, XII, XIII, XIV, XV, and XX GATT 1994. The question remains whether the list under Art. XXIV:8 GATT 1994 is of enumerative or exhaustive character. Arguments in favor of an enumerative nature of the list have also entailed views to include countervailing duties and safeguard measures under Art. XVI GATT 1994 into its scope, given their inherently trade-restrictive character.[92] Yet, whether countervailing duties and safeguard measures are truly trade-restrictive measures is still up for debate.[93] Regarding the extent of the exception, the inclusion of countervailing duties and safeguard measures into the scope of exceptions under Art. XXIV:8 GATT 1994 leads to the question of their administration concerning trade, which is covered by a PTA, and compared trade, which is not covered by a PTA.

The possibility to impose countervailing duties and safeguard measures on goods which were not covered by a PTA, has given rise to assume a principle of parallelism within the exception under Art. XXIV:8 GATT 1994.[94] In line with this principle of parallelism, PTA partners would be required to include *all* trading partners, i.e., specifically their PTA partners in the investigation on the negative trade effect they want to counteract and the application of measures they apply in this regard. The principle of parallelism would therefore not allow for PTA partners to confer privileges on each other because of the interconnectedness of their economies due to the existence of a PTA. In this context, in *Argentina – Footwear*, Argentina could not successfully rely on the invocation of Art. XXIV GATT 1994 as a justification for the introduction of safeguard measures introduced under Art. XIX GATT 1994 and the SG Agreement.[95] The safeguard measure excluded goods that did not originate from Mercosur member states by disregarding PTA partners' footwear suppliers, although they were previously included in the injury investigation and their products were found to cause an injury to the Argentine domestic production.[96] The panel took into account the argument by Argentina that the internal liberalization requirement under Art. XXIV:8 lit. a) GATT 1994 required Argentina to apply safeguard measures only to non-PTA partners, but rejected it on the basis that the MERCOSUR treaty would have still not attained the status of covering

---

[91] The AB has equally left obscure the content of the second element of the internal requirement in two ways. On the one hand, the question on the exact portion of SAT trade remains unsettled; on the other hand, it remains unclear which legal regime applies to the portion of trade that is not covered under the SAT requirement nor is encompassed by the duty to liberalize trade between PTA partners; cf. Sect. 2.3.1.1.3.2.1.2.

[92] Trachtman (2003), p. 483.

[93] For an overview of the debate, cf. Gobbi Estrella and Horlick (2006).

[94] Rodríguez Mendoza et al. (1999), pp. 67–72.

[95] For a detailed overview, cf. de Mestral (2013), pp. 791–794.

[96] WTO Panel, *Argentina — Safeguard Measures on Imports of Footwear (EC)*, WT/DS121R, Judgment of 25 June 1999, para. 8.72.

"substantially all the trade".[97] The panel implied that Art. XXIV GATT 1994 could justify a measure which would have exclusively adverse effects on non-PTA partners. The AB reversed the panel's finding, but solely on grounds derived from the SG Agreement. It did not carry out any analysis under Art. XXIV GATT 1994.[98] Rather, in the view of the AB, the exclusion of non-PTA partners ran against the principle of parallelism established in the SG Agreement.[99] As Argentina did not raise Art. XXIV GATT 1994 as a defense that could justify any violation of the GATT 1994, the AB wished to

"underscore that, [. . .], we [i.e., the AB] make no ruling on whether, as a general principle, a member of a customs union can exclude other members of that customs union from the application of a safeguard measure."[100]

Ultimately, the depth of the justification provided under the provisions of Art. XXIV GATT 1994 and the Enabling Clause are difficult to ascertain concerning the violation of GATT 1994 provisions between and among PTA partners concerning the trade in goods.[101] Especially for the portion of trade that is not covered by the "SAT requirement", it is imaginable that the justification provided by Art. XXIV GATT 1994 could have an impact on the involved PTA partners' rights and obligations arising under WTO rules, at least regarding the MFN treatment among them. In this context, it was argued that the provisions could even constitute an amendment to the provision of the multilateral WTO treaty as so-called *inter se* treaties between PTA partners.[102] Yet, the provision does not contain any explicit information on whether and how a PTA can modify the substantive rights and

---

[97] Ibid., para. 8.98; 8.101.

[98] WTO Appellate Body, *Argentina — Safeguard Measures on Imports of Footwear (EC)*, WT/DS121/AB/R, Judgment of 14 December 1999, para. 114.

[99] Ibid., para. 111. The same approach was taken in WTO Panel, *United States — Definitive Safeguard Measures on Imports of Certain Steel Products*, WT/DS166/R, Judgment of 31 July 2000, para. 8.181., upheld by the AB WTO Appellate Body, *United States — Definitive Safeguard Measures on Imports of Certain Steel Products*, WT/DS166/AB/R, Judgment of 22 December 2000, para. 99. Equally, the AB did not consider Art. XXIV GATT 1994 as a defense to a safeguard measure which exempted PTA partners of the NAFTA from an injury investigation. Under this measure the PTA partners' suppliers were included in the injury investigation and the responsible US authority did not make any statement that only non-PTA partners' product suppliers would be subject to it. In the same vein, cf. WTO Appellate Body, *United States — Definitive Safeguard Measures on Imports of Circular Welded Carbon Quality Line Pipe from Korea*, WT/DS202/AB/R, Judgment of 15 February 2002, para. 198.

[100] WTO Appellate Body, *Argentina — Safeguard Measures on Imports of Footwear (EC)*, WT/DS121/AB/R, Judgment of 14 December 1999, p. 114.

[101] The same problem arises when assessing the legality of countermeasures pursuant to PTA law; cf. Marceau and Wyatt (2010), pp. 73ff.

[102] See Pauwelyn (2003), p. 316, who advances that PTAs amount to an inter se modification of WTO obligations.

obligations of PTA partners arising under WTO rules vis-à-vis each other.[103] The provisions in particular are mute on the prohibition of discrimination of PTA partners within the same PTA.[104] Consequently, it remains possible for PTA partners to maintain and introduce trade-restrictive measures, even if they conform with the liberalization obligation established under Art. XXIV:8 GATT 1994. It follows that generally trade-restrictive measures can continue to exist in a PTA even if they affect the portion of trade to which the liberalization obligation under Art. XXIV:8 GATT 1994 applies, if they conform with the criteria set out above. Conversely, the portion of trade not covered by the "SAT requirement" escapes the ambit of the Art. XXIV GATT 1994, which would consequently allow PTA partners to create individual solutions for the regulation of this part of trade.

Nonetheless, it was argued that the provisions on PTAs cannot serve to carve out other WTO provisions completely between PTA partners.[105] The AB in the case *Peru – Agricultural Products*, facing the contention that an FTA could modify the rights and obligations between the involved WTO Members, argued in the context of Art. XXIV GATT 1994

"[...] that the purpose of a customs union or FTA is 'to facilitate trade' between the constituent members and 'not to raise barriers to the trade' with third countries [and that] paragraph 4 qualifies customs unions or FTAs as 'agreements, of closer integration between the economies of the countries parties to such agreements'. In our view, the references in paragraph 4 to facilitating trade and closer integration are not consistent with an interpretation of Article XXIV as a broad defence for measures in FTAs that roll back on Members' rights and obligations under the WTO covered agreements."[106]

The AB's reading of the provision requires a more extensive argumentation. Neither Art. XXIV GATT 1994 nor the Enabling Clause provide for a textual basis according to which PTA partners are still bound to the MFN principle among themselves within a PTA under these provisions. In order to be still applicable

---

[103] At this point, only the substantive rights and obligations between WTO Members are addressed. The implication of the provisions on PTAs on the procedural right to dispute settlement at the WTO will be addressed separately at Sect. 2.3.1.2.

[104] Whether discriminatory treatment of PTA partners can be mandated under the provisions of PTAs is a crucial question for PTAs with more than two PTA partners. Here, a situation can arise in which one PTA partner (A) provides better treatment of the goods or services of another PTA partner (B) compared to a third PTA partner (C). In this case, C could claim to have the right to receive equal treatment as the one accorded to B—a situation that would normally give rise to the violation of the provisions of Art. I GATT 1994 for trade in goods, or Art. XVII GATS for trade in services. It is doubtful whether these provisions, incorporating the MFN obligations, could still be invoked between PTA partners. Such an understanding of the MFN obligation would require PTA partners to treat each other on an MFN basis depending on the treatment offered to other PTA partners. Consequently, a prohibition of discriminatory treatment among PTA partners could only be inferred from the aforementioned provisions on PTAs. Note that the elements of reciprocity and symmetry, at the qualitative level of the extent of trade liberalization, exist as a direct reflection of the problem to identify the scope of justification provided by the provisions on PTAs.

[105] For an in-depth analysis, cf. Mathis (2001), chap. 9.

[106] WTO Appellate Body, *Peru — Additional Duty on Imports of Certain Agricultural Products*, WT/DS457/AB/R, Judgment of 20 July 2015, para. 5.116.

among PTA partners, the MFN principle would have to be understood as detached from the one stipulated under Art. I GATT 1994—as an abstract value of the GATT 1994. Yet, the wording of Art. I: 1 GATT 1994 sets out only one benchmark for the infringement of the MFN principle. Art. XXIV GATT 1994 and the Enabling Clause serve as a justification and cover exactly this dimension of the MFN infringement.[107] Should such an abstract MFN value exist within the GATT 1994, it could also play a role for the question whether favorable treatment among PTA partners in one PTA should be extended to the same PTA partners within another PTA. Yet, the argumentation of the panel in *Indonesia — Iron or Steel* reads critical to such an understanding of an abstract MFN value. It emphasizes the freedom of WTO Members to negotiate their PTAs as they deem appropriate:

"Article XXIV of the GATT 1994 is a permissive provision, allowing Members to depart from their obligations under the GATT to establish a customs union and/or free trade area, in accordance with specified procedures. Article XXIV does not impose any positive obligation on Indonesia either to enter into free trade agreements (FTAs) or to provide a certain level of market access to its FTA partners through bound tariffs."[108]

In contrast, under Art. 2 lit. c) Enabling Clause, WTO Members are required to reduce *or* eliminate 'tariffs' and 'non-tariff measures' in a PSA. Consequently, elimination of the indicators for hindrances of the trade among them is only optional. Given that Art. 2 lit. c) Enabling Clause lacks a minimum threshold for the reduction of 'tariffs' and 'non-tariff measures', a reduction of the indicators for hindrances of the trade among them can be achieved through their decrease by PTA partners at any level. Pursuant to Art. 2 lit. c) Enabling Clause, the reduction or elimination of 'tariffs' and 'non-tariff measures' should take place in a *mutual* manner. The term clarifies that the higher flexibility on the liberalization of trade should nevertheless be understood to require *all* PTA partners to lower their trade barriers that were in place prior to a PTA's implementation. However, it does not clarify the quality of the elimination or reduction of tariffs and non-tariff measures PTA partners carry out. This makes the debate on the existence of the principles of reciprocity and symmetry equally applicable in the context of the Enabling Clause. At the bottom line, the requirement seems to prevent WTO Members from unilateral trade liberalization which arises when exclusively one of the PTA partners in PSAs is required to implement corresponding measures. Moreover, the Enabling Clause does not contain any exceptions to the obligation to liberalize trade between PTA partners. Pursuant to the rationale underlying Art. 2 lit. c) Enabling Clause to provide developing country WTO Members with more flexibility due to their specific economic situation, it would be nevertheless plausible to assume that the exceptions

---

[107] Opposingly, Mathis (2001), chap. 9.5.

[108] WTO Panel, *Indonesia — Safeguard on Certain Iron or Steel Products*, WT/DS490/R; WT/DS496/R, Judgment of 18 August 2017, para. 7.20.

available under Art. XXIV:8 GATT 1994 to the liberalization obligation are equally available in the context of PSAs.[109]

Concerning the trade in services, Art. V:1 lit. b) GATS prescribes within EIAs discrimination to be *eliminated* or to be *absent*. According to Art. V:1 lit. b) (i) and (ii) GATS, this is to be achieved by PTA partners through the 'elimination of existing discriminatory measures', as well as through a prohibition of 'new' or 'more discriminatory' measures. Concerning S&D treatment in the trade in services, the provisions on PSAs and EIA DCs leave ample room for PTA partners to choose the extent of liberalization they wish to pursue. Regarding EIA DCs, Art.V:3 lit. s) GATS prescribes flexibility to the criteria under Art. V:1 lit. b) GATS 'in accordance with the level of development of the countries concerned' and thereby the extent of trade liberalization. Under EIA DCs, it is therefore likewise possible to assume that any reduction of discriminatory treatment is already sufficient to fulfil this requirement. Regarding the principle of reciprocity in EIA DCs, Art. V:3 GATS provides flexibility on all criteria set out in Art. V:1 lit. b) GATS and could thus provide for a derogation from the principle of reciprocity.[110] Equally, Art. V:1 lit. b) GATS contains an exception to the liberalization obligation and allows maintaining of the respective indicators for hindrances in international trade among PTA partners of EIAs, if they fulfil the provisions of Arts. XI, XII, XIV, and XIV bis GATS. In parallel to the Enabling Clause, EIA DCs are not specifically addressed by the exception under Art. V:1 lit. b) GATS. Regarding the depth of the justification, the panel in *Canada – Autos* stated that

> "the object and purpose of this provision is to eliminate all discrimination among services and service suppliers of parties to an economic integration agreement, including discrimination between suppliers of other parties to an economic integration agreement."[111]

The conclusion reached in this decision is easier to reconcile with wording provided under Art. V GATS, which sets out that within EIAs *all discrimination* must be eliminated.[112] It speaks for an understanding that the MFN principle prevails in the legal relationship between PTA partners—although the provisions on PTAs provide a justification of the violation of the very same principle.

---

[109] See Islam and Alam (2009), p. 22, arguing for a high flexibility of WTO Members that engage in PSAs.

[110] Nwobike (2008), p. 99, analyzing the consequences of the reciprocity requirement for PTAs between Developed and Developing WTO Members (North-South PTAs), taking into account the non-reciprocal principles of Special and Differential (S&D) Treatment; and Ochieng (2007); Bartels (2008), p. 149.

[111] WTO Panel, *Canada — Certain Measures Affecting the Automotive Industry*, WT/DS139/R WT/DS142/R, Judgment of 11 February 2000, para. 10.270.

[112] *Supra* Sect. 2.3.1.1.3.2.1.3.

2.3.1.1.3.2.1.4   Fourth Element: The Temporal Requirement

Additionally, the provisions on PTAs prescribe WTO Members to fulfil trade liberalization within a specific period. This temporal element varies across the different types of PTAs.

Regarding the trade in goods, the provisions on CUs and FTAs prescribe as a general principle that trade liberalization must be accomplished right at the outset of a PTA. Art. XXIV GATT 1994 only provides for one deviation for IAs for which WTO Members must finalize the process of liberalization during a 'reasonable length of time'. Regarding IAs, Para. 3 of the UArt. XXIV 1994[113] sets out that the 'reasonable length of time' referred to in Art. XXIV:5 lit. c) GATT 1994 should exceed 10 years only in exceptional cases. Where PTA partners of an IA believe that this time frame of 10 years would be insufficient, they must provide a full explanation for their need of a longer period to the Council for Trade in Goods, which oversees the review of IAs. The Council for Trade in Goods can propose amendments to the plan for the trade liberalization in the IA pursuant to its authority granted in Art. XXIV:10 GATT 1994. For a better assessment of WTO members' efforts to liberalize trade in an IA, Art. XXIV:5 lit. c) GATT 1994 contains the additional requirement that these PTAs must include a plan and a schedule for their formation within the aforementioned 'reasonable length of time'.

Concerning the trade in services, following the general principle established under Art. XXIV GATT 1994, liberalization of services must be effective in an EIA within its implementation. Equally, the derogation from this principle is uniquely available for EIAs with time frames. Here, too, the effective liberalization can take place 'on the basis of a reasonable time frame', according to Art. V:1 lit. b) (ii) GATS. A clarification on the length of this period as provided under Para. 3 UArt 1994 does not exist for Art. V GATS. It remains entirely obscure.[114]

The flexibility granted in the provisions governing PSAs under the Enabling Clause is reflected equally concerning IEA DCs under Art. V GATS. The provision does not contain any temporal criterion. Here, the liberalization can take place at the WTO Members' required pace, considering the specific economic needs of the involved PTA partners.

2.3.1.1.3.2.2   Ambiguities of the External Requirement

The external requirement arising from the WTO rules on PTAs is equally disputed. Generally, the external requirement is destined to ensure that the economic effects resulting from the implementation of a PTA are not adverse for WTO Members that are not part of it. Panels as well as the AB have refrained from establishing precise economic thresholds to ascertain whether a PTA has adverse economic effects on non-PTA partners among WTO Members.

---

[113] Included under Art. 1.2 lit. c (iv) GATT 1994.

[114] Stephenson (2010), p. 95.

Concerning the trade in goods, under Art. XXIV:5 lits. a) and b) GATT 1994 it is established that 'duties' and 'other restrictive regulations on commerce' must not overall be higher than prior to the conclusion of the respective CU or FTA. The same applies to IAs, which are equally addressed under the same provisions and for which Art. XXIV:5 lit. b) GATT 1994.

Faced with a CU, the panel in *Turkey – Textiles* stated that in sum

"the effects of the resulting trade measures and policies of the new regional agreement shall not be more trade restrictive, overall, than were the constituent countries' previous trade policies."[115]

The panel did not provide additional information how to measure such an effect of the previous trade policies, i.e., those existing prior to the implementation of a PTA. The content of this requirement is heavily debated regarding trade diversion caused by PTAs, as barriers to trade existing prior to the implementation of a PTA can also be maintained thereafter.

Leaving aside the difficulties surrounding the content of this provision, the depth of the justification it entails is highly disputed concerning the effect of trade policies on non-PTA partners among WTO Members. As a flipside to the principle of parallelism, the question arises whether WTO Members can have recourse to the respective justifications offered for PTAs, if they adopt trade-restrictive measures on non-PTA partners among WTO Members arising from the measures implementing a PTA.

Although panels and the AB were already facing the interpretative problems on the depth of the justifications for PTAs, they usually would assume the consistency of PTAs with the relevant provisions,[116] preventing any clarification on this issue. As a general remark on invoking the provisions on PTAs as a justification, the AB noted in the context of a CU in the case *Turkey – Textiles* that the WTO Member invoking Art. XXIV GATT 1994 bears the burden of proof to establish that the PTA is in conformity with the requirements of this provision.[117] Moreover, the AB laid out that Art. XXIV GATT 1994 could be invoked for violations of the GATT beyond the violation of Art. I GATT 1994.[118] This finding confirms the potential of Art. XXIV GATT 1994 to be used as a justification for the violation of other WTO rules vis-à-vis non-PTA partners among WTO Members. In this context, it was claimed that the Turkish import restrictions on textiles violated Art. XI GATT 1994:

---

[115] WTO Panel, *Turkey — Restrictions on Imports of Textile and Clothing Products*, WT/DS34/R, Judgment of 31 May 1999, para. 9.121.

[116] E.g., WTO Panel, *United States — Definitive Safeguard Measures on Imports of Certain Steel Products*, WT/DS166/R, Judgment of 31 July 2000, para. 7.114.

[117] "[. . .] First, the party claiming the benefit of this defence must demonstrate that the measure at issue is introduced upon the formation of a customs union *that fully meets the requirements of sub-paragraphs 8(a) and 5(a) of Article XXIV.*" (emphasis added), cf. WTO Appellate Body, *Turkey — Restrictions on Imports of Textile and Clothing Products*, WT/DS34/AB/R, Judgment of 22 October 1999, para. 58.

[118] Ibid., para. 45.

however, these were introduced in connection with the implementation of a CU between Turkey and the European Communities. Turkey argued that the treaty establishing the CU between the European Communities and itself required it to introduce an import ban on textiles imported by non-PTA partners among WTO Members to prevent the circumvention of the quantitative restrictions upheld by the European Communities against other countries. In response to this discriminatory treatment of non-PTA partners among WTO Members concerning the import restrictions, the AB introduced a soon-to-be-labelled "necessity" test to ensure that such a discriminatory treatment of non-PTA partners could only be justified under Art. XXIV GATT 1994 if it satisfied two conditions: Firstly, the measure must have been introduced *upon the formation* of a CU. Secondly, the measure would have *prevented* the formation of the CU if its introduction was not allowed.[119] The AB suggested that the structure of Art. XXIV GATT 1994 called for a two-pronged test in which the responding party first would have to demonstrate that a CU fulfils the internal and external requirements for the discriminatory measure at issue. Facing the external effects of a measure introduced under a CU, the AB relied on the rationale of the external requirement under Art. XXIV:5 lit. a) GATT 1994 and found that Art. XXIV:5 lit. a) i) GATT 1994 contained a *chapeau*, which governs PTA partners' rights and obligations with regard to the effects of external measures.[120] Under the second prong of the test, the AB considered the legal requirements under the treaty establishing the CU and whether they allowed for the flexible adoption of measures ensuring preservation of its objective.[121] Having found that the treaty establishing the CU between Turkey and the European Communities provided for sufficient flexibility to adopt measures that would lead to less trade-restrictive effects for non-PTA partners among WTO Members, the AB suggested alternatives to the import ban.[122]

The test applied by the AB established a high threshold for measures introduced with the implementation of a PTA that have a trade-restrictive effect on non-PTA partners. It faced severe criticism,[123] as the wording of Art. XXIV:5 GATT 1994 did not to support such an understanding.[124] Presumably the AB approached this problem in this manner despite the lack of a textual basis, as it realized the far-reaching implications of the implementation of PTAs on the multilateral obligations of WTO Members. Only in this way could the AB arrive at the conclusion that

---

[119]Trachtman (2011), pp. 131–132.

[120]Cf. WTO Appellate Body, *Turkey — Restrictions on Imports of Textile and Clothing Products*, WT/DS34/AB/R, Judgment of 22 October 1999, para. 58.

[121]Ibid., para. 50.

[122]Note that the AB's inquiry into the flexibility of the treaty allowed it to sidestep the question whether the CU in fact was in conformity with Art. XXIV:5 lit. a) GATT 1994. Had the provisions been inflexible, the AB would have had to assess the compatibility of the CU with the provision.

[123]Pauwelyn (2004), pp. 130–135.

[124]See instructive for the difficult practicality of the 'necessity-test' under Art. XXIV GATT 1994, WTO Panel, *United States — Definitive Safeguard Measures on Imports of Circular Welded Carbon Quality Line Pipe from Korea*, WT/DS202/R, Judgment of 29 October 2001, para. 7.148.

certain core principles of the WTO prevail independently of the justification provided under Art. XXIV GATT 1994, also in the relationship between PTA partners
and non-PTA partners among WTO Members, ascribing them a quasi-constitutional
character. Whether the legal framework of the WTO indeed provides for such a
constitutional understanding of its principles is the subject of highest controversy.[125]

In *Brazil – Retreaded Tyres*, the panel and the AB omitted to clarify further the
depth of the justification for PTAs. In this context, the AB found a Brazilian import
ban on remolded tyres to be illegal.[126] Following the Mercosur TPR decision, which
held that an import ban on remolded tires originating from PTA partners of the
Mercosur agreement was unlawful under Mercosur rules on trade liberalization,[127]
Brazil allowed imports of remolded tires from its PTA partners of the Mercosur
agreement. However, it maintained the import restriction for non-PTA partners.
Art. XXIV GATT 1994 was not raised as a justification for the maintained import
ban on non-PTA partners. Consequently, the panel as well as the AB only dealt with
the measure's compliance with Art. XX GATT 1994. The panel and the AB agreed
with the arguments of Brazil and found the measure to be necessary to protect public
health as referred to in Art. XX lit. b) GATT 1994, in considering the health risk
arising from tires discarded into the wilderness, which consequently provided a
breeding ground for mosquitoes transmitting malaria. However, the panel and the
AB had diverging views on whether the ban complied with the requirements under
the *chapeau* of Art. XX GATT 1994 regarding the exemption of the import ban
granted to PTA partners. In considering whether the exemption constituted an
arbitrary or unjustifiable discrimination, the panel found that the exemption did
not stem from capricious or unpredictable reasons.[128] The panel argued that the
discrimination of non-PTA partners resulting from applying the import ban to them
compared to PTA partners

> "was adopted specifically in the context of an agreement intended to liberalize trade among
> its members. This type of agreement inherently provides for preferential treatment in favor of
> its members, thus leading to discrimination between those members and other countries. To
> the extent that the existence of some discrimination in favor of other members of a customs
> union is an inherent part of its operation, the possibility that such discrimination might arise
> between members of MERCOSUR and other WTO Members as a result of the implemen-
> tation of the MERCOSUR Agreement is not, in our view, a priori unreasonable."[129]

---

[125] Cottier and Foltea (2006), pp. 56ff. That the provisions on PTAs are superior to PTA treaties and
must come with restrictions is self-evident: Otherwise, the supremacy of the WTO agreement would
lead to a transposition of WTO obligations into the PTA (including its functional structure and
decision-making provisions). Since only selected principles should apply within the PTA, the
argument of prevailing WTO principles among PTAs-partners needs to be treated with caution.

[126] The import ban was introduced on the argument that it was necessary to protect human health, as
the remolded tires were discarded in natural environments and subsequently developed into a threat
to human health, serving as a breeding ground for mosquitoes infected with malaria disease.

[127] TPR, *Laudo N°01/2005*, Judgment of 20 December 2005.

[128] WTO Panel, *Brazil — Measures Affecting Imports of Retreaded Tyres*, WT/DS332/R, Judgment
of 12 June 2007, p. 7.272.

[129] Ibid., p. 7.273.

Although the analysis took only place within the context of Art. XX GATT 1994, the panel reinforced the understanding of a limited scope of justification provided by Art. XXIV GATT 1994, as already argued by the AB in *Turkey – Textiles*, as it did

> "[...] not consider that the fact that the measure may be authorized under Article XXIV dispenses Brazil from complying with the requirements of Article XX, including the requirements of the chapeau."[130]

The AB reversed the panel's finding exclusively under the analysis of Art. XX GATT 1994. It argued that the exemption from the import ban resulted in arbitrary and unjustifiable discrimination of non-PTA partners, as it was not rationally related to the aim of the import ban, and hence would not satisfy the requirements of the *chapeau* of Art. XX GATT 1994.[131] Thus, it did not include any further assessment on the compatibility of the exemption under Art. XXIV GATT 1994.

Art. 2 lit. c) Enabling Clause prescribes a less onerous standard regarding the external requirement for PSAs.[132] Accordingly, PSAs should facilitate and promote trade with developing WTO Members and must not create barriers to, or undue difficulties for, the trade of any WTO Member. Compared with the wording of Art. XXIV:5 GATT 1994, the wording of the Enabling Clause provides for a less strict benchmark for prohibited trade effects on non-PTA partners due to the implementation of a PSA, compared with CUs, FTAs, or IAs. The use of the term 'undue burden' in Art. 2 lit. c) Enabling Clause, as opposed to the mere 'increase' of duties and regulations under Art. XXIV GATT:5 GATT 1994, speaks for such an understanding.

Regarding EIAs, Art. V:4 GATS likewise generally prescribes that these PTAs must not raise the overall level of barriers to trade in services within the respective sectors or subsectors compared to the level applicable prior to the conclusion of such a PTA. For EIA DCs, however, in opposition to the Enabling Clause, the provision does not foresee any more flexible standards for the external requirement.

---

[130] Ibid., n. 1448.

[131] WTO Appellate Body, *Brazil — Measures Affecting Imports of Retreaded Tyres*, WT/DS332/AB/R, Judgment of 3 December 2007, para. 228: "[...] the ruling issued by the MERCOSUR arbitral tribunal is not an acceptable rationale for the discrimination, because it bears no relationship to the legitimate objective pursued by the Import Ban that falls within the purview of Article XX(b), and even goes against this objective, to however small a degree."

[132] In light of the other provisions on the external requirement, the provisions governing PSAs do not require a comparison of the economic situation of WTO Members with the PTA partners *ex ante*, with the economic situation *ex post*, that is, the implementation of the respective PTA. In the case of CUs, FTAs, IAs, and EIAs, where such a comparison renders the result that the implementation of a PTA increases the overall barriers to trade between PTA partners and non-PTA partners, this results in a failure to fulfil the external requirement. By contrast, in the case of PSAs, the increase is supplemented by a qualitative criterion. Here, the comparison must lead to an increase, which results in a *barrier* or *undue difficulties* for the trade between PTA partners and non-PTA partners.

2.3.1.1.4 Legal Overlaps Between and the WTO and PTAs as Source of Diversity

The ambiguities in the WTO provisions, concerning the exact criteria WTO Members are required to comply with when implementing PTAs, make it impossible to separate clearly the regulation of trade at the multilateral level and at the PTA level. Given that the legal framework of the WTO already comprehensively regulates international trade among WTO Members, PTAs have been said to contribute to the diversity of international regulation in the area of the so-called *legal overlaps* between the WTO and PTAs under the *predominantly formalist* approach. As PTAs could also encompass the trade between PTA partners falling within the scope of application of the WTO Agreement, these *legal overlaps* have been identified as generally augmenting diversity in the regulation of international trade. Moreover, the existence of legal overlaps between the WTO Agreement and PTAs has given rise to a broader debate on the institutional and economic consequences for the WTO, in case WTO provisions could not prevail over PTA rules.

The room for maneuver for WTO Members arising from such ambiguities has been understood as constituting a factual obstacle to the hierarchization of WTO rules over PTA rules under the *predominantly formalist* approach. Given that the content of the WTO provisions on PTAs has proven to be only of very limited assistance in establishing limits to the design and content of PTAs, it appears possible that PTAs could provide rules that are incompatible with the legal framework of the WTO, thus counteracting the commitments for trade liberalization at the multilateral level. Therefore, WTO-incompatible provisions that apply to the trade among PTA partners, which is also governed by WTO rules, constitute a veritable legal doctrinal problem. If it remained unresolved, it could harm the centralized legal structure established under the WTO Agreement. Consequently, the rise of PTAs has led to a critical view of their existence, namely as a step backwards to the "à la carte" approach under the GATT 1947, which was successfully terminated with the foundation of the WTO.[133] The *single-undertaking* approach, introduced with the foundation of the WTO, provided the basis for understanding the different legal regimes under the WTO Agreement to amount to a legal system[134] and allowed the AB to describe the WTO Agreement as an "inseparable package of rights and disciplines which have to be considered in conjunction".[135] Against the legal uncertainties arising from the WTO rules on PTAs, PTAs have been regarded as susceptible to adding new and varying obligations within the legal relationships between WTO Members, harming their uniform legal commitments under the *single-undertaking* approach.

---

[133] Hoekman and Mavroidis (2015), p. 323.

[134] Van den Bossche (2005), p. 46.

[135] WTO Appellate Body, *Argentina — Safeguard Measures on Imports of Footwear (EC)*, WT/DS121/AB/R, Judgment of 14 December 1999, para. 81.

These formal legal considerations constitute the starting point on the debate on the diversity of the regulation of international trade concerning the institutional and economic effects on WTO Members. PTAs were equated with the loss of a uniform legal structure on the regulation of international trade under the supremacy of WTO rules in light of the ambiguity of the corresponding WTO rules. The undesirability of such a situation has been backed by several economic analyses which highlighted the insignificant and even counterproductive effects of PTAs on the overall liberalization of international trade. In general, the multilateral approach to trade liberalization has been understood as resulting in greater welfare gains for most of the WTO Members, constituting an argument for a more restrictive understanding of the WTO provisions on PTAs. Consequently, the coexistence and interaction of the different legal regimes of the WTO and PTAs have been characterized as adding complexity to the regulation of international trade,[136] resulting in a hindrance of the creation of free trade.[137] Based on the understanding that creation of free trade depends on the broad participation of countries in the reduction of trade barriers, the effect of trade regulation by PTAs for the creation of free trade was critically assessed and found to be an impediment to this aim. On the one hand, it was argued that the preferential treatment of PTA partners would distort trade flows by creating exclusionary effects with non-PTA partners,[138] instead of creating welfare-enhancing effects by trade creation for all countries.[139] It was said that the MFN principle prevented WTO Members from trade distortion under PTAs and provided for an economic level playing field between all WTO Members.[140] Against such an economic scenario, the multilateral character of the WTO Agreement and the *single-undertaking* approach have been described as effectively minimizing the chances for trade distortion, as they ensured streamlined obligations of WTO Members on international trade. For this aim, WTO rules were already said to provide for the decisive effects on liberalization of international trade due to the elimination and reduction of tariffs and other barriers to trade, making the use of PTAs for this purpose obsolete. It was advanced that the multilateral tariff eliminations on an MFN basis still held the strongest welfare-gaining potential and should be advanced more rigorously to create fewer incentives for the formation of PTAs.[141] The administration of rules on international trade by only one legal framework, as provided under the WTO Agreement, was argued to lower transaction costs for international commercial transactions for all importers due to absence of information asymmetries on the regulation in place. Regarding these findings, only the implementation of PTAs by poorer WTO Members appeared reasonable considering the high potential for the

---

[136] Bhagwati (2008), p. 69.

[137] Ibid., p. 63.

[138] Kim (2014), p. 444.

[139] Already reviewing latest available data on trade-distorting effects, cf. Do and Watson (2006), pp. 13–17; Viner (1924); Viner (2014), pp. 51–93; 159.

[140] Viner (1924), pp. 104–107.

[141] Nken and Yildiz (2021).

reduction of fiscal and non-fiscal barriers to trade between their trade and the resulting potential for welfare gains.[142] The complexity of economic effects resulting from the implementation of PTAs has therefore been compared against the purportedly more streamlined effects resulting from WTO rules. It led to the conviction that PTAs would only contribute to trade liberalization under very limited circumstances, or even not at all. Even in case of a broad enough participation of states in PTAs resulting in potential for trade creation, PTAs were argued to increase complexity of regulation of international trade in general, and therefore transaction costs for international business operations. Consequently, PTAs were considered counterproductive to achieving free trade.[143]

From an institutional point of view, the broad participation in PTAs by WTO Members has been often depicted as evidence of their retraction[144] from or even active undermining[145] of the multilateral legal framework of the WTO. In this context, it has been commented that, especially during the Cancún Ministerial Conference, WTO Members declared they would engage more actively in PTAs than in the negotiations under the WTO.[146] As *Thomas Cottier* and *Marina Foltea* put it:

> "The cyclical proliferation of RTAs in relation to the multilateral trade negotiations shows that WTO Members <u>revert</u> to preferential or regional agreements to the extent that policy goals cannot be sufficiently and promptly achieved in WTO negotiations based upon MFN and formal equality of States."[147] (underline added)

This negative effect of PTAs on the institutional structure of the WTO has been evaluated in light of the genesis of the WTO. The rise in PTAs was regarded as constituting a counter-development to the institutional model of the WTO which created more and diverse venues for the regulation of international trade at the cost of the institutional importance and centrality of the WTO. Given that the *single-undertaking* approach provided for a coherent structure of regulation of international trade, WTO Members also ascribed to the organization itself a high institutional value with its foundation. The inception of the WTO was seen as great progress against the predominantly loose structure of the GATT 1947. This institutional value and design turned out to be an attractive asset for other countries to accede it in the upcoming years. Today, the WTO has attained a quasi-universal character with a high number of Members, a development against which PTAs and their entailed

---

[142] Sutherland et al. (2004), p. 65.

[143] Crawford and Laird (2001), p. 208; Bhagwati (2008), p. 70.

[144] Baldwin and Carpenter (2011), p. 148: "The real threat is that regionalism is becoming so pervasive that it may soon be the rule rather than the exception. It could contribute in a forceful way to the erosion of WTO-centricity in the world trade system."

[145] Bhagwati (2008).

[146] Zeng (2021), p. 464.

[147] Cottier and Foltea (2006), p. 72.

preferentialism stand diametrically opposed.[148] Consequently, due to the rise of PTAs almost simultaneously with the foundation of the WTO, PTAs have been depicted as a counterpart to this organization and its legal framework. The occurrence of PTAs in high numbers has been predominantly depicted as "proliferation"[149] or "mushrooming".[150] This terminology suggests that the number of PTAs has been perceived as excessive, and the corresponding development of the rise of PTAs an anomaly.

Examples exist in which assessing the coexistence of rules under the WTO and PTAs for the governance of international trade has not automatically resulted in a general negative appreciation because it focused on the search for convergences between them. Notably, *Joseph Weiler* advocated the existence of a Common Law of International Trade considering the textual similarities of PTA rules and WTO rules, as well as their shared origins and purposes of the legal frameworks of the WTO, the EU, and NAFTA.[151] In fact, *Weiler* focused on the flipside of fragmentation by examining the convergence of the interpretation of rules on international trade by the WTO-DSM and the Court of Justice of the European Union (CJEU)—the PTA-DSM of the EU. *Weiler's* approach contrasts with the general negative understanding of PTAs, as he finds that WTO rules and EU rules on trade liberalization address "two very different worlds";[152] he forecasts an alignment of the WTO rules to those existing under the legal framework of the EU in the course of their interpretation by the WTO-DSM.

2.3.1.1.5   Diversity due to PTAs: WTO-X Provisions and the Lack of Legal Authority of the WTO

Another issue that has been addressed in the context of diversity of regulation on international trade is that PTAs can augment it by offering varying regulatory approaches towards areas of trade that do not fall within the purview of the WTO Agreement. This has led to the establishment of the classification of PTA provisions as "WTO-plus" or "WTO-X".[153] The term "WTO-X" refers to PTA rules that apply to a type of international trade that, so far, is not captioned by the ambit of the WTO and has the potential to promote trade liberalization between PTA partners, as opposed to the WTO Agreement. Accordingly, PTAs that contain numerous "WTO-plus" and "WTO-X" provisions and contain more potential on trade liberalization were coined as *deep* PTAs, whereas PTAs that depart only minimally from

---

[148] Cottier (2008), p. 4. states without further explanation that "[i]n the meantime, Members resort to transcontinental preferential trade agreements, further undermining the multilateral system."

[149] Crawford and Fiorentino (2005), p. 1.

[150] Davey in Bagwell and Mavroidis (2011), p. 236.

[151] Weiler (2001a).

[152] Weiler (2001b), p. 201.

[153] Horn et al. (2010), p. 1567.

the content of WTO rules and therefore do not contain more potential on trade liberalization are considered *shallow* PTAs. Bearing in mind that there do not exist any legal or institutional constraints on WTO Members to advance regulation of a "WTO-X" nature, controversies nevertheless have surfaced over their effect on international free trade in light of these developments.[154] These argumentative patterns illustrate the institutional dimension of the *predominantly formalist* approach, which focuses extensively on the difficulties arising for the WTO in maintaining its character as the central institution on the "future" regulation of international trade.

2.3.1.2 Diversity of Regulation of International Trade Arising from the Existence of PTA-DSMs

Next to PTAs, PTA-DSMs have been understood as contributing actively to diversity in the regulation of international trade. Their availability was said to create a situation in which identical international trade disputes could be settled in front the WTO-DSM as well as PTA-DSMs on the basis of substantively overlapping WTO and PTA rules. These jurisdictional tensions constitute another reason to anticipate diversity in the regulation of international trade, considering that the WTO-DSM is not able to assert its authority substantively nor procedurally in *all* trade-related disputes.

2.3.1.2.1 Reasons for PTA Partners to Set Up PTA-DSMs

From the perspective of economic theory, the creating of PTA-DSMs has been explained to secure the expected welfare gains negotiated by PTA partners through the effective implementation of these agreements. Consequently, the judicialization of economic relations between PTA partners has been explained to act as a guarantee for the implementation of the provisions on trade liberalization and to ensure that the projected economic-welfare gains will be yielded through the effective compliance with and enforcement of the legal obligations resulting from the respective PTAs.[155] The inclusion of PTA-DSM provisions within a PTA serves the PTA partners' aim to increase each PTA-partner's commitment and willingness to enforce the negotiated legal obligations.

From a legal perspective, the concurrent creation of individual PTA-DSMs, which have the judicial authority to interpret PTA rules autonomously constitutes the main reason for the anticipated diversity in the regulation of international trade under the *predominantly formalist* approach to international trade law. Their judicial activity has exclusively been understood against the substantive legal overlaps

---

[154]Bagwell and Mavroidis (2011), pp. 171–172.

[155]Porges (2011), pp. 467–468.

between WTO rules and PTA rules. This has led to the resurfacing of the institutional debate over the allocation of the appropriate governance between PTAs or the WTO, putting the jurisdictional tensions between PTA-DSMs and the WTO-DSM, which provides formal and binding litigation between WTO Members on WTO rules, in the spotlight.

2.3.1.2.2 Reasons and Causes for Diversity in the Regulation of International Trade due to PTA-DSMs

In correspondence to the 'proliferation' of PTAs, most of these agreements contain provisions on the administration and resolution of disputes arising between PTA partners concerning the application, implementation, and enforcement of PTA rules. According to the RTA IS, out of a total of 294 active, listed PTAs, 261 contain provisions on the settlement of disputes among PTA partners.

The anticipation of diversity in the regulation of international trade due to the activity of PTA-DSMs is multi-faceted. On the one hand, it is based on the jurisdictional ramifications established under the WTO for the adjudication of disputes on WTO rules: firstly, under the WTO-DSM an exclusive and compulsory *judicial* forum for the resolution of disputes among WTO Members is established; secondly, WTO Members themselves are granted wide-ranging procedural rights regarding the access of the WTO-DSM as a correlate of its exclusive and compulsory character; thirdly, the exclusive and compulsory character of the WTO-DSM translates into a broad jurisdiction of panels and the AB. On the other hand, the jurisdictional ramifications established by individual PTA-DSMs are regarded as a major cause for an anticipated diversity of the regulation of international trade. At its core lies the adjudication of substantially convergent rules on international trade existing due to the *legal overlaps* between WTO and PTA rules. According to this understanding, PTA-DSMs could interpret PTA rules legally overlapping with WTO rules and thereby buttress diversity in the regulation of international trade. Given the substantive convergence of the underlying PTA rules with WTO rules, PTA-DSMs were said to be able to issue *incoherent* and *inconsistent* decisions compared to those issued under the WTO-DSM. This development was identified as further exacerbating diversity in the regulation of international trade. It was assumed based on the specific operation of PTA-DSMs, which allows them to engage in autonomous legal reasoning on the interpretation, application, and enforcement of PTA rules, as no obligations for WTO Members exist to subordinate all trade-related measures under the WTO-DSM.

Against this backdrop, the different models of dispute resolution provided by PTA-DSMs have been studied comparatively against the model provided by the WTO-DSM. Consequently, the model of dispute resolution provided by the WTO-DSM has become the departing point for assuming diversity in the regulation of international trade due to the activity of PTA-DSMs. Given that PTA partners may choose from a range of different methods of dispute resolution, judicial models of dispute resolution provided by PTA-DSMs, i.e., those establishing third-party adjudication with no right to veto it, have equally been at the heart of the debate about their contribution to the diversity of regulation of international trade. The categorization of PTA-DSMs according to the different levels of legalism has played a crucial role, as

> "[r]eal risks of forum shopping therefore arise only in the limited instances in which states have agreed to compulsory jurisdiction of several tribunals without the need for a special agreement."[156]

In this context, the WTO-DSM has been considered as providing a highly legalist approach to the resolution of disputes among WTO Members, resulting in the supposition that all other PTA-DSMs providing equally legalist modes of dispute resolution exist in direct competition to it. According to *Chase et al.*, 60% of the analyzed PTA set up quasi-judicial to judicial PTA-DSMs.

Over time, the procedural features of PTA-DSMs were categorized according to the specific means for the resolution of disputes such as consultations, mediation, arbitration, and adjudication by an internal or external third body. PTA-DSMs were classified according to the level of legalism, which is prescribed by the respective provisions. The level of legalism, i.e., the requirement to resort to formal judicial dispute resolution, depends on the availability of judicial methods for dispute resolution and the obligation of PTA partners to use this kind of method. Backed up by this understanding and based on previous efforts to classify the operation of PTA-DSMs,[157] *Chase et al.* assume that all PTAs contain PTA-DSMs. However, they differentiate them according to the level of legalism for which the corresponding provisions provide. Accordingly, they suggest taking into account whether dispute settlement by a third party under an *automatic right to referral* by one of the PTA partners, i.e., in a binding manner, to determine the level of legalism in a PTA-DSM.[158] Pursuant to this approach, the decisive element to ascribe to a PTA-DSM a high level of legalism results from the PTA provisions on dispute settlement, which give PTA partners the right to have unrestrained recourse to adjudication, i.e., that no PTA-partner has a corresponding veto right to obstruct the course of action taken by the other PTA-partner concerning the adjudication of the dispute. Based on this understanding, *Chase et al.* have classified provisions on dispute settlement in PTAs in three categories, namely a political/diplomatic, a quasi-judicial, and a judicial model for PTA-DSMs, which reflect the level of legalism prevailing due to the corresponding provisions.[159] PTAs that do not contain any provisions on dispute settlement belong to the category of the political/diplomatic model.[160] Those PTAs that do contain provisions on dispute settlement and

---

[156]Bruns and Hestermeyer (2008), p. 127.

[157]Jo and Namgung (2012) and Smith (2000).

[158]Chase et al. (2016), pp. 618–621.

[159]Ibid., p. 10; cf. Gantz (2016), pp. 31–33, for an overview of the different existing models for dispute resolution in PTA-DSMs.

[160]Chase et al. (2016), p. 618.

provide for a third-party adjudication with a right to veto it are placed in the category of quasi-judicial PTA-DSMs.

2.3.1.2.2.1   The Exclusive Character of the WTO-DSM for Violations of WTO Rules

The first aspect for the anticipation of diversity in the regulation of international trade lies in the jurisdictional ramifications established under the WTO for resolution of disputes among WTO Members, more precisely: the establishment of an exclusive and mandatory judicial forum by means of the WTO-DSM for this purpose. The provisions of the DSU ensure that WTO Members have the obligation to resort to the WTO-DSM in the case of a dispute over the violation of WTO rules at the expense of all other adjudicative fora potentially available to them. At the same time, this obligation attributes to the WTO-DSM the central and only forum for the interpretation of WTO rules in case of its violation.

Pursuant to Art. 3.2 DSU, the WTO-DSM serves the resolution of disputes between WTO Members under the *covered agreements*.[161] This is also reflected in the standard terms of reference for panels under Art. 7.1 DSU:

> To examine, in the light of the relevant provisions in (name of the covered agreement(s)cited by the parties to the dispute), the matter referred to the DSB by (name of party) in document ... and to make such findings as will assist the DSB in making the recommendations or in giving the rulings provided for in that/those agreement(s).

This clarifies that panels as well as the AB have no general jurisdiction over trade related disputes[162] but only over disputes concerning the interpretation of WTO rules.

Simultaneously, Art. 23.1 DSU sets out the mandatory and exclusive character of the WTO-DSM for WTO Members. Accordingly, when WTO Members consider that other WTO Members violate their obligations under the covered agreements, they are obliged to refrain from any actions other than resorting to the WTO-DSM. Consequently, the obligation to use the WTO-DSM in case of infringement of WTO rules therefore stipulates a mandatory mechanism for the adjudication of trade disputes between WTO Members.

Moreover, Art. 23.1 lit. a) DSU strengthens this authority over the administration of disputes concerning the interpretation and application of WTO rules under the WTO-DSM, as WTO Members are furthermore obliged not to make a determination on the effect that a violation of WTO rules has occurred, except through recourse to dispute settlement in accordance with the rules and procedures of the DSU.

---

[161] In favor of a limiting effect the provisions of the DSU, cf. Bruns and Hestermeyer (2008), pp. 130–131.

[162] For a detailed analysis of the implicit jurisdiction of WTO panels and the AB, see Pauwelyn (2003), p. 442.

The WTO-DSM is determined as the only means of dispute settlement to which WTO Members are allowed to resort, concerning the violation of WTO rules.[163] Within the scope of the covered agreements, Art. 23 DSU stipulates the exclusiveness[164] of the procedures under the WTO-DSM for WTO Members to the detriment of other international fora. The provisions thus establish the WTO-DSM as the only permissible forum to which WTO Members can have recourse when disputes arise under the covered agreements.

Moreover, Art. 23.2 DSU prohibits any *retaliation* other than those authorized by the DSB foreseen by the procedural regulations to which reference is made in the provision.[165] The authority of WTO-DSM as the exclusive adjudicatory forum is therefore further strengthened, as retaliation for the violation of WTO rules remains subject to the authorization of the DSB through the adoption of panel reports (and in cases of appeals AB reports) that contain the corresponding recommendations for authorized retaliation to the DSB.

2.3.1.2.2.2   Wide-Ranging Procedural Rights and Obligations of Disputing WTO Members as a Correlate to the Exclusivity of the WTO-DSM

The exclusive and mandatory character of the WTO-DSM conveys to WTO Members specific procedural rights and obligations concerning their recourse to the WTO-DSM. These rights and obligations exist as a correlate to the exclusive character of the WTO-DSM and therefore have been understood to be wide-ranging. On the one hand, WTO Members have a right to access to the WTO-DSM. On the other hand, WTO Members incur specific procedural obligations that aim at upholding the mandatory and exclusive jurisdiction of the WTO-DSM, as well as remaining available for the settlement of disputes under it.

---

[163] According to *Mbengue*, in light of the negotiating history and experience from dispute settlement under GATT, Art. 23 DSU does not prescribe a monopoly of the WTO-DSM for disputes under the covered agreements. Instead, under the WTO, Art. 23.1 DSU aims at securing the broader multilateral approach, in which dispute settlement under a rule-based system constitutes a means to restrict unilateralism. It is against this backdrop that Mbengue argues on several occasions (e.g., the reasoning of the AB stated in Mexico – Softdrinks) that impediments to the jurisdiction of the WTO-DSM, although not applicable in the given case, could exist. Although this might be true regarding WTO Members' rights to WTO-DSM adjudication, this does modify the fact that WTO Members have accorded the WTO-DSM such a prominent and central role. Even if the WTO-DSM did not have a monopoly on the adjudication of disputes under the covered agreements, any alternative forum would have to suffice as the multilateral threshold, as explained by Mbengue. In particular, this means that there would have to exist an adjudicative body which provides for the same level of accessibility and jurisdiction, as prescribed by Art. 23 DSU. Given the lack of any other alternative for a truly multilateral forum, Art. 23 DSU necessarily implies the WTO-DSM as the central forum for adjudication. Therefore, one could argue that Art. 23.1 DSU, while not establishing a monopoly *stricto sensu*, still results in a requirement for a centralized dispute settlement system, which is in practice very similar to a monopoly, and PTA-DSMs do not have an impact on its status as agreed by the WTO Members under the DSU. Cf. Mbengue (2016).

[164] Kwak and Marceau (2003), p. 103.

[165] Cf. also the finding in WTO Panel, *United States — Sections 301-310 of the Trade Act of 1974*, WT/DS152/R, Judgment of 22 December 1999, para. 7.43.

2.3.1.2.2.3 The Broad Jurisdiction of Panels and the AB Under the WTO-DSM

The exclusive character of the WTO-DSM translates into broad competences for panels and the AB to adjudicate disputes over the violation of WTO rules. Taken together, the exclusive and mandatory character of the WTO-DSB, the negative consensus rule, the competences of panels, and the AB have therefore given rise to understand panels and the AB as having a *jurisdiction* on the settlement of disputes between WTO Members. This makes it highly improbable that panels and the AB will ever conclude a lack of their jurisdiction, or that a WTO Member as party to a dispute could succeed with a claim of a lack of the WTO-DSM's jurisdiction, in case of an alleged violation of WTO rules.

Pursuant to Arts. 1.2 and 2.1 DSU, the DSB administers the rules and procedures of the DSU in the covered agreements as identified in Appendix 2 of the DSU and the consultation and dispute settlement provisions of the covered agreements. Art. 2.1 DSU sets out that the DSB administers an adjudicative structure, the WTO-DSM. According to this provision,

> [...], the DSB shall have the authority to establish panels, adopt panel and Appellate Body reports, maintain surveillance of implementation of rulings and recommendations, and authorize suspension of concessions and other obligations under the covered agreements. (underline added)

In this vein, Art. 11 DSU sets out the function of panels, in that they

> [...] assist the DSB in discharging its responsibilities under [the DSU] [...] and the covered agreements. (underline added)

Due to the so-called *negative consensus rule*,[166] the functioning of the WTO-DSM is *quasi-automatic*, i.e., it is mostly independent of any additional activity of the DSB other than in cases where a negative consensus is reached. Consequently, in line with Art. 6.1 DSU, panels are established, *unless the DSB decides by consensus not to establish a panel at that meeting*. If not appealed, panel reports are adopted by a negative consensus provided by Arts. 16.4 and 2.4 DSU. All disputing parties have an unconditional right to appeal a panel report and thus have unconditional access to the AB, which is charged with the adjudication of appeals pursuant to Art. 17.1 DSU. Once the appeal procedure is concluded, AB reports are likewise adopted, pursuant to the negative consensus rule, as prescribed by Art. 17.14 DSU.

According to Art. 1.1 DSU, the rules and procedure of the DSU apply to disputes arising under the agreements listed in Appendix 1 of the DSU.

Under Art. 3.2 DSU, WTO Members are to recognize that the WTO-DSM

---

[166] As consensus requires WTO Members to vote unanimously against the establishment of a requested panel, or AB report, in practice this principle results in the *de facto* establishment of a panel or adoption of reports by the DSB: A decision against the establishment of a panel or the adoption of a report would require the WTO-Member requesting or winning a dispute to vote against its own demand. Such a scenario is highly unlikely and has never occurred.

serves to preserve the rights and obligations of Members under the covered agreements, and to clarify the existing provisions of those agreements in accordance with customary rules of interpretation of public international law.

Art. 3.2 DSU defines the purpose of this adjudicative structure:

> The dispute settlement system of the WTO is a central element in providing security and predictability to the multilateral trading system. The Members recognize that it serves to preserve the rights and obligations of Members under the covered agreements, and to clarify the existing provisions of those agreements in accordance with customary rules of interpretation of public international law. Recommendations and rulings of the DSB cannot add to or diminish the rights and obligations provided in the covered agreements.

In this context, to fulfil their functions, panels are charged in accordance with Art. 11 DSU to

> [...] make an objective assessment of the matter before it, including an objective assessment of the facts of the case and the applicability of and conformity with the relevant covered agreements, and make such other findings as will assist the DSB in making the recommendations or in giving the rulings provided for in the covered agreements. [...]

Art. 13 DSU sets out a panel's right to seek information and permit panels to seek the information they require to resolve a dispute almost without any restrictions. Art. 13.1 DSU sets out that each

> [...] panel shall have the right to seek information and technical advice from any individual or body which it deems appropriate.

Regarding information from any individual or body within a jurisdiction of a WTO Member, a panel's authority to seek information is adjusted following the second sentence of Art. 13.1 DSU. Accordingly, a panel is required to inform the concerned WTO Member where it seeks such information. The concerned WTO Member is granted the merit of being informed concerning its request for information and

> should respond promptly and fully to any request by a panel for such information as the panel considers necessary and appropriate.

Moreover, from these provisions on the explicit jurisdiction, the panels and the AB are attributed an implicit (or incidental) jurisdiction.[167] To fulfil their function as prescribed under the provisions establishing their explicit jurisdiction, the panels and the AB have the possibility of relying on implicit jurisdictional competences. Implicit jurisdictional competences of panels are said to cover the right to ascertain and identify claims made by the disputing WTO Members, their right to assess independently the existence of its explicit jurisdiction, the right to refrain from exercising validly established jurisdiction, as well as the ancillary right to decide all matters and questions in connection with the substantive matter, for which jurisdiction exists.

These broad competences of panels and the AB make it almost impossible that they would not deal with a dispute over the alleged violation of WTO rules.

---

[167] Pauwelyn (2003), pp. 447–449; Yang (2012), pp. 313–317.

Moreover, they make it extremely unlikely that a party would succeed with a claim to the lack of their jurisdiction. These procedural features of the WTO-DSM have given reason to title it the "jewel in the crown"[168] of the WTO with great regularity.

Regarding PTAs, Para. 12 UArt. XXIV GATT 1994 was introduced to affirm that the panels and the AB can assess the compliance of a PTA with WTO rules under the WTO-DSM:

> The provisions of Articles XXII and XXIII of GATT 1994 as elaborated and applied by the Dispute Settlement Understanding may be invoked with respect to any matters arising from the application of those provisions of Article XXIV relating to customs unions, free-trade areas or interim agreements leading to the formation of a customs union or free-trade area.

At the establishment of the WTO, this addendum became necessary, as GATT panels did not assume authority concerning the legal examination of the compliance of PTAs under Art. XXIV GATT 1947.[169]

2.3.1.2.2.4 Substantive Convergences Between PTA Rules and WTO Rules

Next to the jurisdictional ramifications established under the WTO-DSU for the violation of WTO rules, the aforementioned so-called *legal overlaps* between WTO rules and PTA rules are pivotal to the claim on the anticipated diversity in the regulation of international trade. As both WTO rules and PTA rules address *identical* regulatory objects pertaining to the international trade between PTA partners, the decisions of the respective PTA-DSMs as well as of the WTO-DSM can have a bearing on one another.

Pursuant to the conditions set out under Art. XXIV GATT 1994, a trade-restrictive measure that is justified under Art. XX GATT 1994 does not need to be eliminated within a PTA.[170] On the other hand, PTA partners can choose to interpret their exception clause more narrowly, because Art. XXIV GATT 1994 provides only a minimum standard of liberalization considering the "SAT requirement". In this context, decisions of PTA-DSMs can play a substantive role for panels and the AB when interpreting WTO rules that overlap with PTA rules. Moreover, PTA-DSM decisions can play a procedural role when panels and the AB are called upon to decide in cases in which the actions of WTO Members in front of PTA-DSMs become relevant for the interpretation of WTO rules. This may be the case if panels or the AB under the WTO-DSM were to ascertain claims on the violation of WTO rules that originate from actions taken in a PTA context. Due to their extensive jurisdiction and their additional right to seek information, panels and the AB would be entitled to take these actions into consideration in line with their competence granted under Art. 13.2 DSU. In this regard, disputes that arise concerning PTA rules as well as the corresponding decision of PTA-DSMs can become relevant as a fact

---

[168] Van den Bossche (2005), p. 94.

[169] GATT Panel, *European Communities — Tariff Treatment on Imports of Citrus Products from Certain Countries in the Mediterranean Region*, L/5776, Judgment of 7 February 1985, sec. 4.15.

[170] *Supra* Sect. 2.3.1.1.3.2.1.3.

sounding the case of violation of WTO rules.[171] Moreover, the differentiation between a legal analysis of PTA rules and their acknowledgement as a fact surrounding the dispute is very difficult. Legal arguments surrounding PTAs and PTA-DSMs could especially have an effect on the implicit jurisdiction of panels and the AB, e.g., in cases where the same disputed measure is challenged at the time of the establishment of a panel or has already been challenged in front of a PTA-DSM. Such a situation was discussed to prompt panels or the AB, in line with customary rules of interpretation of public international law, to assume the principle of *lis pendens* or *res judicata* to decline their implicit jurisdiction.[172]

2.3.1.2.2.5 Autonomous PTA-DSMs in Charge with the Interpretation of PTA Rules

Next to the substantive convergences of PTA rules with WTO rules, the competences of PTA-DSMs to interpret PTA rules autonomously constitute the principal cause for an anticipated diversity in the regulation of international trade due to their activity. Although WTO rules entail requirements on the legal design of PTAs to rely successfully on the justification of a violation of the MFN principle, they do not specify any requirements for the relationship between the WTO-DSM and PTA-DSMs.[173] Most importantly, there is no explicit obligation for WTO Members to ensure that the PTA-DSMs follow WTO-DSM decisions given that it only constitutes the exclusive forum for disputes over the violation WTO rules and that no general jurisdiction on all trade related matters is thereby established. Moreover, decisions of the DSB only have an effect between the WTO Members concerned. In light of these deficiencies on the formal coordination of PTA-DSM decisions with the jurisprudence of the WTO-DSM, an implicit jurisdictional authority of the WTO-DSM over PTA-DSMs was argued based on the substantive requirements established under the WTO provisions on PTAs.[174] Even in assuming such broad competences of the WTO-DSM, nothing would preclude PTA-DSMs from still issuing their decisions, as the jurisdictional authority of the WTO-DSM would only be based on substantive WTO rules on PTAs.

---

[171] Marceau and Wyatt (2010), pp. 87–86.

[172] Baldwin and Carpenter (2011), pp. 155–156, Box 3.1.

[173] *Supra* Sect. 2.3.1.1.3.2.1.3, *Brazil — Measures Affecting Imports of Retreaded Tyres*, WT/DS332/R, Judgment of 12 June 2007, para. 7.441, concerning the possibility that trade-restrictive measures in a CU could be justified if they complied with Art. XX GATT 1994. Conversely, a trade-restrictive measure within a PTA would have to comply with Art. XX GATT 1994 in order to comply with the requirements set out under Art. XXIV GATT 1994. Even if this was the case, this would amount to an obligation for WTO Members to ensure that the trade restrictive measures within their PTAs comply with substantive WTO rules. Yet, it does not contain any obligation to ensure this at a procedural level regarding the activity of PTA-DSMs.

[174] Cf. de Mestral (2013).

2.3.1.2.3   Experience from the Interaction of the WTO-DSM Concerning WTO Members' Use of PTA-DSMs

Against this backdrop, the adjudicatory experience made under the WTO-DSM shows that the panels and the AB generally have considered themselves as retaining a *de facto* boundless jurisdiction when confronted with WTO Members' use of PTA-DSMs for the assessment of the violation of WTO rules. Such a stance of the WTO-DSM suggests that PTA-DSMs' decisions are ultimately subject to its review. Nevertheless, the actual clarifications and the thoroughness of the review of PTA-related measures by the WTO-DSM has remained very limited.

Panels and the AB have dealt with the procedural rights and obligations of WTO Members in front of the WTO-DSM for disputes involving PTA rules and the use of PTA-DSMs. They did so without discussing their own potential jurisdictional limitations due to the use of PTA-DSMs. In upholding extensive reading of rights and obligations arising under the legal framework of the WTO, the panels and the AB pronounced several decisions containing basic formal criteria on the wide range of procedural rights and obligations of WTO Members, which did not require them to elaborate on the question of their own jurisdictional limitations when dealing with PTA rules and the use of PTA-DSMs by WTO Members. Consequently, the existence and use of PTA-DSMs have not been considered as having a limiting effect on the jurisdictional competences of panels and the AB, so far.

This result is especially interesting, since panels and the AB simultaneously never denied that such a limiting effect of the use and existence of PTA-DSM could exist. While the precise effects of PTA rules and decisions of PTA-DSMs on procedural aspects of the use of the WTO-DSM have remained obscure, the panels and the AB have been upholding an image of ultimate jurisdictional authority concerning any measure litigated under the WTO-DSM, even in case of prior litigation under a PTA-DSM, at the same time.

2.3.1.2.3.1   *Forum Choice and Forum Exclusion Clauses in PTAs and Their Effect on Procedural Rights of Disputing WTO Members*

Pursuant to WTO-DSM jurisprudence, Art. 23.1 DSU not only sets out the obligation of WTO Members' to take actions that secure the authority of the WTO-DSM in case of a dispute concerning the application and interpretation on WTO rules. It equally grants WTO Members a right to adjudication by the WTO-DSM in case of a dispute.[175] Consequently, the AB in *Mexico – Taxes on Softdrinks* acknowledged the

---

[175] See also Mbengue (2016), p. 238, who makes a distinction between the obligation to engage in multilateral dispute settlement (or refrain from unilateral action) and the right of WTO Members to have access to the WTO-DSM; WTO Appellate Body, *Mexico — Tax Measures on Soft Drinks and Other Beverages*, WT/DS308/AB/R, Judgment of 6 March 2006, para. 53.

panel's finding that Art. 23.1 DSU amounted to such a right. It specified that WTO Members are *entitled* to a ruling by a WTO panel based on this right.[176]

Recognizing such a procedural right has unavoidably set in motion the debate about its dispositive character, since rights—as opposed to obligations—logically may be waived or *relinquished*. The conception of such a right to adjudication by the WTO-DSM therefore plays a crucial role in explaining why WTO Members have argued that the use of a PTA-DSM can constitute a waiver to their right. Supposing that this procedural right was in fact dispositive, WTO Members could agree to give it up once they implement a PTA and designate a PTA-DSM to adjudicate their disputes. Consequently, this would prevent them from claiming this right in front of the panels and the AB under the WTO-DSM to request their decision on WTO rules which are substantively equivalent with PTA rules.

Yet, assuming a dispositive character of a procedural right to adjudication under the WTO-DSM is difficult to reconcile with the understanding of an exclusive and mandatory jurisdiction of the WTO-DSM, as prescribed under Art. 23.1 DSU.[177] It would render the obligation of WTO Members to resort to the WTO-DSM meaningless, if they could agree to waiving their right to adjudication under it.[178] Conversely, the preference for mutually agreed solutions by WTO Members, as prescribed by Art. 3.7 DSU, could constitute an argument in favor of a dispositive character of this procedural right.

Fittingly, the AB in *Peru – Agricultural Products* found the right to adjudication under the WTO-DSM to be in direct opposition to the arrangement of a mutually agreed solution between disputing WTO Members by stating that

> "in order to ascertain whether a Member has **relinquished, by virtue of a mutually agreed solution in a particular dispute, its right to have recourse** to WTO dispute settlement in respect of that dispute, greater scrutiny by a panel or the Appellate Body may be necessary."[179] (emphasis added)

However, the AB equally clarified that a mutually agreed solution was not the only potential means of bringing about the relinquishment of the procedural right to adjudication under the WTO-DSM. It explicitly considered

> "[. . .] the possibility of articulating the relinquishment of the right to initiate WTO dispute settlement proceedings **in a form other than a waiver embodied in a mutually agreed solution** [. . .]." (emphasis added)[180]

---

[176] WTO Appellate Body, *Mexico — Tax Measures on Soft Drinks and Other Beverages*, WT/DS308/AB/R, Judgment of 6 March 2006, para. 52.

[177] *Supra* Sect. 2.3.1.2.2.1.

[178] Upholding a restrictive reading concerning the interpretation of other rules of international law, which would be only allowed if all WTO Members were part of the international agreement under which the rule originates, cf. WTO Panel, *European Communities — Measures Affecting the Approval and Marketing of Biotech Products (Panel)*, WT/DS291, Judgment of 29 September 2006, para. 7.70.

[179] WTO Appellate Body, *Peru — Additional Duty on Imports of Certain Agricultural Products*, WT/DS457/AB/R, Judgment of 20 July 2015, para. 5.19.

[180] Ibid., para. 5.25.

Independently of the means to relinquish this procedural right, the AB tried to add precision to its finding, stating that

"[...] any such relinquishment must be made clearly."[181]

In the end, the AB refused to find that Peru and Guatemala had waived their procedural right to adjudication by the WTO-DSM by means of an FTA between them. However, it made this finding solely based on formal considerations, taking into account that the FTA was still not in force at the time of the dispute at the WTO-DSM. For this reason, the AB argued that it did not qualify for being a mutually agreed solution for the disputing parties within the meaning of Art. 2.7 DSU. The AB also added that, even if the FTA was in force at the time of the dispute, it could not constitute a valid waiver, as it contained elements that were earlier found to be in breach of WTO rules and, hence, barred it from considering the FTA a waiver. This resulted in the FTA being inconsistent with the covered WTO Agreement and against the requirement established under Art. 3.7 DSU.[182]

Concerning the effective relinquishment of the procedural right to adjudication by the WTO-DSM, the panels and the AB have required a high threshold to be fulfilled for this purpose. In *European Communities – Bananas III (Article 21.5 – Ecuador II/Article 21.5 – US)*, the AB already held as a general finding on the status of rights arising under the DSU that

"the relinquishment of rights granted by the DSU cannot be lightly assumed."[183]

With the focus on the *means* to relinquish those rights, the AB specified that

"[...] the language in the Understandings [note: on the relinquishment] must clearly reveal that the parties intended to relinquish their rights."[184]

Against this backdrop, PTA and PTA-DSMs become relevant, as many of them contain provisions regulating the PTA partners' rights to pursue a dispute settlement at other fora, i.e., so-called forum choice or forum-exclusion clauses.[185]

Forum-choice clauses provide PTA partners with the opportunity to decide on the adjudicative forum in which they want to pursue their claims and remedies in case a dispute arises that can be addressed both under PTA and WTO rules. Forum-choice clauses vary in their strictness and formality. Some designate the complaining, some the responding party to the dispute to carry out the actual choice of forum. Other forum-choice clauses require the consent of both parties to lodge their complaint at a specific forum.[186]

---

[181] Ibid., para. 5.25.

[182] Ibid., para. 5.26.

[183] WTO Appellate Body, *European Communities — Regime for the Importation, Sale and Distribution of Bananas Second Recourse to Article 21.5 of the DSU by Ecuador*, WT/DS27/AB/RW2/ECU; WT/DS27/AB/RW/USA, Judgment of 26 November 2008, para. 217.

[184] Ibid., para. 217.

[185] Yang (2014).

[186] Yang (2012), pp. 284–285.

Forum-exclusion clauses preclude PTA partners from filing subsequent disputes on the same subject matter at a different adjudicative forum than the one already solicited with the original dispute. They can appear in connection with forum-choice clauses. Forum-exclusion clauses are often used to mitigate the fear of conflicting decisions issued by PTA-DSMs and the WTO-DSM.[187]

Both forum-choice and forum-exclusion clauses in PTAs were analyzed concerning their effect on constituting a relinquishment of the procedural right to adjudication under the WTO-DSM.[188] The AB in *Peru – Agricultural Products* refused to accept that the specific choice of forum clause in the FTA between Guatemala and Peru could have such an effect, as

> "[. . .] even from the perspective of the FTA, parties to the FTA have the right to bring claims under the WTO covered agreements to the WTO dispute settlement system."[189]

Confronted with a forum-exclusion clause in a PTA between Argentina and Brazil, the panel in *Argentina – Poultry Anti-Dumping Duties* concluded on formal considerations that it was not applicable in the case at hand, since it became effective only after the establishment of the panel.[190]

Consequently, whether the right to have access to the WTO-DSM can be truly relinquished by means of forum-choice or forum-exclusion clauses continues to remain unclear.

2.3.1.2.3.2 Effects of the Use of PTA-DSMs on the Procedural Obligations of Disputing WTO Members

Beyond the question whether WTO Members could be precluded to call on the WTO-DSM due to a past or present dispute at a PTA-DSM because of a waiver to their right to adjudication, the use of PTA-DSMs by WTO Members was equally addressed at the level of procedural obligations of WTO Members. In this context, the use of PTA-DSMs by WTO Members was discussed by panels and the AB regarding their obligation to conduct dispute settlement under the WTO-DSM in good faith. The good-faith obligations, contained in the DSU, limit the WTO Members' range of potential actions while conducting a dispute at the WTO-DSM. The obligation is twofold, as it requires, firstly, WTO Members not to obstruct disputes to emerge under the WTO-DSM and, secondly, once they have emerged, to conduct dispute-settlement proceedings in good faith.

Art. 3.10 DSU sets out this central obligation of WTO Members to perform their actions under the WTO-DSM in good faith:

---

[187] Yang (2014).

[188] Marceau and Wyatt (2010), p. 70.

[189] WTO Appellate Body, *Peru — Additional Duty on Imports of Certain Agricultural Products*, WT/DS457/AB/R, Judgment of 20 July 2015, sec. 5.28.

[190] WTO Panel, *Argentina — Definitive Anti-Dumping Duties on Poultry from Brazil*, WT/DS241/R, Judgment of 22 April 2003, para. 7.38 and n 49.

> It is understood that requests for conciliation and the use of the dispute settlement procedures should not be intended or considered as contentious acts and that, if a dispute arises, all Members will engage in these procedures in good faith in an effort to resolve the dispute. [...]

The principle of good faith entails the WTO Members' obligation to remain generally available for dispute settlement at the WTO-DSM.[191] Consequently, the principle of good faith requires WTO Members actively to pursue settlement of disputes with all means provided under the DSU in a manner that respects the mandatory and exclusive nature of the WTO-DSM and contributes to the settlement of a dispute. In this context, Art. 3.10 DSU expands its full meaning, as it stipulates that requests for conciliation and the use of the dispute-settlement procedures should not be intended or considered as *contentious* acts.

Against this backdrop, the use of PTA-DSMs calls into question whether WTO Members act in conformity with the principle of good faith, if they initiate dispute-settlement proceedings in front of a PTA-DSM, which could have equally been addressed under the WTO-DSM, due to the substantive convergence of WTO and PTA rules.

The panel in *Argentina – Poultry Anti-Dumping Duties* dealt with this question and assessed whether Brazil's action to bring a case in front of the WTO panel after initiating and losing the same case in front of a Mercosur ad hoc arbitral panel could constitute a breach of the principle of good faith and the related principle of estoppel. The panel did not accept the claims of Argentina that the initiation of dispute-settlement proceedings in front of the respective PTA-DSM constituted a breach of the good-faith obligation by Brazil. The panel laid out that the party invoking such a contention, firstly, would have to demonstrate that the bringing of a dispute under the WTO-DSM would violate a WTO provision, and secondly, that this act of bringing a dispute under the WTO-DSM would require being something "more than mere violation".[192] Under this test, Argentina could not demonstrate the first requirement that Brazil violated a WTO provision by bringing the dispute in front of the WTO-DSM. Consequently, the panel abstained from a further analysis on the breach of good-faith obligations. Although the panel in this case did not answer the question whether the invocation of dispute-settlement proceedings at another judicial forum for trade-related disputes could constitute a violation of the good faith obligation under Art. 3.10 DSU, it implicitly denied this possibility by not even considering that a prior judicial proceeding in front of a PTA-DSM could even classify as a breach of this good-faith obligation.

Concerning a potential invocation of the principle of estoppel, Argentina's arguments were especially based on the procedural antecedents of the case at the respective PTA-DSM. Here, the panel did not see the requirements fulfilled that

---

[191] It is not to be confused with the principle of due process, which is directed at ensuring a swift and fair adjudicating procedure by respecting specific time frames and procedural actions; cf. Mitchell (2008), p. 124.

[192] WTO Panel, *Argentina — Definitive Anti-Dumping Duties on Poultry from Brazil*, WT/DS241/R, Judgment of 22 April 2003, para. 7.36.

would allow the principle of estoppel to apply. Based on the consideration that actions of a disputing party need to result in an impediment for the opposing disputing party to make full use of its procedural or substantive rights in dispute-settlement proceedings based on good-faith considerations,[193] the panel declined the application of the principle in this case.[194] Instead, it held that Brazil's repeated initiation of dispute-settlement proceedings at a PTA-DSM and, after its loss, at the WTO-DSM was not enough to amount to the invocation of the principle of estoppel *per se*. Very much comparable to the standard applied under the test for the relinquishment of the procedural right of adjudication under the WTO-DSM, the panel did not recognize the subsequent initiation of disputes to constitute a clear and unambiguous fact not to use the WTO-DSM on which Argentina could rely in good faith.[195] It held that

> "[t]here is no evidence on the record that Brazil made an express statement that it would not bring WTO dispute settlement proceedings in respect of measures previously challenged through MERCOSUR. Nor does the record indicate exceptional circumstances requiring us to imply any such statement."[196]

To clarify the procedural value of repeated initiation of disputes at the PTA-DSM and the WTO-DSM, the panel assessed whether the forum-exclusion clause in the PTA between Argentina and Brazil could have been relied on by Argentina to understand that Brazil would not litigate the same case at the WTO-DSM.[197] The panel could not ascribe any value of implied intent to the forum-exclusion clause in the PTA, as it found it to be inapplicable at time of the establishment of the WTO-DSM panel.[198] Ultimately, the panel acknowledged the existence of other PTA-DSMs dealing with trade-related disputes and the need of WTO Members to initiate proceedings there. However, it did not elaborate on a limiting effect on the initiation of dispute-settlement proceedings in front of the WTO-DSM resulting from the respective WTO Members' breach of procedural obligations under the PTA-DSM.

2.3.1.2.3.3   Substantive Review of Compliance of PTAs with WTO Rules by the WTO-DSM

Pursuant to the Art. 13 of the UArt. XXIV, the AB in *Turkey – Textiles* implied that it would not assume any restriction on its authority to review the compliance of a

---

[193] Cf. Mitchell (2008), p. 117.

[194] WTO Panel, *Argentina — Definitive Anti-Dumping Duties on Poultry from Brazil*, WT/DS241/R, Judgment of 22 April 2003, para. 7.39.

[195] Ibid., para. 7.36.

[196] Ibid., para. 7.38. The panel referred to the GATT panel report on EEC – Bananas I, in which a modification of rights under the GATT 1947 was analyzed.

[197] Ibid., para. 7.38. The panel then turned quickly to the relinquishment of rights to access to the WTO-DSM (which will be reviewed in the following part).

[198] Ibid., para. 7.38.

PTA—in this case a CU—under Art. XXIV 1994.[199] The AB thereby rejected the understanding contained in the appealed panel report that only measures introduced in connection with CUs could be examined by it. Instead, the AB clarified that it had competence to scrutinize a PTA as an international agreement in accordance with requirements established under Art. XXIV GATT 1994.[200]

2.3.1.2.4 No Jurisdictional Limitations Between the WTO-DSM and PTA-DSMs as a Reason for an Anticipated Diversity in the Regulation of International Trade

The WTO Members' adjudicatory experience at the WTO-DSM with the parallel use of PTA-DSMs, on the one hand, and the willingness of WTO Members to use existing formal judicial PTA-DSMs for the resolutions of disputes over substantially convergent PTA rules next to the WTO-DSM, on the other hand, has resulted in their portrayal as contributors of diversity in the regulation of international trade. The jurisprudence developed by the WTO-DSM in view of the WTO Members' use of PTA-DSMs has not helped in defining any clear jurisdictional limitations of the WTO's adjudicative forum. This ambiguity constitutes the main argument for the anticipated diversity of the regulation of international trade due to the PTA-DSMs' activity.

Given the complex interplay of PTA-DSMs at a substantive and procedural level of WTO rules, they have been seen as a potential stumbling block for the formal coordination of the regulation of international trade under the aegis of the WTO. The lack of provisions for the formal coordination between the WTO-DSM and PTA-DSMs, as well as their ability develop autonomously their understanding of PTA rules, have been regarded as a possibility of PTA-DSMs to produce incoherent, inconsistent, and, thus, diverse decisions compared to the jurisprudence of the WTO-DSM. In this context, it has been shown that most PTA-DSMs mimic the provisions on dispute resolution under the WTO-DSM.[201] At the same time, it was argued that PTA partners tend to "want to exclude from dispute settlement areas that are not covered by settled treaty at the WTO".[202]

Against this backdrop, this circumstance was equally regarded critically concerning its impact on the institutional structure of the WTO. It was seen as creating an incentive for WTO Members to engage in forum shopping and resulted in the retraction[203] from the WTO-DSM for the benefit of PTA-DSMs or the

---

[199] WTO Appellate Body, *Turkey — Restrictions on Imports of Textile and Clothing Products*, WT/DS34/AB/R, Judgment of 22 October 1999, para. 60.

[200] WTO Panel, *Turkey — Restrictions on Imports of Textile and Clothing Products*, WT/DS34/R, Judgment of 31 May 1999, para. 9.53.

[201] Rühl (2014).

[202] Froese (2016), p. 582.

[203] Drezner (2013).

obstruction of judicial dispute settlement at the WTO-DSM altogether.[204] Conversely, these courses of action taken by WTO Members were argued as equally increasing the probability of conflicting judgements between the several DSMs.

In this context, it is important to stress that the inclusion of provisions on dispute settlement between PTA partners does not contain information on the actual character of the established PTA-DSM. The concern over judicial PTA-DSMs to constitute competing adjudicative fora vis-à-vis the WTO-DSM explains the research on indicators to identify which kind of PTA-DSM exist in a PTA.[205] Of the different available modes of operation for PTA-DSMs, formal judicial PTA-DSMs constitute the focus of attention regarding the cause of anticipated diversity in regulation of international trade.[206] The reason for focusing on formal judicial PTA-DSMs lies in the character of the WTO-DSM, which offers a binding and formal judicial forum for the resolution of disputes between WTO Members. The WTO-DSM provides WTO Members with decisions of a highly binding character due to concessions made under the DSU. The simultaneous existence of PTA-DSMs that can equally operate at a high level of legalism and issue judgements of a compulsory character with even greater competences for its enforcement demonstrates that other judicial fora exist which can provide a comparable legal character and judicial effect as the WTO-DSM.

Even in the absence of forum shopping, the use of PTA-DSMs by WTO Members was argued as still having adverse effects on the authority and legitimacy of the WTO-DSM as a regulatory and adjudicative forum.[207] This was especially found to be the case in the establishment of a factual hierarchy of regimes, where states would have to decide and justify whether they would follow a judgement of a specific adjudicative body if said body issued a different judgement.[208] Therefore, it was argued that PTA-DSMs could constitute alternatives to a dispute settlement within the WTO-DSM for substantive and procedural reasons at the expense of the use of the WTO-DSM. The claim of PTA-DSMs to constitute judicial bodies that engage on the interpretation of PTA rules at a high degree of isolation was held against the authoritative power of the WTO-DSM in disputes among PTA partners.[209]

Considering this critique, the approach taken by the panels and the AB to confirm their ample competences when dealing with PTAs and the use of PTA-DSMs by WTO Members is very plausible. It appears that the panels and the AB have tried to remedy the missing procedural coordination between PTA-DSMs and the

---

[204] Busch (2007).

[205] Advocating a less formal approach of dispute settlement, namely disputed issues in PTAs, cf. Melillo (2019).

[206] Based on the PTAs listed under the RTA IS up until 2012, these PTA-DSMs with different levels of legalism. 30% of PTAs contain political PTA-DSMs; 65% set up quasi-judicial PTA-DSMs; and 5% set up judicial PTA-DSMs; see Chase et al. (2016), fig. 10.1.

[207] Drahos (2007), pp. 199–200.

[208] Bruns and Hestermeyer (2008), pp. 134–136.

[209] Marceau et al. (2013).

WTO-DSM through an expansive understanding of their judicial competences.[210] Such an approach also nurtured the presumption that the panels and the AB would indeed remain able to find a violation of WTO rules appearing in a PTA context, which allowed the ongoing characterization of PTA-DSMs as drivers of diversity and the fragmentation of international trade law.

Weiler's analysis in this regard is exceptional, as it is based on convergences between the jurisprudence developed under the WTO-DSM and the CJEU. Weiler posits a vision of the rapprochement of the WTO-DSM and the CJEU, making the WTO-DSM legal authority claim irrelevant due to substantive considerations.[211]

2.3.2   Diversity in the Context of the Predominantly Pragmatic Approach Towards International Trade Law: PTA-DSMs as Indications of Diversity

Under the predominantly pragmatic approach towards international trade law, PTAs and PTA-DSMs have been equally considered as contributing to diversity in the regulation of international trade. Pursuant to this understanding, on the one hand, diverse regulation of equivalent regulatory objects give reason to assume that they do not exist for the same pragmatic purposes. On the other hand, formally equivalent rules on which PTA-DSMs issue diverse interpretations constitute a major indication that the existing rules on international trade do not operate systemically, as divergent understandings of the addressed equivalent regulatory objects prevail. In this context, major attempts to rationalize the diversity of rules on international trade with the aim of finding commonalities and recurring patterns, as well as rationalizing the diversity on their interpretation by PTA-DSMs, were already made presupposing a systemic operation of these rules. Refined epistemic interests for the respective equivalent regulatory objects addressed by multiple rules play an important part for this rationalization, which assists in identifying systemic interrelations between them.

2.3.2.1   Measuring Diversity in the Regulation of International Trade due to PTAs Beyond the WTO-PTA Nexus

Beyond the WTO-PTA nexus described above, alternative perspectives on the quantification and qualification of PTAs and PTA-DSMs have emerged, for which the measurement of diversity is not based solely on the requirements established under the legal framework of the WTO. The most prominent example is the research

---

[210]Marceau (1999) and Marceau et al. (2013).

[211]Weiler (2001b).

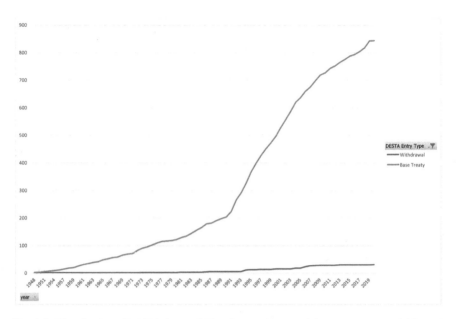

Fig. 2.3 Visualization of DESTA data on PTAs (Source: Data provided by Dür A., Baccini L., and Elsig M. 2014. The Design of International Trade Agreements: Introducing a New Dataset. The Review of International Organizations, 9(3): 353–375; visualization by the author)

project concerning the design of international trade agreements (DESTA),[212] funded by the National Swiss Science Foundation (NCCR Trade Regulation) and hosted at the World Trade Institute. As opposed to the data under the RTA IS, the DESTA project aims at assembling information about all international agreements that have a potential to liberalize trade, independently of their notification status at the WTO. It has not engrained a hierarchical measurement approach to identifying diversity in the regulation of international trade.[213] This database remains based exclusively on the economic potential of the provisions contained in international treaties, and therefore operates outside of the institutional margins established under the WTO provisions on PTAs.

Consequently, the DESTA lists a much higher total number of 842 PTAs (base treaties) that are currently in force, compared to the RTA IS, see Fig. 2.3. Nevertheless, the RTA IS as well as DESTA appear to indicate the same trends, as according to DESTA the number of new PTAs has risen sharply (from 5 to over 40 per year) only in the mid-1990s, but has been steadily declining since then (to around 8 PTAs in 2018).

According to the data provided under DESTA, PTAs remain in force over time. As Fig. 2.3 shows, withdrawals from PTAs constitute a marginal phenomenon, with only 30 withdrawals from base PTAs. From a historical perspective, the data of

---

[212] Dür et al. (2014).

[213] Ibid., p. 1 of the Codebook.

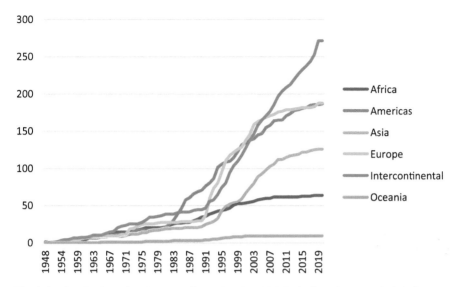

Fig. 2.4 Visualization of DESTA data for regions in which PTAs have been concluded (Source: Data provided by Dür A., Baccini L., and Elsig M. 2014. The Design of International Trade Agreements: Introducing a New Dataset. The Review of International Organizations, 9(3): 353–375; visualization by the author)

DESTA suggests that the composition of PTAs is gradually changing. Whereas PTAs where predominantly a regional phenomenon until the 1990s, the composition of the membership in PTAs has changed to predominantly cross-regional agreements, i.e., in this case intercontinental agreements, see Fig. 2.4.[214]

The high rate of conclusions and implementations of PTAs by relatively few countries or groupings of countries has led to a situation in which most PTAs are interconnected due to the overlap in membership. The networks of PTAs centered around the geographic origin of the membership has given way to a net of different regional hubs of PTAs.[215] For the future, more cross-regionalization is expected, as out of the 82 PTAs under negotiation 57 PTAs are negotiated as inter-regional agreements, see Fig. 2.5.

The current numbers of concluded PTAs are inconclusive concerning the future occurrence of PTAs. According to DESTA, it seems that the overall dynamic on the conclusion of PTAs has not come to a halt yet. According to DESTA, which does not contain data on the effects of Brexit, 89 PTAs are currently being negotiated and could be concluded in the near future. Nevertheless, the general growth in the number of PTAs has been said to slow down and not reach the same pace as it had had before the world economic crisis in 2009.[216]

---

[214] United Nations Conference on Trade and Development (2019), p. 42; Crawford and Fiorentino (2005), pp. 18, 22; Sopranzetti (2018).

[215] Hofmann C et al., *Horizontal depth: a new database on the content of preferential trade agreements*, WPS7981, 22 February 2017, figs 11; 12.

[216] Beyer (2021), p. 4.

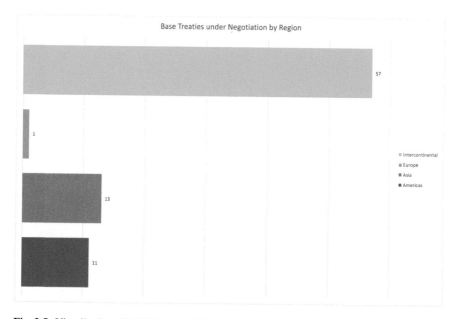

Fig. 2.5 Visualization of DESTA data: PTAs under negotiation per region (Source: Data provided by Dür A., Baccini L., and Elsig M. 2014. The Design of International Trade Agreements: Introducing a New Dataset. The Review of International Organizations, 9(3): 353–375; visualization by the author)

Although the dynamics on the increase of PTAs generally correspond with those available under the RTA IS, research on quantitative textual research on PTA rules shows that their actual substantive diversity is indeed very low. It has been found that most provisions of PTAs are mainly copied and pasted from other PTA provisions.[217] At the same time, most of the existing PTAs contain references to WTO rules and replicate these.[218]

2.3.2.2 Consequences Associated with the Emergence and Diversity of PTA Rules

The emergence of PTA rules and their diversity has been viewed especially critically from an epistemically differently informed legal perspective.

From an economic perspective, the limited openness of PTAs for accession by interested states and the corresponding exclusionary effects of a *de facto* regulation of international trade by PTAs by economically powerful states have been seen particularly critically.[219] Yet, the emergence of new rules on international trade has

---

[217] Allee and Elsig (2016a).

[218] Allee et al. (2017), pp. 361–362.

[219] Hoekman and Sabel (2019).

also been regarded as inevitable, caused by the current institutional structure for the governance of international trade as provided under the legal framework of the WTO. It has been identified as constituting the main cause for the rise of PTAs due to the WTO Members' economic pressure to advance in additional fields of regulation of international trade, in order to ensure trade liberalization at a higher pace than provided for under the current WTO negotiations. Therefore, it has been said that PTAs constitute an important additional regulatory avenue to obtain regulation of controversial aspects of international trade,[220] such as environmental protection[221] or the regulation of new topics such as digital trade,[222] in light of the current stalemate of the Doha Round.[223] Consequently, PTAs were also discussed to create possibilities for new and innovative regulation of international trade for the fields of international trade not yet covered under the legal framework of the WTO. This development was expected to bring faster results, as PTA partners could sidestep the consensus-based negotiations under the WTO. Considering these developments, the study of PTAs, including the diversity of their rules, has gradually gained momentum. Much of the research surrounding PTAs as legal tools for the process of trade liberalization has focused on the assembly of data, which goes beyond their tracking and tracing by means of the taxonomy provided by the legal framework of the WTO. Most importantly, this measurement has not taken place to establish the formal coordination of PTA rules with WTO rules. Rather, the research has focused on identifying factual coordination between rules of different PTAs, thus emphasizing the *diversity-reducing* quality of PTA rules. Consequently, the inclusion of substantive identical rules in PTAs compared to WTO rules was argued as speaking for the importance of the obligations arising under WTO rules, which PTA partners equally wish to respect among them in PTAs.[224] It was said that WTO Members take their obligations arising under WTO rules rather seriously and do not aim at a complete retraction from the multilateral system.[225]

In the same vein, inquiries into the *rapprochement* between legal regimes by means of the development of common standards through mutual recognition between legal regimes and, e.g., by inquiring the regulatory convergence between PTAs[226] have also been advanced. The mutual recognition between legal regimes and the *rapprochement* between legal regimes by means of the development of common standards are other examples of how the potential diversity of PTA rules has been addressed.[227]

Consequently, assumed *diversity-creating* effects of PTA rules have regularly been the starting point of the corresponding research, leading to outcomes that have rather stressed the *diversity-reducing* quality of their design. As opposed to the understanding of international trade law under the *predominantly formalist* approach

---

[220] *Supra*, the notion of "WTO-X" and "WTO-plus" provisions, at Sect. 2.3.1.1.5.

[221] Morin and Jinnah (2018).

[222] Burri and Polanco (2020).

[223] Sutherland et al. (2004), paras 62–63; Do and Watson (2006), p. 22.

[224] Allee and Elsig (2016a).

[225] Allee et al. (2017), pp. 361–362.

[226] Lazo and Sauvé (2018).

[227] Peters (2017) and Walker (2008).

towards international trade law, the findings were not evaluated concerning the effect on the institutional structure of the WTO. Instead, the measurement was dealing with the economic advantages and disadvantages incurred by PTA partners, rather than on the repercussions for the system of international trade law, which included—but was not limited to—the multilateral legal framework of the WTO.

2.3.2.3   Measuring Diversity in the Regulation of International Trade due to PTA-DSMs

Measuring diversity in the regulation of international trade due to the activity of PTA-DSMs continues to remain scarce under the *predominantly pragmatic* approach towards international trade law. Equally under this alternative approach, PTA-DSMs continue to be understood as venues or interfaces for interaction between PTA partners on the implementation of PTA policy goals, in line with a rationalist-functionalist understanding of the legalization of disputes. This means of institutionalized communication gateways was argued to allow for better exchange between PTA partners and, hence, to improve the efficiency of an agreement, "expose free-riding and, if judgments are binding and enforceable, penalize non-compliance".[228] However, alternative approaches also explain the phenomenon: Liberal-institutionalist theories explain the existence of legalized dispute settlement due to the preference in democratic politics for review of the executive power; realist theories explain their occurrence with the regional hegemons' choice of legalized dispute settlement as the least expensive method to get other countries to comply with certain policy choices; and policy-diffusion theorists have argued that legalized dispute settlements allow states to learn together and from each other in addressing certain areas of policy, most likely resulting in "systematic transmission belts" of certain global norms and values.[229] Challenges to the systemic operation on the rules on international trade resulting from the decisions of PTA-DSMs have not been considered, because usually the "co-existence of multiple governance actors with overlapping mandates [have not been regarded] as a pathology ('overlap' or 'fragmentation') that threatens governance effectiveness through redundancy, inconsistency and conflict."[230] This can be explained due to the fact that, under the *predominantly pragmatic* approach towards international trade law, differences between compliance and actual effects of PTA-DSMs are much more distinguishable.[231]

In this context, DESTA includes data on PTA-DSMs that are somewhat more refined than the RTA IS, including proxies for the quality of dispute settlement mechanisms, such as the availability of alternative means for dispute resolution like consultations or mediation available to PTA partners. Moreover, the stability of

---

[228] Alter and Hooghe (2016), p. 548.

[229] Ibid., pp. 548–550.

[230] Abbott et al. (2014), p. 7.

[231] Alter and Hooghe (2016), pp. 551–554.

PTA-DSMs is equally reflected, containing data on the availability of standing or ad-hoc dispute-resolution bodies, as well as the availability of choice of forum provision. Finally, the bindingness and the enforcement of the decisions of PTA-DSMs are equally considered, as the research design provides information on whether the PTA-DSMs are set up, which issue explicitly non-binding decisions. The DESTA data reveal that, out of 621 listed PTAs, 530 contain provisions on dispute settlements among PTA partners. Of the PTAs that contain provisions on the settlement of disputes, 26 create an own standing legal body, while 161 delegate disputes to an external adjudicative body. Moreover, 270 PTAs provide for arbitration and 128 for mediation procedures. 153 PTAs contain provisions on the choice of forum by any of the PTA partners. Overall, 85% of all PTAs listed in DESTA include provisions on dispute settlement.

Moreover, the creation of diversity in the regulation of international trade due to the activity of PTA-DSMs has been regarded as rather exceptional. Scholars have approached the problem without primarily considering the institutional friction between the WTO-DSM and PTA-DSMs. Instead, they rather tended to rely—whether explicitly or implicitly—on the hypothesis advocated by *Anne-Marie Slaughter* on the so-called *Global Community of Courts*. *Slaughter* argues that the methodologies required by the adjudicators of international courts create among them an awareness of belonging to a united epistemic group.[232] Based on these premises, research exists that tends to depart from the understanding that PTA-DSMs do not engage in isolationist law-making, due to the adherence of the members of the judiciary to a common epistemic community. Consequently, common procedural interpretation maxims of international courts and tribunals[233] were assumed to have a limiting effect on PTA-DSMs for the diversification in the regulation of international trade due to their activity. The reciprocal acknowledgement of different PTA-DSM decisions or the common application of a balancing test for exception clauses[234] have been advanced as examples for this. Equally, non-judicial regime interaction such as politicization, e.g., by inquiring into the driving forces of regulation of international trade,[235] were argued as being another important factor for the ability of PTA-DSMs to create diversity in regulation of international trade.

Nevertheless, *Karen Alter* and *Laurence Helfer* found that the CJEU and the Tribunal of Justice of the Andean Community (TJCAN),[236] the latter one being a legal transplant for the adjudication of community-law disputes, have developed differences in their subsequent operation in the different regional constellations. Equally, they found that these courts have developed different legal reasonings despite the shared purpose of their underlying legal frameworks.

---

[232] Slaughter (2003), p. 192.

[233] Jemielniak et al. (2016), p. 11; Slaughter (2003).

[234] Sweet and Mathews (2008), pp. 139–158.

[235] Allee and Elsig (2016b).

[236] Original title: Tribunal de Justicia de la Comunidad Andina.

2.3.2.4 Consequences Associated with Diversity in the Regulation of International Trade due to PTAs and PTA-DSMs

Diversity in the regulation of international trade due to the activity of PTA-DSMs has been regarded as an inevitable possibility, without giving rise to a discussion of PTA-DSMs to constitute an institutional threat to the WTO-DSM. Consequently, the reasons for PTA partners to set up PTA-DSMs in their PTAs has been said to take place due to a broad range of motives. Given the similarities with the data under the RTA IS, most of the explanations regarding the integration of provisions on dispute settlement and the creation of PTA-DSMs have supported the insurance hypothesis already used in the context the assessment of PTA-DSMs under the *predominantly formalist* approach towards international trade law. The insurance hypothesis, however, also encompasses the fact that PTA partners anticipate experiencing difficulties while making use of the legal framework of the WTO as WTO Members. According to *Marc Froese*, PTA partners set up PTA-DSMs to insure their negotiation outcomes on trade liberalization especially at the backdrop of a potentially unstable WTO-DSM.[237] Moreover, the insurance hypothesis also aligns with veritable legal considerations of PTA partners, namely to include PTA-DSMs in PTAs to secure judicial independence, thus ensuring that the content of a respective PTA will not be the result of the economic and political powers of involved PTA partners.[238] In this context, it has been argued that PTA partners include provisions on PTA-DSMs for especially costly policy objectives. Confirming this hypothesis, *Todd Allee and Manfred Elsig* demonstrated that the more ambitions the commitments PTAs contain, the more likely it is that they will also contain provisions on strong PTA-DSMs.[239] Therefore, the integration of PTA-DSMs has been assumed to take place if PTA partners require an assurance that the specific policy goals in a PTA can be attained by ensuring a constant—sometimes legalized—dialogue. The insurance hypothesis also resonates with other observations, such as the suggestion that PTAs safeguard the security of global value chains to counter protectionist policy changes by PTA partners.[240] Given that legal overlaps have not posed a doctrinal or institutional problem under the *predominantly pragmatic* approach, PTAs, as well as PTA-DSMs, were characterized as simply building "upon the existing architecture of global trade governance in order to *customize* it for regional potential",[241] thereby dropping the claim that PTA-DSMs constitute an institutional threat to the WTO and WTO-DSM.

---

[237] Froese (2014).

[238] Cf. "an agreement lacking a DSM validates the suspicion that an independent mechanism is impossible within the particular historical institutional context of regional trade relations." ibid., p. 385.

[239] Allee and Elsig (2016b), p. 116.

[240] Kimura (2021).

[241] Froese (2016), pp. 582–583 (emphasis added).

The uncertainty on the exact operation of PTA-DSMs at the substantive level was only addressed conceptually, giving rise to assume their functioning as a *Global Community of Courts* versus PTA-DSMs supporting their distinctive narratives to confirm their own superiority.[242] The latter characterization has been generally seen to be conceptually problematic, allowing one to presume that PTA-DSMs are able to create diversity in the regulation of international trade. *Alter* and *Helfer* have identified the differences in operation of CJEU and TJCAN and sought to provide reasons for it by considering the differences in the political systems of the CAN member states. The authors found that these differences have not allowed the TJCAN to engage in an identical legal reasoning as its blueprint, the CJEU.[243] These findings still suggest that the activity as well as the doctrinal stance of PTA-DSMs may in fact develop differently in the different regional contexts and depend on factors going beyond their legal design, even if PTAs and PTA-DSMs exist to further an identical goal.[244] Nevertheless, *Alter* and *Helfer* also attributed positive effects to the diverse operation of the compared international courts, focusing on their importance to constrain the power of national authorities by highlighting, e.g., the TJCAN's contribution to securing the rule of law in the region, or the generally availability of a body that can carry out legal review on state conduct.

2.4 Conclusion

The assessment of the fragmentation of international trade law requires an understanding of the different emphases entailed by the two different *predominantly formalist* and *predominantly pragmatic* approaches towards international trade law. Under both approaches, fragmentation of international trade law is perceived as a development or situation that has the potential to create diversity in regulation of international trade. Whereas the understanding of the system of international trade law under the *predominantly formalist* approach essentially builds on securing the hierarchy of WTO rules over PTA rules to ensure that diversity in regulation of international trade does not arise concerning an identical regulatory object addressed by WTO and PTA rules, the understanding of the system of international trade law under the *predominantly pragmatic* approach focuses instead on the shared logic of rules addressing an equivalent regulatory object and potential diversity in this regard. The two approaches to international trade law are reflected in the apprehension of the relationship of the WTO-DSM with PTA-DSMs: under the *predominantly formalist* approach, PTA-DSMs pose an institutional threat to the WTO-DSM, whereas under the *predominantly pragmatic* approach, the range of different purposes for which

---

[242] Weiler (2001a), p. 1.

[243] Alter and Helfer (2017), pp. 108–110.

[244] Alter and Helfer (2017).

PTA-DSMs are set up by PTA partners is very broad. Pursuant to this broad range of possible motivations of PTA partners to set up PTA-DSMs, scholars have mainly focused on the shared commonalities and differences of these adjudicative bodies, taking the WTO-DSM into account as a fact instead of a legal premise.

References

Abbott KW, Genschel P, Snidal D, Zangl B (2014) Orchestration. In: Abbott KW, Genschel P, Snidal D, Zangl B (eds) International organizations as orchestrators. Cambridge University Press, Cambridge, pp 3–36

Acharya R (2016) Some conclusions. In: Acharya R (ed) Regional trade agreements and the multilateral trading system, 1st edn. Cambridge University Press, Cambridge, pp 703–706

Acharya R, Crawford J-A, Maliszewska M, Renard C (2011) Landscape. In: Preferential trade agreement policies for development. World Bank Publications, Washington D.C., pp 37–76

Allee T, Elsig M (2016a) Are the contents of international treaties copied-and-pasted? Evidence from preferential trade agreements. World Trade Institute working papers working paper no. 8

Allee T, Elsig M (2016b) Why do some international institutions contain strong dispute settlement provisions? New evidence from preferential trade agreements. Rev Int Organ 11:89–120. https://doi.org/10.1007/s11558-015-9223-y

Allee T, Elsig M, Lugg A (2017) The ties between the World Trade Organization and preferential trade agreements: a textual analysis. J Int Econ Law 20:333–363. https://doi.org/10.1093/jiel/jgx009

Alter KJ, Helfer LR (2017) Transplanting international courts: the law and politics of the Andean Tribunal of Justice, 1st edn. Oxford University Press, Oxford

Alter KJ, Hooghe L (2016) Regional dispute settlement. In: Börzel TA, Risse T (eds) The Oxford handbook of comparative regionalism. Oxford University Press, Oxford, pp 538–559

Bagwell KW, Mavroidis PC (eds) (2011) Preferential trade agreements: a law and economics analysis. Cambridge University Press, Cambridge

Baldwin R, Carpenter T (2011) Regionalism: moving from fragmentation towards coherence. In: Delimatsis P, Cottier T (eds) The prospects of international trade regulation: from fragmentation to coherence. Cambridge University Press, Cambridge, pp 136–166

Baldwin RE, Robert-Nicoud F (2000) Free trade agreements without delocation. Can J Econ/Revue Canadienne d'Economique 33:766–786. https://doi.org/10.1111/0008-4085.00040

Bartels L (2008) The trade and development policy of the European Union. Oxford University Press, Oxford

Beyer V (2021) Dispute settlement in preferential trade agreements and the WTO: a network analysis of idleness and choice of forum. Eur J Int Law 32(2):433–456. https://doi.org/10.1093/ejil/chab011

Bhagwati JN (2008) Termites in the trading system: how preferential agreements undermine free trade. Oxford University Press, Oxford

Bruns V, Hestermeyer H (2008) Where unity is at risk: when international tribunals proliferate. In: König D, Stoll P-T, Röben V, Matz-Lück N (eds) International law today: new challenges and the need for reform? Springer, Heidelberg, pp 123–140

Bureau J-C, Guimbard H, Jean S (2019) Competing liberalizations: tariffs and trade in the twenty-first century. Rev World Econ. https://doi.org/10.1007/s10290-019-00346-1

Burri M, Polanco R (2020) Digital trade provisions in preferential trade agreements: introducing a new dataset. J Int Econ Law 23:187–220. https://doi.org/10.1093/jiel/jgz044

Busch ML (2007) Overlapping institutions, forum shopping, and dispute settlement in international trade. Int Organ 61:735–761. https://doi.org/10.1017/S0020818307070257

Cattaneo O (2009) The political economy of PTAs. In: Lester S, Mercurio B (eds) Bilateral and regional trade agreements. Cambridge University Press, Cambridge, pp 28–51

Chase C, Yanovich A, Crawford J-A, Ugaz P (2016) Mapping of dispute settlement mechanisms in regional trade agreements–innovative or variations on a theme? In: Acharya R (ed) Regional trade agreements and the multilateral trading system. Cambridge University Press, Cambridge, pp 608–702

Cottier T (2008) Challenges ahead in international economic law. J Int Econ Law 12:3–15. https://doi.org/10.1093/jiel/jgp005

Cottier T, Foltea M (2006) Constitutional functions of the WTO and regional trade agreements. In: Regional trade agreements and the WTO legal system. Oxford University Press, Oxford

Cottier T, Delimatsis P, Gehne K, Payosova T (2011) Introduction: fragmentation and coherence in international trade regulation: analysis and conceptual foundations. In: Cottier T, Delimatsis P (eds) The prospects of international trade regulation. Cambridge University Press, Cambridge, pp 1–66

Crawford J-A, Fiorentino RV (2005) The changing landscape of regional trade agreements. World Trade Organization, Geneva

Crawford J-A, Laird S (2001) Regional trade agreements and the WTO. N Am J Econ Financ 12:193–211. https://doi.org/10.1016/S1062-9408(01)00047-X

de Córdoba SF, Laird S, Maur J-C, Serena JM (2006) Adjustment costs and trade liberalization. In: Laird S, de Córdoba SF (eds) Coping with trade reforms: a developing country perspective on the WTO industrial tariff negotiations. Palgrave Macmillan, London, pp 66–85

de Mestral ACM (2013) Dispute settlement under the WTO and RTAs: an uneasy relationship. J Int Econ Law 16:777–825. https://doi.org/10.1093/jiel/jgt032

Devuyst Y, Serdarevic A (2007) The World Trade Organization and regional trade agreements: bridging the constitutional credibility gap. Duke J Comp Int Law 18:1–76

Do VD, Watson W (2006) Economic analysis of regional trade agreements. In: Bartels L, Ortino F (eds) Regional trade agreements and the WTO legal system. Oxford University Press, Oxford

Drahos P (2007) Weaving webs of influence; the United States; free trade agreements and dispute resolution. J World Trade 41:191–210

Drezner DW (2013) The tragedy of the global institutional commons. In: Finnemore M, Goldstein J (eds) Back to basics: state power in a contemporary world. Oxford University Press, New York

Dür A, Elsig M (eds) (2015) Trade cooperation: the purpose, design and effects of preferential trade agreements. Cambridge University Press, Cambridge

Dür A, Baccini L, Elsig M (2014) The design of international trade agreements: introducing a new dataset. Rev Int Organ 9:353–375. https://doi.org/10.1007/s11558-013-9179-8

Froese M (2014) Regional trade agreements and the paradox of dispute settlement. Manchester J Int Econ Law 11(3):367–339

Froese MD (2016) Mapping the scope of dispute settlement in regional trade agreements: implications for the multilateral governance of trade. World Trade Rev 15:563–585. https://doi.org/10.1017/S1474745616000057

Gantz DA (2016) Assessing the impact of WTO and regional dispute resolution mechanisms on the world trading system. In: Jemielniak J, Nielsen L, Olsen HP (eds) Establishing judicial authority in international economic law. Cambridge University Press, Cambridge, pp 31–77

Gobbi Estrella AT, Horlick GN (2006) Mandatory abolition of anti-dumping, countervailing duties and safeguards in customs unions and free-trade areas constituted between World Trade Organization members: revisiting a long-standing discussion in light of the Appellate Body's Turkey — textiles ruling. J World Trade 40:909–944

Grossman GM, Horn H (2013) Why the WTO? An introduction to the economics of trade agreements. In: Horn H, Mavroidis PC (eds) Legal and economic principles of world trade law: economics of trade agreements, border instruments, and national treasures. Cambridge University Press, Cambridge, pp 9–67

Hamanaka S (2012) Unexpected usage of enabling clause? Proliferation of bilateral trade agreements in Asia. J World Trade 6:1239–1260

Harrison J (2014) The case for investigative legal pluralism in international economic law linkage debates: a strategy for enhancing the value of international legal discourse. London Rev Int Law 2:115–145. https://doi.org/10.1093/lril/lru002

Hart HLA (2012) The concept of law, 3rd edn. Oxford University Press, Oxford

Hoekman BM, Mavroidis PC (2015) WTO 'à la carte' or 'menu du jour'? Assessing the case for more plurilateral agreements. Eur J Int Law 26:319–343. https://doi.org/10.1093/ejil/chv025

Hoekman B, Sabel C (2019) Open plurilateral agreements, international regulatory cooperation and the WTO. Glob Policy 10:297–312. https://doi.org/10.1111/1758-5899.12694

Horn H, Mavroidis PC, Sapir A (2010) Beyond the WTO? An anatomy of EU and US preferential trade agreements. World Econ 33:1565–1588. https://doi.org/10.1111/j.1467-9701.2010.01273.x

Islam MR, Alam S (2009) Preferential trade agreements and the scope of GATT Article XXIV, GATS Article V and the enabling clause: an appraisal of GATT/WTO jurisprudence. Netherlands Int Law Rev 56:1. https://doi.org/10.1017/S0165070X09000011

Jemielniak J, Nielsen L, Olsen HP (2016) Introduction. In: Jemielniak J, Nielsen L, Olsen HP (eds) Establishing judicial authority in international economic law. Cambridge University Press, Cambridge, pp 1–28

Jo H, Namgung H (2012) Dispute settlement mechanisms in preferential trade agreements: democracy, boilerplates, and the multilateral trade regime. J Confl Resolut 56:1041–1068

Kelsen H (2003) Principles of international law, 5th edn. The Lawbook Exchange, Ltd., Clark

Kelsen H (2017) Reine Rechtslehre, 1st edn. Mohr Siebeck, Tübingen

Kim JB (2011) WTO legality of discriminatory liberalization of internal regulations: role of RTA national treatment. World Trade Rev 10:473–496

Kim JB (2014) Entrenchment of regionalism: WTO legality of MFN clauses in preferential trade agreements for goods and services. World Trade Rev 13:443–470. https://doi.org/10.1017/S1474745613000311

Kim JB (2018) Adaptation of internal trade requirements in RTAs: substandard internal trade liberalization. J World Trade 375–392

Kimura F (2021) International production networks and required new global governance: mega-FTAs and the WTO. In: Ogawa E, Raube K, Vanoverbeke D et al (eds) Japan, the European Union and global governance. Edward Elgar, Cheltenham

Koskenniemi M (2007) Fragmentation of international law: difficulties arising from the diversification and expansion of international law. Erik Castrén Institute of International Law and Human Rights

Koskenniemi M (2014) What is international law for? In: Evans MD (ed) International law. Oxford University Press, Oxford, pp 28–50

Kreuder-Sonnen C, Zürn M (2020) After fragmentation: norm collisions, interface conflicts, and conflict management. Glob Con 9:241–267. https://doi.org/10.1017/S2045381719000315

Kwak K, Marceau G (2003) Overlaps and conflicts of jurisdiction between the World Trade Organization and regional trade agreements. Can Yearb Int Law 41:83–152

Lazo RP, Sauvé P (2018) The treatment of regulatory convergence in preferential trade agreements. World Trade Rev 17:575–607. https://doi.org/10.1017/S1474745617000519

Marceau G (1999) A call for coherence in international law—praises for the prohibition against 'clinical isolation' in WTO dispute settlement. J World Trade:87–152

Marceau G, Wyatt J (2010) Dispute settlement regimes intermingled: regional trade agreements and the WTO. J Int Dispute Settlement 1:67–95. https://doi.org/10.1093/jnlids/idp009

Marceau G, Izaguerri A, Lanovoy V (2013) The WTO's influence on other dispute settlement mechanisms: a lighthouse in the storm of fragmentation. J World Trade 47:481–574

Mathis JH (2001) Regional trade agreements in the GATT/WTO: Article XXIV and the internal trade requirement. T.M.C. Asser Press, Den Haag

Mavroidis PC (2005) The general agreement on tariffs and trade: a commentary. Oxford University Press, Oxford

Mavroidis P (2007) Trade in goods: an analysis of international trade agreements. Oxford University Press, Incorporated, Oxford

Mbengue MM (2016) The settlement of trade disputes: is there a monopoly for the WTO? Law Pract Int Courts Tribunals 15:207–248. https://doi.org/10.1163/15718034-12341320

Melillo M (2019) Informal dispute resolution in preferential trade agreements. J World Trade 53: 95–127

Mitchell AD (2008) Legal principles in WTO disputes. Cambridge University Press, Cambridge

Morin J-F, Jinnah S (2018) The untapped potential of preferential trade agreements for climate governance. Environ Polit 27:541–565. https://doi.org/10.1080/09644016.2017.1421399

Navarro PE, Rodríguez JL (2014) Deontic logic and legal systems. Cambridge University Press, Cambridge

Nken M, Yildiz HM (2021) Implications of multilateral tariff bindings on the extent of preferential trade agreement formation. Econ Theory. https://doi.org/10.1007/s00199-020-01338-1

Northrup CC et al (2015) Imperialism. In: Encyclopedia of world trade from ancient times to the present. Routledge, New York

Nwobike C (2008) The WTO compatible ACP-EU trade partnership: interpreting the reciprocity requirement to further development. Asper Rev Int Bus Trade Law 8:87–124

Ochieng CMO (2007) The EU–ACP economic partnership agreements and the 'development question': constraints and opportunities posed by Article XXIV and special and differential treatment provisions of the WTO. J Int Econ Law 10:363–395. https://doi.org/10.1093/jiel/jgm009

Organisation for Economic Co-operation and Development (2003) Regionalism and the multilateral trading system. OECD Publishing, Paris

Pauwelyn J (2003) Conflict of norms in public international law: how WTO law relates to other rules of international law. Cambridge University Press, Cambridge

Pauwelyn J (2004) The puzzle of WTO safeguards and regional trade agreements. J Int Econ Law 7: 109–142. https://doi.org/10.1093/jiel/7.1.109

Peters A (2017) The refinement of international law: from fragmentation to regime interaction and politicization. Int J Constitutional Law 15:671–704. https://doi.org/10.1093/icon/mox056

Petersen J (2009) Max Webers Rechtssoziologie und die juristische Methodenlehre. De Gruyter, Berlin

Porges A (2011) Dispute settlement. In: Preferential trade agreement policies for development. The World Bank, pp 467–501

Posner RA (2004) Legal pragmatism. Metaphilosophy 35:147–159. https://doi.org/10.1111/j.1467-9973.2004.00310.x

Prost M (2012) The concept of unity in public international law. Hart, Oxford

Raiser T (2008) Max Weber und die Rationalität des Rechts. JuristenZeitung 63:853–859. https://doi.org/10.1628/002268808785849654

Rigod B (2013) Enforcement of the WTO 'regional exceptions': a comparative institutional analysis. In: Cremona M, Hilpold P, Lavranos N et al (eds) Reflections on the constitutionalisation of international economic law: Liber Amicorum for Ernst-Ulrich Petersmann. Nijhoff, Leiden, pp 425–439

Rodríguez Mendoza M, Low P, Kotschwar B (eds) (1999) Trade rules in the making: challenges in regional and multilateral negotiations. Organization of American states. Brookings Institution Press, Washington, D.C.

Rosenstock J, Singelnstein T, Boulanger C (2019) Versuch über das Sein und Sollen der Rechtsforschung: Bestandsaufnahme eines interdisziplinären Forschungsfeldes. In: Boulanger C, Rosenstock J, Singelnstein T (eds) Interdisziplinäre Rechtsforschung. Springer Fachmedien Wiesbaden, Wiesbaden, pp 3–29

Rühl J (2014) Design by diffusion: dispute settlement mechanisms in preferential trade agreements. Graduate Institute of International and Development Studies

Schwartz WF, Sykes AO (1996) Toward a positive theory of the most favored nation obligation and its exceptions in the WTO/GATT system. Int Rev Law Econ 16:27–51. https://doi.org/10.1016/0144-8188(95)00053-4

Seinecke R (2015) Das Recht des Rechtspluralismus. Mohr Siebeck, Tübingen

Slaughter A-M (2003) A global community of courts focus: emerging fora for international litigation (part 2). Harv Int Law J:191–220

Smith JM (2000) The politics of dispute settlement design: explaining legalism in regional trade pacts. Int Organ 54:137–180

Sopranzetti S (2018) Overlapping free trade agreements and international trade: a network approach. World Econ 41:1549–1566. https://doi.org/10.1111/twec.12599

Stephenson SM (2010) Services trade in the western hemisphere: liberalization, integration, and reform. Brookings Institution Press, Washington D.C.

Sutherland P et al (2004) The future of the WTO: addressing institutional challenges in the new millennium. World Trade Organization

Sweet AS, Mathews J (2008) Proportionality balancing and global constitutionalism. Columbia J Transnatl Law 47:72–164

Tamanaha BZ (2004) On the rule of law: history, politics, theory. Cambridge University Press, Cambridge

Trachtman JP (2003) Toward open recognition? Standardization and regional integration under Article XXIV of GATT. J Int Econ Law 6:459–492

Trachtman JP (2011) The limits of PTAs. In: Bagwell KW, Mavroidis PC (eds) Preferential trade agreements. Cambridge University Press, Cambridge, pp 115–149

United Nations Conference on Trade and Development (2019) The shifting contours of trade under hyperglobalization. In: Trade and Development Report 2018. UN, pp 35–67

Valcke C (2018) Comparing law: comparative law as reconstruction of collective commitments, 1st edn. Cambridge University Press

Van den Bossche P (2005) The law and policy of the World Trade Organization: text, cases and materials. Cambridge University Press, Cambridge

Viner J (1924) The most-favored-nation clause in American commercial treaties. J Polit Econ 32:101–129. https://doi.org/10.1086/253580

Viner J (2014) The customs union issue. Oxford University Press, New York

Walker N (2008) Beyond boundary disputes and basic grids: mapping the global disorder of normative orders. Int J Constitutional Law 6:373–396. https://doi.org/10.1093/icon/mon016

Weber M (2010) Max Weber-Gesamtausgabe, 1st edn. Mohr Siebeck, Tübingen

Weber M, Rheinstein M, Shils E (1954) Max Weber on law in economy and society. Harvard University Press, Cambridge

Weiler JHH (ed) (2001a) Cain and Abel—convergence and divergence in international trade law. In: The EU, the WTO, and the NAFTA: towards a common law of international trade? Oxford University Press, Oxford, pp 1–4

Weiler JHH (ed) (2001b) Epilogue: towards a common law of international trade. In: The EU, the WTO, and the NAFTA: towards a common law of international trade? Oxford University Press, Oxford, pp 201–222

Winters LA (2017) The WTO and regional trading agreements: is it all over for multilateralism? In: Elsig M, Hoekman B, Pauwelyn J (eds) Assessing the World Trade Organization. Cambridge University Press, Cambridge, pp 344–375

Yang S (2012) The key role of the WTO in settling its jurisdictional conflicts with RTAs. Chin J Int Law 11:281–319. https://doi.org/10.1093/chinesejil/jms036

Yang S (2014) The solution for jurisdictional conflicts between the WTO and RTAs: the forum choice clause. Mich State Int Law Rev 23:107–152

Zeng L (2021) New tendency of the regional trade agreements and its negative impacts on the Doha round. In: Contemporary international law and China's peaceful development. Springer, Singapore, pp 455–473

Chapter 3
Revisiting Methodological Shortcomings for Assessing the Role of PTA-DSMs for the Fragmentation of International Trade Law

Both notions of diversity identify distinct reasons for diversity connected with the PTA-DSMs' activity and consequently focus on different potential for their contribution to the fragmentation of international trade law. Each of the different notions of diversity contains shortcomings concerning the assessment of the common problem that PTA-DSMs may be installed for different reasons and consequently operate differently, impairing the systemic operation of multiple rules on international trade.

While under the *predominantly formalist* approach, the notion of diversity is well-suited to identifying institutional deficiencies for the WTO-DSM resulting from the activity of PTA-DSMs, it does not allow the development of a method that would provide for precise substantive and procedural limits to their activity. Conversely, although under the *predominantly pragmatic* approach *all* rules and actors on international trade can be taken into account, under this approach the assessment and comparison of PTA-DSM activity concerning a specific substantive matter remains neglected. Consequently, this approach has not brought clarity concerning the salient doctrinal problem on the validity of rules on international trade so far.

3.1 Opportunities and Limits Arising from the Understanding of Diversity Under the *Predominantly Formalist* Approach Towards International Trade Law

Assessing diversity under the *predominantly formalist* approach contains a strong emphasis on the formal coordination of multiple rules in the realm of international trade law. It departs from an understanding that a legal system on international trade can be created by substantive and procedural means of hierarchization. Thus, it offers the opportunity to optimize a legal system, with the aim of making it work efficiently and effectively by designating a key-operator for its coordination, namely the WTO with its WTO-DSM. Both terms of efficiency and efficacy act as measurements which are deeply linked to the prevalent perception of legitimacy of a legal system.[1] Moreover, it is most beneficial from a perspective of litigation: It contributes to high accuracy for the calculation of risks and chances arising from the possibility of initiating litigation leading to the enforcement of PTA rules. The understanding of diversity under the *predominantly formalist* approach therefore corresponds best with epistemic interests that require the systemic operation of international trade to be calculable and open to its effective modification.

In the context of international trade law, this understanding of diversity in the regulation of international trade constitutes the main driver for the perceived centrality of the WTO as a key-operator for the establishment of system of international trade law. Consequently, the establishment of the WTO as well as its predecessor the GATT 1947 have been perceived as pivotal points for the systematic operation of international trade law, ascribing the rules contained in their legal frameworks' constitutional value. For the classification of PTAs, WTO rules therefore constitute the "main analytical lens"[2] through which PTAs are perceived as a social and legal phenomenon. Given this normative value assigned to WTO rules, it is has become challenging under the *predominantly formalist* approach to consider PTAs as self-standing international trade agreements, given that the benchmark for preferential treatment to which they apply is inherently linked to the trading conditions that were established together with the rules under the GATT 1947 and the WTO Agreement. Facing an increasingly sophisticated network of PTAs therefore appears as a setback considering the systemic operation of multiple rules on international trade under the WTO Agreement as a key-operator for it.[3] In this context, experience from the past of the successful use of the WTO-DSM "with teeth" for the systemic operation of multiple rules on international trade on the procedural level has led many to expect an "advent of judicial review"[4] of PTAs with finding and resolving conflicts between WTO and PTA rules.

Nonetheless, this understanding of diversity also has its limitations regarding the apprehension of a systemic operation of *all* rules on international trade, which goes beyond their formal coordination. After all, the existence of *any* legal discipline on PTAs and PTA-DSMs and its enforcement constitutes only one possibility to understand fragmentation of international trade law. It is heavily informed by the

---

[1]Walker (2008), pp. 391–396; Cottier et al. (2011), pp. 41–42; Armingeon et al. (2011), p. 74.

[2]Using the term to describe a methodology which allows to legally assess the same set of facts from different legal perspectives and normative backgrounds in international law, cf. Harrison (2014), p. 124.

[3]Pauwelyn and Alschner (2014).

[4]Cottier and Foltea (2006), pp. 59–61.

aim of finding a remedy for its effective prevention.[5] By establishing the rules of the legal framework of the WTO as the yardstick for the systemic operation of international trade, this perception will always remain limited to assessing the *incompatibility* of PTA rules with WTO rules and will therefore produce analytical blind spots for the development of a systemic operation of multiple rules on international trade beyond the margins of the WTO. Moreover, the prevailing pessimistic stance concerning the conclusion of PTAs and the activity of PTA-DSMs merits heavy criticism, since the requirements under the legal framework of the WTO on PTAs and PTA-DSMs do not provide for precise conditions that could serve as a basis for a comprehensive inquiry into their incompatibility with WTO rules. Consequently, the continuing pessimistic narratives on PTAs and the activity of PTA-DSMs can be easily exposed as an "ideological exercise"[6] to secure the hegemony[7] of the WTO by securing its authority as the central platform for the systemic operation of multiple rules on international trade.[8] It only remains possible if the incompatibility of PTAs and PTA-DSMs with the corresponding WTO rules is maintained at an utmost abstract and ideal-type understanding derived from the corresponding requirements under the WTO. And it only remains accurate if the ambiguities of the WTO rules on PTAs are not mentioned.[9] The reiteration of the experience of the prior successful use of the WTO-DSM to clarify ambiguous legal requirements contained in WTO rules constitutes a significant element to uphold this claim.

---

[5]On the possibility of applying the principles of *lex generalis*, *lex specialis*, *lex anterior*, and *lex posterior* in the context of the WTO-DSM vis-à-vis PTAs, cf. Pauwelyn (2003), chap. 7; Sacerdoti (2008), pp. 9–22.

[6]Cf. also Koskenniemi (2014), pp. 44–46, referring to a "hegemonic struggle" engrained in the debate on the fragmentation of international law; Advancing a hypothesis of the re-appropriation of social capital in international law and strategies of self-representation by general lawyers to depict fragmentation as a 'pathological development', see Prost (2012), pp. 201–211.

[7]The term "master weaver" to refer to integration of international rules of different origins to regard allowing for conclusions on the legal authority of the international legal system is used by Broude (2008), p. 120.

[8]This becomes especially clear regarding the dynamic of "proliferation" of PTAs. Whether an unobjectionable number of PTAs exists has never been addressed by the users of this terminology. Rather it was the high number of PTAs itself that represented a deviation from the prevailing standard in the regulation of international trade.

[9]It should be pointed out that the enforcement of norms by means of adjudication in itself already constitutes a self-standing normative statement pursuant to which the lack of enforcement of norms in itself already constitutes a deviation from the ideal. The consequence of such an understanding of international trade law limits the assessment of fragmentation to the possibility of successful adjudication of a specific phenomenon. In this regard, Navarro and Rodríguez (2014), p. 72. Note that following the pragmatic reading of norms "the norm itself is constitutive of which possible worlds the norm-giver considers normatively ideal in relation to the actual world."

3.2   Opportunities and Limits Arising from the Understanding of Diversity Under the *Predominantly Pragmatic* Approach Towards International Trade Law

The understanding of diversity under the *predominantly pragmatic* approach has a strong emphasis on identifying recurring patterns in multiple rules in the realm of international trade to confirm their systemic operation. This aim of finding recurring patterns is equally reflected in the analysis of the activity of PTA-DSMs. The understanding of diversity under the *predominantly pragmatic* approach comes with the opportunity of methodological pluralism. It provides an enriched yardstick to measure the phenomenon of PTAs and PTA-DSMs, which goes beyond the respective requirements stipulated under the legal framework of the WTO. Therefore, it can also capture more realistically the actual legal architecture for the regulation of international trade. This realist approach is deferential to the availability of a *quasi-automatic* functioning of the WTO-DSM and its role for understanding the systemic operation of international trade law. Although the WTO-DSM has contributed much to an observable implementation of WTO rules, this notion of diversity can take this development into account as a *factor* having an effect on *all* rules on international trade, but not as its *constituent* for their systemic operation. Most importantly, it can contain information on the operation of international trade law beyond the PTA-WTO nexus. For this purpose, the GATT 1947 as well as the legal framework of the WTO can be conceived less as legal conditions applying to PTAs and PTA-DSMs and more as a legal fact surrounding them. The categorization of PTAs as self-standing international trade agreements thus becomes feasible. Such an understanding also aligns with the general historical understanding that the regulation of international trade has always been a history of international trade agreements,[10] in which PTAs of themselves have always played their part.

Although this different understanding of diversity can serve to confirm whether PTA-DSMs interpret equivalent rules on international trade in a uniform manner, and can provide information on the means employed by PTA-DSMs to arrive at this uniform understanding, this has rarely been addressed. The salient doctrinal question on the validity of rules on international trade was only addressed on a very abstract level, not leading to the identification of *incommensurability* of decisions issued by different adjudicative authorities. According to *Cass R. Sunstein*:

> "Incommensurability occurs when the relevant goods cannot be aligned along a single metric without doing violence to our considered judgments about how these goods are best characterized."[11]

---

[10]Concerning the origins of international trade agreements, cf. Northrup et al. (2015a), pp. 443–446 at p. 444; concerning reasons on the conclusion of PTAs, cf. Northrup et al. (2015b), pp. 491–499 at p. 444 under New Imperialism; for a historical overview, cf. World Trade Organization (2011), pp. 48–54.

[11]Sunstein (1993), p. 796.

Neil Walker describes as follows the consequence of the incommensurability of rules and decisions—in his words, authority claims—issued by different adjudicative authorities:

> "In explanatory terms, it means that there is no sure basis of historical knowledge – no Archimedean point – from which we can evaluate the strength and validity of the different, and in some respects contending, authority claims [...]. [I]n normative terms [...] [this] means that the idea of a fully consensual 'sharing', 'pooling' 'division' or 'co-ordination' of authority between units, still less of the transcendence of the need for a vocabulary of authority in a 'post-sovereign' future, can never be more than an aspiration whose full realization is frustrated by the resilient distinctiveness and authoritativeness-in-the-last-instance of the units who might pursue it."[12]

From these definitions, it becomes clear that the analysis of PTA-DSM decisions concerning their *incommensurability* makes it possible to address the validity of rules as understood by PTA-DSMs engaging in their interpretation. Given that *incommensurability* encompasses more than mere incompatibility, because the single metric for the measurement of court decisions can be composed of a multitude of aspects,[13] this methodological pluralism is simultaneously the greatest weakness of this notion of diversity: The findings appear rather descriptive than normative[14] and are therefore not able to cater to the epistemic interest of proactively shaping a legal system aspired to under the *predominantly formalist* approach. Consequently, the finding on incommensurability in the regulation of international trade makes it prone to criticism, given the broad range of aspects of regulation it can encompass.[15]

In light of this critique, the analysis of incommensurability of PTA-DSM decisions can indeed be valuable if the single metric is not overly broad. This can be ensured by applying it to a selected area of regulation of international trade. The rather descriptive findings resulting from an inquiry into the incommensurability of PTA-DSM decisions can be useful in refining the debate over their contribution to the regulation of international trade and the fragmentation of international trade law overall. The review of the incommensurability of PTA-DSM decisions allows verification whether these adjudicative bodies have given rise to varying interpretations on substantively equivalent rules on international trade. Therefore, it allows us to verify whether the PTA-DSMs, in applying and interpreting these rules, accept

---

[12] Walker (2002), pp. 338–339. Note that Walker uses units instead of contributors or legislatures to describe the origin of the rules in question.

[13] Sunstein (1993), pp. 854–856.

[14] Rosenstock et al. (2019), pp. 11–16.

[15] This is especially true for PTAs for which no definite clarity on the principal outcome pursued exists. For a good overview on legal considerations, cf. Cottier and Foltea (2006), pp. 44–47; for a good overview on economic considerations, cf. Panagariya (2000). The criticism applies equally to the findings of *Alter and Helfer*, because it remains unclear for which actual purposes the TJCAN has been endorsed by CAN member states, given that they find it to be less exigent on certain aspects. Ultimately, this may be due to the very broad base of comparison chosen for the review of their activity. Alter and Helfer (2017), pp. 92–98.

them as valid and resort to the same logic for this purpose, an aspect that can be found at the core of the debate under the *predominantly formalist* approach.

3.3 The Necessity for a Reassessment of the Role of PTA-DSMs for the Fragmentation of International Trade Law

Depending on the approach taken on the diversity in international trade law, the review of the study of active PTA-DSMs uncovers theoretical discrepancies or analytical blind spots calling for a reassessment of their role for the fragmentation of international trade law. Concerning the notion of diversity under the *predominantly formalist* approach, the explanations provided thereunder cannot be reconciled with the *actual* low activity of PTA-DSMs experienced to date. Given that, pursuant to the understanding of diversity under the *predominantly pragmatic* approach, the enforcement of substantively equivalent rules on international trade through PTA-DSMs has not been addressed, an answer to the question on the *actual* contribution of PTA-DSMs to the diversity in the regulation of international trade is still missing. Given that the approach was not sufficiently informed by the substantive provisions PTA-DSMs have included in their legal reasoning so far, this also speaks for a reassessment of their role for the fragmentation of international trade law under this perspective.

3.3.1 Theoretical Frictions Under the Predominantly Formalist Approach Towards International Trade Law

As it stands now, the low activity of PTA-DSMs reveals that the concerns over their excessive use, resulting in a detriment of the WTO-DSM have been unfounded. Instead, they rather speak for theoretical frictions on this topic, resulting from a schematic approach to the phenomenon of PTA-DSMs, which excessively draws on the experience of dispute resolution made under the WTO-DSM. Although there exists no central database tracking the activity of PTA-DSMs,[16] only very few of the PTA-DSMs have been called upon to for the resolution of disputes.[17] At the outset, this indicates that the abstract characterization of PTA-DSMs as contributors to the

---

[16] Porges (2011), pp. 491–492.

[17] On the advantages of the WTO-DSM vis-à-vis other PTA-DSMs and the low use of the latter, see Gantz (2016), pp. 74–76; see, moreover, Melillo (2019), who analyzes venues for informal dispute resolution; see also Porges (2011), pp. 468–475 who places an emphasis on the judicial review by third-party adjudication.

diversity in the regulation of international trade is difficult to reconcile with their actual performance experienced so far.

The low activity of PTA-DSMs under the *predominantly formalist* approach has been addressed primarily from an angle of its deficiency due their low-level use via-à-vis the high-level use of the WTO-DSM. Most authors have searched for compelling reasons for why WTO Members still resort to the WTO-DSM despite the existence of PTA-DSMs. This search has been stimulated by the extraordinary dynamics surrounding the use of the WTO-DSM for the adjudication of violations of WTO rules in the realm of international trade.[18] These dynamics were assumed to constitute a blueprint for a litigious approach in international trade law aiming at the clarification of rules on international trade.[19] The use of the WTO-DSM has been understood as being far less costly compared to maintaining an institutional setting at the level of a PTA-DSM.[20] This perspective has been enriched by highlighting the specific procedural nature of the PTA-DSM, which offers a highly collective surrounding for the settlement of disputes. It was understood to play an important role for its frequent use.[21] With the realization that WTO Members in fact do not engage in forum shopping, this specific feature of the WTO-DSM with its greater potential for effective community pressure exerted by other WTO Members was argued to constitute one of the main reasons to abstain from forum shopping.[22] New research on the preference of WTO Members for the WTO-DSM equally places this understanding under scrutiny, since only a portion of 6% of cases that were argued under the WTO-DSM could have also been argued under a PTA-DSM due to the existing assignment of PTA rules to a specific adjudicative forum. This finding refutes the assumption of a *genuine preference* for the WTO-DSM by PTA partners.[23] Rather, in the context of the existence of PTA-DSMs as an "incomplete set" for the resolution of disputes on PTA rules, it was argued that PTA partners still require the competencies of the WTO-DSM as a fallback option in the legal administration of their trade relations.[24]

As it stands now, the prediction of an excessive activity of PTA-DSMs and the related effects on the diversification of the regulation of international trade has proven to be inaccurate. This inaccuracy speaks rather for theoretical frictions concerning the understanding of PTA-DSMs: They can assume functions beyond those known under the WTO-DSM. This constitutes a circumstance that could be reflected by their low activity. At the same time, the comparison of dispute settlement under PTA-DSMs with the one experienced under the WTO-DSM has led to a schematic understanding of the resolution of disputes concerning international trade.

---

[18] Saluste and Hoekman (2021), p. 2.

[19] Sacerdoti (2015), p. 153.

[20] Porges (2011), p. 474.

[21] Carmody (2008), p. 532.

[22] Vidigal (2017).

[23] Beyer (2021).

[24] Froese (2016), p. 582.

The inaccuracy in the prediction of the activity of PTA-DSMs demonstrates that the experience of dispute resolution under the WTO-DSM is not as easily transferable to other fora adjudicating rules on international trade. Very broadly, it also speaks against the assumption of fragmentation of international trade law through the activity of PTA-DSMs. Simultaneously, it has dimmed the vision on examining their role independently of their coexistence with the WTO-DSM.

Considering, on the one hand, the fact that not a single panel or the AB has declared a PTA to violate the corresponding WTO rules and, on the other hand, that WTO Members have clearly abstained from bringing this issue under the purview of the WTO-DSM, this shows that the expectation was clearly disappointed. Moreover, the failure of WTO Members to contribute to the clarification on the content of the corresponding PTA provisions provided under the legal framework of the WTO technically prevented the WTO-DSM from finding a rule of conflict between WTO and PTA rules and putting it to practice.[25] Furthermore, the understanding of diversity under the *predominantly formalist* approach becomes increasingly debatable in light of a newly evolving situation of political economy: In light of the demise of the AB and an inherently weakened stance of the WTO for the regulation of international trade, the WTO-DSM can contribute even less clarification on WTO rules overall as it stands now.[26]

3.3.2 Analytical Blind Spots for Identifying Diversity in the Regulation of International Trade Under the Predominantly Pragmatic Approach Towards International Trade Law

Research not focusing on the interaction of PTA-DSMs with the WTO-DSM has uncovered very important additional insight on their actual purpose and function in PTAs. However, this strand of research has not delved sufficiently into the substantive problems that arise from the interpretation of substantively equivalent rules by PTA-DSMs and their effects on the regulation of international trade. Consequently, until today no sufficient insights exist that shed light on the significance and validity of rules on international trade as applied and understood by PTA-DSMs.

---

[25] On the possibilities of rule conflicts and their resolution, cf. Waltermann et al. (2020), pp. 20–25.
[26] Pauwelyn (2019).

3.3.2.1   Lost Purpose or Different Functions of PTA-DSMs as an Explanation for Their Low Activity

Under the *predominantly pragmatic* approach, the fact that PTA-DSMs are not being used frequently has created momentum for discussing potential alternative tasks assigned to PTA-DSMs, going beyond those known under the WTO-DSM.

Since newer PTAs in particular do not remain limited to regulation of trade issues, but also include investment provisions, as well as other abstract provisions on, e.g., labor standards and protection of the environment and fundamental rights, this makes the precise economic assessment of PTAs more complex. Explanations on the inclusion of such non-trade aims under economic theory become gradually more difficult and serve as an argument that PTAs target other purposes than trade liberalization only. Considering the observation that almost all states participate in the conclusion of PTAs, it appears that their implementation is not economically efficient in all instances. Consequently, the fact that PTA partners possibly implement PTAs counterfactually from an economic perspective was argued as speaking against their function exclusively to administer the economic process of trade liberalization. The motivations for states to implement PTAs can range from altruist agendas to rather self-centered aims of securing a critical mass concerning a specific regulatory topic, which would then allow maintaining a specific type of regulation that best suits the predominant economic models of one or all PTA partners.[27] Therefore, the research on heterogenic non-economic motives for states to conclude PTAs has gradually become more popular due to the higher visibility of non-economic objectives in the texts of the PTAs.[28] In this vein, the rise of PTAs was also explained as serving equally strategic interests of the involved countries. For instance, the existence of PTAs has been explained as a means for political dominance of "user" states over "taker" states of pre-negotiated PTAs.[29] Equally, it has been shown that the drafting process of PTAs depends on the power of the states involved, rather than on the specific economic considerations relevant for the involved states.[30]

The low use of PTA-DSMs allows us to assume two scenarios outside their function to contribute to the administration of trade liberalization by contributing guidance on the content of PTA rules. On the one hand, PTA-DSMs may not be used to assist in the process of trade liberalization, because PTAs themselves do not necessarily have to aim at this economic function. Consequently, it is imaginable that PTA-DSMs could have lost their purpose in PTAs as instruments for the clarification of the economic content of PTA rules that are not exclusively of an economic nature. On the other hand, diverse models of trade liberalization in PTAs could be accompanied by the assignment of totally different tasks going beyond the

---

[27]Mavroidis and Sapir (2015).

[28]Meissner and McKenzie (2019).

[29]Mavroidis and Sapir (2015).

[30]Lugg et al. (2019).

ones known and experienced under the WTO-DSM,[31] resulting in their low activity. This understanding is backed by research investigating the, *inter alia*, non-economic purposes of PTAs or the inability of PTA-DSMs to deliver the economic outcomes that are aimed at thereunder. In this context, varying PTA rules have cast doubts concerning their single purpose to regulate trade among PTA partners. This has called in question whether PTAs are being used as legal tools for the economic process of trade liberalization between PTA partners. These doubts on the economic purpose of PTAs have their origin in the increasingly difficult endeavor to realign them with insights from economic theory due to the diversity of PTA rules.

Ultimately, this has led scholars to assume that PTAs are implemented for goals other than the legal administration of trade liberalization:[32] On the other hand, research exists supporting the claim that effective trade liberalization is much less a process that can be administered and designed legally, but is much more dependent on other factors not tied to legal questions. In this context, recent data on the effects of PTAs for the liberalization of trade provide for a nuanced picture of their effects for trade liberalization. These data speak rather for exogenous factors responsible for successful trade liberalization, i.e., factors that cannot be accomplished solely by the legal design of PTAs rules. It has been shown that the configuration of PTAs as well as their composition concerning the economic status of states participating in it are extremely decisive for an actual welfare-enhancing effect. Based on an ex-post analysis on the effects of PTAs, *Chafer et al.* have found that bilateral PTAs dispose over almost no trade-creating effect, while plurilateral PTAs contribute to the creation of trade between PTA partners.[33] Consequently, a change in the landscape of PTAs was prognosticated from a participation of economies of all sizes to the conclusion of PTAs between relatively large economies.[34] Pursuant to these insights, only PTAs with a high number of participating states could lead to a veritable removal of barriers in international trade.[35] The addition of non-traditional trade issues such as investment-protection provisions were suggested as having a positive effect on trade creation, but the exact effects still remain too uncertain to be measured.[36] The economic perspective has become further enriched by additional variables on the calculation of welfare gains, which take into account more complex aspects of the liberalization and integration by so-called "non-trade"[37] provisions within PTAs. This circumstance might speak for the low use of PTA-DSM as

---

[31] Hauser and Roitinger (2004); cf. Jensen (2012), p. 6, who refers to the function of constitutionalization of certain PTA-DSMs.

[32] Rosen (2004).

[33] Chafer et al. (2021).

[34] Baier et al. (2019), p. 1.

[35] Already reviewing the latest available data on trade-distorting effects, cf. Do and Watson (2006), pp. 13–17; Viner (2014), pp. 51–93; 159.

[36] Baier et al. (2019), p. 48.

[37] For other political motives to engage in PTAs, cf. Damro (2006), pp. 29–38; Sutherland et al. (2004), para. 87.

adjudicative venues for the clarification of this process. In other words, as states might not be able to arrive at the economic goals they aim for due to the lack of certain economic predispositions, PTA-DSMs, which usually have the purpose of overseeing litigation on the economic content of PTA rules, might be superfluous because considerable gains from litigation cannot be expected. Moreover, a varying strictness on the enforcement of these provisions by means of PTA-DSMs speaks for the PTA partners' aim of approaching the settlement of disputes concerning specific PTA rules differently from the procedures established under the WTO-DSM. *Simon Wüthrich and Manfred Elsig* argue that prior dispute-settlement experiences at the WTO-DSM of future PTA partners lead to the inclusion of more flexible and shallow provisions on dispute settlement.[38]

3.3.2.2 Research Dealing with the Analysis of the Few Active PTA-DSMs Adjudicating the Obligations to Liberalize Trade

Regarding the few active PTA-DSMs, only some analyses allow us to draw conclusions on their contribution to the diversity of regulation of international trade. Insights on this topic require the merging of procedural and substantive aspects of PTA rules and activity for the interpretation of their respective resulting caseloads. The few analyses in which substantive and procedural aspects of the operation of PTA-DSMs have been merged nevertheless remain highly abstract, creating analytical blind spots for the debate on the fragmentation of international trade law.

Research exploring active PTA-DSMs recognizes their general function towards contributing to the legal administration of the economic process of trade liberalization. Regarding the activity of PTA-DSMs, "the increasing importance of law in the shadow of power"[39] constitutes the backbone of their comparison under the *predominantly pragmatic* approach. Yet, only scarce research exists that deals with the comparison of different PTA-DSMs. Often the claim that the regulation from one specific functional origin follows a distinct logic, and therefore makes it not suitable for comparison, has prevented such an analytical stance towards PTA-DSM activity.[40] The few existing comparisons of active PTA-DSMs have mainly dealt with such PTA-DSMs that applied a model of highly institutionalized operation given the difficulty to identify PTA-DSM activity.[41] The scarcity of PTA-DSM decisions has resulted in few possibilities to review their activity from a comparative aspect on a procedural *and* a substantive level. Therefore, comparisons of PTA-DSMs decisions have rather often dealt with abstract doctrinal commonalities to rationalize their operation instead of focusing on their precise legal reasoning concerning detailed substantive questions arising under PTA rules. The method dealing with

---

[38] Wüthrich and Elsig (2021).

[39] Froese (2014), p. 387.

[40] Referring to "ideational fragmentation" Peters (2017), p. 675.

[41] Porges (2011), p. 491.

predominantly abstract doctrinal commonalities is inspired by the understanding of PTA-DSMs constituting a *Community of Courts* and underlines their potentially unifying features throughout their activity. The downside of this research methodology, which focuses on commonalities, is that it does not contain information on a potential diversification of the regulation of international trade, which lies at heart of the debate on the fragmentation of international trade law under the *predominantly formalist* approach.

A notable exception is the work of *Alter* and *Helfer* on the "Divergent Jurisprudential Paths"[42] of the CJEU and TJCAN. It needs to be mentioned that *Alter* and *Helfer* do not intend to contribute to the debate on the fragmentation of international trade law. Nonetheless, their analysis provides information on divergent results that have emanated throughout the activity of the CJEU and the TJCAN concerning the integration process initiated under their respective community laws. Consequently, *Alter* and *Helfer*'s work also becomes available as an argument for the fragmentation of international trade law, given that the community laws of the EU and CAN equally contain regulation of international trade. Nevertheless, the entirely procedural emphasis chosen by the authors in this case is highly abstract and does not allow us to identify diversification of regulation of international trade due to the activity of PTA-DSMs in an equally substantive fashion. *Alter* and *Helfer* address the different developments that both PTA-DSMs have taken concerning specific doctrines that have been traditionally regarded as typical for the activity of the CJEU. These doctrines include the stance of the CJEU on the supremacy of EU law, its direct effect, and the implied powers of community organs and human rights authorities. All these doctrinal approaches have usually been used to explain the high activity of the CJEU and have served as an explanation for the increased efficiency of the enforcement of EU law elsewhere, too.[43] *Alter* and *Helfer* identify divergent and convergent approaches of the TJCAN on these issues. Their analysis is very insightful regarding the operation of the TJCAN and the leeway available to this court to equally apply the above-mentioned doctrinal approaches as developed by the CJEU in an entirely different political context. Nevertheless, the focus remains predominantly procedural concerning the operation of both PTA-DSMs.[44] *Alter* and *Helfer*'s work does not provide consistently additional substantive context on the specific legal issue in question. Their findings therefore remain of limited help to identify diversity in the regulation of international trade due to activity of PTA-DSMs within the meaning of the *predominantly pragmatic* approach.

---

[42] Alter and Helfer (2017), p. 91.

[43] Hinton (1998).

[44] Cf. Alter and Helfer (2017), p. 95, concerning the constitutionalization of CAN law, stating that "[...] there are some differences in the applicable legal rules, such as the Andean Free Trade Programme, but law alone cannot explain why the ATJ is less willing to constitutionalize the treaty."

3.4 Conclusion

The role of PTA-DSMs for the fragmentation of international trade law needs to be reassessed given the theoretical shortcomings under both approaches to international trade law. Under the *predominantly formalist* approach to international trade law, the sole focus on the legal relationship between the WTO and PTAs does not help us to ascertain whether PTA-DSMs resort to the same logic within their legal reasoning as an indication whether their activity has contributed to the diversity of regulation of international trade. Such an analytical stance, however, would allow us to verify the validity of the rules on international trade that active PTA-DSMs apply and interpret. This methodological shortcoming stems from the predominant research interest to safeguard the institutional significance of the WTO and the WTO-DSM, considering the very ambiguous legal disciplines under the legal framework of the WTO on the design and operation of PTAs and PTA-DSMs. Consequently, the focus has remained on the analysis of PTA-DSMs issuing hypothetically *incompatible* decisions with the rules of the WTO legal framework or decisions of the WTO-DSM as a backbone to the claim over their contribution to the incoherence and inconsistency of international trade law. At the same time, the approach does not provide any precise legal requirements that would confirm this claim. Concerning the *predominantly pragmatic* approach to international trade law, an analysis on whether PTA-DSMs are dealing with substantively equivalent rules on international trade and resort to the same logic within their legal reasoning has not taken place yet. Consequently, both inquiries on the activity and practice of PTA-DSMs have remained focused on a rather abstract examination of PTA-DSMs, without confirming or refuting the salient issue of the incommensurability of PTA-DSM decisions of substantively equivalent rules originating under different PTAs.

References

Alter KJ, Helfer LR (2017) Transplanting international courts: the law and politics of the Andean Tribunal of Justice, 1st edn. Oxford University Press, Oxford

Armingeon K, Milewicz K, Peter S, Peters A (2011) The constitutionalisation of international trade law. In: Cottier T, Delimatsis P (eds) The prospects of international trade regulation. Cambridge University Press, Cambridge, pp 69–102

Baier SL, Yotov YV, Zylkin T (2019) On the widely differing effects of free trade agreements: lessons from twenty years of trade integration. J Int Econ 116:206–226. https://doi.org/10.1016/j.jinteco.2018.11.002

Beyer V (2021) Dispute settlement in preferential trade agreements and the WTO: a network analysis of idleness and choice of forum. Eur J Int Law 32(2):433–456. https://doi.org/10.1093/ejil/chab011

Broude T (2008) Fragmentation(s) of international law: on normative integration as authority allocation. In: The shifting allocation of authority in international law: considering sovereignty, supremacy and subsidiarity, 1st edn. Hart, Oxford

Carmody C (2008) A theory of WTO law. J Int Econ Law 11:527–557. https://doi.org/10.1093/jiel/jgn017

Chafer C, Gil-Pareja S, Llorca-Vivero R (2021) Warning: bilateral trade agreements do not create trade. Bull Econ Res 2021:1–10. https://doi.org/10.1111/boer.12281

Cottier T, Foltea M (2006) Constitutional functions of the WTO and regional trade agreements. In: Regional trade agreements and the WTO legal system. Oxford University Press, Oxford

Cottier T, Delimatsis P, Gehne K, Payosova T (2011) Introduction: fragmentation and coherence in international trade regulation: analysis and conceptual foundations. In: Cottier T, Delimatsis P (eds) The prospects of international trade regulation. Cambridge University Press, Cambridge, pp 1–66

Damro C (2006) The political economy of regional trade agreements. In: Bartels L, Ortino F (eds) Regional trade agreements and the WTO legal system. Oxford University Press, Oxford

Do VD, Watson W (2006) Economic analysis of regional trade agreements. In: Bartels L, Ortino F (eds) Regional trade agreements and the WTO legal system. Oxford University Press, Oxford

Froese M (2014) Regional trade agreements and the paradox of dispute settlement. Manchester J Int Econ Law 11(3):367–396

Froese MD (2016) Mapping the scope of dispute settlement in regional trade agreements: implications for the multilateral governance of trade. World Trade Rev 15:563–585. https://doi.org/10.1017/S1474745616000057

Gantz DA (2016) Assessing the impact of WTO and regional dispute resolution mechanisms on the world trading system. In: Jemielniak J, Nielsen L, Olsen HP (eds) Establishing judicial authority in international economic law. Cambridge University Press, Cambridge, pp 31–77

Harrison J (2014) The case for investigative legal pluralism in international economic law linkage debates: a strategy for enhancing the value of international legal discourse. London Rev Int Law 2:115–145. https://doi.org/10.1093/lril/lru002

Hauser H, Roitinger A (2004) Two perspectives on international trade agreements. Zeitschrift für ausländisches öffentliches Recht und Völkerrecht 64:641–658

Hinton EF (1998) Strengthening the effectiveness of community law: direct effect, Article 5 EC, and the European Court of Justice. N Y Univ J Int Law Polit 31:307–348

Jensen T (2012) The role of dispute settlement mechanisms in the constitutionalization of regional trade agreements. Library and Archives Canada = Bibliothèque et Archives, Ottawa

Koskenniemi M (2014) What is international law for? In: Evans MD (ed) International law. Oxford University Press, Oxford, pp 28–50

Lugg A, Lund N, Allee T, Elsig M (2019) Determining the authorship of preferential trade agreements: a new technique using a supervised author topic model v2.0. In: The political economy of international organization. Salzburg

Mavroidis PC, Sapir A (2015) Dial PTAs for peace: the influence of preferential trade agreements on litigation between trading partners. J World Trade 49:351–372

Meissner KL, McKenzie L (2019) The paradox of human rights conditionality in EU trade policy: when strategic interests drive policy outcomes. J Eur Public Policy 26:1273–1291. https://doi.org/10.1080/13501763.2018.1526203

Melillo M (2019) Informal dispute resolution in preferential trade agreements. J World Trade 53: 95–127

Navarro PE, Rodríguez JL (2014) Deontic logic and legal systems. Cambridge University Press, Cambridge

Northrup CC et al (2015a) Hanseatic League. In: Encyclopedia of world trade from ancient times to the present. Routledge, New York

Northrup CC et al (2015b) Imperialism. In: Encyclopedia of world trade from ancient times to the present. Routledge, New York

Panagariya A (2000) Preferential trade liberalization: the traditional theory and new developments. J Econ Lit 38:287–331. https://doi.org/10.1257/jel.38.2.287

Pauwelyn J (2003) Conflict of norms in public international law: how WTO law relates to other rules of international law. Cambridge University Press, Cambridge

Pauwelyn J (2019) WTO dispute settlement post 2019: what to expect? J Int Econ Law 22:297–321. https://doi.org/10.1093/jiel/jgz024

Pauwelyn J, Alschner W (2014) Forget about the WTO: the network of relations between PTAs and 'Double PTAs'. SSRN Electron J 39. https://doi.org/10.2139/ssrn.2391124

Peters A (2017) The refinement of international law: from fragmentation to regime interaction and politicization. Int J Constitutional Law 15:671–704. https://doi.org/10.1093/icon/mox056

Porges A (2011) Dispute settlement. In: Preferential trade agreement policies for development. The World Bank, pp 467–501

Prost M (2012) The concept of unity in public international law. Hart, Oxford

Rosen H (2004) Ch 3, free trade agreements as foreign policy tools: the US-Israel and US-Jordan FTAs. In: Schott JJ (ed) Free trade agreements: us strategies and priorities. Peterson Institute for International Economics, Washington, DC, pp 51–78

Rosenstock J, Singelnstein T, Boulanger C (2019) Versuch über das Sein und Sollen der Rechtsforschung: Bestandsaufnahme eines interdisziplinären Forschungsfeldes. In: Boulanger C, Rosenstock J, Singelnstein T (eds) Interdisziplinäre Rechtsforschung. Springer Fachmedien Wiesbaden, Wiesbaden, pp 3–29

Sacerdoti G (2008) WTO law and the 'fragmentation' of international law: specificity, integration, conflicts. In: Janow ME, Donaldson V, Yanovich A (eds) The WTO: governance, dispute settlement and developing countries. Juris Publishing, Huntington, pp 595–609

Sacerdoti G (2015) Resolution of international trade disputes in the WTO and other fora. J Int Trade Law Policy 14:147–156. https://doi.org/10.1108/JITLP-11-2015-0036

Saluste M, Hoekman BM (2021) Informing WTO reform: dispute settlement performance, 1995-2020. J World Trade 55

Sunstein CR (1993) Incommensurability and valuation in law. Mich Law Rev 92:779–861

Sutherland P et al (2004) The future of the WTO: addressing institutional challenges in the new millennium. World Trade Organization

Vidigal G (2017) Why is there so little litigation under free trade agreements? Retaliation and adjudication in international dispute settlement. J Int Econ Law 20:927–950. https://doi.org/10.1093/jiel/jgx037

Viner J (2014) The customs union issue. Oxford University Press, New York

Walker N (2002) The idea of constitutional pluralism. Mod Law Rev 65:317–359. https://doi.org/10.1111/1468-2230.00383

Walker N (2008) Beyond boundary disputes and basic grids: mapping the global disorder of normative orders. Int J Constitutional Law 6:373–396. https://doi.org/10.1093/icon/mon016

Waltermann A, Arosemena G, Hage J (2020) Exceptions in international law. In: Bartels L, Paddeu F (eds) Exceptions in international law. Oxford University Press, Oxford, pp 11–34

World Trade Organization (ed) (2011) The WTO and preferential trade agreements: from co-existence to coherence. WTO, Geneva

Wüthrich S, Elsig M (2021) Challenged in Geneva: WTO litigation experience and the design of preferential trade agreements. Bus Polit 23:1–20. https://doi.org/10.1017/bap.2020.20

Chapter 4
Developing the Ramifications for the Analysis on the Contribution of Active PTA-DSMs to the Diversity in the Regulation of International Trade

The review of the theoretical frictions under the *predominantly formalist* approach, as well as the analytical blind spots contained under the *predominantly pragmatic* approach towards international trade law, can be used to develop a methodology that may assist in identifying diversity in the regulation of international trade due to the activity of PTA-DSMs. As explained above, under the excessively narrow understanding of the system of international trade law of the *predominantly formalist* approach, ascertaining the role of PTA-DSMs for the fragmentation of international trade law can only take place insufficiently when the research remains with the corresponding limited notion of diversity.

Consequently, carrying out an analysis that builds on the broader notion of diversity of the *predominantly pragmatic* approach is preferable. This means that the WTO rules as a reference point for the activity of PTA-DSM should not be considered. Yet, to prevent the analytical blind spots from the past from recurring, the analytical stance should instead focus on divergence instead of convergence of the decisions issued by PTA-DSMs, thus taking into account both substantive and procedural aspects of PTA rules. Moreover, to enable a truly pragmatic discussion on the issue of PTA-DSM activity, the question should be approached empirically in order also to allow an assessment of its overall relevance.

4.1 Identifying Diversity in a Setting of Commonalities

First and foremost, to identify diversity in the regulation of international trade due to the activity of PTA-DSMs, the methodological focus should lie on finding divergence in a setting of commonalities, instead of identifying commonalities in a setting of divergence. A methodology building on such an understanding delivers interesting results from two perspectives: Firstly, it allows us to surpass the exclusively negative appraisal of PTA-DSM activity that evolved under the *predominantly*

P. Wasilczyk, *Fragmentation of International Trade Law Reassessed*, EYIEL Monographs - Studies in European and International Economic Law 32, https://doi.org/10.1007/978-3-031-40601-0_4

formalist approach and to rectify the assumption that active PTA-DSMs have contributed to the diversity in the regulation of international trade. Secondly, it provides more accurate information on a potentially existing diversity of the regulation of international trade, which has led scholars under the *predominantly pragmatic* approach to focus primarily on the commonalities and convergence in PTA-DSM activity.

4.2   Due Consideration of the Context of Substantive and Procedural Elements Governing International Trade

The existing scholarship on active PTA-DSMs demonstrates that an alternative methodology that is supposed to deliver results on the diversity of the regulation of international trade due to PTA-DSM activity requires both substantive and procedural elements to be covered. On the one hand, a comparison of the activity of PTA-DSMs, based on a substantive basis, clearly delineates the field of discourse on the fragmentation of international trade law.[1] It allows us to surpass issues pertaining to competing legal authorities of PTA-DSMs with the WTO-DSM where convergences in the legal reasoning of PTA-DSMs are found. Where divergences exist, such a methodology allows us better to analyze the reasons for their emergence. Consequently, combining substantive and procedural aspects enable us to answer more precisely whether a specific legal reasoning applied by PTA-DSMs on the certain rules governing the liberalization of trade has developed in light of the specific substantive contexts in which they are operating, or the procedural contexts, or both. Moreover, elements derived from the substantive rules on international trade in PTAs allow an effective narrowing down of the research field, instead of covering an overly broad range of regulatory contexts.

4.3   Empirical Approach Towards the Assessment of Active PTA-DSMs on the Diversity of Regulation of International Trade

Research of PTA-DSM activity from a *predominantly formalist* approach in particular reveals that the question of fragmentation of international trade law has been addressed primarily from a doctrinal point of view, which did not require relying on empirical findings. This has led to a very selective approach towards PTA-DSM or WTO-DSM decisions, which ultimately resulted in the confirmation of a beholder's

---

[1] Froese (2016), p. 571.

claim regarding the role of PTA-DSMs for the regulation of international trade. Given the large-scale phenomenon of PTA-DSMs, an entirely doctrinal approach that does not take empirical findings into account does not appear to be adequate anymore. Therefore, any methodology that aims at identifying diversity in the regulation of international trade should also include an empirical analysis of the actual activity of PTA-DSMs. Such an empirical analysis can result in a better understanding of the quantitative and qualitative dimensions of diversity in regulation of international trade presumably resulting from PTA-DSM activity. Moreover, the relevance of the claim over the fragmentation caused by the activity of PTA-DSMs can be put into perspective by considering the *actual* contribution of the relevant PTA-DSMs, i.e., by identifying the exact decisions that can be considered as adding to the diversity in the regulation of international trade.

4.4   Exclusion of WTO Rules and Corresponding WTO-DSM Decisions from the Assessment

Finally, any methodology aiming to identifying diversity in the regulation of international trade due to PTA-DSM activity should not take into account WTO-DSM decisions. The different economic rationales predominantly aspired to under the legal framework of the WTO and PTAs justifies the exclusion of WTO-DSM decisions as a factor to verify whether PTA-DSMs have engaged in diverse legal reasonings on the same substantive issues. Concerning the multilateral and the preferential dimension of trade liberalization, the WTO-DSM and PTA-DSMs constitute different legal tools for the attainment of the desired level of trade liberalization within the respective legal arrangement. These different legal arrangements set out different pragmatic goals and speak for an assessment of PTA-DSM decisions separately from the decisions of the WTO-DSM.[2] Most importantly, exempting WTO-DSM decisions from the assessment will help us better to address *how* PTAs and PTA-DSMs contribute to the fragmentation of international trade, instead of focusing on the—until now—predominant question of *whether* they are responsible for it.

Ultimately, this approach also allows us to surpass the discourse under the *predominantly formalist* approach that deals with securing the legal authority of the WTO-DSM over PTA-DSMs. Considering the unresolved substantive ambiguities of WTO provisions on PTAs and PTA-DSMs, such a methodology results in a change of perspective: Instead of asking whether PTA-DSMs issue incompatible and

---

[2]Cf. Ortino (2004), arguing for different depths of trade liberalization, depending on the specific method applied for this purpose; differently in this regard, cf. Weiler (2001), pp. 230–231, who perceives a general trend of convergence between jurisprudence on WTO law and EU law.

conflicting[3] decisions, compared to those issued by the WTO-DSM, we can assess whether PTA-DSMs deliver incommensurable decisions when they are compared exclusively with each other.

4.5   Conclusion

Based on the understanding of international trade law under the *predominantly pragmatic* approach, in order to ascertain better the role of active PTA-DSMs for the fragmentation of international trade law, the developed methodology strives to identify diversity in a setting of commonalities and, consequently, through detecting divergent PTA-DSM decisions in *recurring case groups*. It encompasses the procedural and substantive bases on which PTA-DSMs have engaged in legal reasoning and issued their decisions. Moreover, such an alternative methodology should also encompass the empirical assessment of issued PTA-DSM decisions considering the theoretical frictions that have so far prevented verification of their *actual* role under the *predominantly formalist* approach. Finally, the methodology excludes WTO-DSM decisions from the analysis, given the fundamentally different purposes of PTAs and the WTO for the liberalization of international trade.

References

Froese MD (2016) Mapping the scope of dispute settlement in regional trade agreements: implications for the multilateral governance of trade. World Trade Rev 15:563–585. https://doi.org/10.1017/S1474745616000057

Hart HLA (1983) Kelsen's doctrine of the unity of law. In: Essays in jurisprudence and philosophy. Oxford University Press, Oxford

Ortino F (2004) Basic legal instruments for the liberalisation of trade: a comparative analysis of EC and WTO law. Hart, Oxford

Weiler JHH (ed) (2001) Epilogue: towards a common law of international trade. In: The EU, the WTO, and the NAFTA: towards a common law of international trade? Oxford University Press, Oxford, pp 201–222

---

[3]The term "conflict" is often used in this context. Incommensurable results would not only encompass a situation of a conflict but extend to situations that go beyond it. For a critique on the understanding of the term conflict, cf. Hart (1983), pp. 324–334.

Chapter 5
Putting the Revisited Methodology Into Practice

In the following, the proposed alternative methodology to identify an active role of PTA-DSMs for the fragmentation of international trade law will be used to review PTA-DSM decisions on PTA rules concerning the so-called General Exception Clause. This substantive basis for the inquiry allows us to verify whether the activity of PTA-DSMs contributed to the diversity of regulation of international trade and acts as a precondition to engage in the debate on fragmentation of international trade law as an empirically verifiable fact based on the identification of incommensurable results.

The focus on PTA-DSM decisions concerning the General Exception Clause encompasses PTA-DSMs' legal reasoning on the whole "legal compound" of trade liberalization striven for within a PTA: firstly, it provides information on the PTA-DSMs' understanding of the obligation to liberalize trade among PTA partners; and, secondly, it shows their understanding of the exceptions to it. So far, research on the exceptions to trade liberalization has gained only marginal attention under both the *predominantly formalist* and the *predominantly pragmatic* approach to international trade law. To identify diversity in a setting of commonalities, the analysis focuses on divergent legal reasoning in PTA-DSM decisions where they have been dealing with a substantially equivalent legal basis concerning comparable *recurring case groups*. PTA-DSM decisions containing a legal reasoning regarding the General Exception Clauses under the respective PTAs constitute one suitable area of law for verifying whether these PTA-DSMs have issued diverse decisions in this regard. The shared legal design of General Exception Clauses, and their high availability in almost all PTAs, allows for an easy identification of diverse decisions rendered by PTA-DSMs in a setting of commonalities. In this context, diverse PTA-DSM decisions can be detected by assessing them against their content, namely the declaration of the lawfulness of a disputed trade-restrictive measure for each adjudicated case.

Consequently, diverse decisions of PTA-DSMs for comparable *recurring case groups* indicate that they are incommensurable. They sustain the claim on their role for the fragmentation of international trade law. Reversely, the lack of diversity in the decisions of PTA-DSMs in comparable *recurring case groups* can serve as an argument against the fragmentation of international trade law due to the activity of PTA-DSMs.

At this point, it needs to be granted that developing such a methodology appears especially difficult and also prone to criticism in the context of international law.[1] As *Rodrigo Polanco Lazo* and *Pierre Sauvé* note regarding the comparison of PTA rules and its interpretation of PTA-DSMs:

> "Equal rules may mean different things under differing legal systems (e.g. same rule, different meaning) or within differing implementation cultures (e.g. same rule, different application)."[2]

A solution to this problem can be to consider the formal dimension of the wording of the provisions under analysis and the pragmatic reason for their existence. The inclusion of the (presumed) pragmatic reason for the existence of specific rules on international trade can help us to ascertain how the law in the books has developed vis-à-vis the law in action, and whether PTA-DSMs have interpreted the rules in the books in a way that amounts to diversity in the regulation of international trade.

Consequently, the methodology requires us to find substantive equivalence between of the PTA rules administering the process of trade liberalization including the corresponding General Exception Clauses.

5.1   Developing Criteria for the Identification of *Recurring Case Groups*

Given that each dispute in front of a PTA-DSM remains *unique*, identifying *recurring case groups* ultimately allows an approximation concerning a similar factual backdrop against which PTA-DSMs have engaged in a legal reasoning concerning equivalent substantive PTA rules. In defining *recurring case groups*, this study builds on a most-similar case design. *Recurring case groups* contain PTA-DSM decisions that are highly similar concerning their factual composition on the disputed trade-restrictive measure, as well as the reason for their justification under the General Exception Clause, and which have been adjudicated by more than one PTA-DSM. It enables the identification of divergent legal reasonings of PTA-DSMs on the respective General Exception Clauses. The review on the equivalence of General Exception Clauses, including the obligations to liberalize trade amongst PTA partners, allows us to develop criteria by means of which such *recurring case groups* can be detected for the aforementioned purpose. The availability of *recurring case groups* permits us to select PTA-DSM decisions that have

---

[1] Roberts et al. (2018).

[2] Lazo and Sauvé (2018), p. 577.

been most similar and therefore especially suitable for an analysis concerning their incommensurability.

Bearing in mind that the analysis only covers the specific part of trade in goods, and the legitimate objective invoked in the context of the respective General Exception Clauses, the results of such an analysis cannot speak for the global activity of PTA-DSMs with regard to their overall practice of issuing incommensurable decisions. Naturally, the conclusions reached in this context cannot speak directly to the fragmentation of international trade law in its entirety, but remain limited to these specific aspects. However, they can serve as indicators that can be used to confirm or dismiss the concept of PTA-DSMs issuing *incommensurable* decisions on substantially equivalent and hence commensurable rules on trade liberalization. Consequently, results from this study can be utilized to confirm or refute the accuracy of PTA-DSM characterization as a systemic threat to the system of international trade law.

Not all PTA-DSMs provide sophisticated research tools for retrieving PTA-DSM decisions issued in the context of the respective General Exception Clauses.[3] For this reason, PTA-DSM decisions were screened concerning the reference to the respective General Exception Clauses within the text of the decision. Subsequently, information on the nature of the disputed trade-restrictive measure—i.e., concerning its fiscal or non-fiscal character, the number of legitimate objectives invoked under the respective General Exception Clause, as well as procedural aspects (such as the specific procedure under which the PTA-DSM was approached to issue a decision), the date of the decision, and the parties involved in the dispute—was added to the resulting dataset on relevant PTA-DSM decisions. Moreover, the cases were coded according to the specific decision taken by the PTA-DSM, namely whether the decisions contained a decision on the illegality of the measures, were subject to the respective enforcement provisions under the PTA, or whether the PTA-DSM referred the case back to the domestic court in preliminary rulings to issue a final ruling on the case at hand.

Concerning the substantive aspects of the PTA-DSM decisions, in a second step the identified PTA-DSM decisions were coded according to the dichotomous structure of the provisions governing the process of trade liberalization among PTA partners contained in the respective PTAs. Accordingly, PTA-DSM decisions were coded based on the information they contained regarding the first element, that is, the specific type of obligation to liberalize trade, which was allegedly violated; and the second element, that is, the legitimate objective pleaded in front of a PTA-DSM to justify the existence of a trade-restrictive measure. Consequently, the relevant PTA-DSM decisions were coded according to the specific trade-restrictive measure that was identified by the PTA-DSM to be in dispute, namely whether a quantitative restriction (QR) or a measure of equivalent effect as quantitative restriction (MEQR) was at issue. Where the PTA-DSM did not make an explicit finding on this topic, the

---

[3] Note that the CJEU is the only PTA-DSM to offer a very powerful search engine for research on its decisions.

measure was classified as QR when it provided for a quota for imports or exports, and as MEQR if this was not the case; but the PTA-DSM nevertheless insisted on a justification for this measure, thereby indicating its trade-restrictive character. This methodology, applied here, has important implications regarding the number of PTA-DSM decisions, which were analyzed for the purpose of this study. PTA-DSM decisions were considered relevant if the decision of the individual PTA-DSMs was based on the respective General Exception Clauses, or if PTA-DSMs carried out a justification analysis in the context of the invocation of the General Exception Clauses, independently of the specific legitimate objective used for this purpose. This allows us to consider not only the legal reasoning of PTA-DSMs concerning the formal requirements contained within the General Exception Clauses themselves, but also to trace the practice of PTA-DSMs that has developed in the context of the reference to General Exception Clauses, namely in which settings they have allowed PTA partners to rely on a justification of a trade-restrictive measure, irrespectively of whether the relied-on legitimate objective was encompassed by the respective General Exception Clauses. Ultimately, such a methodology enables us to verify whether PTA-DSMs have in practice broadened or narrowed the scope of the General Exception Clause for the purpose of justifying trade-restrictive measures.[4] Consequently, the relevant PTA-DSM decisions were coded according to the legitimate objective that was invoked under the respective General Exception Clause by the responding party or the PTA-DSM itself. The dataset contains information on whether the legitimate objective was included in the text of the provision of the respective General Exception Clause under the corresponding PTA or not, i.e., whether it formally constitutes an *additional* legitimate objective.

Given that PTA-DSM decisions can contain a legal assessment of more than one trade-restrictive measure, and that it can affect more than one type of good, and taking into account that more than one legitimate objective can be invoked to justify it, for the purpose of coding PTA-DSM decisions a separate entry in the database was created for every individual trade-restrictive measure and the individual type of good it affected, in addition to each legitimate objective invoked by a PTA-partner or analyzed by a PTA-DSM. Against the broad universe of goods which QRs and MEQRs can affect, and the different scopes of application of the reviewed PTAs, the disputed measures were coded according to the goods that they were affecting—i.e., imported goods and goods destined for export—or coded according to whether they established general requirements for all goods being marketed within a PTA-partner's economy. The coding for the specific goods affected by these

---

[4] Note that this methodology goes beyond the confirmation of whether PTA-DSMs have resorted to the same legal reasoning under the specific requirements of the respective General Exception Clauses. It enables a perspective on their interpretative practice when facing this provision. This has important implications regarding the case selection of the CJEU, which has developed a sophisticated doctrine on the invocation of legitimate objectives for the justification of trade-restrictive measures that are not encompassed under the respective General Exception Clause; see *infra* Sect. 5.4.2.1.2.

measures was carried out in accordance with the Harmonized Commodity Description and Coding System, the Harmonized System (HS), resulting in a specific HS Code Nomenclature. For this purpose, the most approximate HS tariff line was taken. For more abstract trade-restrictive measures, the HS chapter number was used or, if this was not possible, a proxy for a generally trade-restrictive measure was created.

Additionally, the relevant PTA-DSM decisions were coded according to the analysis they carried out, i.e., whether they were successfully or unsuccessfully invoked, and the reason for this outcome is coded: Considering the equivalent doctrines developed by all PTA-DSM on the use of the respective General Exception Clauses, which generally require a proportionality analysis thereof, the measures were coded along with the respective PTA-DSM's evaluation of whether it was considered suitable, necessary, or excessive for the protection of the legitimate objective invoked. Additionally, the cases were coded based on the information whether the respective PTA-DSMs contemplated precise alternative measures or simply found the measure to be illegal.

Finally, to understand better the methodological openness of the different PTA-DSMs, and to identify a potential transjudicial dialogue between them, the decisions were coded based on whether they contained references to other non-PTA documents and non-PTA sources, as well as on the respective types of said references.

The resulting different datasets, firstly, provide insights on the procedural background in which PTA-DSMs have operated in the context of the interpretation of the respective General Exception Clauses. Secondly, they contain substantive information on the conclusion reached by PTA-DSMs in these decisions and on the quality of their legal reasoning. Thirdly, they provide information on the specific use on non-PTA sources which have become relevant for reaching this conclusion.

The development of these proxies is based on the common characteristics that can be found throughout the operation of PTA-DSMs at the procedural and substantive level.

5.2   Substantive and Procedural Limitations Resulting from the Review of PTA-DSM Decisions on General Exception Clauses

The aforementioned methodology is employed exclusively for the review of PTA-DSM decisions on General Exception Clauses which exist in the context of the respective PTA partners' trade-liberalization obligations concerning the trade in goods. It finds support in the overarching logic of trade liberalization that can be found in virtually all PTAs, and which has been reconfirmed as playing the same role in dispute settlement under PTA-DSMs. This choice is made in purview of a high normative value of this part of jurisprudence developed under PTA-DSMs. It is based on the importance of regulating the trade in goods as a basic element in PTAs, as well as on the long-standing tradition of regulation regarding this type of trade and the influence it has on other areas of regulation of international trade.[5] The choice of this methodology initially suggests that PTA-DSMs should have a uniform understanding of the obligations and exceptions existing under the process of trade liberalization within PTAs. Such a uniform understanding of the provisions indicates that different legal reasonings of PTA-DSMs concerning the respective General Exception Clauses are less likely to occur, given that PTA-DSMs are therefore inclined to understand them as sharing the same logical commonalities. This would allow us to conclude that these substantially equivalent rules in fact do operate systemically.

5.2.1 Explaining the Incorporation of General Exception Clauses for the Trade in Goods in PTAs

Until now, the invocation of General Exception Clauses in international trade disputes has been subject to little attention. This has been the case despite General Exception Clauses constituting an integral part of the legal frameworks of all economic-integration agreements, including the legal framework of the WTO as well as PTAs.[6] Generally, General Exception Clauses are incorporated to signal to the involved parties the existence of "socio-political values that are so vital and compelling to the parties that they transcend economic and commercial interests."[7] Consequently, the obligations for PTA partners to liberalize trade are not boundless and prevent them from equating trade liberalization with economic deregulation.[8] For this purpose, General Exception Clauses provide some leeway for PTA partners to deny the process of trade liberalization for a certain portion of trade. They nevertheless exert a strong influence for the part of trade underlying the process of trade liberalization. This so-called antecedent[9] of the respective General Exception Clauses highlights the overarching obligation of PTA partners to liberalize trade by reconfirming the legal rule for which any deviation requires a proper justification.[10] Concerning the General Exception Clauses under the WTO's legal framework, it has therefore been argued that the "[. . .] true concern [of General Exception Clauses] is with *normalcy*",[11] namely with the effective implementation of the obligations to

---

[5] Sauvé (2019).

[6] For a general overview, cf. Bartels and Paddeu (2020).

[7] Kurtz (2016), p. 169.

[8] In the context of trade liberalization in the EU, cf. Maletić (2013), pp. 9–10.

[9] Cf. Dolcetti and Ratti (2020), p. 111.

[10] Waltermann et al. (2020), p. 18.

[11] Pelc (2016), p. 5. He continues: "Treaty negotiators know they can do little to affect behavior during emergencies. They internalize the old legal maxim according to which 'necessity knows no

liberalize trade within the respective PTA—instead of serving the obstruction of trade liberalization.

As a result, the review of all jurisprudence on General Exception Clauses offers a complete picture of the PTA-DSMs' understanding of the process of trade liberalization, as they encompass the whole spectrum of the respective obligations incurred by PTA partners to implement trade liberalization contained under PTA rules. The PTA-DSMs' decisions concerning General Exception Clauses as 'case-legal consequence pairs'[12] "define the outcome of all the interacting original rules"[13] under the legal framework of any respective PTA. By reviewing these *derived rules*[14] on the liberalization of trade by PTA-DSMs, deviating decisions can be easily detected and allow identification of diversity in the regulation of international trade.

Finally, such a review of the jurisprudence on the respective General Exception Clause equally may provide information on the predominant claim that PTA partners set up PTA-DSMs to maximize their flexibility concerning the process of trade liberalization. Deviating decisions could confirm this claim given that PTA-DSMs may use their autonomy to base their decisions on other additional factors than those prescribed by PTA rules on trade liberalization.

Bearing the specifics of General Exception Clauses in mind, the review of the corresponding decisions by PTA-DSMs does not encompass all PTA-DSM decisions on the obligation for PTA partners to liberalize trade. For this purpose, this research relies on the respective doctrine to explain the function of the respective General Exception Clauses within the individual legal frameworks of the PTAs under which they have been issued.

5.2.2   Procedural Criterion for the Review of Active PTA-DSMs

The review of PTA-DSM decisions concerning their legal reasoning on the General Exception Clauses for the liberalization of trade in goods remains limited to decisions of PTA-DSMs operating at a high level of legalism. Decisions of PTA-DSMs operating under the model of high legalism are intended to have enforceable consequences for the parties involved in a dispute, and consequently have a definitive effect on the dispute as prescribed in their respective underlying PTAs. Under the proposed methodology, the identification of diversity in international trade due

---

law.' [. . .] But escape clauses are nonetheless required to carve out and distinguish these instances from normal circumstances [. . .]. [. . .] In short, flexibility provisions exist to prevent behavior under extraordinary circumstances from spilling over onto normal times. They are not concerned with hard times per se, but with what comes after."

[12] Waltermann et al. (2020), p. 30.

[13] Ibid., p. 31.

[14] Ibid., para. 10.

PTA-DSM activity is based on the understanding that only legally binding and definitive decisions of PTA-DSMs can be considered truly to verify the claim concerning the diversity in the regulation of international trade. Departing from the underlying logic of the assumed existence of a *Global Community of Courts*, only members of PTA-DSMs that issue binding decisions and are aware of their competences will be recognized as belonging to the same epistemic group.

By contrast, legally non-binding decisions issued by PTA-DSMs—such as those issued by PTA-DSMs operating under a diplomatic model—cannot be ascribed sufficient evidentiary value for the identification of diversity in regulation of international trade. These PTA-DSMs are not intended to have direct legal consequences on PTA partners, nor to equip PTA partners with enforceable PTA-DSM decisions against each other. Once again, departing from the logic of the existence of a *Global Community of Courts*, members of these PTA-DSMs are equally aware of the non-binding character of their decisions they issue. This awareness allows them to identify as a members of another, distinct epistemic community among PTA-DSMs, that have additional flexibly to approach disputes among PTA partners.

Regarding the definitive character of decisions issued by PTA-DSMs, only successfully appealed decisions that have been rectified by a superseding adjudicative body within the PTA-DSMs can be taken into account. Appealed cases do not have any legal effect on the disputing parties and cannot be considered for the contribution of diversity in the regulation of international trade. Conversely, decisions that might still be appealed if an appeal procedure is available continue to have this legal effect on the parties. Therefore, where appeal procedures remain possible, the latest decision of the PTA-DSM is considered definitive. Where appellate proceedings have been concluded, the latest decision in this case is considered definitive. All decisions that contain information on the content of the respective General Exception Clauses are considered, irrespectively of the specific procedure that led the respective PTA-DSM to deliver a legal reasoning in this matter.[15]

5.2.3   Exclusion of WTO-DSM Decisions on Art. XX GATT 1994

At this point, it is noteworthy to recall *Weiler's* approach to the fragmentation of international trade law, given that WTO-DSM decisions on Art. XX GATT 1994 are excluded from this analysis. According to *Weiler*, the legal frameworks of the EU and the WTO share common origins and purposes justifying their direct comparison, reflected in the textual similarities of EU rules on the free movement of goods, as

---

[15]Cf. Beyer V, Dispute Settlement in Preferential Trade Agreements and the WTO: A Network Analysis of Idleness and Choice of Forum, ID 3667796, 26 May 2020, pp. 17–18, who takes only inter-state disputes into account.

well as the WTO rules on non-discrimination.[16] This comparability of WTO and PTA rules has allowed *Weiler* to compare the decisions of the WTO-DSM with those of a PTA-DSM.

Regardless of the exact notion of diversity instructing *Weiler's* approach, it is highly doubtful whether his analysis can be sustained, particularly regarding the different purposes of PTAs and the legal framework of the WTO. Consequently, decisions on the invocation of the General Exception Clauses under these different types of agreements should not be compared with one another.

Whether *Weiler's* choice can really speak for the development of a common law of international trade or not is not self-evident from his chosen standard of comparison. This is because the legal framework of the WTO and PTAs in general contain different economic principles and conceptually applie to a different level of trade liberalization. The underlying economic and legal rationale contained under the legal framework of the WTO, which allows WTO Members to engage in a more ambitious economic integration between them by means of PTAs, is to prevent any damage to the multilateral concessions already achieved under the WTO. This is in line with the overall goal of the WTO to remove gradually *all* barriers to trade in order to tap the whole potential of welfare-enhancing effects of free trade between all WTO Members.[17] In this sense, the exceptions granted to WTO Members, which allow them to engage in PTAs, are generally aimed at achieving overall higher levels of economic integration that effectively surpass the level of concessions offered by the multilateral legal framework of the WTO.[18] In this vein, at least the GATT 1994 deals primarily with *competitive opportunities* that *convey* a certain market access to imported goods—as opposed to *a right to market access* as such under PTAs.

At the outset, under the legal framework of the WTO, goods need to exist on an exporting WTO Member's market, and consequently *competitive opportunities* for these goods need to exist on this market. Should this be the case, WTO Members incur the obligation to extend these existing *competitive opportunities* to *like* existing goods originating from importing WTO Members. This extension of competitive opportunities conveys a certain right to market access to the importing WTO Members. The MFN principle ensures that *competitive opportunities* for goods are extended to imported 'like' goods if goods from another WTO Member already exist in the exporting WTO Member's market. The NT principle secures the extension of *competitive opportunities* to imported goods if these *like* goods exist because they are domestically produced. The extension of *competitive opportunities* under the MFN and NT principles to imported goods consequently translates into a *limited right to market access* of the importing WTO Member. Consequently, market access for WTO Members under the GATT 1994 always remains *conditional*, as it

---

[16] Weiler (2001a).

[17] Cf. First recital of the WTO Agreement.

[18] Cf. the wording of Art. XXIV:4 GATT: [...] recognize the desirability of increasing freedom of trade by the development, through voluntary agreements, of closer integration between the economies of the countries parties to such agreements.

essentially depends on the pre-existence of the goods in question on the market of the importing WTO Members.[19] In this sense, the prohibition of quantitative restrictions under Art. XI GATT 1994 on imported goods cannot exist without understanding that the imported good in question, which is affected by a restriction, could be hypothetically marketed on the importing WTO Member's market—absent the limiting measure that is being enforced at the border.[20] For WTO Members that wish to export a good that has no 'like' counterpart available on the market of an importing WTO Member, relying on the MFN as well as the NT principle will not result in market access for this specific good.[21] Therefore, the scope of the GATT 1994 cannot prohibit WTO Members from generally denying the marketing of a specific good. Consequently, WTO Members remain competent to amend their domestic regulation of the overall economic activity of their market—and, with it, the degree of trade liberalization they aim for under the legal framework of the WTO. They retain the possibility of completely banning specific products form their markets, which results in protecting *only existing* and not potential trade on an importing WTO Member's market under Arts. I, III, and XI GATT 1994.

By contrast, PTA rules on trade liberalization usually confer to PTA partners an *unconditional* right to market access for the respective covered goods through the elimination of *all* trade-restrictive measures.[22] In correspondence with the substantive requirement to eliminate *all tariffs and other restrictive regulations on commerce* under Art. XXIV GATT 1994, the respective PTA partners are required to provide the same competitive opportunities not only to the goods originating from their PTA partners, which already exist on the market, but also to *all future and potential* goods, which do not exist on the market of the WTO-Member at the moment of engaging in a PTA, but that are encompassed by the specific scope of the PTA as expressed in the tariff lines covered by it. In opposition to the general situation as provided under Art. I, III, and XI GATT 1994, the rationale of Art. XXIV GATT 1994 therefore ultimately results in PTA partners effectively granting *an unconditional right to market access* on all products, irrespectively of their

---

[19] Cf. Weiler (2001b), p. 211, who does not further elaborate on the nature of the market access under GATT rules.

[20] This becomes particularly palpable after a comparison of Art. XI GATT 1994 and Art. 34 TFEU. Whereas Art. XI:1 GATT 1994 addresses 'prohibitions or restrictions other than duties, taxes or other charges, whether made effective through quotas, import or export licenses or *other measures*' (emphasis added), Art. 34 TFEU speaks directly of 'quantitative restrictions on imports and *all measures having equivalent effect*' (emphasis added).

[21] Barnard (2019), pp. 24–26, concerning the distinction between a market access approach and discrimination tests under EU rules on free trade; Pauwelyn (2005), p. 141, concerning the distinction between domestic regulation as a market access restriction versus import bans: "the mandate of the WTO does not, in principle, extend to identifying appropriate domestic regulation, the mandate of the EC and especially that of the US does include the harmonization of domestic regulation."

[22] Weiler (2001b), p. 216, observes this for Art. 34 TFEU by noting: "The Court's choice to conflate in the non-pecuniary area Market Access and Market Regulation and subject both to an obstacle-based test [. . .]."

existence on their markets, often leading to the establishment of a *single market* in the case of a wide PTA coverage. Pursuant to this understanding, from the conception of Art. XXIV GATT 1994 there should be no space available for WTO Members that engage in a PTA to shut off their markets for existing *and future* international trade with their PTA partners, except for the cases for which a justification can be invoked.

This important aspect on the comparability of WTO rules and PTA rules is not sufficiently taken into account by *Weiler*. Therefore, it allows him to assume a basis for comparison of the rules under the WTO and the EU to identify convergence between them. Given the different rationales of the multilateral and preferential approaches to the *right to market access* for imported goods, *Weiler's* approach to the comparison of decisions of the WTO-DSM and PTA-DSMs is not reproduced here.

5.2.4   Empirical Approach: Reviewing All Available Decisions on the Respective General Exception Clauses

The methodology of using a "most significant"[23] case study can be of limited use in providing information on the contribution of PTA-DSMs to the diversity of regulation of international trade. It is not employed here. Considering the weakness of an empirically unfounded finding on the diversity in the regulation of international trade law, all decisions of all PTA-DSMs active in issuing decisions on the respective General Exception Clauses are reviewed.

Weiler's conclusion on an emerging convergence between WTO rules and EU rules on market access should be equally taken into account concerning this point. It is based on the single decision in the case *European Communities – Hormones (Canada)* on Art. XI GATT 1994, in which the panel abstained from deciding on this matter.[24] If anything, Canada advanced an argumentation on the content of Art. XI GATT 1994 which could resemble the understanding of quantitative restrictions as developed by the jurisprudence of the CJEU on Art. 34 TFEU, but which was not further addressed by the European Communities as a respondent.[25] Against this finding, *Weiler's* methodology testifies that an actual convergence between the interpretation of the rules of market access by the CJEU as well as the WTO-DSM has indeed not taken place. Although he shows an awareness that his attempt

---

[23] Ibid., p. 203.

[24] WTO Panel, European Communities — Measures Concerning Meat and Meat Products (Hormones) Complaint by Cananda, WT/DS26/R/CAN, Judgment of 18 August 1997, para. 8.275-8.276.

[25] Ibid., para. IV.354.

contains "shortcomings",[26] nevertheless the different aims of WTO and PTA rules have cast doubt as to whether his claim can be supported.

5.3 Case Selection and Caseload

The proposed methodology limits the review of the overall performance of active PTA-DSMs for identifying diversity in the regulation of international trade, due to the substantive and procedural criteria set out above.

Bearing this classification in mind, only a very small number of PTA-DSMs have been active in adjudicating General Exception Clauses for the trade in goods. In total, the search for relevant PTA-DSM decisions encompassed all adjudicative bodies established in PTAs which have been active and were able to issue decisions on the General Exception Clauses contained in the respective PTAs, namely the Court of Justice of the Caribbean Community (CARICOM),[27] the Court of Justice of the Common Market for Eastern and Southern Africa (COMESA),[28] the East African Court of Justice,[29] the Central American Court of Justice,[30] the Community

---

[26] Weiler (2001b), p. 201.

[27] According to Arts. 72 and 91 of the revised Treaty of Chaguaramas, CARICOM member states shall not apply quantitative restrictions among them, but can justify their maintenance pursuant to the so-called General Exceptions contained in Art. 226 of this treaty. The Court of Justice of the CARICOM has *original jurisdiction* over these matters, in line with Art. 211 of this treaty. The Court of Justice of the CARICOM has become active in the field of its *original jurisdiction*, but has not issued any decision on the provisions regulating the trade in goods and the corresponding General Exception Clause so far. Cf. also Berry (2014), p. 288.

[28] According to Art. 49 of the Treaty establishing the COMESA (COMESA Treaty), COMESA member states shall remove all existing non-tariff barriers to the import of goods among them. They can justify their existence by having recourse to Art. 50 of the COMESA Treaty, which contains the General Exception Clause. Pursuant to Art. 23 of the COMESA Treaty, the Court of Justice of COMESA has jurisdiction over all matters that may be referred to it pursuant to the COMESA treaty. Until today, the Court of Justice of COMESA has issued only one decision concerning the international trade among COMESA member states, namely concerning the imposition of custom duties. Cf. Gathii (2018).

[29] According to Art. 75 of the Treaty for the Establishment of the East African Community (EAC Treaty), EAC member states establish a Customs Union. Pursuant to Art. 75 lit. b) and c) of the EAC Treaty, EAC member states shall eliminate all internal tariffs and other charges of equivalent effect as well as non-tariff barriers. Art. 22 of the Protocol on the Establishment of the East African Customs Union contains the General Exception Clause pursuant to which restrictions and prohibitions to trade may be justified. The East African Court of Justice has jurisdiction over these matters in line with Art. 27.1 of the EAC treaty. On the limited role of the East African Court of Justice concerning the adjudication of trade disputes, cf. Possi (2018), pp. 30–32.

[30] Pursuant to Art. 3 lit. e) of the Tegucigalpa Protocol establishing the Central American Integration System (Sistema de la Integración Centroamericana, hereinforth SICA), SICA member states have entered into an economic union. In line with Art. 7 of the subsequently negotiated Guatemala Protocol, SICA member states shall remove all tariff and non-tariff barriers between them, including quantitative restrictions on imports for goods originating in one of the SICA member states. The

Court of Justice of the Economic Community of West African States (ECOWAS),[31] the Economic Court of the Commonwealth of Independent States,[32] the CJEU, the General Secretariat of the Andean Community (SGCAN)[33] and TJCAN, the Mercosur's ad-hoc arbitral panels, and the Permanent Review Court (TPR), as well as the EFTA Court.

Until 1 December 2021, only the PTA-DSMs of the four latter PTAs of the EU, the CAN, the Mercosur, and EFTA have issued decisions on the content of the respective General Exception Clauses contained within their legal frameworks, of which the exact number of analyzed decisions becomes visible in Fig. 5.1. The inactivity of PTA-DSMs in general, and on issuing decisions concerning General Exception Clauses in particular, is remarkable. All of the aforementioned PTA-DSMs have jurisdiction over disputes arising with regard to the liberalization of trade among the respective PTA partners and the invocation of the General Exception Clauses contained in the respective PTAs. Nevertheless, the inactivity

---

provision equally contains the General Exception Clause, pursuant to which SICA member states may justify the existence of the restrictions on trade. The Central American Court of Justice (Corte Centroamericana de Justicia) has jurisdiction over all disputes arising on the interpretation of these provisions according to Arts. 35 and 12 of the Tegucigalpa Protocol. So far, the Central American Court of Justice has become active in adjudicating trade disputes regarding the imposition of custom duties; cf. O'Keefe (2000).

[31] According to Art. 3.2 lit. d) of the Revised Treaty establishing the ECOWAS (ECOWAS Treaty), ECOWAS member states establish a common market in which customs duties and non-tariff barriers are abolished concerning the trade among them. Art. 41.1 of the ECOWAS treaty contains the details on the implementation of the common market regarding the prohibition of quantitative restrictions on community goods. Art. 41.3 of the ECOWAS Treaty contains the General Exception Clause to this duty. Art. 76.2 of the ECOWAS treaty designates the Community Court of Justice of the ECOWAS as the competent court concerning any dispute arising on the interpretation or application of the ECOWAS treaty. The Community Court of Justice of the ECOWAS has remained predominantly active within the field of human rights adjudication. Concerning the reasons for its virtually non-existent activity in trade related matters, cf. Alter et al. (2013), pp. 758, 772–775.

[32] According to Art. 19 of the Charter of the Commonwealth of Independent States (CIS Charter), CIS member states establish a common market which enables the free movement of goods. The Economic Court of the CIS, according to Art. 32 of the CIS Charter, has jurisdiction over disputes arising in the performance of economic obligations. Under this provision the court has the right to provide for the interpretation of agreements and other acts of the CIS. However, Art. 4 of the CIS Statute clarifies that these interpretations merely constitute recommendations to the disputing CIS member states. Consequently, the decisions of the Economic Court of the CIS are not considered for analysis. On the uncertain nature of the CIS decisions, cf. Danilenko (1998), pp. 906–908; in the same vein, cf. Dragneva (2018), p. 309. One of the legal acts of the CIS granting jurisdiction to the Economic Court is the CIS Free Trade Area (CISFTA). Pursuant to Art. 3 CISFTA, signatories shall remove quantitative restrictions on their mutual trade except for those permitted under Art. XI GATT 1994. Art. 15 CISFTA contains the General Exception Clause referring to the legitimate objectives under Art. XX GATT 1994. Art. 19 CISFTA designates the Economic Court of the CIS as the competent authority for the settlement of disputes concerning this treaty.

[33] Original title: Secretaría General de la Comunidad Andina.

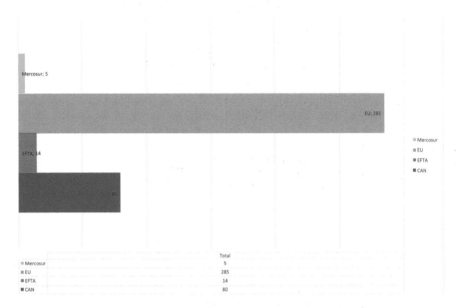

Fig. 5.1 Overall Identified Decisions Dealing with the Respective General Exception Clauses. *Source:* Autor's novel dataset

of PTA-DSMs and the absence of relevant cases among active PTA-DSMs is not surprising. It aligns with the general observations on the overall low activity of PTA-DSM.[34]

Moreover, among the aforementioned four active PTA-DSMs, the overall caseload on the respective General Exception Clauses is distributed unevenly.

One factor contributing to this uneven distribution certainly is the different periods during which the respective PTA-DSMs have been established and operational. As Fig. 5.2 shows, PTA-DSMs existing for a longer time were able become more active and issue more decisions containing legal reasoning on the respective General Exception Clause more often.

Nonetheless, it is also worthwhile to take into account other factors for the uneven distribution of the overall caseload. The analysis of the active PTAs, as well as the legal design of the respective PTA-DSMs, shows that the uneven distribution of cases may be impacted by procedural and substantive circumstances arising thereunder.

Concerning the procedural dimension, the review of the statutory rules of the four active PTA-DSMs shows different legal requirements concerning the ways of recourse, and therefore access to them. Multiple types of proceedings under which PTA-DSMs engage in legal reasoning on the respective General Exception Clauses may contribute to their higher activity in this regard. Also, the right to initiate such

---

[34] *Supra*, Sect. 3.3.1.

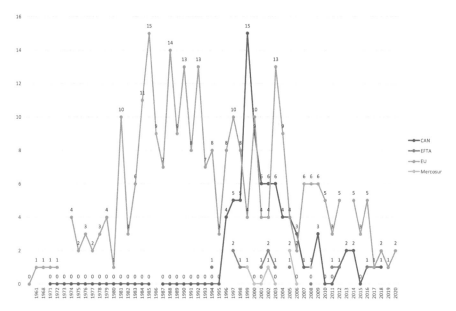

Fig. 5.2   PTA-DSM Activity Over Time. *Source:* Autor's novel dataset

proceedings, i.e., the standing of different parties in a dispute, can have an impact on the performance of PTA-DSMs. In this context, it can be observed that standing may be granted to the PTA partners for the purpose of carrying out interstate disputes only, or additional agencies may be set up with the aim of supporting the initiation of proceedings in front of a PTA-DSM in order to surveil the enforcement of PTA rules. Next to such entities, individuals may also be granted standing to have direct access to a PTA-DSM. The design of the standing in proceedings in front of PTA-DSMs can result in higher or lower legal obstacles to have recourse to a PTA-DSMs, resulting in issuing of relatively more or fewer decisions on the respective General Exception Clauses compared to other PTA-DSMs. Another procedural factor for the uneven distribution of the caseload could be the question whether PTA-DSM are assigned exclusive and mandatory jurisdiction. PTA partners that are legally required to use their PTA-DSMs in disputes involving the respective General Exception Clause may result in the PTA-DSM's higher activity record. On the other hand, the lack of exclusive and mandatory jurisdiction may cause PTA-DSMs to have fewer disputes pending overall, having lower numbers of cases submitted, as alternative adjudicative fora also remain available to PTA partners for the resolution of their disputes. Formal cooperation between two PTA-DSMs may result in fewer proceedings being brought to the PTA-DSM, which is legally required to follow the decisions of another PTA-DSM. Given that the outcome of a similar case is already approximately known by the partners from another PTA, the decision issued by the cooperating PTA-DSM may lead to fewer incentives to initiate similar proceedings—which are not only time-consuming, but require the allocation of significant human resources—in front of the own PTA-DSM.[35] Finally, the existence of mechanisms to enforce PTA-DSM decisions, i.e., the prospect of having the decisions successfully implemented, may constitute another factor that decides over the PTA partners' willingness to initiate proceedings in front of PTA-DSMs.. The PTA partners' willingness to pursue dispute resolution under the PTA-DSMs can be influenced considerably by the probability of the enforcement of a PTA-DSM's decision, as well as different proceedings regarding their correct implementation.

Concerning the substantive dimension, the different scopes of application of the PTAs in question and their legal ambit concerning the liberalization of trade can have an important influence on the performance of PTA-DSMs on delivering decisions on the respective General Exception Clauses. These different scopes of PTAs may preclude PTA partners from PTA-DSMs being able to issue a decision that includes information on the respective General Exception Clauses if the specific substantive context is not covered under a PTA.

5.3.1   Caseload of the Court of Justice of the European Union and Factual Background of the European Union

Within the EU, the CJEU issued a total of 285 decisions dealing with the General Exception Clause under Art. 36 Treaty on the Functioning of the EU (TFEU),[36] since its foundation in 1952. This amounts to ca. 4.1 decisions per year of its activity. The relevant decisions were identified by using the *InfoCuria* database provided by the CJEU, listing all decisions in which a reference to Art. 36 TFEU was contained in the operative part and the grounds of judgment.[37] This study includes all cases issued by 1 December 2021.

5.3.1.1   Conclusion of EU Treaties and their Scope

Pursuant to Art. 3 (4) TEU and Arts. 26, 27 TFEU, one of the main economic objectives under the legal framework of the EU is the creation of a single market

---

[35] E.g., this is the case between the CJEU and the EFTA Court, due to the *principle of judicial homogeneity*, inscribed in the EEAA. Concerning the activity of the EFTA court, cf. Baudenbacher (2005), p. 412.

[36] (2020) Consolidated Version of the Treaty on the Functioning of the European Union.

[37] Although the reviewed decisions should encompass virtually all decisions issued by the CJEU on Art. 36 TFEU, decisions in which the provision was neither cited in the operative part nor in the grounds of the judgement could not be considered. This has important implications on the completeness of the search on decisions by the CJEU on Art. 36 TFEU, for decisions in which the relevance of Art. 36 TFEU becomes apparent when the arguments of the parties have been reviewed, e.g., CJEU, *Commission v Lithuania*, C-61/12; ECLI:EU:C:2014:172, Judgment of 20 March 2014, para. 28. On the search criteria in the *InfoCuria* database, see CJEU (2019) InfoCuria Online help.

between the EU member states.[38] Trade liberalization resulting in the establishment of the single market requires all factors of production to move freely, independently of the borders between EU member states. Regarding the trade in goods within the EU, this is ensured through the establishment of the so-called *free movement of goods*, and the exceptions to it, which are governed by Arts. 28-37 TFEU. The scope of the provision of trade liberalization is very broad. Accordingly, the current legal framework of the EU provides for comprehensive liberalization of all trade between EU Members, in particular for all physical and non-physical goods without limitations to the scope of the covered goods.[39] However, this does not apply to agricultural products, which are governed by Arts. 38 ff. TFEU and benefit from a slower pace of liberalization. Under the free movement of goods, the EU member states' obligation to establish a single market encompasses fiscal and non-fiscal measures that can affect the trade of goods between EU member states.[40] The General Exception Clause under Art. 36 TFEU justifies *a priori* breaches of the legal principle of the free movements of goods for non-fiscal measures governed by Arts. 34 and 35 TFEU, namely the prohibition of quantitative restrictions (QRs) and measures of equivalent effects (MEQRs) for imports and exports.

5.3.1.2   PTA-DSM at the EU: The CJEU

Art. 344 TFEU sets out the compulsory and exclusive authority of the CJEU concerning all disputes arising within the underlying legal framework of the TFEU. Pursuant to Art. 19:1 TEU, the CJEU[41] 'shall ensure that in the interpretation

---

[38] Note that the legal framework of the EU is understood to have developed gradually over time in roughly three steps of reform and treaty negotiations, from the European Economic Community (EEC) to the European Communities (EC) up to the EU; cf. Craig (2011). In the following, Arts. 28-37 TFEU will be referred to as the latest relevant provisions for the trade in goods between EU Members including all preceding equivalent provisions under the preceding European treaties, which can be ascertained by means of the so-called Table of References. For a Table of References including all preceding European treaties, see the very good overview in Barnard and Peers (2020). Equally, the term 'EU member states' includes all preceding memberships, including the EEC and EC member states. Equally, the reference to the CJEU includes the preceding terminology on the European Court of Justice (ECJ) before the (2007) Treaty of Lisbon Amending the Treaty on European Union and the Treaty Establishing the European Community.

[39] Note that the free movement of goods in the EU was introduced through the gradual removal of fiscal and non-fiscal barriers to trade; cf. Title I of the (1957) Treaty Establishing the European Economic Community.

[40] This is only an outline of the substantive law of the EU. Refer to Barnard (2019), pp. 36–37 for an extensive analysis. As the history of the formation of the EU shows, this has not always been the case. The provisions on trade liberalization in the previous treaties between European countries did not cover all goods and services, but provided for progressive liberalization schemes concerning the external and internal tariffs (cf. Arts. 14-17 and 31 (2), Treaty Establishing the European Economic Community [EEC], as well as Art. 3, Treaty Establishing the European Communities [TEC Maastricht]) and the prohibition of import restrictions (cf. Arts. 31-33 EEC, and continuing in Arts. 30-34 [TEC Maastricht]).

[41] The abbreviation is used in accordance with the general usage when it comes to the complex of EU courts as set out in the TFEU. Cf. Lenaerts et al. (2014), para. 2.03.

and application of the Treaties the law is observed'. Moreover, Art. 344 TFEU underlines the obligation of EU member states to secure the CJEU's compulsory and exclusive character by following the dispute settlement provisions as set out in the TFEU:

> Member States undertake not to submit a dispute concerning the interpretation or application of the Treaties to any method of settlement other than those provided for therein.

Based on these two obligations, it has been maintained that the CJEU is the constitutional and supreme court of the EU and thereby ensures the uniform application of, *inter alia*, the rules on trade liberalization under the corresponding legal framework of the EU.[42] Its decisions result in immediate and legal force for EU member states and must be complied with by their national courts and EU member states' national authorities. Pursuant to this objective, any entity or judicial arrangement between EU member states that is capable of rendering an interpretation of EU rules outside the judicial system established by the TEU and TFEU is therefore deemed in breach of the principle of autonomy of EU law, as well as the corresponding judicial autonomy of the CJEU.[43]

The adjudication of Art. 36 TFEU by the CJEU can take place in the context of the different existing proceedings in front of the CJEU that regulate the access to this PTA-DSM. Proceedings exist under which the actions of the EU member states as well as proceedings under which the actions of the organs of the EU are subject to legal review of the CJEU. Usually, Art. 36 TFEU is invoked in the context of disputes over the legality of trade-restrictive domestic measures in the so-called proceedings for the Action for Infringement. Hereunder, the executive organ of the EU, the EU Commission (EC), and the EU member states are given the right to have recourse to the CJEU to determine whether another EU Member State has acted in breach of EU rules. Pursuant to Art. 258 TFEU, the EC is given the right to act as applicant for this type of proceeding, which delivers a reasoned opinion (so-called formal letter)[44] before the proceedings. Art. 259 TFEU regulates the right of EU member states to act as applicants for this type of proceedings, which requires that the complaining EU Member State communicate its observation on an alleged breach of EU rules by another EU Member State. Following the contact by the complaining EU Member State, the EC can deliver a reasoned opinion concerning the infringement of EU rules that was alleged by the complaining EU Member State. However, whether the EC in fact delivers an opinion remains at its discretion, as there is no due date prescribed by Art. 259 TFEU for this specific communication. On the contrary, the complaining member is merely precluded from having recourse to the CJEU within a three-month period, starting from its first contact with the EC.

---

[42] Ibid., para. 2.21.

[43] CJEU, *Slovak Republic v Achmea*, C-284/16; ECLI:EU:C:2018:158, Judgment of 6 March 2018, para. 57.

[44] Lenaerts et al. (2014), para. 5.41-5.50.

Individuals are not granted a right to act as applicant for this type of proceeding and therefore do not have direct access to the CJEU. Their access to the CJEU concerning the violation of EU rules by EU member states remains limited to approaching the EC and informing it about it. The EC has formalized its contact between itself and EU citizens by providing a form on its website for individual claims.[45]

Preliminary Rulings constitute another type of proceeding in which the CJEU can indirectly review the legality of trade-restrictive measures introduced or maintained by an EU Member State. Under these proceedings, governed by Art. 267 TFEU, domestic courts act as applicants to the CJEU. Preliminary Rulings take place in the spirit of cooperation of national courts with the CJEU and provide them with the possibility of inquiring about the interpretation of EU rules for cases in which they deem the application and interpretation of the EU treaties (Art. 267 (1) lit. a) TFEU) or the validity and interpretation of acts of the institutions, bodies, offices, or agencies of the Union (Art. 267 (1) lit. b) TFEU) pertinent to deciding the respective cases before them.[46] Domestic courts of the EU member states have the right, and in specific cases the duty, to address the CJEU to obtain its interpretation on EU rules.[47] Pursuant to Art. 267 (2) TFEU, solicitation of the CJEU for preliminary rulings is generally within the discretion of the national court. However, Art. 267 (3) TFEU sets out that any domestic court has the duty to request a Preliminary Ruling by the CJEU, against whose decisions there is no judicial remedy under national law, requiring especially the highest domestic courts to cooperate with the CJEU. It is possible for the CJEU to request further information regarding the facts of the case,[48] to reformulate the question asked by the national court,[49] and to refer the case back to the national court for further fact-finding.[50]

According to Art. 260 (1) TFEU, EU member states are obliged to take all necessary actions to ensure the implementation of the decisions of the CJEU. Should an EU Member State not comply with this obligation arising under Art. 260 (1) TFEU, further Action of Infringement proceedings concerning this failure to comply remain possible. Additionally, concerning Actions for Infringement initiated by the EC pursuant to Art. 258 TFEU, a sanctioning procedure under Art. 260 (2) TFEU is available. Hereunder, the EC can again initiate proceedings in front of the CJEU for the imposition of a penalty payment on the relevant EU Member State. These penalty payments are aimed at increasing the pressure on the concerned EU Member State to give in to the decision of the CJEU, thereby terminating its

---

[45] Complaint Form for breach of EU law – European Commission. https://ec.europa.eu/assets/sg/report-a-breach/complaints_en/. Accessed 3 September 2023.

[46] Lenaerts et al. (2014), para. 6.19.

[47] See Art. 267 (3) TFEU, which reads: "Where any such question is raised in a case pending before a court or tribunal of a Member State against whose decisions *there is no judicial remedy* under national law, that court or tribunal *shall bring the matter before* the Court" (emphasis added).

[48] Lenaerts et al. (2014), para. 6.21.

[49] Ibid., para. 6.22.

[50] Ibid., para. 6.25.

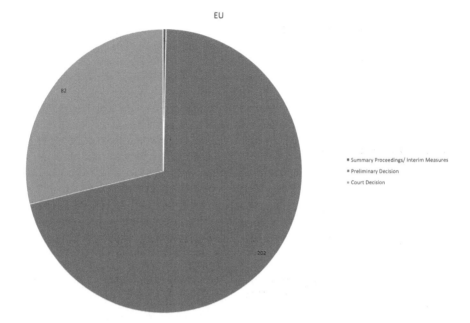

Fig. 5.3 Type and Proportion of Proceedings Regarding Decisions Dealing with the General Exception Clause Regarding the PTA-DSM of the EU. *Source:* Autor's novel dataset

breach of the EU rules in question.[51] Additionally, as a decentral mechanism to incentivize EU member states to enforce EU rules, the CJEU has developed its doctrine on state liability for damages resulting to individuals in the EU, if EU rules are not observed by EU member states or not transposed by them into their domestic legal systems.[52]

The content of the Preliminary Rulings, and its interpretation of the EU rule in question, is communicated in form of a decision and equally becomes part of EU law. It has a mandatory effect[53] on all national courts and the EU member states regarding the specific interpretation rendered by it for all future[54] proceedings conducted in front of the national courts of the EU member states. Where national courts fail to comply with the interpretation encompassed by the Preliminary Ruling, this results in the breach of EU law and can be challenged through the Action for Infringement pursuant to Art. 258-260 TFEU.[55]

As Fig. 5.3 shows, overall, of the 285 cases in which the CJEU dealt with the invocation of the General Exception Clause under Art. 36 TFEU, Preliminary Rulings have proven to be the most significant type of proceeding in which

---

[51]Wennerås (2017), pp. 89–96.

[52]Reich (2017).

[53]Lenaerts et al. (2014), para. 6.31.

[54]Ibid., p. 6.33.

[55]Ibid., p. 6.29.

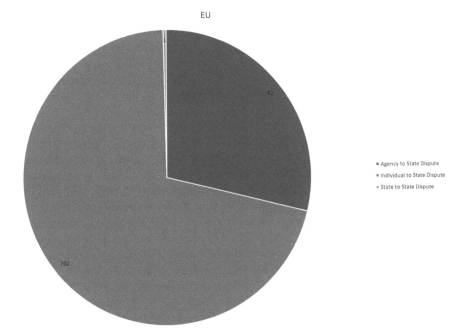

Fig. 5.4 Type and Proportion of Participants Involved in Proceedings Regarding the PTA-DSM of the EU. *Source:* Autor's novel dataset

interpretations on the content of this provision was rendered. A total of 202 Preliminary Proceedings were carried out in front of the CJEU, while 83 Action for Infringement Proceedings were conducted in the context of Art. 36 TFEU. Within these 83 Action for Infringement Proceedings, only one interstate dispute was carried out, and one interim measure proceeding was initiated, while the rest of the 81 cases were initiated by the EC, see Fig. 5.4.

5.3.2   Caseload of the EFTA Court and Factual Background of the European Economic Area

Within the European Economic Area (EEA), the EFTA Court, since its foundation in 1994, has issued 14 decisions dealing with the General Exception Clause under Art. 13 of the EEA agreement (EEAA).[56] This amounts to 0.5 decisions per year of its

---

[56](1994) Agreement on the European Economic Area.

activity. The cases were identified by screening all available decisions on the website of the EFTA Court for Art. 13 EEAA.[57] This study includes all decisions issued by the EFTA Court by 1 December 2021.

5.3.2.1 Conclusion of EEA Treaty and Its Scope

The EEAA expands the EU single market to three states of the European Free Trade Association (EFTA), namely Iceland, Norway, and Liechtenstein (thereby omitting Switzerland as a fourth EFTA Member State, hereafter EEA parties), and at the same time establishes a Free Trade Area between them.[58] The EEAA predominantly contains rules that aim at building an internal market between the EU and the EEA parties. This includes the liberalization of trade in goods, as already known under the corresponding rules of the legal framework of the EU.[59] Concerning the trade in goods, pursuant to Art. 8:3 lit. a) and b) EEAA, it covers an extensive list of products including some, but not all, agricultural and fishery products, and hence not the entirety of all imaginable products as compared to the scope of the legal framework of the EU.[60] Pursuant to Part II EEAA, liberalization of the trade in goods is established by prohibiting trade-restrictive fiscal and non-fiscal measures. Arts. 11 and 12 EEAA prohibit QRs and MEQRs for imports and exports. Art. 13 EEAA, containing the General Exception Clause, provides a justification for the introduction of trade-restrictive measures.

5.3.2.2 PTA-DSM in the European Economic Area: The EFTA Court

The EFTA Court emerged as part of the so-called two-pillar structure under the EEAA and as an alternative to an all-encompassing EEA court after being declared incompatible with the legal framework of the EU by the CJEU.[61] It is charged with ensuring the homogeneity of rules under the legal frameworks of the EU and the EEAA in disputes over EEA rules.[62] This two-pillar structure has resulted in the establishment of the EFTA Surveillance Authority (EFTA-SA) as an approximation to the EC. It is responsible for the implementation and enforcement of EEA rules by

---

[57] The Court. In: EFTA Court. https://eftacourt.int/the-court/. Accessed 15 December 2021. The software *DocFetcher* was used to identify decisions that dealt with Art. 13 EEAA until this date. The key words were: "Art. 13", "Art. 10", "restriction", "justification", and "protection".

[58] Baur (2020), pp. 2–6.

[59] Ibid., pp. 130–135.

[60] Ibid., p. 136.

[61] Fredriksen (2010), p. 486.

[62] Baur (2020), pp. 138–144.

the EEA parties that are not EU member states.[63] Implementation and enforcement of EEA rules is made effective through the foundation of the EFTA Court overseeing their interpretation. Art. 3 Para. 2 of the Surveillance and Court Agreement (SCA)[64] embeds the *principle of judicial homogeneity* between EU and EEA rules for the operation of the EFTA Court.[65] Accordingly, the EFTA Court is legally bound to take into consideration the relevant rulings of the CJEU for the interpretation of EEA rules, if they are identical in substance with rules available under the legal framework of the EU:[66] Concerning decisions that took place prior to the conclusion of the EEAA, the EFTA Court is obliged to interpret EEA rules in conformity with CJEU decisions; regarding subsequent decisions of the CJEU after the conclusion of the EEAA, the EFTA Court is required to take "due account" of them. Therefore, the *principle of judicial homogeneity* and the resulting duty for homogeneous interpretation of EEA rules with the rules under the legal framework of the EU should not be confused with a principle of direct transposition of the jurisprudence of the CJEU by the EFTA Court or the "formal acceptance of the ECJ as the supreme authority on EEA law".[67] Rather, the EFTA Court has leeway to adapt the jurisprudence of the CJEU to the conditions set out by the EEA treaty.[68] Given the complex task of the EFTA Court to ensure the *principle of judicial homogeneity*, this has resulted in an equally complex jurisdiction of this PTA-DSM. Pursuant to Art. 107 EEAA, the national courts of the EEA parties can ask the CJEU about the interpretation of EEA rules. Unlike the CJEU, the EFTA Court therefore has no exclusive mandate as a "pre-eminent interpreter of EEA law".[69] Consequently, in line with Art. 35 SCA, the EFTA Court only has unlimited jurisdiction regarding penalties imposed by the EFTA SA in antitrust matters under Arts. 53 and 54 EEAA.[70] On the other hand, according to Art. 33 SCA, the EEA parties shall take the necessary measures to comply with the judgement of the EFTA Court. Exclusive and compulsory jurisdiction of the EFTA Court concerning disputes over EEA rules is therefore not provided expressly,[71] but rather practiced by the individual EEA parties.[72] This practice is

---

[63] Note that the EFTA SA does not play any role in the legislative process of the EEA parties; cf. Björnsson (2013), p. 67.

[64] Agreement Between the EFTA States on the Establishment of a Surveillance Authority and a Court of Justice.

[65] Baur (2020), pp. 140–141.

[66] Cf. Skouris (2005), p. 124.

[67] Fredriksen (2010), p. 486.

[68] Baur (2020), p. 141; Skouris (2005), p. 124.

[69] Fredriksen (2010), p. 487.

[70] Björnsson (2013), p. 67.

[71] Baur et al. (2018), para. 208: "[...] in EEA law there is no single Court that has the final competence to decide, with effect for the entire EEA system, on the correct interpretation of the EEA Agreement. In the absence of an EEA Court, this task is now divided between the EFTA Court, having the competence to clarify the obligations of the EFTA States, and the ECJ with the competence to give the final interpretation of EEA law in the EU member states."

[72] Fredriksen (2010), pp. 488.

based on the EEA member states' individual treaty obligation to ensure the *principle of judicial homogeneity* between EEA and EU rules.

The EFTA Court offers several proceedings that became relevant for the interpretation of the General Exception Clause under Art. 13 EEA. Pursuant to Arts. 31 and 32 SCA, Action of Infringement proceedings exist under which the EFTA SA and the EEA parties themselves may have access to the court. Moreover, in line with Art. 34 SCA, the EFTA Court may issue Advisory Opinions on the interpretation of EEA rules. According to this provision, the request for such an Advisory Opinion by the EFTA Court is at the discretion of the domestic courts of the respective EEA party requesting it. Consequently, it has been held that the Advisory Opinion itself would not be directly of binding effect for the dispute at the level of the national court requesting it. Nevertheless, national courts have understood them to be directly binding in practice once they made a request to the EFTA Court, due to their concurrent legal obligations under the EEA treaty, to ensure for themselves judicial homogeneity between EEAA and EU rules.[73]

There is no enforcement mechanism available for the implementation of decisions issued by the EFTA Court.[74] Despite this lack of compliance procedures for the decisions of the EFTA Court, their implementation is assumed to take place nonetheless. This is said to be accomplished through the factual level of coercion resulting from the drastic economic consequences that could be incurred by EEA parties should the EU decide to terminate the PTA due to the effective breach of the *principle of judicial homogeneity*.[75] Regarding decentralized mechanisms that ensure the implementation of decisions of the EFTA Court, in parallel to the CJEU, the EFTA Court has developed the doctrine of state liability for damages incurred by EEA individuals due to the breach of EEA rules.[76]

As Fig. 5.5 shows, in a total of 14 cases that dealt with the invocation of the General Exception Clause under Art. 13 EEA treaty, Advisory Opinion proceedings have proven to be the most significant: Eleven decisions involving the interpretation of the General Exception Clause were issued by the EFTA Court within this specific procedure. By contrast, only three decisions involving the interpretation of the General Exception Clause were issued under the Infringement Proceedings. In this context, dispute resolution has remained predominantly driven by the EFTA SA, with all three Infringement Proceedings initiated by it, see Fig. 5.6. Moreover, the EEA parties have abstained from resorting to interstate dispute resolution provided by Art. 32 SCA to obtain an interpretation of Art. 13 EEA treaty.

---

[73] Concerning Advisory Opinions issued by the EFTA Court, cf. Baudenbacher (2005), p. 412; Björnsson (2013), p. 79.

[74] Björnsson (2013), pp. 80–82.

[75] Ibid., p. 81.

[76] Fredriksen (2010), pp. 490–491.

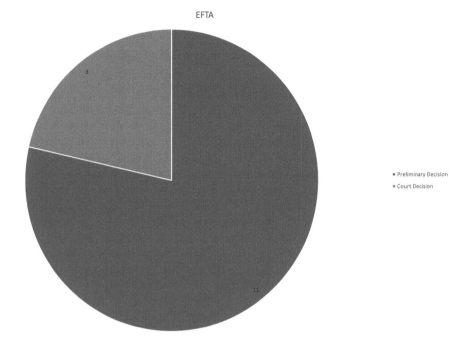

Fig. 5.5 Type and Proportion of Proceedings Regarding Decisions Dealing with the General Exception Clause Regarding the PTA-DSM of the EEA. *Source:* Autor's novel dataset

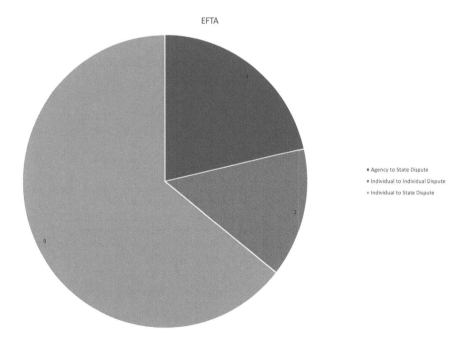

Fig. 5.6 Type and Proportion of Participants Involved in Proceedings Regarding the PTA-DSM of the EEA. *Source:* Autor's novel dataset

5.3.3   Caseload of the General Secretariat of the Andean Community, Tribunal of Justice of the Andean Community, and Factual Background of the Andean Community

From 1969 until today, the CAN, the SGCAN, and, from 1984 until today, the TJCAN issued a total of 50 decisions dealing with the General Exception Clause under Art. 73 of the Cartagena Agreement (AdC).[77] These decisions build on a total of 79 proceedings—57 conducted in front of the SGCAN and 22 conducted before the TJCAN. This amounts to 1.09 decisions per year before the SGCAN and 0.8 decisions per year during the existence of the TJCAN. The decisions were identified by screening all available decisions on the websites of the SGCAN[78] and the TJCAN[79] on Art. 73 AdC.[80] This study includes all decisions issued by the SGCAN and TJCAN by 1 December 2021.

5.3.3.1   Conclusion of the Cartagena Agreement and Its Scope

Per Art. 1 AdC, the PTA between Bolivia, Colombia, Ecuador, and Peru, joined by Venezuela from 1973 until 2003, was established in foresight of a future creation of a Latin-American common market. The highly-staked aim of this agreement needs to be understood at the backdrop of the regulatory agenda under the Treaty of Montevideo (TdM).[81] The TdM was concluded in 1980 between 13 counties of the South American continent and constitutes the founding act of the Latin American Integration Association (ALADI)[82] and its predecessor the Latin American Free Trade Association (ALALC),[83] which extends over the majority of Latin American countries.[84] The ALADI provides for a loose legal and political framework for the

---

[77] Original title: Acuerdo de Integración Subregional Andino "Acuerdo de Cartagena". Comunidad Andina (2003) Decisión 563 Codificación del Acuerdo de Integración Subregional Andino (Acuerdo de Cartagena).

[78] Normativa Andina – Comunidad Andina. https://www.comunidadandina.org/normativa-andina. Accessed 15 December 2021.

[79] (2019) Jurisprudencia. In: Tribunal de Justicia de la Comunidad Andina. https://www.tribunalandino.org.ec/index.php/jurisprudencia/. Accessed 15 December 2021.

[80] The software *DocFetcher* was used to identify decisions that dealt with Art. 72 AdC until 15 December 2021. The key words were: "Art. 72", Art. 70", "restricción/restricciones", "gravamen/es", "import*", "justificación", "justificad*", "protección", "protec*", as well as "Art. 40" and "Art. 42" considering the original AdC.

[81] (1980) Tratado De Montevideo.

[82] Original title: Asociación Latinoamericana de Integración / Associação Latino-Americana de Integração (LAIA / ALADI).

[83] Original title: Asociación Latinoamericana de Libre Comercio.

[84] Susani (2010), p. 73; Malamud (2010), pp. 23–25.

purpose of economic cooperation between Latin American countries, which includes the offering of tariff preferences for the less developed countries of the ALADI, regionally, as well as particular partial-scope agreements covering critical aspects of commercial policy among them.[85] According to Art. 3 lit. d) AdC, the PTA aims at heightening the commitments made under the TdM by introducing a so-called *Liberalization Program*,[86] which is supposed to aim at the establishment of a subregional market between CAN member states. Chapter VI AdC contains the rules of the *Liberalization Program* that apply to the trade in goods between CAN member states. The provisions of this *Liberalization Program* apply to goods originating in other CAN member states:

> with the aim to arrive at their total liberalization of trade in goods within the time limits and modalities set forth in the AdC.[87]

These time limits and modalities are enumerated under Art. 76 lit. a) – d) AdC and have provided for a gradual liberalization of trade of the specific types of goods mentioned therein. Regarding this gradual liberalization of trade in goods among CAN member states, the process is said to be completed by now.[88] Agricultural goods are subject to the distinct disciplines of Chapter IX AdC. The *Liberalization Program* applies to fiscal and non-fiscal measures having a trade-restrictive effect on the trade amongst CAN member states. The General Exception Clause contained in Art. 73 AdC applies to all measures encompassed by the *Liberalization Program* under Chapter VI AdC.

5.3.3.2 PTA-DSM in the CAN: The SGCAN and the TJCAN

The PTA-DSM of the CAN is two-tiered regarding disputes over the introduction and maintaining of trade-restrictive measures in violation of the obligations under the *Liberalization Program*. Under the first tier for dispute settlement, the SGCAN and its predecessor, the Junta, are assigned as competent bodies to resolve disputes among CAN member states on the identification of duties and restrictions prohibited under the *Liberalization Program*. According to Art. 74 AdC, the SGCAN is conferred exclusive authority[89] to identify and determine whether CAN member states have introduced or maintained trade-restrictive measures falling afoul of the

---

[85] Secretaría General de la ALADI (ed) (2020) Serie Fichas ALADI - El TM80 - sus principios y mecanismos - Ficha N° 1, p. 2.

[86] Original wording: Programa de Liberación.

[87] Original wording of Art. 76 AdC: "El Programa de Liberación será automático e irrevocable y comprenderá la universalidad de los productos, salvo las disposiciones de excepción establecidas en el presente Acuerdo, para llegar a su liberación total en los plazos y modalidades que señala este Acuerdo."

[88] For a historical overview of the gradual expansion of the scope of goods covered under the *Liberalization Program* of the CAN, cf. Castro Bernieri (2003), pp. 117–119.

[89] Reyes Tagle (2018), p. 236.

Liberalization Program.[90] This procedure is established through the CAN Commission's Decision 425 (D.425).[91] The SGCAN is charged with finding whether CAN member states have introduced prohibited import duties or restrictions on trade, which also includes invocations of the General Exception Clause under Art. 73 AdC by the investigated CAN member states. Findings of the SGCAN are pronounced by means of a so-called *resolution.*[92] Generally, *resolutions* closely resemble administrative acts of governmental agencies on the national level and are referred to by the TJCAN as administrative acts of the CAN juridical order.[93] Pursuant to Art. 47 D.425, these *resolutions* must contain specific information, such as the precise identification of the measure as well as the goods affected under the CAN tariff code. Moreover, *resolutions* must include specific formal requirements (Title I, Chapter II D.425); they must not give rise to nullity (Title II, Chapter II D.425); and they must be published in the Official Journal of the Cartagena Agreement to be of full legal effect (Title III, Chapter II D.425 and Art. 3 TJCAN-FA). This means that the findings of the SGCAN, as well as the recommendations concerning the lifting of a previously found illegal measure, are fully legally binding. The obligation continues to exist until the respective *resolution* is modified or revoked by the SGCAN or, alternatively, declared void in the Action for Annulment by the TJCAN[94] *resolutions* by the SGCAN on the existence of prohibited import duties or restrictions on trade prohibited under Art. 72 AdC have a definitive and immediate effect on the concerned CAN Member State.[95] In carrying out the investigation, the

---

[90] Orinignal wording: Investigaciones que tengan por objeto determinar la posible existencia de gravámenes o restricciones aplicados por Países Miembros al comercio intrasubregional de mercancías, Art. 1 lit. c Dec. 425.

[91] Comisión (1997) Decisión 425.

[92] The determination of measures in violation of Art. 72 AdC is only one of the in a total of seven different competences to issue *resolutions* in different areas of the CAN legal order. Under Art. 1 lit. a) D.425, the SGCAN is charged with the procedural overview for the so-called pre-judicial phase in Action of Infringement proceedings between CAN member states, as well as CAN member states and individuals. Art. 1 lit. b) D.425 sets out the broad competence of the SGCAN to pronounce findings in proceedings where it acts *ex officio.* Art. 1 lit. d) D.425 established the competence of the SGCAN to make findings on the infringement of CAN law. Art. 1. Lit. e) D.425 charges the SGCAN with investigations within the field of CAN's competition and antitrust policy and allows it to identify in CAN member states the existence of dumping, subsidies, and other trade-distorting practices. Under Art. 1 lit. f) D.425, the SGCAN can authorize the introduction of safeguard measures in CAN member states. Finally, pursuant to Art. 1 lit. g) D.425, the SGCAN is charged with all proceedings in which it is required to issue so-called *resolutions.*

[93] TJCAN, *5-AN-97*, Judgment of 8 June 1998, pp. 10–15.

[94] Original wording: Acción de Nulidad.

[95] Cf., e.g., TJCAN, *43-AI-99*, Judgment of 13 October 2000, p. 13: "As a consequence of the principle of immediate and direct application of the acts and rules forming up to the legal order of the Andean Community, Member Countries are obliged to take the necessary measures to ensure compliance with them, following their approval by the Andean Council of Foreign Ministers or by the Commission of the Andean Community, in the case of Decisions, and from their publication in the Official Journal of the Cartagena Agreement, in the case of Resolutions issued by the General Secretariat."

SGCAN faces CAN member states as the bearer of the community interest and must therefore investigate all evidence pertinent to the case, without relying only on the evidence provided by the petitioner.[96]

If the decisions of the SGCAN remain unappealed in front of the TJCAN, they become part of CAN law, which therefore constitute an important contribution to the interpretation of Art. 73 AdC. Nevertheless, the exclusive authority of the SGCAN regarding the identification of prohibited measures under Art. 72 AdC is reflected by strict procedural elements under D.425, which prioritize the proceedings in front of this body. The right to appear as an applicant in front of the TJCAN within the Action of Infringement proceedings is conditional upon the SGCAN having already provided a *resolution* where it had the authority to do so.[97] Only if the SGCAN remains inactive and does not issue a *resolution*, or if it does not respect the timeframes set out in D.245, do the proceedings in front of the SGCAN for the access to the TJCAN become irrelevant pursuant to Art. 4 D.245. In these two cases of inactivity or delayed activity on the part of the SGCAN, the complaining CAN Member State retain its right to appear without further requirements as applicant in front of the TJCAN.[98]

Original wording: "Como consecuencia del principio de aplicación inmediata y directa de los actos y normas que conforman el ordenamiento jurídico de la Comunidad Andina, los Países Miembros se encuentran obligados a adoptar las medidas que sean necesarias para asegurar su cumplimiento, a partir de su aprobación por el Consejo Andino de Ministros de Relaciones Exteriores o por la Comisión de la Comunidad Andina, en el caso de las Decisiones, y a partir de su publicación en la Gaceta Oficial del Acuerdo de Cartagena, cuando se trate de Resoluciones expedidas por la Secretaría General."

[96] Ibid., p. 8: „In this respect, the General Secretariat has a role to play in representing the public and Community interests and cannot therefore limit itself to what the parties have decided, but must investigate the facts and conduct an informal inquiry into the proceedings."

Original wording: "La Secretaría General cumple, en este sentido, un papel de representante de los intereses público-comunitarios, y por tal motivo no puede limitarse a lo que dispongan las partes, sino que deberá indagar sobre los hechos e instruir oficiosamente el procedimiento." Cf. *infra* Sect. 8.2.2, Table 8.1.

[97] Cf. TJCAN, *12-AN-99*, 12-AN-99, Judgment of 24 September 1999, para. 2.2.3. A comparison between the provisions for the proceedings on the identification of prohibited levies and restrictions of imports under Title V, Chapter I, and the provisions on the pre-judicial phase for the action of infringement under Title V, Chapter II, clarifies that the access to the TJCAN in cases where the SGCAN does not provide a *resolution* is barred, as opposed to the provision under Art. 67 D.245, which does not contain such a requirement. If the SGCAN does not issue its *resolution* within the three months following the date of presentation of the claim, or if finds that the responding party does not comply with CAN law, the complaining CAN Member State may go directly to the Tribunal.

Original wording: Si la Secretaría General no emitiere su Resolución dentro de los tres meses siguientes a la fecha de presentación del reclamo o si su determinación no fuere de incumplimiento, el país reclamante podrá acudir directamente al Tribunal.

[98] Likewise, when the General Secretariat refrains from carrying out an activity to which it is expressly bound by the legal system of the CAN or, in any circumstance, the time limits for its pronouncement expire, the complaining CAN Member State may go directly to the Court, in accordance with the provisions of Articles 42 and 43 of these Regulations.

Under the second tier of dispute resolution in the CAN, the TJCAN is assigned the competence to resolve all disputes arising in the context of all CAN rules, including the rules under the *Liberalization Program*. Faced with this double structure for dispute resolution under the CAN, it is worthwhile to mention that the existence of the TJCAN was not envisaged within the original founding treaty of the CAN concluded in 1969 by Bolivia, Colombia, Ecuador, and Peru. It was only 15 years after the coming into force of the AdC that the TJCAN became operational.[99] The TJCAN is said to be closely modelled after the structure and legal architecture of the CJEU.[100] Pursuant to Art. 47 AdC, all disputes arising from the application of CAN rules are subject to the jurisdiction of the TJCAN. Moreover, the compulsory and exclusive jurisdiction of the TJCAN over disputes over CAN law is prescribed by Art. 74 Founding Act of the TJCAN (TJCAN-FA),[101] according to which

> Member States shall not submit any dispute arising out of the application of the rules establishing the legal order of the Andean Community to any court, arbitration system or procedure other than those provided for in this Treaty.[102]

In parallel to the CJEU, the Action for Infringement[103] and Preliminary Rulings[104] are the most important proceedings[105] in which the TJCAN can deliver interpretations on the provisions on the liberalization of trade in goods, and consequently the

---

Original wording: Igualmente, cuando la Secretaría General se abstuviere de cumplir una actividad a la que estuviere obligada expresamente por el ordenamiento jurídico de la Comunidad Andina o, en cualquier circunstancia, vencieren los plazos para su pronunciamiento, el país reclamante podrá acudir directamente al Tribunal, de conformidad con lo previsto en los artículos 42 y 43 del presente Reglamento.

[99] Sasaki Otani (2012), p. 304. In addition to the mainly political dispute-settlement system provided under the Latin American Integration Association, see *Asociación Latinoamericana de Integración* – ALADI, succeeding the Latin American Free Trade Association, Asociación Latinoamericana de Libre Comercio – ALALC (for a historical overview of the development of this specific free trade agreements, cf. Piérola Castro (2006), p. 18, fn. 40–41, to which all CAN member states are likewise parties; cf. Pizzolo (2010), p. 980; Rojas Penso (2004), p. 134.

[100] Cf. first recital of the TJCAN-FA.

[101] Orinignal title: Tratado de Creación del Tribunal de Justicia de la Comunidad Andina (CAN).

[102] Original wording: Los Países Miembros no someterán ninguna controversia que surja con motivo de la aplicación de las normas que conforman el ordenamiento jurídico de la Comunidad Andina a ningún tribunal, sistema de arbitraje o procedimiento alguno distinto de los contemplados en el presente Tratado. Also affirming the compulsory jurisdiction for the CAN member states of the TJCAN, cf. Pizzolo (2010), p. 981.

[103] Original wording: Acción de Incumplimiento.

[104] Original wording: Interpretación Prejudicial.

[105] For an overview of all types of proceedings in front of the TJCAN, Pizzolo (2010), pp. 983–1007.

General Exception Clause under Art. 73 AdC. Arts. 23, 24, and 25 TJCAN-FA governs the Action of Infringement proceedings which set out the right of the SGCAN, CAN member states, and individuals from CAN member states to appear as applicants in front of the TJCAN to bring forward an alleged breach of CAN rules by one of the CAN member states. The recourse to the TJCAN is conditional upon the completion of pre-judicial proceedings pursuant Art. 23 TJCAN-FA, D.425, and Decision 623 (D.623),[106] Section I. The pre-judicial proceedings are initiated with a so-called *comment note*[107] by the SGCAN, in which the precise violation of CAN law is indicated, Art. 4 D.623. The concerned CAN Member State is given the opportunity to comment and react to this indication within a maximum of 60 days. Upon the expiration of this deadline, the SGCAN is obliged to issue an *Opinion*, within a maximum of 15 days,[108] on whether the violation of the CAN rules is ongoing. If the SGCAN considers that the violation of CAN rules persists, it is obliged to initiate proceedings for the Action of Infringement in front of the TJCAN.[109] According to Art. 24 TJCAN-FA and D.623,[110] Section II, for CAN member states the right to appear as applicants of Action of Infringement proceedings is equally conditional upon the completion of pre-judicial proceedings. Similarly to the situation where the SGCAN appears as applicant in the Action of Infringement proceedings, the pre-judicial proceedings for the case in which CAN member states appear as applicants likewise involves the indication of an allegedly illegal measure to the SGCAN, which then must issue an *Opinion* on its legality.

---

[106] 2005, Decisión 623 'Reglamento de la Fase Prejudicial de la Acción de Incumplimiento' (Decision 623), Consejo Andino De Ministros De Relaciones Exteriores de la Comunidad Andina (CAN).

[107] Original wording: nota de observaciones, Art. 4 D.623.

[108] Original wording: Dictamen.

[109] This means that the SGCAN has considerably less flexibility in the initiation of Action of Infringement proceedings in front of the TJCAN compared to the EC in front of the CJEU. The TFEU does not contain any obligation of the EC to prosecute the infringement of EU law and leaves ample discretion as to how the EC conducts the pre-judicial proceedings with the concerned EU Member State. In fact, the initiation and conclusion of these proceedings is not reviewable by the public, as the EC does not have to issue an opinion on the state of infringement by the EU Member State. However, the EC has introduced, subject to its own discretion, a so-called "Pilot Mechanism" that continuously monitors the status of the purported EU law infringement by the EU Member States, cf. EU Pilot - European Commission. https://single-market-scoreboard.ec.europa.eu/enforcement-tools/eu-pilot_en. Accessed 3 September 2023. In stark contrast to this, the SGCAN has formal requirements how to frame its notes of comments, Art. 4 D.623, opinions, Art. 9 D.623, as well as the obligation to publish all documents assembled throughout the pre-judicial phase, Art. 26 D.623.

[110] 2005, Decisión 623 'Reglamento de la Fase Prejudicial de la Acción de Incumplimiento' (Decision 623), Consejo Andino De Ministros De Relaciones Exteriores de la Comunidad Andina (CAN).

Pursuant to Arts. 32 ff TJCAN-FA, the TJCAN pronounces Preliminary Rulings[111] on questions on the interpretation of CAN rules directed by domestic courts of the CAN member states

in order to ensure its uniform application in the territory of the Member Countries.[112]

Domestic courts have discretion to address the TJCAN for the interpretation of CAN rules, when it is applicable to the case at hand as long as domestic law provides for an appeal procedure against the decision by a superior domestic court, Art. 33 Para. 1 TJCAN-FA. Pursuant to Art. 33 Para. 2 TJCAN-FA, however, domestic courts have the obligation to address the TJCAN and suspend the proceedings *proprio motu* or at the request of one of the parties in the dispute if the respective judgement could not be appealed under domestic law.[113]

Due to the aforementioned procedural particularities of dispute settlement in front of the SGCAN, Action for Annulment proceedings pursuant to Arts. 17 ff TJCAN-FA[114] in front of the TJCAN play an equally important role for the interpretation of Art. 73 AdC. These proceedings are directed at revoking acts of the organs of the CAN which are incompatible with its legal framework.[115] Accordingly, CAN member states can appeal the decisions of the SGCAN to the TJCAN should they believe that the SGCAN wrongly identified the existence of duties and restrictions prohibited under the *Liberalization Program*. Since under these proceedings the TJCAN reviews the contested decision of the SCAN in purview of the provisions under the *Liberalization Program*, it can equally interpret the content of the General Exception Clause under Art. 73 AdC. Proceedings for the Action for Annulment are only available within 2 years after the issuance of the concerned act of the CAN organ by the aforementioned parties. After the lapse of this period, domestic judges of the CAN member states remain the only party eligible to have recourse to the CAN, if an act of the CAN organ is pertinent for the decision of an ongoing dispute, Art. 20 TJCAN-FA.

Decisions of the TJCAN resulting from the proceedings for Actions of Infringement of the TJCAN can be enforced under the procedure established within the TJCAN-FA. According to Art. 29 TJCAN-FA, the CAN Member State that was found to be in breach of CAN rules has 90 days to implement the corresponding decision. After the lapse of this period, so-called *Summary Proceedings for contempt of judgements in Action for Infringement Proceedings* can be initiated pursuant to Art. 112 ff. of the Statue of the TJCAN (St-TJCAN).[116] Hereunder, the respective

---

[111] Original wording: Interpretación Prejudicial.

[112] Original wording of Art. 32 TJCAN-FA: [...] con el fin de asegurar su aplicación uniforme en el territorio de los Países Miembros.

[113] Original wording of Art. 343 TJCAN-FA: [. . .] Si llegare la oportunidad de dictar sentencia sin que hubiere recibido la interpretación del Tribunal, el juez deberá decidir el proceso.

[114] Original wording: Acción de Nulidad.

[115] Pizzolo (2010), pp. 984–985, refers for a classification of internal and external illegality derived from French adminstrative legal doctrine.

[116] Original title: Estatuto del Tribunal de Justicia de la Comunidad Andina.

CAN Member State can react to the court's comments on its failure to implement its foregoing decision. If the breach of CAN rules persists, the TJCAN can determine the sanctions against the CAN Member State, which can result in the revocation of the advantages accruing from the *Liberalization Program,* pursuant to Art. 119 St-TJCAN. Examples for such sanctions were the introduction of a penalty tariff on products originating from this country, or rendering certain products ineligible for intra-CAN commerce by suspending the issuing of certificates of origin, making them subject to the tariffs payable by third countries.[117] Regarding decentralized mechanisms to incentivize the implementation of decisions issued by the TJCAN, Art. 30 TJCAN-FA stipulates the principle of state liability for the violation of CAN rules. It clarifies that the decision on the infringement of CAN rules enables individuals to claim damages against the CAN Member State resulting from its breach of these obligations.[118]

After the successful initiation of Action for Annulment proceedings in front of the TJCAN, the TJCAN issues a decision declaring the challenged act of the CAN organ null and void, if it violates CAN law. Regarding *resolutions* issued by the SGCAN made under the procedure of D.425, these *resolutions* lose their status as an integral part of CAN law and do not have any further effect on the respective CAN Member State, including the duty to enact the recommendations of the SGCAN with a corresponding declaration of the TJCAN.

As Fig. 5.7 shows, the procedure in front of the SGCAN for the clarification and identification of trade-restrictive measures has proven to be most important for the interpretation of Art. 73 AdC. Out of the total 51 cases relevant in the context of the General Exception Clause, 40 were conducted in front of the SGCAN, and 21 were also concluded at this stage. For the remaining 14 cases, the decisions of the SGCAN were challenged at the TJCAN. Six cases were dealt with directly by the TJCAN in the course of Infringement Proceedings, and another nine in Preliminary Proceedings, see Table 8.7.[119]

As Table 5.1 shows, most of the proceedings were initiated by the SGCAN, either as investigating authority at its own behalf in the procedure for the clarification and identification of trade-restrictive measures, or as a complaining party in Infringement Proceedings in front of the TJCAN in 33 out of 79 proceedings. Apart from the SGCAN, the review of all relevant proceedings for the interpretation of the General Exception Clauses shows a strong interstate character. 28 out of 79 relevant proceedings were initiated by either of the CAN member states against another CAN Member State. Moreover, the standing of individuals in the proceedings in front of the CAN had an equally important impact on the use of the PTA-DSM of the CAN. Nine proceedings were initiated by individuals, eight of them directed against trade-restrictive measures introduced or maintained by one of the CAN member states, and one of them directed against an organ of the CAN (Comisión) for the adoption of

---

[117] Sasaki Otani (2012), p. 315.

[118] Ibid., p. 322.

[119] Cf. infra Sect. 8.2.3, Table 8.2.

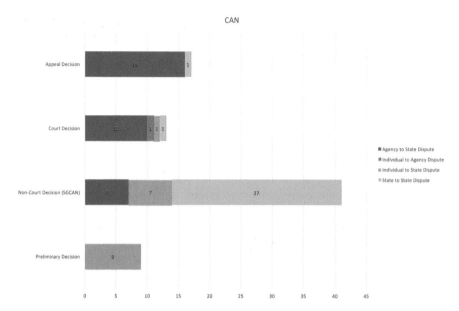

Fig. 5.7 Type and Proportion of Participants Regarding the PTA-DSM of the CAN. *Source:* Autor's novel dataset

presumably trade-restrictive CAN legislation. Additionally, nine Preliminary Proceedings dealt with the interpretation of domestic legislation involving the content of Art. 73 AdC.

5.3.4 Caseload of the Ad-hoc Arbitral Panels and the Permanent Review Court and Factual Background of the Mercosur

Since 1991, within the Mercosur, ad-hoc arbitral panels (and, since 2002, the TPR)[120] have issued three decisions dealing with the General Exception Clause under Art. 50 TdM until today. These three decisions involved three proceedings adjudicated by ad-hoc arbitral panels and two proceedings in front of the TPR. This amounts to an activity of roughly 0.1 decisions per year at the level of ad-hoc arbitral panels and—since its existence—of the TPR. The decisions were identified by screening all available decisions of ad-hoc arbitral panels and the TPR on the website

---

[120] Original title: Tribunal Permanente de Revisión.

Table 5.1 Type and Proportion of Participants Regarding the PTA-DSM of the CAN

Type of proceedings/Participants in proceedings	Agency vs. State (SGCAN/Junta)	Individual vs. Agency	Individual vs. State	State vs. State	
Preliminary Proceedings			9	9
Non-Court Decision (SGCAN/ Junta)	7		7	27	41
TJCAN Decision	10	1	1	1	13
Appeal Decision	16			1	17
Grand Total	**33**	**1**	**17**	**29**	**80**

Source: Autor's novel dataset

of Mercosur on Art. 50 TdM.[121] This study includes all decisions issued by the ad-hoc arbitral panels and the TPR by 1 December 2021.

5.3.4.1 Conclusion of Mercosur Treaty and Its Scope

Parallel to the development of the CAN, in 1991 the Mercosur emerged from the existing ALADI framework under the Treaty of Asunción (TdA).[122] As per now, the countries of Argentina, Brazil, Paraguay, and Uruguay[123] form part of the Mercosur.[124] The TdA contains provisions on the liberalization of trade in goods among the member states with the aim of establishing a single market among them. The so-called *Trade Liberalization Program* (TdA-TLP),[125] in Annex I TdA, primarily governs the process of trade liberalization among Mercosur member states. The TdA interweaves obligations arising from the pre-existing cooperation agreement and legal framework of ALADI with the new legal framework of Mercosur, as can be seen in the multiple references to the TdM in the preamble of the TdA.

Pursuant to Art. 1 TdA-TLP, the *Trade Liberalization Program* aims at accomplishing a common market between the Mercosur member states. At the outset, the TDA-TLP covers all imaginable goods[126] and stipulates, in the first recital of Art. 1 TDA-TLP, the obligation for member states to eliminate gradually all duties and other restrictions by 31 December 1994.[127] These timeframes were eventually prolonged by the so-called *Adaptation Program*, terminating at the end of 1998 for Brazil and Argentina, and in 1999 for Uruguay and Paraguay, respectively.[128] Under Art. 6 TdA-TLP, member states are granted a fixed number of tariff lines, which serves to exclude specific goods from the relief schedule. However, in accordance with Art. 7 TdA-TLP, this number decreases annually by a specific percentage set out for each Member State, which becomes higher within the course of the relief schedule. Moreover, the scope of the *Trade Liberalization Program* was

---

[121]Laudos. In: MERCOSUR. https://www.mercosur.int/quienes-somos/solucion-controversias/laudos/. Accessed 15 December 2021. The software *DocFetcher* was used to identify decisions which were dealing with Art. 50 TdM until this date. The key words were: "Art. 50"; "restriccion/es"; "gravamen/es"; "import*"; "justificación"; "justificad*"; "protección"; "protec*", as well as "liberación".

[122](1991) Tratado Para La Constitución De Un Mercado Común.

[123]Until 5 August 2017, Venezuela was also a Mercosur Member State; cf. (2017) Suspensión de Venezuela en el MERCOSUR.

[124](2020) MERCOSUR Countries. In: MERCOSUR. https://www.mercosur.int/en/about-mercosur/mercosur-countries/. Accessed 3 September 2023. Note that the membership of Venezuela is temporarily suspended, cf. (2017) Suspensión de Venezuela en el MERCOSUR.

[125]Original wording: Programa de Liberación Comercial.

[126]Pizzolo (2010), p. 767.

[127]By means of the second recital of Art. 1 TdA-TLP, the member states Paraguay and Uruguay benefited from an altered timeframe for the implementation of this obligation and were granted additional time until 31 December 31 1995, in accordance with Art. 7 TdA-LTP.

[128]CMC (1994a) Régimen de Adecuación; CMC (1994b) Régimen de Adecuación.

modified subsequently by exempting the trade in used goods by virtue of Resolution 109/94. Equally, the automotive[129] and sugar sector[130] remain subject to more specific sectorial liberalization obligations under Art. 5 lit. d) TdA, exempting them from the general rules on trade liberalization under the TdA-TLP.[131]

Pursuant to Art. 2 TdA-TLP, trade-restrictive measures between Mercosur member states are classified in accordance with their fiscal and non-fiscal nature. Art. 2 lit. b) TdA-TLP contains a broad and general notion of restrictions of trade between member states, which includes measures of fiscal and non-fiscal character. Moreover, the wording of the provisions provides for a wide scope of prohibited trade-restrictive measures, encompassing not only trade-restrictive measures on imports, but also on exports.[132] Art. 1, first recital TdA, sets out that

> The free movement of goods, services and factors of production between countries, through, inter alia, [encompasses] the elimination of customs duties and non-fiscal restrictions on the movement of goods and any other equivalent measures.[133]

Art. 2 lit. b), second sentence TdA-TLP, constitutes the General Exception Clause for the *Trade Liberalization Program,* which contains a reference to Art. 50 TdM.

In this context, pursuant to Decision 03/94,[134] Mercosur member states record non-fiscal trade-restrictive measures in specific lists with the goal of eliminating or harmonizing them over time. These lists have a partially legitimizing effect as Mercosur member states explicitly acknowledge their existence and determine their termination in the future. Nonetheless, more recent Mercosur legislation explicitly allows their member states to resort to dispute resolution should they experience being negatively affected by them.[135] According to Art. 2 Decision 03/94, the process of harmonizing or eliminating these measures was supposed to be completed by 31 December 1994. Yet, this practice appears to continue even after the envisaged end date.

---

[129] CMC Adecuación Regimen Automotriz Dec. 29/94.

[130] CMC Sector Azucarero Dec. 19/94.

[131] See Art. 10 of CMC Arancel Externo Comun Dec. 07/94; cf. also Fuders (2010), p. 91; cf. Klumpp (2013), p. 13.

[132] Note, e.g., under Art. 72 AdC, the wording for only a prohibition of restrictions on imports.

[133] Original wording of Art. 1 first recital TdA: La libre circulación de bienes, servicios y factores productivos entre los países, a través, entre otros, de la eliminación de los derechos aduaneros y restricciones no arancelarias a la circulación de mercaderías y de cualquier otra medida equivalente [...].

[134] CMC Restricciones No Arancelarias Dec. 03/94.

[135] Cf. Art. 5 in CMC Restricciones no arancelarias Dec. 27/07.

5.3.4.2 PTA-DSM in the Mercosur: The Ad-hoc Arbitral Panels and the TPR

Mercosur member states have agreed on various means of dispute settlement which are often characterized as mainly diplomatic[136] due to their varying compulsory character. The now existing provisions on the resolution of disputes under the legal framework of the Mercosur, which institutionalize dispute settlement between Mercosur member states, were only gradually adopted within the course of this PTA's development. Initially, only a negotiations-based approach to dispute settlement was foreseen in Annex III TdA, which has been gradually "revamped"[137] towards institutionalized, non-political, third-body adjudication as a reaction the weak enforcement of Mercosur provisions at the beginning of the agreement's implementation.[138]

The current provisions on dispute settlement in the Mercosur therefore offers informal and formal instruments for dispute resolution. On the one hand, the so-called diplomatic dispute resolution can take place in the Common Market Group (CMG), which is characterized by its informal and voluntary character pursuant to Annex III TdA.[139] On the other hand, a formalized DSM exists for which Mercosur member states, under certain conditions, are entitled to the establishment of ad-hoc arbitral panels and the possibility of reviewing the awards issued by them by the TPR. The legal basis for ad-hoc arbitration is found in the Brasília Protocol of 1991, which was replaced by the Olivos Protocol for Dispute Settlement in Mercosur (PO)[140] in 2002.[141]

The establishment of an ad-hoc arbitral panel within the Mercosur is elective. It is not the only method for formal dispute resolution between Mercosur member states, since Art. 1.2 PO contains a so-called forum choice clause allowing them to submit their disputes to the WTO-DSM or any other PTA-DSMs to which an individual Mercosur member states is a party, if the dispute arises under the legal framework of the Mercosur pursuant to Art. 1.1. PO. The execution of the choice of forum is carried out by the complaining party.[142] Moreover, Mercosur member states are free

---

[136] Susani (2010), p. 76; Pizzolo (2010), n. 43, p. 1041.

[137] Susani (2010), p. 74.

[138] Ibid., pp. 73–74.

[139] Ibid., n. 20, p. 76.

[140] (2002) Protocolo de Olivos para la Solución de Controversias en el Mercosur.

[141] Susani (2010), p. 75.

[142] Art. 1.2. PO: Disputes falling within the scope of this protocol that may also be submitted to the dispute-settlement system of the World Trade Organization or other preferential trade schemes to which individual Mercosur States Parties are party. They may be submitted to either forum at the choice of the claimant. Notwithstanding the foregoing, the parties to the dispute may, by mutual agreement, agree on the forum. Original wording: Las controversias comprendidas en el ámbito de aplicación del presente Protocolo que puedan también ser sometidas al sistema de solución de controversias de la Organización Mundial del Comercio o de otros esquemas preferenciales de comercio de que sean parte individualmente los Estados Partes del Mercosur, podrán someterse a

to agree mutually to submit their dispute to ad-hoc arbitral panels pursuant to the last sentence of Art. 1.2 PO. The choice of forum is definitive, which only after its execution establishes a compulsory and exclusive jurisdiction of ad-hoc arbitral panels pursuant to Art. 33 PO. The admissibility of adjudication by an ad-hoc arbitral panel is dependent on the conclusion of a so-called pre-arbitral procedure, which is regulated by the PO and its implementing provisions (PO Imp).[143] According to Arts. 9 ff. PO, arbitration is available for disputes that could not have been settled during direct negotiation (Arts. 5 ff PO) or the recourse to the CMG (Arts. 6 ff PO). When a conflict materializes, direct negotiations are compulsory[144] (Art. 4 PO, Art. 26.1 PO Imp) and require initiation by means of a written request. This request must include preliminary and basic information on the disputed matter by the complaining party. Moreover, Mercosur member states must specify the time and date for the direct negotiations in their request (Art. 14 PO Imp). If the dispute cannot be resolved during direct negotiations, and/or if the disputing members agree, they can bring the dispute in front of the CMG (Art. 6.1 and 6.2 PO). Their request for review by the CMG needs to fulfil precise formal criteria on the legal understanding of the dispute, its surrounding facts, as well as the foregoing negotiation process (Art. 15.3 PO Imp). In this respect, it is necessary to clarify that the outcomes reached in the pre-arbitral phase in front of the TMC and CMG do not qualify as legally binding decisions between the disputing parties.[145] Art. 7 PO sets out that the CMG can only comment or make recommendations in a dispute. Therefore, Mercosur member states are not bound by these decisions and remain free to initiate dispute-settlement proceedings under the ad-hoc arbitration, the TPR, or the WTO-DSM after they have been concluded.[146]

The TPR primarily assumes the function of a court of appeals for the arbitral awards issued under the ad-hoc arbitration proceedings, pursuant to Art. 15 PO. In line with the optional character of dispute resolution under Mercosur, the TPR becomes the competent judicial authority only if the complaining Mercosur Member State has chosen to resolve its dispute within the Mercosur's own institutional framework. Once the choice of forum has been executed, the TPR automatically and irrevocably becomes the competent court for any appeal on the ad-hoc arbitration procedure, Chapter VII PO, or as a court of first instance, Art. 23 PO, pursuant to Art. 33 PO.

---

uno u otro foro a elección de la parte demandante. Sin perjuicio de ello, las partes en la controversia podrán, de común acuerdo, convenir el foro.

[143] 2003, 'Reglamento Del Protocolo De Olivos Para La Solución De Controversias En El Mercosur' (PO-Imp), MERCOSUR/CMC/DEC. N° 37/03 (Mercosur).

[144] Pizzolo (2010), p. 1065.

[145] Mercosur ad hoc arbitral panel (Brasília), Laudo "Subsidios a La Produccion Y Exportacion De Carne De Cerdo", Judgment of 27 September 1999, paras 35 and 38.

[146] Franch (2006), n. 5. Note that this stands in stark opposition to the pre-judicial phase at the CAN, where the resolutions of the SCGAN amount to the status of CAN law, if the concerned CAN member states do not take procedural actions to annul them. *Supra* Sect. 5.3.3.2.

In the efforts to obtain a more uniform interpretation and application of the Mercosur rules, Mercosur member states have enabled domestic courts to obtain so-called Consultative Opinions from the TPR, pursuant to Arts. 2 ff. RoPPO.[147] As the term suggests, consultative opinions do not constitute a part of any compulsory proceedings.[148] Moreover, their content does not constrain domestic courts in making their decision based on Mercosur rules as they understand them, since they remain non-binding and non-obligatory pursuant to Art. 11 RoPPO. Rather, Consultative Opinions are supposed to provide simple advice on the interpretation of Mercosur rules.[149] Therefore, there is no guarantee that they will be enforced by domestic courts, nor does their non-implementation constitute a violation of Mercosur law.

Individuals are not entitled to initiate any judicial and binding proceedings on a violation of Mercosur rules. The only option remaining is to bring their claims over the violation of Mercosur rules to the attention of Mercosur member states. Chapter XI PO provides for an institutionalized procedure for individuals to bring their complaints over the violation of Mercosur rules to the attention of the respective Member State. Claims of individuals over legal or administrative measures that have a restrictive or discriminatory effect or lead to unfair competition, in violation of the agreements listed in Art. 33 PO, can result in the member states' obligation to conduct consultations, Art. 41.1 PO, and the failure to settle a dispute obliges them to call upon the CMG, Art. 42 PO. Yet, a further unsuccessful settlement of the issue in front of the CMG does not require the concerned Mercosur member states to initiate ad-hoc arbitral proceedings. Rather, the CMG has the power to reject a claim by an individual or to deal with the contentious question, Art. 42.1 PO, but is obliged, on the other hand, to establish an "expert group" on the matter, Art. 42.2 PO. In any case, the opinion of the "expert group" does not amount to a legally binding decision, and any remedy against an illegal measure would have to be claimed independently in an ad-hoc arbitral procedure, Art. 41.1.i PO. Ultimately, Mercosur member states themselves remain exclusively responsible for clarifying the claims by individuals through adjudication. This leaves them with a high degree of discretion to initiate such proceedings.[150]

According to Art. 26 PO, the decisions of ad-hoc arbitral panels and the TPR are binding upon the disputing Mercosur member states. They must be complied with within 30 days of their issuance, if not specified differently, according to Art. 29 PO, which provides for additional and separate proceedings for clarifying the process of

---

[147] Consejo del Mercado Común, Reglamento Del Procedimiento Para La Solicitud De Opiniones Consultivas Al Tribunal Permanente De Revisión Por Los Tribunales Superiores De Justicia De Los Estados Partes Del Mercosur.

[148] In opposition to the preliminary proceedings at the EU and CAN level.

[149] Susani (2010), pp. 84–85.

[150] Cf. Franch (2006), p. 185, clarifying that the procedure for individual claims does not amount to a locus standi for individuals at ad-hoc proceedings.individual.

Table 5.2 Type of Proceedings and Individual Relevant Cases in front of the PTA-DSM of the Mercosur

Type of proceedings (case sequence number)	Appellate	Ad-hoc	Total
Merocsur-Ad-hoc-11	1		1
Merocsur-Ad-hoc-1		1	1
Merocsur-Ad-hoc-7		1	1
Grand total	**1**	**2**	**3**

Source: Autor's novel dataset

compliance by the losing disputing party.[151] If not complied with, Mercosur member states have the possibility to introduce countervailing duties against the infringement of Mercosur rules, in line with Art. 31 PO. Mercosur member states can decide autonomously on the amount and the design of such countervailing measures, but need to respect the proportionality criteria contained in Art. 31 Para.2 PO.[152] Pursuant to Art. 32 PO, additional proceedings exist under which the Mercosur Member State affected by the countervailing measures can address either the ad-hoc arbitral panel or the TPR to examine the legality of such countervailing measures, depending on the last competent judicial authority in the case at hand.

Despite the built-in choice of forum clause, the DSM of the Mercosur has become active in the past. Dispute resolution through ad-hoc arbitration has remained the most important procedure in the context of which findings have been issued on Art. 50 TdM. Two relevant cases were dealt with by ad hoc arbitral panels and completed at this level. One relevant case has also been disputed in addition to the ad-hoc level at the TPR. The possibility of obtaining Consultative Opinions by the TPR has proven to be of no relevance for the interpretation of the General Exception Clause under the legal framework of Mercosur, see Table 5.2.

5.4   Confirming the Equivalence of the Respective General Exception Clauses

Given that the proposed methodology aims at identifying divergence in a setting of commonalities to identify diversity in the regulation of international trade, the review of PTA-DSM decisions concerning the respective General Exception Clauses for the trade in goods can only encompass those decisions that were rendered based on equivalent PTA rules applied by these PTA-DSMs.

---

[151] Klumpp (2013), pp. 254–255.
[152] On the importance of the sanctioning mechanism under the legal framework of the EU, cf. ibid., pp. 255–259.

5.4.1 Confirming Equivalence by Means of Treaty Interpretation: Ordinary Meaning Analysis

Ultimately, affirming the equivalence of rules under international trade law is a highly interpretative task.[153] As can be upheld by reference to Art. 31 (1) VCLT, confirming that rules under international law are equivalent can be based on their formal similarity, i.e., the ordinary meaning of the wording used in these provisions. Therefore, the departing point for the confirmation of equivalence of the respective international rules naturally is the existence of identical wording in different provisions. At the same time, to assume equivalence of different provisions under international law based exclusively on their identical wording creates tensions with the principle of autonomous interpretation of international treaties. This principle suggests that provisions in international treaties should be regarded as autonomous in their content, except where something different is indicated.

In this field of tension between formality and functionality of provisions under international law,[154] the principle of contextual interpretation enshrined in Art. 32 (2) VCLT can serve to confirm equivalence between the provisions on the obligation to liberalize the trade in goods by PTA partners, as well as the corresponding General Exception Clauses within the legal frameworks of the EU, EFTA, CAN, and Mercosur. The principle of contextual interpretation suggests that—even in the case of formally identical international provisions—their content, and hence their function, can differ considerably, depending on the historical, political, economic, or territorial context, as well as on the object and purpose of a treaty. Simultaneously, the principle of contextual interpretation allows us to consider the shared context in which they all have been negotiated. In this regard, the essential role of the GATT 1947 for the negotiation of PTAs must be acknowledged, in addition to its longstanding tradition to provide for multilateral regulation in international trade.[155] Given that all PTAs have been negotiated and concluded under the simultaneous existence of the GATT 1947, their provisions on trade liberalization make reference to the same general nomenclature of different types of domestic trade-restive measures that hinder the international free trade in goods. Equally, the general dichotomous design of the rules of and exceptions to the process of trade liberalization contained within the GATT 1947 is equally reflected by the different PTA provisions for the liberalization of trade in goods providing for the identification of various impediments to international trade. Likewise, the enumeration of almost identical policy areas legitimizing the introduction or maintenance of trade-restrictive measures in the context of the General Exception Clauses, the so-called legitimate objectives, likewise need to be understood in the context provided under Art. XX GATT 1947. This applies especially to the rules contained

---

[153] *Supra*, 5, Putting the Revisited Methodology into Practice.

[154] Siems (2018), p. 24.

[155] Armingeon et al. (2011), pp. 72–73, on the nature of the GATT as a constitutional treaty.

under the legal framework of the EU, but also generally to all other PTA provisions on the process of trade liberalization. At the same time, the PTA provisions of the EFTA, CAN, and Mercosur have always been negotiated with the purview of other pre-existing PTA provisions on the process of trade liberalization, adding another layer for the contextual interpretation, which allows us to assume their equivalence.

Against this context, the almost identical wording and architecture of general obligation to liberalize trade in goods as well as the respective General Exception Clauses in PTAs speaks for a setting of commonalities, in which the respective General Exception Clauses assume a highly similar purpose, namely to strike a balance between the obligation to liberalize trade and to protect the *regulatory autonomy* of PTA partners within the course of trade liberalization.[156]

Consequently, the underlying provisions on the liberalization of trade in goods in PTAs can be generally presumed to refer to the same object—the covered goods under a PTA and the same legitimate objectives referred to in the respective General Exception Clauses.

5.4.1.1 Relevant Provisions under the Legal Framework of the EU

The freedom of movement of goods under the legal framework of the EU encompasses, *inter alia*, the prohibition of non-fiscal measures in the form of quantitative restrictions (QRs) on imports and export, as well as measures having an equivalent effect (MEQRs) as quantitative import or export restrictions between EU member states; they are governed by Arts. 34 and 35 TFEU, respectively:

Article 34 TFEU (ex Article 28 TEC) Quantitative restrictions on imports and all measures having equivalent effect shall be prohibited between Member States.

Article 35(ex Article 29 TEC) Quantitative restrictions on exports, and all measures having equivalent effect, shall be prohibited between Member States.

The wording of Art. 36 TFEU explicitly qualifies it as a justification in its first sentence.

Article 36 (ex Article 30 TEC) The provisions of Articles 34 and 35 shall not preclude prohibitions or restrictions on imports, exports or goods in transit justified on grounds of public morality, public policy or public security; the protection of health and life of humans, animals or plants; the protection of national treasures possessing artistic, historic or archaeological value; or the protection of

---

[156] Regarding the exception clauses under the WTO Agreement, cf. Howse (2012), pp. 441–442.

industrial and commercial property. Such prohibitions
or restrictions shall not, however, constitute a means of
arbitrary discrimination or a disguised restriction on
trade between Member States.

In total, the provision enumerates 12 legitimate objectives that allow for the
justification of an *a priori* breach of Arts. 34 and 35 TFEU. These legitimate
objectives are put together in compounds and separated by a semicolon. In total,
this results in four groupings of legitimate objectives under Art. 36 TFEU:

1st grouping: public morality, public policy, or public security;
2nd grouping: the protection of health and life of humans, animals or plants;
3rd grouping: the protection of national treasures possessing artistic, historic or
    archaeological value;
4th grouping: the protection of industrial and commercial property

Finally, trade-restrictive measures that qualify as QRs and MEQRs, and are introduced for the legitimate objectives enumerated above, have to be
non-discriminatory, as prescribed by Art. 36 TFEU:

> Such prohibitions or restrictions shall not, however, constitute a means of *arbitrary dis-
> crimination* or *a disguised restriction on trade* between Member States. (emphasis added)

5.4.1.2   Relevant Provisions Under the Legal Framework of the EEAA

The freedom of movement of goods under the legal framework of the EEAA
encompasses, *inter alia*, the prohibition of non-fiscal measures in the form of
quantitative restrictions (QRs) on imports and export, as well as measures having
an equivalent effect (MEQRs) to quantitative import or export restrictions between
EU member states; they are governed by Arts. 11 and 12 EEAA, respectively:

Article 11 EEAA *Quantitative restrictions on imports and all measures having equiv-*
alent effect shall be prohibited between the Contracting Parties.

Article 12 EEAA *Quantitative restrictions on exports and all measures having*
equivalent effect shall be prohibited between the Contracting
Parties.

The wording of the provision explicitly qualifies it as a justification in its first
sentence:

Article 13 EEAA *The provisions of Articles 11 and 12 shall not preclude pro-*
hibitions or restrictions on imports, exports or goods in transit
justified on grounds of public morality, public policy or public
security; the protection of health and life of humans, animals or
plants; the protection of national treasures possessing artistic,
historic or archaeological value; or the protection of industrial

and commercial property. Such prohibitions or restrictions shall not, however, constitute a means of arbitrary discrimination or a disguised restriction on trade between the Contracting Parties.

5.4.1.3   Relevant Provisions Under the Legal Framework of the CAN

Art. 72 AdC contains the agenda for the liberalization of trade in goods between CAN Member States. Under this provision, it is stated that

> [...] the purpose of the Liberalization Program is to eliminate all duties and restrictions of any kind that affect the importation of products originating in the territory of any CAN Member State.[157]

The first paragraph of Art. 73 AdC provides for the definitions of these trade-restrictive measures, namely 'duties' and 'restrictions of any kind'. Accordingly, 'duties'

> shall mean customs duties and any other surcharges of equivalent effect, whether of a fiscal, monetary or exchange nature, which affect imports. This concept shall not include similar rates and surcharges when they correspond to the approximate cost of the services rendered.[158]

Restrictions of any kind' are defined as

> any administrative, financial or exchange measure by which a Member State, by unilateral decision, prevents or hinders imports.[159]

Under Art. 73 AdC, it is set out that the concept of prohibited import duties and restrictions of all kinds

---

[157] Original wording of Art. 72 AdC: El Programa de Liberación de bienes tiene por objeto eliminar los gravámenes y las restricciones de todo orden que incidan sobre la importación de productos originarios del territorio de cualquier País Miembro.

[158] Original wording of Art. 73, 1st paragraph: Se entenderá por "gravámenes" los derechos aduaneros y cualesquier otros recargos de efectos equivalentes, sean de carácter fiscal, monetario o cambiario, que incidan sobre las importaciones. No quedarán comprendidos en este concepto las tasas y recargos análogos cuando correspondan al costo aproximado de los servicios prestados.

Given the fact that levies remain partially in place even for the importation of goods between CAN member states, and also due to the fact the AdC allows for the imposition of safeguard measures (Chapter XI AdC) and anti-dumping and countervailing duties (Decisión 283), the provision takes an important place within the legal order of the CAN and the jurisprudence of SGCAN, as well as TJCAN. It plays a particularly important role in assessing the legality of fees levied for custom services upon importation, which are exempted from the prohibition by means of Art. 73 AdC.

[159] Original wording of Art. 73, 1st paragraph: Se entenderá por "restricciones de todo orden" cualquier medida de carácter administrativo, financiero o cambiario, mediante la cual un País Miembro impida o dificulte las importaciones, por decisión unilateral.

shall not include the adoption and enforcement of measures aimed at[160]

seven non-economic[161] legitimate objectives enumerated thereunder:

(a) Protection of public morality;
(b) Enforcement of security laws and regulations;
(c) Regulation of imports or exports of arms, munitions and other war materials and, in exceptional circumstances, of all other military items, provided that they do not interfere with the provisions of treaties on unrestricted free transit in force between Member Countries;
(d) Protection of human, animal and plant life and health;
(e) Import and export of metallic gold and silver;
(f) Protection of national treasures of artistic, historical or archaeological value;
(g) and
(h) Export, use and consumption of nuclear materials, radioactive products or any other material usable in the development or use of nuclear energy.[162]

5.4.1.4 Relevant Provisions Under the Legal Framework of the Mercosur

According to Art. 2 lit. b) TDA-TLP, 'restrictions' are defined as

[...] any measure of an administrative, financial, exchange-rate or other nature, by which a State party unilaterally prevents or impedes reciprocal trade.

Moreover, Art. 2 lit. b) TdA-TLP is complemented by several other provisions within the general part of TdA, reaffirming the wide scope of the provision. In this context, Art. 1, first recital TDA, clarifies that the establishment of a common market implies

---

[160] Original wording of Art. 73, 2nd paragraph: No quedarán comprendidas en este concepto la adopción y el cumplimiento de medidas destinadas a la [...].

[161] Cf. Raygada (2003), p. 307; Reyes Tagle (2018), p. 28, distinguishing between economic and non-economic exceptions. Safeguard, antidumping, and balance of payments measures are counted as economic exceptions in the context of the CAN in the legal scholarship.

[162] Original wording of Art. 73 AdC, 2nd paragraph: a) Protección de la moralidad pública; b) Aplicación de leyes y reglamentos de seguridad; c) Regulación de las importaciones o exportaciones de armas, municiones y otros materiales de guerra y, en circunstancias excepcionales, de todos los demás artículos militares, siempre que no interfieran con lo dispuesto en tratados sobre libre tránsito irrestricto vigentes entre los Países Miembros; d) Protección de la vida y salud de las personas, los animales y los vegetales; e) Importación y exportación de oro y plata metálicos; f) Protección del patrimonio nacional de valor artístico, histórico o arqueológico; y g) Exportación, utilización y consumo de materiales nucleares, productos radiactivos o cualquier otro material utilizable en el desarrollo o aprovechamiento de la energía nuclear.
Note that the structure of the provision shares similarities with Art. 36 TFEU: It contains identical legitimate objectives, as included within the thematic fields of Art. 36 TFEU, namely objectives under field 1 (Art. 73 lit. a) and b), field 2 (Art. 73 lit. d AdC), and field 3 (Art. 73 lit. f)). However, Art. 73 AdC contains three additional legitimate objectives under lit. c), e), and g).

[t]he free movement of goods, services and factors of production between countries, through, inter alia, the elimination of customs duties and non-tariff restrictions on the movement of goods and *any other equivalent measures.* (emphasis added)

Equally, Art. 5 first recital TdA stipulates that the TLP consists of a

[. . .] progressive, linear and automatic tariff reductions, accompanied by the elimination of non-fiscal restrictions or equivalent measures, as well as other restrictions on trade between the States Parties, leading to 31 December 1994 at zero tariff, without non-fiscal restrictions on the entire tariff system (Annex I).[163]

In the context of the definition of 'restrictions' under Art. 2 lit. b) TdA-TLP,

[t]he measures adopted by virtue of the situations foreseen in Article 50 of the Treaty of Montevideo 1980 are not included in this concept.

In turn, Art. 50 TdM lists seven groupings of legitimate objectives, which can serve to legitimize the maintenance or introduction of 'other restrictions':

Nothing in this Treaty shall be construed as preventing the adoption and enforcement of measures aimed at

(a) Protection of public morals;
(b) Enforcement of security laws and regulations;
(c) Regulation of imports or exports of arms, munitions, and other war material and, in circumstances exceptional, of all other military items
(d) Protection of the life and health of humans, animals and plants;
(e) Import and export of gold and silver metals;
(f) Protection of national heritage of artistic, historical, or archaeological value; and
(g) Export, use and consumption of nuclear materials, radioactive products or any other material usable in the development or use of nuclear energy.[164]

---

[163] Original wording of Art. 5 First Rectial TdA: Un Programa de Liberación Comercial, que consistirá en rebajas arancelarias progresivas, lineales y automáticas, acompañadas de la eliminación de restricciones no arancelarias o medidas equivalentes, así como de otras restricciones al comercio entre los Estados Partes, para llegar al 31 de diciembre de 1994 con arancel cero, sin restricciones no arancelarias sobre la totalidad del universo arancelario (Anexo I).

[164] Orginal wording of Art. 50TdM: Ninguna disposición del presente Tratado será interpretada como impedimento para la adopción y el cumplimiento de medidas destinadas a la:

(a) Protección de la moralidad pública;
(b) Aplicación de leyes y reglamentos de seguridad;
(c) Regulación de las importaciones o exportaciones de armas, municiones y otros materiales de guerra y, en circunstancias excepcionales, de todos los demás artículos militares;
(d) Protección de la vida y salud de las personas, los animales y los vegetales;
(e) Importación y exportación de oro y plata metálicos;
(f) Protección del patrimonio nacional de valor artístico, histórico o arqueológico; y
(g) Exportación, utilización y consumo de materiales nucleares, productos radiactivos o cualquier otro material utilizable en el desarrollo o provechamiento de la energía nuclear.

5.4.1.5 Caveats Resulting from the Wording of the Provisions on the Liberalization of Trade in Light of the Respective General Exception Clauses

The review of all provisions on the liberalization of trade between PTA partners and the corresponding General Exception Clauses shows that certain exceptions to trade liberalization are not covered by all the provisions for which the active PTA-DSMs have issued decisions.

Regarding the obligations to liberalize trade, the provisions under the legal framework of the EU and the EFTA only encompass non-fiscal measures for which the respective General Exception Clauses under Art. 36 TFEU and Art 13 EEAA apply, see Table 5.3. The limited scopes of application of these PTAs result in different extents of the obligation of PTA partners to liberalize trade. Consequently, the respective General Exception Clauses do not apply as broadly as is the case under the rules of the legal frameworks of the CAN and Mercosur. This constitutes an important caveat for the comparison of the activity of all four PTA-DSMs, which limits the analysis to non-fiscal measures only. Moreover, trade-restrictive measures pertaining to state monopolies are governed under the specific provisions in all PTAs and will be not considered here either.

Moreover, as Table 5.4 shows, concerning the provisions containing the General Exception Clauses, the review of all legitimate objectives contained therein exposes certain limitations to their scopes of application: On the one hand, Art. 36 TFEU and Art. 13 EEAA provide for justification of trade-restrictive measures for the protection of industrial and commercial property, which cannot be found in the wordings of Art. 73 AdC and Art 50 TdM. In the context of the CAN, the protection of industrial and commercial property was subsequently introduced by Decision 85,[165] which has subsequently proven to constitute an important basis for the activity of the TJCAN.[166] Equally, the recourse to the legitimate objectives concerning the protection of the trade in arms and military supplies and concerning the trade in radioactive or fissionable materials, as included under Art. 73 AdC and Art. 50 TdM, is not foreseen under the General Exception Clauses under Art. 36 TFEU and Art. 13 EEAA.[167] For this reason, no comparative analysis will take place concerning these legitimate objectives. Although all General Exception Clauses do not contain the legitimate objective of the protection of the environment explicitly in the wording of their provisions, the review of the PTA-DSM decisions shows that this legitimate objective has nevertheless been constantly invoked by PTA partners across all

---

[165] As amended by the decisions 311, 313, 344 and 486, cf. Talavera et al. (2003), p. 249.

[166] Alter and Helfer (2017), pp. 74–77.

[167] Instead, Art. 346 TFEU and Art. 123 EEAA stipule so-called Security Exceptions, which withhold even further the areas of military activity from the purview of the respective agreements. Concerning the trade in nuclear materials, the Euratom treaty (Consolidated Version of the Treaty Establishing the European Atomic Energy Community.) regulates the use of nuclear material for the purpose of nuclear energy for peaceful purpose. Cf. Kanellakis et al. (2013). It contains a separate General Exception Clause in Art. 96 of the Euratom Treaty.

Table 5.3 Schematic Overview of All Provisions Mandating the Liberalization in Goods Within the Relevant PTAs

Liberalization commitment/ provision in PTA	EU	CAN	Mercosur	EEAA
Coverage	All products, separate policy area for agricultural goods	All products, separate policy areas for agricultural goods	Range of products gradually increasing; used products agricultural products and goods from the automotive sector exempted	Selected products
Provision on coverage	Art. 28.1 TFEU	Art. 76 AdC	Annex I, Art. 4 TdA	Art. 8.3 EEAA
Duties	Prohibition of customs duties on imports and exports	Elimination of customs duties on imports	Elimination of customs duties which affect foreign trade.	Prohibition of customs duties, as well as custom duties of a fiscal nature on imports and exports.
Charges	Prohibition of all charges having equivalent effect as duties.	Elimination of any other charges having equivalent effect as duties, whether of a fiscal, monetary, or exchange-rate nature, which have an impact on imports	Elimination of any other charges having equivalent effect, of fiscal, monetary, exchange or any other nature, which affect foreign trade.	Prohibition of charges having an equivalent effect as customs duties.
Provision on duties and charges	Art. 30 TFEU	Arts. 72, 73 first paragraph AdC	Art. 1 first recital TdA; Art. 2 lit. a) Annex I	Art. 10 EEAA
Quantitative restrictions on imports	Prohibition of quantitative restrictions on imports and all measures having equivalent effect.	Prohibition of restrictions of any kind: any measure of an administrative, financial, or exchange nature by which a Member Country unilaterally prevents or hinders imports.	Prohibition of restrictions: any measure of an administrative, financial, exchange, or any nature whatsoever, by which a State Party, by unilateral decision, prevents or hinders reciprocal trade.	Quantitative restrictions on imports and all measures having equivalent effect shall be prohibited between the Contracting Parties.

(continued)

Table 5.3 (continued)

Liberalization commitment/ provision in PTA	EU	CAN	Mercosur	EEAA
Provision on quantitative restrictions on imports	Art. 34 TFEU	Arts. 72 AdC, 73 second paragraph AdC	Arts. 1.1, 1.2 TdA ; Art. Art. 1 lit. b) Annex I	Art. 11 EEAA
Quantitative restrictions on exports	Prohibition of quantitative export restrictions and all measures having equivalent effect.	The AdC does not apply to quantitative export restrictions or measures having equivalent effect.	Prohibition of quantitative export restrictions and all measures having equivalent effect. Arg. ex. reciprocal trade.	Quantitative restrictions on exports and all measures having equivalent effect shall be prohibited between the Contracting Parties.
Provision on quantitative restrictions on exports	Art. 35 TFEU	n/a	Arts. 1.1, 1.2 TdA; Art. Art. 1 lit. b) Annex I	Art. 12 EEAA

Source: Author

PTA-DSMs.[168] It will be therefore included in the further comparative analysis. Against the growing importance of the environmental protection, it serves to confirm whether the PTA-DSMs under review have accepted PTA partners in disputes to have recourse to it, independently of whether it was explicitly provided within the respective legal framework.

Consequently, the actual number of PTA-DSM decisions suitable for an analysis are fewer than those identified above, namely 255 decisions of the CJEU, 11 decisions issued by the EFTA Court, 21 decisions issued under the PTA-DSM of the CAN, and three decisions issued by the PTA-DSM of the Mercosur.[169]

5.4.2 Confirming the Equivalence of General Exemption Clauses: Contextual Analysis Based on the Doctrine Developed by PTA-DSMs on Their Use

Against the remaining potential uncertainties on the equivalence of the respective General Exception Clauses resulting from their analysis concerning their ordinary meaning, their equivalence can be confirmed through an additional contextual

---

[168] Cf. *infra* Sect. 5.4.2.5.

[169] For a list of all decisions, cf. infra Sect. 8.2.1.

Table 5.4 Overview of All Provisions Encompassing the General Exception Clause in the Relevant PTAs.

Original wording of the General Exception Clauses/ translation	EU – Art. 36 TFEU	CAN – Art. 73 AdC	Mercosur – Art. 50 Tratado de Montevideo	EFTA – Art. 13 EEAA
Original wording		No quedarán comprendidas en este concepto la adopción y el cumplimiento de medidas destinadas a la: a) Protección de la moralidad pública; b) Aplicación de leyes y reglamentos de seguridad; c) Regulación de las importaciones o exportaciones de armas, municiones y otros materiales de guerra y, en circunstancias excepcionales, de todos los demás artículos militares, siempre que no interfieran con lo dispuesto en tratados sobre libre tránsito irrestricto vigentes entre los Países Miembros; d) Protección de la vida y salud de las personas, los animales y los vegetales; e) Importación y exportación de oro y plata metálicos; f) Protección del patrimonio nacional de valor artístico, histórico o arqueológico; y g) Exportación, utilización y consumo de	Ninguna disposición del presente Tratado será interpretada como impedimento para la adopción y el cumplimiento de medidas destinadas a la: a) Protección de la moralidad pública; b) Aplicación de leyes y reglamentos de seguridad; c) Regulación de las importaciones o exportaciones de armas, municiones y otros materiales de guerra y, en circunstancias excepcionales, de todos los demás artículos militares; d) Protección de la vida y salud de las personas, los animales y los vegetales; e) Importación y exportación de oro y plata metálicos; f) Protección del patrimonio nacional de valor artístico, histórico o arqueológico; y g) Exportación, utilización y consumo de	

(continued)

Table 5.4 (continued)

Original wording of the General Exception Clauses/ translation	EU – Art. 36 TFEU	CAN – Art. 73 AdC	Mercosur – Art. 50 Tratado de Montevideo	EFTA – Art. 13 EEAA
		materiales nucleares, productos radiactivos o cualquier otro material utilizable en el desarrollo o aprovechamiento de la energía nuclear.	materiales nucleares, productos radiactivos o cualquier otro material utilizable en el desarrollo o aprovechamiento de la energía nuclear.	
Translation (emphasis added)	The provisions of Articles 34 and 35 **shall not preclude** prohibitions or restrictions on imports, exports, or goods in transit **justified** on grounds of **public morality, public policy or public security**; the protection of **health and life of humans, animals or plants**; the protection of **national treasures possessing artistic, historic or archaeological value**; or the **protection of industrial and commercial property**. Such prohibitions or restrictions shall not, however, constitute a means of **arbitrary discrimination or a disguised restriction on trade** between Member States.	This concept **shall not include** the adoption and enforcement of measures **intended for** this purpose: (a) **Protection of public morality**; (b) **Application of safety laws and regulations**; (c) Regulation of imports or exports of *arms, munitions and other war materials* and, in exceptional circumstances, of all other *military articles*, provided that they do not interfere with the provisions of treaties on unrestricted free transit in force among Member Countries; (d) Protection of **human, animal and plant life and health**; (e) Import and export of metallic **gold and silver**; (f) Protection of	**Nothing** in this Treaty shall **be construed to preclude** the exercise of any right of the adoption and enforcement of measures **intended for** the: (a) Protection of **public morality**; (b) Enforcement of **security laws and regulations**; (c) Regulation of *imports or exports of arms, munitions and other war materials* and, in exceptional circumstances, of all other military goods. (d) Protection of **human, animal and plant life and health**; (e) Import and export of metallic **gold and silver**; (f) Protection of **national heritage of artistic, historical or**	The provisions of Article 7 **shall not preclude** prohibitions or restrictions on imports, exports, or goods in transit **justified** on grounds of **public morality,; public policy**, or **public security**; the protection of **health and life of humans, animals, or plants**; the protection of **national treasures possessing artistic, historic, or archaeological value**; or the protection of **industrial and commercial property**. Such prohibitions or restrictions shall not, however, constitute a means of **arbitrary discrimination** or a **disguised restriction** on

(continued)

Table 5.4   (continued)

Original wording of the General Exception Clauses/ translation	EU – Art. 36 TFEU	CAN – Art. 73 AdC	Mercosur – Art. 50 Tratado de Montevideo	EFTA – Art. 13 EEAA
		national trea-sures of artistic, historical or archaeological value; and (g) Export, use and consumption of *nuclear materials, radioactive products* or any other material usable in the development or use of nuclear energy.	**archaeological value**; and (g) Export, use and consumption of *nuclear materials, radioactive products* or any other material usable in the development or use of nuclear energy.	trade between the Member States.

Source: Author

analysis that takes into consideration the legal concepts developed by the respective PTA-DSMs at the level of the rule to liberalize trade and the exception to it. Consequently, the equivalent understanding of the respective General Exception Clauses by the individual PTA-DSMs make their decisions available for identifying divergence in a setting of communalities.

As can be concluded from the comparison of the provisions administering the process of trade liberalization under the legal frameworks of the EU, EFTA, CAN, and Mercosur, the provisions amount to two elements: firstly, an obligation to eliminate trade-restrictive measures and, secondly, a justification for the violation of this general obligation, if PTA partners introduce trade-restrictive measures protecting specified legitimate objectives. This dichotomous structure for administering the process of trade liberalization has led PTA-DSMs to an equivalent understanding of both elements. A review of the doctrine established by the different PTA-DSMs on the obligation to liberalize trade and the respective General Exception Clauses shows that these provisions have generally been understood in the same manner concerning the concepts of prohibited trade-restrictive measures and the use of the General Exception Clauses, despite other institutional and substantive differences existing in this context.[170]

Despite the different scopes of application concerning the first element, which can cover *fiscal* as well as *non-fiscal* trade-restrictive measures, the reviewed PTA-DSMs have developed an equivalent understanding of *non-fiscal* trade-

---

[170] See *infra* at Sect. 5.4.2.1–5.4.2.4.

restrictive measures, encompassing equivalent concepts of quantitative and other restrictions on intra-PTA trade. In response to these equivalent understandings on trade-restrictive measures, PTA-DSMs have approached the legal analysis of the justification provided under the respective General Exception Clauses equivalently. In this regard, the use of principles of proportionality and corresponding legal analyses resulting in their restrictive understanding have played a significant role. Nevertheless, the review of the PTA-DSMs' doctrine on the use of General Exception Clauses has given rise to different approaches concerning the invocation of *additional* legitimate objectives for the justification of trade-restrictive measures, which could initially call into question the PTA-DSMs' equivalent understanding of these provision.

A closer look at the record of the PTA-DSM decisions reviewed here, however, shows that all PTA-DSMs have been exposed to the PTA partners' attempts to justify trade-restrictive measures through the invocation of *additional* legitimate objectives while relying on the respective General Exception Clauses.[171] In response to these invocations, PTA-DSMs have handled the successful invocation of these *additional* legitimate objectives differently. Nevertheless, the differences in the PTA-DSMs' approaches to rely successfully on *additional* legitimate objectives under the respective General Exception Clause cannot contest their equivalent understanding of their invocation. On the contrary, the differences in the approaches towards the successful invocation of *additional* legitimate objectives essentially depend on the quality of measures PTA-DSMs have been called upon to adjudicate: Where the adjudicative record of PTA-DSMs shows that they have been requested to adjudicate trade-restrictive measures that have the potential for high adjustment costs due to trade liberalization, PTA partners could rely more often on more *additional* legitimate objectives. As the adjudicative record of the PTA-DSMs reviewed here differs in this regard, the PTA-DSMs haven been precluded from developing an equivalently sophisticated doctrine on the use of *additional* legitimate objectives. Concerning PTA-DSMs that have developed doctrinal responses to the invocation of *additional* legitimate objectives, the analysis of successfully invoked *additional* legitimate objectives shows that they have remained only a marginal phenomenon within the context of the invocation of the General Exception Clauses, since the PTA-DSMs have handled these invocations restrictively. Against the common feature of all reviewed PTA-DSMs in handling cases restrictively involving the adjudication of *additional* legitimate objectives, their equivalent understanding of the respective General Exception Clauses can therefore still be maintained.

5.4.2.1 Liberalization of Trade in Goods Under EU Rules

Liberalization of trade in goods under the legal framework of the EU is administered by Chapter 1 TFEU, in which the General Exception Clause under Art. 36 TFEU

---

[171] See *infra* at Sect. 5.4.2.5.

plays a central role regarding the prohibition of *non-fiscal* trade-restrictive measures in the form of quantitative restrictions (QRs) on imports and exports, as well as measures of equivalent effect as quantitative restrictions (MEQRs) on imports and exports, as stipulated under Arts. 34 and 35 TFEU.

5.4.2.1.1 First element: Prohibition of QRs and MEQRs on Imports and Exports Under Arts. 34 and 35 TFEU

The concept of the prohibition of QRs encompassed under Chapter 1 TFEU contains a straightforward prohibition of restriction on imports and exports expressed by a certain numerical limitation. Consequently, all measures restricting the quantities of goods eligible for imports and exports to a specific quota are encompassed by the prohibition of QRs. The concept of prohibited MEQRs is much more complex and has been subject to multiple refinements by the CJEU over time. Confronted with a broad prohibition of MEQRs on import restrictions, which allowed a challenge of every domestic measure that related to cross-border trade between EU member states simply due to its effect on international trade, the CJEU had to develop a concept of MEQRs allowing a distinguishing between measures having a *regulating* effect on international trade from measures having a *limiting* effect for market access of imported and exported goods. Such a differentiation became important over time in order not to render the notion of a single market synonymous with absolutely liberalized and therefore unregulated trade in goods between EU member states. This has resulted in a very complex structure of case law and legal doctrine, shaping the content of these provisions. In this regard, three principles—namely, concerning the general level, width, and depth of trade liberalization between the EU member states—are important to mention.

5.4.2.1.1.1 *On the General Level of Trade Liberalization:* Dassonville *and the Concept of QRs and MEQRs on Imports under Art. 34 TFEU*

In *Dassonville,* the CJEU set out that MEQRs on imports need to be understood as all domestic measures that could in fact or potentially, i.e. even if the affected goods are currently not present on the market of the respective EU Member State, have a limiting effect on the trade of goods between EU member states.[172] The finding that even any potential limiting effect on imports was prohibited under Art. 34 TFEU created an almost irrebuttable presumption that a domestic measure that has any effect on international trade between EU member states was prohibited if a good, firstly, was not able to access another EU Member State's market and, secondly, if the challenged measure was linked to the market access of the unavailable product. The CJEU established an unconditional right to market access, subject only to the prerequisite that any good from another EU member states be lawfully produced in this country of origin. It follows from *Dassonville* that no *a priori* limitation of the

---

[172] CJEU, *Procureur Du Roi v Dassonville*, 8/74; ECLI:EU:C:1974:82, Judgment of 1974.

trade inflow, and therefore no degree of trade liberalization between the EU member states, was foreseen. This has resulted in a judicial concept encompassing a very high level of trade liberalization aimed at under the TFEU: absolutely free trade for which all deviations require a justification.[173]

The *Dassonville* formula has resulted in high pressure on domestic measures, placing on existing domestic rules on trade among EU member states the presumption of violating Art. 34 TFEU due to their regulating and, hence, inherently limiting effect on trade flows. Moreover, the subsequent jurisprudence gradually turned to classifying all measures resulting in higher costs for importation of goods into a respective EU Member State's market as measures having an equivalent effect of quantitative restrictions.[174]

Only on rare occasions did the CJEU find that the presumption established under *Dassonville* could not be applied, because a measure had a too distant connection to the marketing of a certain good in question.[175] However, a general standard on the exact proximity, which would make a measure liable for a potentially limiting effect in imports, was not developed.

It was against this pressure on domestic legislatures that the CJEU was confronted with balancing the EU member states' need to maintain this regulation of trade grounded in a cultural, historical, and social understanding of trade against their obligation to liberalize their markets in a non-discriminatory manner.

5.4.2.1.1.2 On the Width of Trade Liberalization: Cassis de Dijon and A New Approach for MEQRs

With *Cassis de Dijon*, the CJEU explicitly accepted that measures that had a negative impact on trade among EU member states could continue to exist under the legal disciplines of the TFEU without being explicitly justified under Art. 36 TFEU.[176] This new logic created less pressure on EU member states to give way to unrestricted free trade on the European Single Market. Under *Cassis de Dijon*, the CJEU was confronted with a measure that set out minimum alcohol content requirements for certain alcoholic beverages marketed in Germany.

---

[173] As opposed to a test where less favorable treatment of other like goods, either on another PTA-partner (MFN) or the domestic market (NT) would be required. Cf. also Perišin (2008), pp. 20–25 and 200–201: "When interpreting the relevant provisions of the GATT [...], one has to bear in mind that the intention of this agreement is not to attain the ambitious level of integration that are the core of the EU, but merely to tackle protectionism by limiting its means to tariffs. Therefore, when analyzing whether a non-pecuniary trade restriction is contrary to the GATT, one has to check whether its *purpose is protectionism*."

[174] CJEU, *Commission v Italy*, C-270/02; ECLI:EU:C:2004:78, Judgment of 5 February 2004, para. 19.

[175] CJEU, *CIA Security v Signalson and Securitel*, C-194/94; ECLI:EU:C:1996:172, Judgment of 30 April 1996.

[176] CJEU, *Rewe v Bundesmonopolverwaltung für Branntwein*, 120/78; ECLI:EU:C:1979:42, Judgment of 20 February 1979.

Although the measure effectively prevented alcoholic beverages from other member states from being imported into Germany if their alcohol content was below the German minimum alcohol content, Germany argued that the disputed measure was not aimed at the discrimination of imports. Instead, it argued that the measure applied indistinctly to all products marketed on the German market. Accordingly, Germany argued that the measure was not prohibited by Art. 34 TFEU. In this context, it proposed to distinguish between *distinctly* and *indistinctly* applied measures on imports and domestic goods, which would allow EU member states to maintain measures dealing generally with the safeguarding of, e.g., public health, life, or consumer protection. Specifically, in the case at hand, Germany argued that the ability to market alcoholic beverages on the German market which satisfied a *minimum* alcohol requirement would protect the life and health of the public by minimizing the danger of alcoholism and serving consumer-protection purposes, as consumers would be sure to buy alcoholic beverages at the expected amount of alcohol. The CJEU did not accept these arguments, as it could neither be convinced that a *minimum* alcohol requirement prevented the dangers of alcoholism, nor that consumers could only be protected by allowing products on the German market which had characteristics that consumers *expected* them to have. Instead, the CJEU argued that consumers would only require appropriate information on the product they wanted to buy to make their decision to purchase it.

Yet, the CJEU accepted that EU member states could introduce or maintain measures of a *per se* negative impact in trade, if they were introduced for so-called *mandatory requirements*, i.e.,

"necessary [...] [for the] fiscal supervision, the protection of public health, the fairness of commercial transactions and the defence of the consumer."[177]

The introduction of the *mandatory requirements* doctrine carved out a substantial part of measures with a negative impact on trade from the ambit of the prohibition of MEQRs established under Art. 34 TFEU. The CJEU thereby acknowledged the need of EU member states to introduce or maintain trade regulation subject to the condition it applied *indistinctly* to domestic and imported goods alike, i.e., if it was *de jure* and *de facto* origin-neutral.

At the same time, the introduction of *mandatory requirements* limited the leeway of EU member states for introducing or maintaining measures of a *per se* negative impact on trade solely based on the argument that they would apply indistinctly to all goods on the market. Instead, the CJEU established that the negative impact would have to remain limited to a *specific* public-interest policy, introducing a *rule of reason*:[178] Measures having a negative impact on trade among EU Members could exist if they appeared reasonable to the court. This modified understanding of MEQRs lowered in practice the degree of trade liberalization among EU member states previously built up under *Dassonville*, giving way to a more restrictive concept

---

[177] Ibid., para. 8.
[178] Alter and Meunier-Aitsahalia (1994), pp. 539–541.

of trade liberalization under which EU member states would be allowed to resort to some sort of non-discriminatory regulation of their economy. The approach by the CJEU was heavily debated, as the CJEU's reasoning remained very difficult to reconcile with the text of the TFEU, which contained explicit justifications for trade-restrictive measures under the General Exception Clause under Art. 36 TFEU.[179] However, it constituted the only way post-*Dassonville* under which a measure having a negative impact on intra-EU trade would not be automatically encompassed by the prohibition of MEQRs and *a priori* violate Art. 34 TFEU, which would require a justification under Art. 36 TFEU. At the same time, this approach ensured that the regulation of a trade-restrictive effect would remain open to the scrutiny of the CJEU, since such a measure would not only have to aim at the so-called *mandatory requirements*, but would also have been necessary and proportionate.[180]

At the same time, the approach taken under *Cassis de Dijon* to review *the mandatory requirements* strengthened the so-called *principle of equivalence* or *mutual recognition*.[181] The review of *mandatory requirements* by the Court had the effect that goods from EU member states could not be denied market access on the importing EU member states' market, simply because different standards were applied to these products in the respective EU member states. Instead, the lawful production of a good on the market of one EU Member State created a presumption that it was produced under standards equivalent to those existing in any other EU Member State. This effectively contributed to an increase of competition between the different existing standards, and hence regulatory systems of the EU member states.[182]

5.4.2.1.1.3 On the Depth of Trade Liberalization: Keck *and the Differentiation Between Product Requirements and Certain Selling Arrangements*

Even after having clarified that EU member states could maintain regulations of the economic activity on the domestic markets, thereby affecting the international trade between them, the CJEU was confronted with measures that would not directly impede market access on the domestic markets of EU member states, but instead would hamper the participation of imported goods within these markets, i.e., their *marketing*. For this purpose, the CJEU introduced in *Keck* a distinction between product requirements and all other measures that have an impact on trade, such as

---

[179] Barents (1981), pp. 283–291.

[180] CJEU, *Rewe v Bundesmonopolverwaltung für Branntwein*, 120/78; ECLI:EU:C:1979:42, Judgment of 20 February 1979, paras 13–14.

[181] Ibid., para. 14; Barnard (2019), p. 93.

[182] Barnard (2019), p. 89; Perišin (2008), p. 10, argues that the competition between the legislation of the EU member states results from a competitive model of integration, which constitutionalizes negative integration by allowing all legally marketed goods of one EU Member State to be marketed on the markets of all other EU member states.

Certain Selling Arrangements,[183] thus providing further guidance on the depth of trade liberalization between the EU member states. Following *Cassis de Dijon*, distinguishing between these two sorts of measures became important, because, by resorting to *mandatory requirements* under Art. 34 TFEU, EU member states would be allowed to maintain measures that would have a limiting effect on trade between EU member states, subject to the condition that they applied indistinctly to all imported and domestic goods. So-called Domestic Selling Arrangements determine the structure of a marketplace and decide over the modalities how goods can be sold or purchased by consumers in a respective EU Member State without laying down specific product characteristics. They can be designed in a way that effectively prevents imported goods from being marketed and sold as effectively as domestic ones, which would amount to a violation of Art. 34 TFEU in the *Dassonville* sense. The CJEU clarified that Certain Selling Arrangements must be distinguished from product requirements. It established a presumption of legality for Certain Selling Arrangements, as opposed to product requirements which that could internalize domestic standards and favor the sale of domestic products, because

> "the application of such rules to the sale of products from another Member State meeting the requirements laid down by that State is *not by nature* such as to prevent their access to the market or to impede access any more than it impedes the access of domestic products."[184] (emphasis added)

The presumption of legality is subject to two conditions: firstly, the Certain Selling Arrangement in question applies to all goods marketed within the EU Members State (principle of universality) and, secondly, the Certain Selling Arrangement in question does not discriminate either in law or in fact (principle of neutrality).[185]

Upon introduction of this test, from a bird's eye perspective the CJEU was primarily concerned with creating equal opportunities of marketing for the goods admitted on the exporting market within the marketing structure established by domestic legislation. Yet, Certain Selling Arrangements would not have to be analyzed under the concept of MEQRs by the CJEU if they were operating in a *de facto* non-discriminatory way and therefore provided equal opportunities for imported goods to be marketed. The approach under *Keck* secured a large portion of the regulatory autonomy of EU member states and enabled them to shape the modalities of commercial activity on their markets.[186] Nonetheless, it seems as if the CJEU has started to revisit its position on the review of equal opportunities for

---

[183] According to *Barnard*, the CJEU now distinguishes between certain selling arrangements as a distinct group and furthermore created, for all other origin-neutral measures that are not product requirements, a new test under Art. 34 TFEU. Cf Barnard (2019), pp. 135–141.

[184] CJEU, *Keck and Mithouard*, C-267/91; C-268/91; ECLI:EU:C:1993:905, Judgment of 24 November 1993, para. 17.

[185] Ibid., para. 16.

[186] As Barnard (2019), pp. 135–141, notes that such a restrained approach to market access might have changed in the most recent jurisprudence, where the sole existence of a regulation that did not allow market access of goods that were lawfully produced in other EU member states was sufficient for the CJEU to conclude a violation of Art. 34 TFEU.

imported goods being marketed on EU member states' markets. As the CJEU held in *Commission v Italy*, Certain Selling Arrangements would still fall within the ambit of MEQRs even if they are universal and neutral and consequently need to fulfil the criteria of mandatory requirements established under *Cassis de Dijon*.[187] Consequently, EU member states would still need to provide reasons for the existence of a Certain Selling Arrangement having a negative impact on imported goods if it resulted in an increase of costs for marketing.[188] Even more recently, the carve-out for Certain Selling Arrangements has been further narrowed as the CJEU scrutinized the effects of domestic legislation on the *use* of imported goods. Approaching the issue from a bottom-up perspective, the CJEU assumed that bans on the use of certain goods have a considerable impact on the economic decisions of consumers to purchase them. The CJEU found that they would equally fall within the scope of MEQRs.[189] As a result, EU member states cannot argue anymore that a ban restricting the specific use of goods is comparable to a Certain Selling Arrangement, since it applies to all goods on the domestic market, irrespectively of their origin.[190] Rather the potentially disincentivizing effects for the demand of goods lawfully manufactured on another EU Member State's market suffices for a measure to constitute an MEQR, which requires justification by having recourse to the doctrine of *mandatory requirements*.

5.4.2.1.1.4 Export Restrictions

Art. 35 TFEU prohibits QRs and MEQRS on exports. Domestic producers of goods that encounter restrictive effects on export into other EU member states due to domestic legislation are entitled to challenge such discrimination. As the limiting effect of domestic measures lies at the heart of Art. 35 TFEU, it has been argued that it only covers distinctly applied measures, i.e., where the exports to other EU member states are restricted vis-à-vis production and sale for the domestic market.[191] Accordingly, the CJEU found that, next to export licenses, the requirement to carry out quality checks for goods destined for export, in the absence of such a requirement for the domestic market, constituted a violation of Art. 35 TFEU.[192] Concerning indistinctly applied measures, the CJEU held that disadvantages to domestic producers for the possibility to export due to domestic regulation do not

---

[187] CJEU, *Commission v Italy*, C-270/02; ECLI:EU:C:2004:78, Judgment of 5 February 2004, paras 22–24.

[188] Equally in the CJEU, *Commission v Italy*, C-110/05; ECLI:EU:C:2009:66, Judgment of 10 February 2009, para. 57, the effect on the reduced demand for nationals of Italy to buy trailers specifically to be towed by motorbikes was already enough to establish that the Selling Arrangement constituted an infringement of Art. 34 TFEU (Art. 28 EC).

[189] Ibid., para. 57.

[190] Barnard (2019), p. 134.

[191] Craig and De Búrca (2015), p. 650; Barnard (2019), p. 101.

[192] CJEU, *Procureur De La République v Bouhelier*, 53/76; ECLI:EU:C:1977:17, Judgment of 3 February 1977, para. 18.

amount to a violation of Art. 35 TFEU. In this context, a prohibited production method in the Netherlands, which did not allow the production horsemeat in the same slaughterhouse as other kinds of meat, did not violate Art. 35 TFEU, only because domestic producers had difficulties with supplying horsemeat for export to other EU member states. Since the prohibition of the production method applied to all domestic producers, independently of the destination of the product, the CJEU argued that this was not a measure discriminating against exports.[193]

5.4.2.1.2 Second Element: The General Exception Clause Under Art. 36 TFEU

In view of a growing body of secondary EU legislation, the CJEU has specified on several occasions that the invocation of the General Exception Clause under Art. 36 TFEU is only possible where secondary EU legislation has not resulted in a full harmonization of laws at the EU level between the member states. Consequently, Art. 36 TFEU can only be invoked where EU member states have retained their authority to set own policy goals concerning the legitimate objectives.

Generally, the provision needs to be understood narrowly, and the list of the legitimate objectives for the justification of trade-restrictive measures cannot be extended.[194] Corresponding to the principle of narrow interpretation of the General Exception Clause, recourse to Art. 36 TFEU is only available for trade-restrictive measures with policy goals of a non-economic nature.[195] Moreover, it is mainly the last aspect under Art. 36 TFEU, namely that the measure in question should not create disguised restrictions on the trade between EU member states, nor constitute a means of arbitrary discrimination amongst them, which has given rise to the CJEU applying a *proportionality test*.[196] It involves a test including elements of suitability, necessity, and proportionality *stricto sensu* of the disputed measure in question to attain the legitimate objective invoked by the EU Member State, carried out in two or three steps.[197]

---

[193] CJEU, *Groenveld v Produktschap Voor Vee En Vlees*, 15/79; ECLI:EU:C:1979:253, Judgment of 8 November 1979, para. 7.

[194] Barnard (2019), pp. 146–147.

[195] Cf., e.g., CJEU, *Commission v Italy*, C-7/61; ECLI:EU:C:1961:31, Judgment of 19 December 1961, pt. C lit. d); CJEU, *Evans Medical and Macfarlan Smith*, C-324/93; ECLI:EU:C:1995:84, Judgment of 28 March 1995, para. 36.

[196] The proportionality test is inspired by legal tests available under German jurisprudence, known as the "Verhältnismäßigkeitsprüfung", and the British reasoning developed under the Wendesbury principle. It entails a specific rationality assessment for the justification of a measure, where alternative ways of action for the protection of a legitimate objective are imaginable. Advocating a separate function of Art. 36, second sentence TFEU, cf. Barnard (2019), p. 166; on the disputed function of Art. 36, second sentence TFEU, as an origin of the proportionality analysis under EU rules on trade, cf. Snell (2002), p. 181.

[197] Perišin (2008), p. 48; Snell (2002), p. 196.

The CJEU's modified understanding of MEQRs, developed under the landmark cases *Dassonville*, *Cassis de Dijon*, and *Keck*, pursuant to which measures having a negative impact on intra-EU trade do not constitute MEQRs if they are maintained to satisfy so-called *mandatory requirements*, gradually developed an impact on the justification provided under Art. 36 TFEU. Traditionally, the concept of *mandatory requirements* was only available to indistinctly applicable measures. It already applied at the level of the rule to liberalize trade among EU Members, namely Arts. 30 and 34 TFEU. This resulted in a legal concept according to which measures having a negative impact on intra-EU trade would not require a justification under Art. 36 TFEU because they technically did not constitute MEQRs. All distinctly applicable measures automatically qualified as MEQRs, as they were presumed to have a negative effect on intra-EU trade and consequently would have to be justified under Art. 36 TFEU. In line with the principle of restrictive interpretation of this provision, Art. 36 TFEU would continue to provide exclusively the explicitly provided legitimate objectives for EU member states to justify their trade-restrictive measures. The CJEU was still able to practice a narrow reading of Art. 36 TFEU, while the generally boundless concept of *mandatory requirements* offering a theoretically open list of policy objectives only applied to indistinctly applicable measures having a negative effect on intra-EU trade.

Despite this logical differentiation between measures having a negative impact on trade and prohibited MEQRs, the distinction built by the CJEU has been gradually dissolving: The scope of applying the concept of *mandatory requirements*, on the one hand, and the legitimate objectives contained under Art. 36 TFEU, on the other, have gradually merged. Considering the extremely similar structure of tests that the concept of *mandatory requirements* calls for and the legal analysis of Art. 36 TFEU, the CJEU in several cases applied *mandatory requirements* not to exempt measures having a negative impact on trade from the scope of the prohibition of MEQRs. Instead, it has shifted to using them as an additional justification, once it has established that a measure has a negative impact on trade and is indeed a MEQR. This has important implications on the CJEU's doctrine pursuant to which it often does not determine anymore whether an indistinctly applicable measure having a negative impact on intra-EU trade might be still exempted from the ambit of the prohibition of MEQRs, or whether it already considers the measures MEQRs— which is justified because it aims at one of the *mandatory requirements*. Technically, this practice amounts to an actual broadening of the concept of justification of MEQRs, which cumulates the use of Art. 36 TFEU with the use of *mandatory requirements*.[198]

---

[198] Cf. CJEU, *Canadian Oil Company Sweden und Rantén*, C-472/14; ECLI:EU:C:2016:171, Judgment of 17 March 2016, para. 45: "In accordance with settled case-law, a measure having equivalent effect to a quantitative restriction on imports can be justified, for example, on grounds of the protection of the health and life of humans, under Article 36 TFEU, only if that measure is appropriate for securing the achievement of the objective pursued and does not go beyond what is necessary in order to attain it (judgment in Scotch Whisky Association and Others,C-333/14, EU: C:2015:845, paragraph 33). Furthermore, national measures that are capable of hindering intra-

Moreover, along with the use of *mandatory requirements* as justification, the differentiation concerning their scope of application has also been gradually dissolving. Consequently, cases exist in which the CJEU has argued *mandatory requirements* as being available as a justification for distinctly applicable MEQRs, too, i.e., discriminating *de jure* or *de facto* against imported goods or products destined for export within the meaning of Art. 35 TFEU.[199] Regularly, in the context of Art. 36 TFEU, the CJEU therefore firstly addresses whether *mandatory requirements* can be invoked by the EU member states and scrutinizes whether the measure in question respects the principles of universality and neutrality.[200] This has important consequences for the search of relevant cases suitable for analysis: Where the CJEU has brought forward that *mandatory requirements* are available as a justification next to Art. 36 TFEU, these cases are considered as relevant concerning the CJEU's legal reasoning on the General Exception Clause.

5.4.2.1.2.1   Suitability to Protect One of the Legitimate Objectives

Under the first element of the proportionality test involving the suitability of the disputed measure in question, the CJEU regularly assesses whether the measure is logically and technically able or apt to protect any of the legitimate objectives contained under Art. 36 TFEU. The measure taken needs to be causal for the protection of the claimed legitimate objective.[201]

Regarding the invocation of the legitimate objectives which the measure aims at protecting, the parallel availability of the *mandatory requirements* and legitimate objectives contained in Art. 36 TFEU has given rise to the availability of *mandatory requirement* also for measures that distinctly prevent market access for imported goods. Due to the similarity of the structure developed for the *mandatory requirements* test regarding the proportionality of the measure, legitimate objectives under Art. 36 TFEU and *mandatory requirements* are often invoked side by side.

5.4.2.1.2.2   Necessity of the Measure to Protect One of the Legitimate Objectives

Under the second step under the proportionality test, the CJEU carries out a twofold assessment of the trade-restrictive measures regarding its necessity to protect one of the invoked legitimate objectives. Firstly, the CJEU scrutinizes whether the introduced measure is the most effective way to protect the legitimate objective pursued, by comparing it with alternative measures that are equally able to do so. The

---

Community trade may be justified by *overriding requirements* relating to protection of the environment (see, to that effect, judgment in Ålands Vindkraft,C-573/12, EU:C:2014:2037, paragraph 77)." (emphasis added)

Note that this has an important impact on the identification of cases in which the CJEU allowed the recourse to additional legitimate objectives; cf. *infra* Sect. 5.4.2.5.2.1.

[199] Barnard (2019), pp. 82–83.

[200] Cf. *supra*, at Sect. 5.4.2.1.1.2.

[201] Snell (2002), pp. 196–197.

existence of alternative measures that are equally capable of protecting the legitimate objective is said to uncover hidden protectionism.[202] It is noteworthy that the CJEU has not remained limited to assessing alternative measures that correspond to the technical capabilities of EU Member State to protect a legitimate objective invoked. Lack of administrative structures or internal processes in an EU Member State has not precluded the CJEU from contemplating alternatives that would require it to establish additional infrastructure facilitating the collaboration between the EU Member State invoking the legitimate objective and the other EU member states from which the goods originate. This has led the CJEU to require cooperation from domestic administrative agencies of different EU member states to prevent duplication of administrative requirements, as well as the design of domestic administrative practices that are necessary for the market placement of goods.[203] Secondly, among several measures that can attain the invoked legitimate objective, preference is given to the measure that has the least trade-restrictive effect on international trade between EU member states. In other words, for a measure to sustain the legal test at this point, an EU member states would have to have implemented the most effective and least trade-restrictive measure available for the protection of the legitimate objective invoked.

5.4.2.1.2.3 *Proportionality of a Measure* Stricto Sensu*: Cost-Benefit-Analysis Involving the Importance of the Legitimate Objective Invoked and the Repercussions on Intra-EU Trade*

Finally, the third step of the proportionality test developed by the CJEU regularly involves the assessment of a measure regarding its proportionality *stricto sensu*. It involves a final cost-benefit analysis of a trade-restrictive measure by weighing its negative effect on the free movement of goods between EU member states and the importance of the legitimate objective pursued. The boundaries between an analysis under a measure's necessity and the legitimate objective pursued are blurred, resulting in considerations of the level of protection effectively realized by the measure in question at this point by the CJEU.[204] The reference for the trade impact applied by the CJEU has been said to vary from the assessment of a measure's general effect on intra-EU trade to its effect on intra-EU trade by safeguarding the exact domestic policy aimed at by the EU Member invoking the legitimate objective.[205] Ultimately, under this last step of the proportionality analysis, the CJEU assesses whether a trade-restrictive measure is compatible with the fundamental obligations to liberalize trade and, thus, the economic integration process as

---

[202] Poiares Maduro (1998a), p. 308.

[203] On the proceduralization of proportionality, see Barnard (2019), pp. 188–190; Snell (2002), p. 199.

[204] Perišin (2008), pp. 49–50.

[205] Poiares Maduro (1998a), p. 307.

administered by legal framework of the EU.[206] Consequently, a cost-benefit analysis of a trade-restrictive measure results in a favorable finding by the CJEU, depending on how important the protected legitimate objective is and how far-reaching the repercussions on the free movement of goods are. Which legitimate objectives enumerated under Art. 36 TFEU and the *mandatory requirements* rank amongst the highest cannot be stated clearly. The CJEU has repeatedly stated that the protection of life and health of humans is one of the most important values, which can justify even severe repercussions on the free movement of goods.[207]

5.4.2.2   Liberalization of Trade in Goods Under EEAA Rules

Liberalization in the trade in goods within EFTA is administered under Chapter 1 of the EEAA. In parallel to the provisions contained in the TFEU, Art. 13 EEAA constitutes the General Exception Clause of this agreement. It can be invoked to justify the existence of *non-fiscal* trade-restrictive measures, namely QRs and MEQRs on imports and exports prohibited under Arts. 11 and 12 EEAA.

5.4.2.2.1   First Element: Prohibition of QRs and MEQRs on Imports and Exports Under Arts. 11 and 12 EEAA

Given that Art. 6 EEAA stipulates the principle of homogeneity between EU rules and EEAA rules in their implementation and application, the concept of QRs and MEQRs as developed by the CJEU over time equally applies within the EEAA context.[208] In this context, the EFTA Court unequivocally confirmed the broad concept of MEQRs, stating that Art. 11 EEAA "is not conditional upon proof that the measure in question actually restricts imports; it is sufficient that it potentially has an effect on trade".[209] Equally, the concept of *mandatory requirements* has been transferred by the EFTA Court in the context of MEQRs developed under *Cassis de Dijon*. In *Ullensaker kommune and Others v. Nille AS*, the EFTA Court generally accepted the availability of *mandatory requirements* as developed by the CJEU and applied the corresponding legal test accordingly. Ultimately, it refused mandatory requirements to be invoked because the disputed measure amounted to discriminatory application, which precluded their application.[210]

---

[206] Snell (2002), p. 200.

[207] E.g., CJEU, *The Scotch Whisky Association*, C-333/14; ECLI:EU:C:2015:845, Judgment of 23 December 2015, para. 35.

[208] Pétursson (2018), para. 1.

[209] EFTA Court, *Ravintoloitsijain Liiton Kustannus Oy Restamark*, E-1/94, Judgment of 16 December 1994, para. 47.

[210] EFTA Court, *Ullensaker kommune and Others v. Nille AS*, E-5/96, Judgment of 26 February 1997, para. 30.

5.4.2.2.2   Second Element: Doctrine Developed by the EFTA Court
            on the Invocation of Art. 13 EEAA

In line with the understanding of the limited availability of the General Exception
Clause developed by the CJEU considering the growing body of secondary EU
legislation, the EFTA Court likewise held that Art. 13 EEAA is not applicable where
secondary legislation has fully harmonized the specific policy in question.[211] Moreover, in holding the concepts of MEQRs and *mandatory requirements* equally
applicable in the context of the legal framework of the EEAA, the scope of
application of the General Exception Clause under Art. 13 EEAA equally results
in its limited availability, namely to distinctly applicable measures only.[212] In
parallel to the understanding of the CJEU of the General Exception Clause under
Art. 36 TFEU, the EFTA Court confirmed the narrow understanding of Art.
13 EEAA, which generally precluded broadening the scope of the provision by
introducing additional legitimate objectives.[213] However, whether the EFTA Court
assumes that legitimate objectives available under Art. 13 EEAA and *mandatory
requirements* are available in parallel for the justification of trade-restrictive measures at the same time and in line with the CJEU is not evident. Finally, the EFTA
Court applies a proportionality analysis in the sense of the practice of the CJEU,
given that Art. 13 EEAA contains the prohibition to use the General Exception
Clause as a means of arbitrary discrimination or a disguised restriction on trade
between EEA parties.[214]

5.4.2.3   Liberalization of Trade in Goods Under CAN Rules

Liberalization of trade in goods is governed by Chapter VI of the AdC, in which the
General Exception Clause under Art. 73 AdC plays an important role for the
justification of all restrictions on imports, as defined in Arts. 72 and 73 AdC,
introduced between CAN member states.[215]

---

[211] EFTA Court, *Ferskar kjötvörur ehf. and The Icelandic State*, E-17/15, Judgment of 1 February
2016, para. 52.

[212] Cf. e.g. EFTA Court, *Ullensaker kommune and Others v. Nille AS*, E-5/96, Judgment of
26 February 1997, para. 30.

[213] Ibid., para. 33.

[214] Cf., e.g. EFTA Court, Fagtún ehf. and Byggingarnefnd Borgarholtsskóla, the Government of
Iceland, the City of Reykjavík and the Municipality of Mosfellsbær, E-5/98, Judgment of 12 May
1999, para. 37; EFTA Court, Pedicel AS and Sosial- og helsedirektoratet (Directorate for Health and
Social Affairs), E-4/04, Judgment of 25 February 2005, para. 51.

[215] Note that the provisions in the original AdC were contained in Arts. 41 and 42, (1988) Acuerdo
De Cartagena (original).

5.4.2.3.1   First Element: Prohibition of Restrictions on Trade Under Arts.
72 and 73 AdC

The elimination of 'restrictions of any kind' encompasses a broad variety of fiscal and non-fiscal trade-restrictive measures. The Financial and exchange measures are captioned by this concept, which according to the TJCAN is "one of the main mechanisms foreseen by the [AdC] to achieve the objectives of the integrationist process and, in particular, to obtain the gradual formation of a common market."[216] The TJCAN established a broad obligation to liberalize trade in goods amongst CAN member states concerning trade-restrictive measures on imports only.[217] Considering such a broad scope of the prohibition under Art. 73 AdC, the TJCAN was faced with making the provision operational regarding the different kinds of imaginable trade-restrictive measures. It stated in this regard that "it is clear that to restrict means to diminish an *existing* capacity to do something and 'restrictions of all kinds', supposes a general globalization, of any attitude that diminishes powers or rights *existing previously*, in any form or way, that means a situation less favorable than the one existing before the new restriction was dictated."[218] Consequently, the TJCAN departs from a prohibition of measures that restrict numerically, i.e., *on the face* and only for *existing* imports, the importation of goods from other CAN member states, much comparable to the concept of QRs under Arts. 34 and 35 TFEU. This has important consequences for the level of trade liberalization aimed at by the TJCAN. As other measures do not impede the market access of imported goods, but nevertheless could have a negative effect on trade flows of goods among CAN member states, they were originally not directly covered by TJCAN's doctrine on the prohibition of 'restrictions of any kind'. Confronted with a Venezuelan import prohibition on roasted coffee from CAN member states, in *3-AI-96* the TJCAN changed its understanding of the prohibition of import restrictions under Art. 73 AdC. In *3-AI-96*, it laid the groundwork for the adoption of the concept of MEQRs.[219] It held that "the Andean Subregional Agreement does not contain

---

[216]TCJAN, *1-IP-90*, Judgment of 19 September 1990, p. 6. Original wording: "[. . .] uno de los principales mecanismos previstos por el Acuerdo de Cartagena para lograr los objetivos propios del proceso integracionista y, en especial, para obtener la formación gradual de un mercado común."

[217]Art. 3 of Decision 284 regulates the procedure in front of the SGCAN to identify export restrictions and prescribe remedies against them. So far, the SGCAN dealt only once with allegations brought forward by Venezuela concerning the prohibition of exports of live animals introduced by Colombia. Venezuela argued that such a measure would be in breach of Art. 72 AdC; it did not conclude anything on the legality of this export restriction and instead abstained from a finding, cf. SGCAN, *Resolución 570*, Judgment of 30 November 2001.

[218]Cf. TJCAN, *5-IP-90*, Judgment of 22 July 1994, p. 10.
Original wording: "En todo caso, queda claro que restringir significa disminuir una capacidad *existente* de hacer algo y "Restricciones de todo orden", supone una globalización general, de cualquier actitud que disminuye facultades o derechos *existentes anteriormente*, de cualquier forma o manera, que signifiquen una situación menos favorable a la existente antes de dictarse la nueva restricción." (emphasis added)

[219]See also Reyes Tagle (2012).

substantive rules concerning measures of equivalent effect as contained in Article 30 of the European Economic Community Treaty [now Art. 34 TFEU]; however, this provision can constitute a valuable supplementary source of law–together with the rules applying to quantitative restrictions at the level of the World Trade Organization–for the conclusion that an obstacle or impediment to the free importation of goods [. . .], which goes beyond the specific object of the measure [. . .] by making the importation of a certain product unjustifiably impossible or more difficult or more costly, may qualify as a restriction on trade, and even more so if such a measure has a discriminatory character."[220]

The SGCAN picked up the doctrinal supplementation of the TJCAN and, on occasion, of a Colombian law on import declarations, which mandated a penalty fee of 200% of the value of the imported product where these declarations were not completed: In *Resolution 047*, it declared that the prohibition of import restrictions under Art. 73 AdC also encompassed *measures of equivalent effect as quantitative restrictions*. Although under the original concept of MEQRs, pursuant to the doctrine of the CJEU, fiscal measures usually are not captioned,[221] the SGCAN specified that Art. 73 AdC was inspired by the Treaty of Rome, in "which also [. . .] the term 'measure' [should be] understood as any act of a regulatory or administrative nature or any actual or potential conduct or practice which has the effect of limiting, hindering, preventing or in any way restricting imports or making them more burdensome, as confirmed by the case law of the Court of the European Communities in a number of judgments, including the Simenthal [sic], Cassis de Dijon and Keck cases."[222]

---

[220]TJCAN, *3-AI-96*, 3-AI-96, Judgment of 24 March 1997, p. 17.

Original wording: "Para la identificación de la correspondencia entre la medida restrictiva y el objeto específico de protección de la salud vegetal, por ejemplo, el Acuerdo Subregional Andino no contiene norma sustantiva relativa a las medidas de efecto equivalente contenidas en el artículo 30 del Tratado de la Comunidad Económica Europea; sin embargo ésta puede constituir valiosa fuente supletoria del derecho – junto con las normas aplicables al tema de restricciones cuantitativas a nivel de la Organización Mundial de Comercio – para concluir que un obstáculo o impedimento a la importación libre de mercancías que se salga del objeto específico de la medida – en este caso la salud de la producción agrícola – dirigiéndose a imposibilitar injustificadamente la importación de un determinado producto o de hacer la importación más difícil o más costosa, pueda reunir las características de restricción al comercio y más aún, si una medida tiene el carácter discriminatorio."

[221] In this context, it should be noted that, due to the distinction of fiscal and non-fiscal measures and a general prohibition of the collection of duties on intra EU-trade under the legal framework of the EU, the CJEU could not be confronted substantively with such an issue. That said, we should bear in mind that the imposition of fiscal measures such as antidumping measures – with the authorization of the SGCAN – under Chapter X AdC and safeguard measures under Chapter XI AdC still remains possible under the legal framework of the CAN. This context may contribute to our understanding why the SGCAN was motivated to apply the concept of MEQRs regarding a fiscal measure.

[222]SGCAN, *Resolución 047*, Judgment of 23 January 1998, p. 6.

Original wording: "Resulta ilustrativo señalar que el Artículo 73 del Acuerdo de Cartagena se inspiró en el artículo 30 del Tratado de Roma el cual tampoco limita el término "medida" entendiéndolo como cualquier acto de carácter normativo, administrativo o cualquier conducta o práctica de carácter real o potencial que tenga por efecto limitar, dificultar, impedir o de algún modo restringir las importaciones o hacerlas más onerosas, según lo confirma la jurisprudencia del

The TJCAN confirmed the SGCAN's approach in the corresponding process. In *2-AN-98*, it defined that, "to be classified as a restriction on trade, a measure must come from a body exercising public functions, whether governmental, legislative, administrative, supervisory or judicial. This type of measure may take the form of a legal rule of general effect–even though it may affect only one sector in particular–, a decision or ruling effectively *inter partes* or *erga omnes*, material or physical operations, omissions or, finally, any positive or negative attitude, including administrative practices outside the law or even derived from it. Furthermore, it must be capable of 'preventing or hindering' imports, regardless of whether that was the intention or purpose of the measure",[223] including a reference to *3-AI-96* in this regard.

5.4.2.3.2   Second Element: General Exception Clause Under Art. 73 AdC

The second sentence of Art. 73 AdC, serving as General Exception Clause, contains several requirements that were clarified by the SGCAN and TJCAN over time. The nature of the provision is still contested, as the wording 'shall not include' in the second paragraph of Art. 73 AdC calls into question whether it serves as a justification or whether measures taken pursuant to this provision are carved out from the disciplines of the first sentence of Art. 72 AdC. In this regard, the SGCAN and TJCAN generally apply the second sentence of Art. 73 AdC as a justification.[224] Nevertheless, it appears that the TJCAN does not fully differentiate between the existence of a trade-restrictive measure and that measure being potentially justified. This sentence, which is often referred to in several cases by the TJCAN, makes this clear:

> "As a result, a measure that *constitutes* a restriction on trade is only *justified* if it is fully demonstrated that it is subsumed under one of the exceptions set out in the second paragraph of Article 73. For this purpose, the SGCAN, on its own initiative or at the request of a party,

---

Tribunal de la Comunidades Europeas en sendas y reiteradas sentencias entre las cuales se pueden citar los casos Simenthal, Casis de Dijon y Keck, entre otros."

[223]TJCAN, *2-AN-98*, Judgment of 2 June 2000, p. 10. Original wording: "Para catalogar una medida como restricción al comercio debe provenir de un órgano en ejercicio de funciones públicas, sean gubernativas, legislativas, administrativas, de control, o judiciales. Este tipo de medidas puede revestir la forma de una norma jurídica de efectos generales – aunque pudieren afectar, particularmente a un solo sector –, de una decisión o resolución con eficacia inter partes o erga omnes, de operaciones materiales o físicas, de omisiones o, en fin, cualquier actitud positiva o negativa, incluidas las prácticas administrativas al margen de la ley o incluso derivadas de ésta. Por otra parte, debe ser susceptible de "impedir o dificultar" las importaciones, sin que interese que esa haya sido la intención o el propósito de la medida."

[224]SGCAN, *Resolución 2019*, Judgment of 14 August 2018, para. 91; SGCAN, *Resolución 1695*, Judgment of 6 June 2014, pt. 3; SGCAN, *Resolución 1564*, Judgment of 14 April 2013, pt. 1.3; TJCAN, *02-AN-2015*, Judgment of 26 August 2016, para. 1.5.4.

shall determine, where appropriate, whether a measure taken unilaterally by a member country *constitutes* a restriction."[225] (emphasis added)

The approach by the TJCAN has given rise to some controversy, as once a measure constitutes a restriction on trade it still pertains to exist, notwithstanding the fact that it can be justified. In other words, the circumstances that a measure constitutes a restriction on trade, and at the same time is justified, does not alter the measure's trade-restrictive effect. In the same vein, *Yovana Reyes Tagle* criticizes that the TJCAN has been inconsistent with its approach so far.[226]

Whether Art. 73 AdC can be invoked even if secondary CAN legislation exists regarding the disputed measure is not entirely clear from the doctrine of the TJCAN. The General Exception Clause can be regularly invoked for all measures found inconsistent with Art. 72 AdC. Specific subject matters, such as the notification, authorization, and inscription in the registry of sanitary and phytosanitary (SPSCAN) measures under Decision 328, safeguard measures, and countervailing duties under Decision 456,[227] have been found to serve as a justification for the existence of non-fiscal and fiscal trade-restrictive measures. Concerning the provisions on the notification, authorization, and inscription of SPSCAN measures under Art. 10 Decision 328, the doctrine of the SGCAN and TJCAN allows us to understand them as more specific justifications vis-à-vis the General Exception Clause under Art. 73 AdC regarding the protection of human, animal and plant life, and health. Nonetheless, SGCAN and TJCAN have nonetheless referred to Art. 73 AdC, even if they found a measure to fall within the ambit of Decision 328. As the interpretation of Art. 73 AdC remained relevant even for measures that fell within the scope of Decision 328, it appears that Art. 73 AdC retains a quasi-constitutional character regarding the justification of all trade-restive measures within the legal ambit of the CAN rules.[228] Consequently, it appears more

---

[225] TJCAN, *01-AN-2014*, Judgment of 19 January 2017, para. 3.2.14. Original wording: "Como consecuencia de ello, una medida que constituya una restricción al comercio solo se encontrarla justificada si se demuestra cabalmente que se encuentra subsumida en alguna de las excepciones estipuladas en el segundo párrafo del Artículo 73. Para tal efecto, la SGCA, de oficio o a petición de parte, determinará, cuando así corresponda, si una medida adoptada unilateralmente por un país miembro constituye o no una restricción."

[226] Reyes Tagle (2012), p. 11.

[227] Comisión (1999) Decisión 456.

[228] TJCAN, *1-AN-97*, Judgment of 26 February 1998, pp. 31–32: "In the case of accepting for the sake of the argument the discussion that the contested Resolution has as a background the registration of a sanitary norm based on Decision 328, this does not have the virtuality of preventing the Board, with the general competence assigned – Article 15, (30 of the current) – from declaring that the Venezuelan norm constituted a restriction, because a country which uses a health standard as a disguised restriction on intra-subregional trade fails to comply with the objective of the Agreement as regards the free movement of goods, and in such a case the action of the Board, based on Article 73, becomes necessary to prevent the excesses which occur in over-registration of a health standard."

Original wording: "En el supuesto de aceptar en gracia de discusión que la Resolución impugnada tiene como antecedente el registro de una norma sanitaria con base en la Decisión

appropriate to speak of Decision 328 as an *addendum* rather than a concretization of the more comprehensive General Exception Clause of Art. 73 AdC.

Another interesting development of legal doctrine concerning this provision could be witnessed regarding the application of the *principle of reasonableness*, a legal analysis resembling the *proportionality test* equally applied by the CJEU. The reference to the *principle of reasonableness* by the SGCAN and TJCAN is remarkable because the wording of Art. 73 AdC does not contain elements that would give rise to a corresponding test. To remedy their absence, in *3-AI-96* the TJCAN declared that the Treaty of Rome as well as the WTO Agreement constituted a valuable supplementary means of interpretation for the General Exception Clause for the AdC.[229] By referring to both legal sources, the TJCAN identified specific criteria

---

328, ésta no tiene la virtualidad de impedir que la Junta, con la competencia general asignada – artículo 15, (30 del actual) – de declarar que la norma venezolana constituía una restricción, porque un País que utiliza una norma sanitaria como restricción encubierta al comercio intrasubregional, incumple el objetivo del Acuerdo en cuanto a la libre circulación de mercancía, y en tal caso la actuación de la Junta, basada en el artículo 73 se hace necesaria para prevenir los excesos que se produzcan sobre registro de una norma sanitaria."

[229]TJCAN, *3-AI-96*, 3-AI-96, Judgment of 24 March 1997, p. 17: "For the restriction to acquire the status of justification, according to the competence assigned to the Board, the internal act of the Member Country must be inspired by the *principle of proportionality* between the restrictive measure and the specific purpose for which it is intended, which must appear *as a direct and immediate cause for the solution* of the plant-protection problems. This is the only way to ensure that there is no room for doubt that the internal measure may surreptitiously threaten the essential purpose of integration, which is the free movement of goods. For the identification of the correspondence between the restrictive measure and the specific object of plant-health protection, for example, the Andean Subregional Agreement does not contain substantive rules concerning measures of equivalent effect contained in *Article 30 of the European Economic Community Treaty*; however, this can constitute a valuable *supplementary source of law* – together with the rules applicable to the subject of quantitative restrictions at the level of the *World Trade Organization* – to conclude that an obstacle or impediment to the free importation of goods that goes *beyond* the specific object of the measure – in this case, the health of agricultural production – and is aimed at making the importation of a certain product unjustifiably impossible or at making importation more difficult or more costly may have the characteristics of a restriction on trade, and even more so if a measure is *discriminatory* in nature. In the same vein, it can be concluded whether the purpose of the "domestic measure" could have been *achieved by other means* that do not hinder trade." (emphasis added)

Original wording: "Para que la restricción adquiera la categoría de justificatoria, según la competencia asignada a la Junta, es necesario que el acto interno del País Miembro esté inspirado en el principio de proporcionalidad entre la medida restrictiva y el objeto específico a que ella vaya dirigida, el cual deberá aparecer como causa directa e inmediata para la solución de los problemas fitosanitarios. Sólo así se garantiza que no haya lugar a duda de que la medida interna pueda amenazar subrepticiamente el propósito esencial de la integración consistente en la libre circulación de mercancías. Para la identificación de la correspondencia entre la medida restrictiva y el objeto específico de protección de la salud vegetal, por ejemplo, el Acuerdo Subregional Andino no contiene norma sustantiva relativa a las medidas de efecto equivalente contenidas en el artículo 30 del Tratado de la Comunidad Económica Europea; sinembargo ésta puede constituir valiosa fuente supletoria del derecho – junto con las normas aplicables al tema de restricciones cuantitativas a nivel de la Organización Mundial de Comercio – para concluir que un obstáculo o impedimento a la importación libre de mercancías que se salga del objeto específico de la medida - en este caso la

that a measure would have to satisfy to be justified. These criteria covered aspects of suitability of the trade-restrictive measure ("direct and immediate cause for the solution [of the problem addressed by the measure]"), necessity ("[solution could] have achieved by other means that do not hinder trade"), and the importance of non-discrimination throughout the application of the measure. The explanations of the court reproduced the Junta's approach in the corresponding *resolution* on the measure. However, the Junta did not elaborate on the criteria under the legal analysis nor on their origin.[230] In *3-AI-96*, the *principle of reasonableness* was not put into practice by the TJCAN, given that it upheld the primacy of proceedings in front of the SGCAN. Consequently, Action of Infringement proceedings were found to be the incorrect procedural action to be taken by CAN member states to challenge *resolutions* issued by the Junta or the SGCAN. Instead, the TJCAN held the Action for Nullity proceedings as incorrect and took only *subsidiary* procedural action to challenge Decisions issued by the SGCAN. In its place, the appeal procedure in front of the SGCAN should have been used by CAN member states for disputes over trade-restrictive measures. For this reason, the TJCAN abstained from making a legal finding under Art. 73 AdC.[231]

Subsequent practice of the SGCAN and TJCAN has shown some degree of variation concerning the criteria that need to be included in the test under Art. 73 AdC.[232] The legal doctrine developed by the SGCAN and TJCAN on the use of Art. 73 AdC remains sometimes difficult to grasp, due to partly missing textual foundations in the AdC and the intuitive approach taken by the SGCAN and TJCAN for the legal analysis of disputed measures. The following order of the legal analysis under Art. 73 AdC is based on the approach taken by the TJCAN in *02-AN-2015*.

5.4.2.3.2.1 Non-discrimination of CAN Member States in the Application of the Trade-Restrictive Measures

The disputed trade-restrictive measure must be first and foremost of a non-discriminatory nature in order comply with the principle of reasonableness under Art. 73 AdC. This requirement needs to be fulfilled for a trade-restrictive measure to be justified successfully under the General Exception Clause.[233] It is

---

salud de la producción agrícola - dirigiéndose a imposibilitar injustificadamente la importación de un determinado producto o de hacer la importación más difícil o más costosa, pueda reunir las características de restricción al comercio y más aún, si una medida tiene el carácter discriminatorio. En igual sentido cabe concluir si el objeto que persigue la "medida interna" podría haberse alcanzado por otros medios que no obstaculizaran el comercio."

[230] JUNAC, *Resolución 379*, Judgment of 27 September 1995.

[231] TJCAN, *3-AI-96*, 3-AI-96, Judgment of 24 March 1997, p. 25.

[232] Most illustrative in this regard TJCAN, *02-AN-2015*, Judgment of 26 August 2016, pt. 3.3. The TJCAN does not require the SGCAN always to apply the same test; rather, it verifies whether the specific criteria of 03-AI-96 were applied.

[233] Ibid., para. 3.4.2. lit. a).

considered as an outflow of the general principle of proportionality.[234] When a measure applies distinctly to imported goods, a non-discrimination analysis including aspects on the discrimination among imported goods (MFN dimension) and imported vis-à-vis domestic goods (NT dimension) takes place.[235] Moreover, the non-discrimination requirement also encompasses *de facto* discrimination of imported goods on the domestic market.[236]

A finding of discriminatory treatment of imported goods originating in other CAN member states indicates that a justification under Art. 73 AdC will not be successful. In this case, it is understood that the trade-restrictive measure does not encompass all goods that could constitute a risk to the legitimate objective invoked for its protection and speaks for its flawed design. The ineffective contribution of the disputed measure to the protection of the invoked legitimate objective makes the subsequent analysis of the measure's suitability for the protection of the legitimate objective redundant and gives rise to assume its arbitrary character.[237] The elevated

---

[234] E.g., SGCAN, *Resolución 681*, Judgment of 20 December 2002, p. 5: "That, with regard to the first condition, this General Secretariat considers that by prohibiting the importation of explosives of similar characteristics to those that exist in Peru, it cannot be justified that there is proportionality between this rule and the specific object to which it is addressed (theoretically, protect the national security or reduce the possibility of subversive attacks), because the rule is *discriminatory*, since the sale of imported explosives similar to those produced in Peru is prohibited, while the sale of domestic like products is permitted with some controls (emphasis added). SGCAN, *Resolución 710*, Judgment of 21 March 2003, para. 1. However, for cases where the non-discriminatory nature of a measure was not carried out as a fist part of the analysis, cf., as suggested in TJCAN, *241-IP-2015*, Judgment of 12 June 2017, para. 3.7.

[235] TJCAN, *02-AN-2015*, Judgment of 26 August 2016, para. 3.4.11-3.4.12; SGCAN, *Resolución 2019*, Judgment of 14 August 2018, paras 79–90.

[236] TJCAN, *02-AN-2015*, Judgment of 26 August 2016, para. 3.4.11. In the given case, the TJCAN found an Ecuadorian tariff regime on imports of parts for the assembly of cars (so-called Completely Knocked Down parts for the assembly of cars, CKD), constituted discriminatory treatment of imports from Colombia. It did so by arguing that the tariff amount, due at the border, became progressively lower the higher the amount was of domestically produced or available CKD that were used in the assembly of the final car in Ecuador.

[237] SGCAN, *Resolución 897*, Judgment of 4 February 2005, p. 4.: "That although the Government of Ecuador has invoked Article 73(d) of the Cartagena Agreement, that Government has not justified that the products of the Subregion and particularly of Colombia, falling under the tariff subheadings NANDINA 2501.00.11 (table salt), 2501.00.19 (other salts, including denatured salts), and 2501.00.90 (other, sea water) could affect human health. Nor has the Government of Ecuador demonstrated a direct link between the suspension of imports of products falling within the aforementioned tariff subheadings and the legitimate objective of protection of health provided for in Article 73 of the Cartagena Agreement; that the fact that at some point products that do not comply with Ecuador's health legislation have entered Ecuador – as can be seen from COMEXI Resolution 274 – does not justify the adoption of a measure suspending all imports of products corresponding to tariff subheadings NANDINA 2501.00.11 (table salt), 2501.00.19 (other, including denatured products), and 2501.00.90 (other, sea water). That, in this regard, the measure applied by the Government of Ecuador is disproportionate to the objective it would allegedly pursue." Original wording: "Que si bien el Gobierno del Ecuador invocó el literal d) del artículo 73 del Acuerdo de Cartagena, dicho Gobierno no ha justificado que los productos de la Subregión y particularmente de Colombia, comprendidos en las subpartidas arancelarias NANDINA 2501.00.11

role of non-discrimination of a trade-restrictive measure as a preliminary requirement for the invocation of the General Exception Clause creates uncertainties
regarding its purpose. After all, Art. 73 AdC should be able to serve as a justification
even for distinctly applicable trade-restrictive measures, without amounting to
discriminatory treatment because they properly serve a legitimate objective. This
might especially be the case for trade-restrictive measures that aim at the protection
of legitimate objectives emanating from goods that are presently not available on the
market of the importing CAN Member State. Nonetheless, the analysis of the
discriminatory character of the measure in the first place rather speaks for a focus
on the measure's effects on intra-CAN trade and its potential excessiveness.[238] It
serves to indicate a protectionist purpose of measure due to its arbitrary construc-
tion.[239] The design of a trade-restrictive measure to be distinctly applicable does not
necessarily render it unavailable for a justification under the General Exception
Clause. Consequently, the SGCAN engaged in an analysis of *de facto* discrimination
for distinctly applicable security checks for imports of cement, due to a risk of the
product being misused to produce cocaine, and still held Art. 73 AdC to be
applicable in this case.[240] On the other hand, the character of a distinctly applicable
trade-restrictive measure does not always lead to a discrimination analysis for the
purpose of its justification. For instance, in the case of requirements to furnish
pharmaceuticals with a certificate of compliance of goods manufacturing at their
importation, the SGCAN did not analyze the non-discrimination requirement of the
measure.[241]

(sal de mesa), 2501.00.19 (las demás sales, incluidas las desnaturalizadas) y 2501.00.90 (los demás,
agua de mar) puedan afectar la salud de las personas. El Gobierno del Ecuador tampoco ha
demostrado una vinculación directa entre la suspensión de las importaciones de los productos
comprendidos en las mencionadas subpartidas arancelarias y el objetivo legítimo de protección a la
salud previsto en el artículo 73 del Acuerdo de Cartagena; Que el hecho de que hubieran ingresado
en algún momento al Ecuador productos que no cumplen la legislación sanitaria de ese país – según
se desprende de la Resolución 274 del COMEXI – no justifica la adopción de una medida que
suspenda todas las importaciones de los productos correspondientes a las subpartidas arancelarias
NANDINA 2501.00.11 (sal de mesa), 2501.00.19 (los demás, incluidas las desnaturalizadas) y
2501.00.90 (los demás, agua de mar); que, en este sentido, la medida aplicada por el Gobierno del
Ecuador resulta desproporcionada con el objetivo que supuestamente perseguiría."

[238] Such an analysis equally takes place as the last element under the proportionality test under Art.
36 TFEU, which gives meaning to the requirement of the justified measure not to constitute an
arbitrary discrimination or a disguised restriction on trade; cf. *supra*, at Sect. 5.4.2.1.2.3.

[239] Cf. Appleton (1997), p. 135.

[240] SGCAN, *Resolución 2019*, Judgment of 14 August 2018, paras 80–90. However, note that Art.
75 AdC contains a separate NT obligation concerning the favorable treatment of imports from CAN
member states. Additionally, Art. 139 AdC stipulates a separate MFN obligation to extend
preferential treatment of import from non-CAN countries to CAN member states. A limitation of
the scope of application of Art. 73 AdC to only non-discriminatory measures is therefore questionable, as the provision could become meaningless considering the parallel existing NT and MFN
obligations under Arts. 75 and 139 AdC. After all, under the broad concept of MEQRs, the violation
of the NT and MFN obligations are equally encompassed.

[241] SGCAN, *Resolución 576*, Judgment of 12 December 2001, p. 5.

The emphasis on the non-discriminatory character of a trade-restrictive measure for it be justified under Art. 73 AdC has important practical consequences for the process of trade liberalization among CAN member states. As a prerequisite for the invocation of Art. 73 AdC it effectively decreases the regulatory autonomy of the CAN member states, given that the approach prohibits the introduction of product-specific requirements by means of import prohibitions. Instead, for CAN member states successfully to rely on Art. 73 AdC as a justification, the doctrine requires them to design and enforce trade-restive measures that are framed as neutrally as possible, demanding domestic legislators also to encompass domestic goods and identify characteristics *allowing* their marketing, instead of prohibiting them.[242] Such a reading of the General Exception Clause assesses the neutrality of trade-restrictive measures instead of justifying trade restrictions.[243]

5.4.2.3.2.2   Measures Aimed at the Protection of One of the Listed Legitimate Objectives

SGCAN and TJCAN have reiterated that the legitimate objectives included in Art. 73 AdC constitute a closed list and need to be interpreted restrictively.[244] In order to rely successfully on Art. 73 AdC as a justification, a measure must generally aim only at the protection of the legitimate objectives specified in the provision. Never-theless, the TJCAN accepted the approach of the SGCAN to include the protection of consumer rights as another legitimate objective that can justify a trade-restrictive measure.[245] It did so by reciting the finding of the SGCAN and other objectives encompassed by laws on the standardization in the CAN legal order:

> "to the extent that such domestic regulations are intended to ensure objectives of general interest *worthy of protection in the light of Community law*, such as *consumer protection*, which, in addition to being *recognized by constitutional traditions of the countries of the Community*, is also consistent with the aim of 'seeking a persistent improvement in the

---

[242] The SGCAN found the inspection of imports of cement into Colombia for drug-prevention purposes to be of a non-discriminatory nature because it regulated the whole production cycle of cement, cf. SGCAN, *Resolución 2019*, Judgment of 14 August 2018, para. 88.

[243] Note that this logic is applied with exceptions: The TJCAN found that a product-specific import restriction is not discriminatory if there is no domestic production of the banned good in the CAN Member State prohibiting it; cf. TJCAN, *02-AN-2015*, Judgment of 26 August 2016, para. 3.4.5. In line with the principle of neutrality, such a finding can only hold true if it is guaranteed that no domestic production of the prohibited good will be established in the aftermath of an import restriction. Given the fast pace in the adaptation to an ever-changing economic situation of a country, such a finding remains doubtful. Moreover, such a limited understanding of discrimination, i.e., by omitting a *de facto* analysis, is difficult to reconcile with the almost all-encompassing notion of trade restriction under Art. 72 AdC, which also addresses potential and hypothetical difficulties for the circulation of goods.

[244] In this context, the TJCAN speaks of the exhaustive and restrictive character of the envisaged exceptions. Original wording: "carácter taxativo (y restrictivo) de las excepciones previstas", cf. TJCAN, *01-AN-2014*, Judgment of 19 January 2017, para. 3.2.17.

[245] TCJAN, *125-AI-2004*, Judgment of 13 July 2006, p. 13.

standard of living of the inhabitants of the Subregion' pursued by the Cartagena Agreement."[246] (emphasis added)

Moreover, in several *resolutions* the SGCAN explicitly left open that trade-restrictive measures could be introduced for statistical purposes.[247]

5.4.2.3.2.3 Suitability of the Measure (Idoneidad, Causalidad de la Medida)

Trade-restrictive measures must be suitable to protect the legitimate objectives invoked for CAN member states to justify them successfully under Art. 73 AdC. Consequently, the measure must result in a higher protection thereof, as compared to the situation without the trade-restrictive measure. Without providing information on the suitability of a measure by the invoking CAN Member State, neither SGCAN and TJCAN were able to confirm that a trade-restrictive measure satisfies this requirement.[248]

Both the SGCAN and TJCAN argued that the notion of suitability[249] or causality,[250] or these two aspects combined,[251] originate from the general principle of proportionality, which applies in the context of Art. 73 AdC. The TJCAN held that

"according to the principle of proportionality between the restrictive measure and the specific purpose for which it [i.e., the measure] is intended, [the measure] must appear as a *direct and immediate cause* for the solution of the problems." (emphasis added)[252]

---

[246] Original wording: "que tales reglamentaciones internas tengan por finalidad garantizar objetivos de interés general *dignos de protección a la luz del Derecho comunitario*, como lo es *la protección del consumidor*, la cual, además de ser reconocida por las tradiciones constitucionales de los países de la Comunidad, también resulta congruente con la finalidad de 'procurar un mejoramiento persistente en el nivel de vida de los habitantes de la Subregión' que persigue el Acuerdo de Cartagena" (emphasis added), see SGCAN, *Resolución 759*, Judgment of 29 August 2003, p. 4.

[247] SGCAN, *Resolución 184*, Judgment of 29 January 1999, p. 4; SGCAN, *Resolución 407*, Judgment of 22 June 2000, p. 5; however, far more restrictive concerning measures for trade statistics, see SGCAN, *Resolución 638*, Judgment of 3 July 2002, p. 4.

[248] Cf. SGCAN, *Resolución 897*, Judgment of 4 February 2005, p. 4; SGCAN, *Resolución 1289*, Judgment of 11 November 2009, p. 19.

[249] Original wording: "idonéidad". For examples for the use of this term, see SGCAN, *Resolución 440*, Judgment of 9 October 2000, p. 3; SGCAN, *Resolución 449*, Judgment of 2 November 2000a, p. 5; SGCAN, *Resolución 047*, Judgment of 23 January 1998, p. 6.

[250] Original wording: "causalidad". Examples for the use of this term, see SGCAN, *Resolución 2019*, Judgment of 14 August 2018, para. 77; SGCAN, *Resolución 1289*, Judgment of 11 November 2009, p. 2; SGCAN, *Resolución 966*, Judgment of 20 October 2005, p. 6; SGCAN, *Resolución 1564*, Judgment of 14 April 2013, p. 4; SGCAN, *Resolución 1622*, Judgment of 15 November 2013, p. 2; SGCAN, *Resolución 823*, Judgment of 5 May 2004, p. 2; TCJAN, *125-AI-2004*, Judgment of 13 July 2006, p. 8.

[251] *Supra* note 517, at 3.4.14.

[252] Original wording: "en el principio de proporcionalidad entre la medida restrictiva y el objeto específico a que ella vaya dirigida, [. . .] [la medida] deberá aparecer como causa directa e inmediata para la solución de los problemas"; see SGCAN, *Resolución 1622*, Judgment of 15 November 2013, p. 17; reconfirmed in TJCAN, *02-AN-2015*, Judgment of 26 August 2016, para. 3.3.10–3.3.11.

The criterion of suitability is used to assess the causality or link between the legitimate objective allegedly aimed at and a measure's actual effects on trade.[253] Therefore, in order to rely successfully on Art. 73 AdC, a disputed trade-restrictive measure needs to identify products by defining properties that have a connection with the substantive content of the legitimate objective. These properties need to correspond with the legitimate objective that a trade measure is aimed at. Concerning, e.g., the protection of plant life and health, the SGCAN and TJCAN have found repeatedly that processed products are not able to produce a threat of proliferating agricultural diseases in live plants due to their distinct physical properties, which make them inactive for live plants due to their processing[254] (e.g., roasted coffee[255] and processed sugar).[256]

The concept of suitability does not remain limited to the characteristics of a good that might have a negative impact on the legitimate objective invoked. Additional aspects that are not directly included in the design of the trade-restrictive measure can also have an impact on the assessment of this criterion. In this context, the SGCAN assumed that the existing legislation establishing a specific market structure in a CAN Member State equally plays a role for the assessment whether a trade-restrictive measure can directly protect a legitimate objective. In the case of a measure regulating the import and sales of explosives in Ecuador, the SGCAN held that it could generally be justified under Art. 73 lit. c) AdC. Nevertheless, analyzed in conjunction with the Ecuadorian market structure on the sale of domestic explosives, the measure did not satisfy the requirement of suitability, because the domestic legislation did not contribute to the protection of the legitimate objective invoked. The sole establishment of a state monopoly for the sale of explosives was found not to protect human life and health sufficiently, making the provision unavailable as a justification for the trade-restrictive effect from the regulation of imported explosives.[257] Similarly, an Ecuadorian ban of imports of sulfuric acid—a chemical agent used for the extraction of alkaloids in coca leaves and, hence, essential for the production of cocaine—could not satisfy the requirement of suitability for the protection of human health by the SGCAN. In the view of the SGCAN, the measure solely aimed at reducing imports of sulfuric acid to Ecuador, without encompassing reductions of the domestic production. This created a

---

[253] Original wording: "vinculación", cf. SGCAN, *Resolución 184*, Judgment of 29 January 1999, p. 6.

[254] TJCAN, *43-AI-99*, Judgment of 13 October 2000, pp. 17–18.

[255] JUNAC, *Resolución 397*, Judgment of 18 March 1996; TJCAN, *3-AI-96*, 3-AI-96, Judgment of 24 March 1997.

[256] SGCAN, *Resolución 209*, Judgment of 24 March 1999; SGCAN, *Resolución 230*, Judgment of 21 May 1999; SGCAN, *Resolución 248*, Judgment of 8 July 1999; TJCAN, *43-AI-99*, Judgment of 13 October 2000.

[257] SGCAN, *Resolución 201*, Judgment of 15 March 1999, p. 3.

circumstance under which the trade-restrictive measure alone could not effectively diminish the overall availability of the restricted good.[258]

On the other hand, in cases in which the market structure of a CAN Member State did not affect the protection of a legitimate objective by a disputed trade-restrictive measure, any contribution to its protection was found sufficiently to fulfil this criterion. Confronted with a solely quantitative assessment of the SGCAN concerning import restrictions on CKDs (disassembled vehicles) by Ecuador, the TJCAN found such an approach inadmissible to verify a measure's suitability. Opposing the finding of the SGCAN that the reduction of only 3% of all greenhouse-gas emissions in Ecuador would not be sufficient to establish the suitability of a measure, the TJCAN held that any measure which contributing to the attainment of the legitimate objective, "however little its contribution",[259] would fulfil the test under the suitability requirement of Art. 73 AdC.

5.4.2.3.2.4 Proportionality and Irreplaceability of a Trade-restrictive Measure for the Protection of a Legitimate objective (Proporcionalidad, Insustituibilidad de la Medida)

Finally, a trade-restrictive measure needs to satisfy the criteria of proportionality and irreplaceability to rely successfully on Art. 73 AdC as a justification. The assessment involves a two-tiered test.

The first element involves an analysis of the availability of alternative, less trade-restrictive measures. TJCAN and SGCAN refer to it as the *proportionality test*. It serves to clarify whether a measure is "not excessive in relation to the purpose for which it is intended".[260] The identification of alternative measures is often accompanied by questions about the scientific state of the art and, accordingly, their

---

[258] SGCAN, *Resolución 308*, Judgment of 27 October 1999, p. 4. For a similar argumentation concerning the sale of explosives and the protection of human health, see SGCAN, *Resolución 681*, Judgment of 20 December 2002; SGCAN, *Resolución 739*, Judgment of 7 July 2003. It is imaginable that the domestic market structure could have played a role in other requirements under the test of Art. 72 AdC. The actual domestic-market situation and its relevance for the protection of the legitimate objective could likewise be treated under the availability of Art. 72 AdC for exclusively non-economic trade restrictive measures. The principle was deducted from the systemic overview of exceptions provided under the AdC and the differentiation between economic and non-economic justifications for trade-restrictive measures. In contrast to trade-restrictive measures that are introduced for alleviating a CAN Member State's economic hardship, such as BoP issues, safeguard measures, or countervailing duties, which allow for the preservation of domestic industries in order to counteract these economic pressures, Art. 72 AdC is reserved for non-economic reasons only, i.e., the preservation or protection of a legitimate objective. In this case, a measure aiming at the preservation of specific branches of the economy could not be regarded as non-economic. On the other hand, the exclusive ban of imports of a certain good could likewise be regarded as violating the non-discrimination obligation.

[259] TJCAN, *02-AN-2015*, Judgment of 26 August 2016, para. 3.4.19.

[260] Original wording: "que no resulte una medida excesiva respecto de la finalidad que persigue", see SGCAN, *Resolución 1289*, Judgment of 11 November 2009, p. 19.

technical feasibility or implementation.[261] Alternative measures suggested by the SGCAN have to constitute veritable substitutes to a disputed measure, referring to the same economic sector as the disputed measure does. In connection with an import restriction on CKDs (disassembled vehicles) into Ecuador, aimed at the protection of human health through the reduction of greenhouse gases, the TJCAN found that CAN member states can choose from a variety of measures suitable for protecting a legitimate objective. Alternative measures proposed by the SGCAN, such as setting up infrastructure for transportation through communal means of transport or bicycles, which equally have an impact on the reduction of greenhouse gases, were complementary at best. The alternative measures in the case would have to deal with "the use of automotive vehicles; otherwise, we could go into the absurdity of considering, as an alternative measure, that, for example, Ecuadorian citizens go on foot (walking) to their centers of work."[262]

The second element requires an inquiry into the level of protection achieved by the disputed measure. It is referred to as an *irreplaceability test* and serves to find, among "all the measures that can be taken to prevent damage [to the legitimate objective], [...] those that impose the lowest costs on the consumer and on subregional trade".[263] A measure is deemed irreplaceable if no other less trade-restrictive measures exist, which can attain at least the same level of protection of the legitimate objective in question. Identifying the least costly or invasive measure, however, is limited to the chosen level of protection by the respective CAN Member State.

> "In the absence of Community rules or in the absence of harmonization of the conditions of manufacture, marketing or consumption of certain products, the Member Countries are in principle competent to issue regulations aimed at preserving legitimately protected objectives, provided that such conditions of access to the market are not disproportionate to the aim pursued."[264]

Generally, the SGCAN and the TJCAN have found that penalty fees of 200% of the value of imports for the omission on import documentation were excessive,[265] without further explaining the threshold of excessive costs on free trade among CAN member states. Likewise, the SGCAN found that the prescription of a metal coating for batteries had an excessively limiting effect on CAN Member State trade,

---

[261] E.g., SGCAN, *Resolución 1289*, Judgment of 11 November 2009.

[262] Original wording: "La medida alternativa debe implicar el uso de vehículos automotores; de lo contrario, podríamos llegar al absurdo de considerar, como medida alternativa el que, por ejemplo, los ciudadanos ecuatorianos vayan a pie (caminando) a sus centros de trabajo. See TJCAN, *02-AN-2015*, Judgment of 26 August 2016, para. 3.4.30.

[263] SGCAN, *Resolución 1289*, Judgment of 11 November 2009, p. 19.

[264] Original wording: "Frente a la ausencia de una normativa comunitaria o ante la falta de armonización de las condiciones de fabricación, comercialización o consumo de determinados productos, los Países Miembros, en principio, son competentes para expedir reglamentaciones dirigidas a preservar fines legítimamente protegidos, siempre que tales condiciones de acceso al mercado no resulten desproporcionadas con el fin perseguido." See SGCAN, *Resolución 576*, Judgment of 12 December 2001, p. 4.

[265] Cf. TJCAN, *2-AN-98*, Judgment of 2 June 2000, pp. 10–11.

because any coating could not prevent the leakage of batteries, and thus the protection of human health at all.[266] On the other hand, the SGCAN likewise found that a measure introduced to promote dolphin-safe fishing was not demanding enough,[267] because its trade-restrictive requirements were kept in place for only several months of the year, creating too high a burden for trade among CAN member states.

According to the SGCAN and the TJCAN, the two-tiered test originates from a general *rule of reason* that is inherent to the application of General Exception Clauses, by referencing the decision of the CJEU in *Cassis de Dijon* and the Spanish legal textbook on EU law by *Honrubia et al.*[268] Both tests are complementary: Only the identification of an alternative, less trade-restrictive measure allows the inquiry into the quality of the level of protection and the evaluation whether it can be equally attained by such an alternative measure.

5.4.2.3.2.5 Irreplaceability

Under the irreplaceability test under Art. 73 AdC, the justification of trade-restive measures is limited to the one measure with the lowest impact on the free trade of goods among CAN member states.

The test for the irreplaceability of a measure thus needs to take into account a CAN Member State's chosen level of protection for a respective legitimate objective aimed at by the disputed trade-restrictive measure, compared against the identical level of protection achieved by other alternative, less-trade-restrictive measures. In this regard, a general principle cannot be given concerning the excessive interference of trade-restrictive measures, justified *a priori*, into the free trade in goods among CAN member states. However, TJCAN and SGCAN have found certain general

---

[266] SGCAN, *Resolución 1289*, Judgment of 11 November 2009, sec. D.3.

[267] SGCAN, *Resolución 986*, Judgment of 15 December 2005, p. 3.

[268] TJCAN, *3-AI-97*, Judgment of 8 December 1998, p. 27.: "Among Europeans, the way in which reasonableness is measured is conceived in terms of not arbitrary discrimination or a restriction on trade, which must meet three criteria: causality, proportionality and irreplaceability.

– The first criterion requires a cause-and-effect relationship between the regulation and the mandatory requirement.
– The second requires that the regulation be appropriate and not excessive in relation to the end pursued, and
– The Third, that there is no other means of achieving the same end. (García Enterría, p. 90)".

Original wording: "Entre los europeos la forma de medir la razonabilidad está concebida en términos de que no se trate de una discriminación arbitraria ni de una restricción al comercio, la que debe responder a tres criterios: el de causalidad, el de proporcionalidad y el de insustituibilidad.

– El primero exige la relación causa-efecto entre la reglamentación y la exigencia imperativa.
– El segundo que la reglamentación sea apropiada y no excesiva con respecto al fin perseguido, y
– El Tercero, que no exista otro medio de obtener el mismo fin. (García Enterría, pág. 90)"

Note, the TJCAN makes here reference to the work by Note that the TJCAN here makes reference to the work by Abellán Honrubia et al. (1986).

criteria that play a significant role in this consideration. In the context of measures introduced for statistical purposes, the TJCAN clarified that, even if statistical purposes constituted another legitimate objective under Art. 73 AdC, any trade-restrictive measure would certainly have to be below the level of excessiveness.[269] Consequently, a certain degree of trade-restrictiveness would be justified by such measures if all other requirements were fulfilled.

5.4.2.4   Liberalization of Trade in Goods Under Mercosur Rules

Liberalization of trade in goods in the Mercosur is governed by Annex I TdA, the TdA-TLP. It contains a reference in Art. 2 lit. b), second sentence TdA-TLP to Art. 50 TdM, which acts a General Exception Clause for the violations of the obligation stipulated under Art. 2 lit. b), first sentence TdA-TLP to eliminate all restrictions on Mercosur trade.

5.4.2.4.1   First Element: Prohibitions of All Restrictions on Trade Under Art. 2 lit. b) TDA-TLP

In opposition to the clearly-defined scope of Art. 2 lit. a) TdA-TLP, which encompasses duties and charges for customs enforcement, i.e., measures of a predominantly fiscal character, Art. 2 lit. b) TdA-TLP constitutes a subsidiary provision, covering all other restrictions on the *reciprocal trade* between Mercosur member states, including all remaining fiscal and additionally non-fiscal measures. In line with the distinction under Art. 2 TdA-TLP, Mercosur ad-hoc arbitral panels, examined under Art. 2 lit. b) TdA-TLP, measures both fiscal measures, such as antidumping duties,[270] safeguard measures,[271] and subsidies,[272] as well as non-fiscal measures, such as import licenses,[273] import bans,[274] and other measures that

---

[269] TJCAN, *2-AN-98*, Judgment of 2 June 2000, p. 10.

[270] Mercosur ad hoc arbitral panel (Brasília), Laudo "Aplicación De Medidas Antidumping Contra La Exportación De Pollos Enteros, Provenientes De Brasil, Resolución N° 574/2000 Del Ministerio De Economía De La República Argentina", Judgment of 21 May 2001.

[271] Mercosur ad hoc arbitral panel (Brasília), Laudo 'Aplicación De Medidas De Salvaguardia Sobre Productos Textiles (Res. 861/99) Del Ministerio De Economia Y Obras Y Servicios Publicos', Judgment of 2 March 2000.

[272] Mercosur ad hoc arbitral panel (Brasília), Laudo 'Subsidios a La Produccion Y Exportacion De Carne De Cerdo', Judgment of 27 September 1999.

[273] Mercosur ad hoc arbitral panel (Brasília), Laudo Arbitral "Controversia sobre Comunicados N° 37 del 17 de diciembre de 1997 y N° 7 del 20 de febrero de 1998 del Departamento de Operaciones de Comercio Exterior (DECEX) de la Secretaría de Comercio Exterior (SECEX): Aplicación de Medidas Restrictivas al Comercio Recíproco", Judgment of 28 April 1999.

[274] Mercosur ad hoc arbitral panel (Brasília), Laudo "Prohibición de Importación de Neumáticos Remoldeados (Remolded) Procedentes de Uruguay", Judgment of 9 January 2002.

allegedly restrict intra-PTA trade. On several occasions, ad-hoc arbitral panels have rigorously emphasized that under Mercosur law the duty to liberalize trade should be understood extensively, and derogations from it can only exist if they are expressly contained in the legal framework.[275]

Regarding non-fiscal trade-restrictive measures captioned by the TdA-TLP, Art. 10, first sentence TdA-TLP, Mercosur member states remain able to apply them partially throughout the trade-liberalization process. This provision establishes a moratorium on the introduction of new non-fiscal restrictions on trade, except for those contained under the Supplementary Notes to the Complementary Agreement of the Mercosur (ACE 18):[276]

> Until 31 December 1994, State Parties may apply to products covered by the relive schedule only those non-fiscal restrictions expressly stated in the Supplementary Notes to the Complementary Agreement to be concluded by the States Parties under the Treaty of Montevideo, 1980.

The provision contains two clarifications on how to operationalize the duty to eliminate non-fiscal trade-restrictive measures in the legal framework of Mercosur: On the one hand, a specific list of non-fiscal trade-restrictive measures contained in the ACE 18 allows the maintenance and imposition of specific and enumerated trade barriers. On the other hand, the obligation not to impose trade-restrictive measures extends only to the goods covered under the TdA-TLP and therefore does not prevent Mercosur member states from maintaining or introducing trade-restrictive measures for goods that are not covered under the relief schedule, such as those referred to in Art. 6 TdA-TLP. In the context of non-fiscal restrictions, pursuant to Decision 03/94,[277] Mercosur member states record and collect all non-fiscal restrictions on trade in specific lists, which is then used as a basis for their elimination or harmonization. According to Art. 2 of Decision 03/94, the process of harmonizing or eliminating these measures was supposed to be completed by 31 December 1994. And according to Art. 8 of Decision 03/94, the CMG is set as the authority supervising it.

Although the inscription of non-fiscal measures in this list might appear to have a legitimizing effect, the first ad-hoc arbitral panel set out that the trade-restive character of a measure depends on the kind of commitment made under Decision 03/94 by Mercosur member states either to eliminate or to harmonize a trade-restrictive measure. In the latter case, a finding of the CMG on a measure's trade-restrictiveness is required, which initiates its harmonization process.[278] Nonetheless, the same ad-hoc arbitral panel held that trade-restrictive measures, independently of

---

[275] Mercosur ad hoc arbitral panel (Brasília), Laudo "Aplicación De Medidas Antidumping Contra La Exportación De Pollos Enteros, Provenientes De Brasil, Resolución N° 574/2000 Del Ministerio De Economía De La República Argentina", Judgment of 21 May 2001, pp. 131–148.

[276] (1991) Acuerdo de Alcance Parcial - Complementación Económica 18.

[277] CMC Restricciones No Arancelarias Dec. 03/94.

[278] Mercosur ad hoc arbitral panel (Brasília), Laudo Arbitral "Controversia sobre Comunicados N° 37 del 17 de diciembre de 1997 y N° 7 del 20 de febrero de 1998 del Departamento de Operaciones de Comercio Exterior (DECEX) de la Secretaría de Comercio Exterior (SECEX): Aplicación de Medidas Restrictivas al Comercio Recíproco", Judgment of 28 April 1999, para. 38.

their status as listed or not, would nonetheless have to comply with the requirements of the General Exception Clause under Art. 50 TdM.[279]

Although the practice to list non-fiscal trade-restrictive measures continues to exist even after the envisaged end date under Decision 03/94, recent Mercosur legislation on this matter explicitly allows member states to use the PTA-DSM in case they are negatively affected by them.[280]

The remaining leeway to adopt non-fiscal trade-restrictive measures, resulting from Art. 10, first sentence TdA-TLP, is fully reduced by Art. 10, second sentence TdA-TLP, which provides for a full operationalization of the duty to eliminate non-fiscal barriers to trade by 31 December 1994, which was later amended within the course of the *Adaptation Program* to 31 December 1999:

> By 31 December 1994 all non-fiscal restrictions will be eliminated within the scope of the Common Market.[281]

Since this provision applies to the scope of the Common Market, and therefore not only to the goods covered under the TdA-TLP, Art. 10, second sentence TdA-TLP makes clear the obligation to eliminate *all* non-fiscal trade-restrictive measures on the entirety of trade in goods covered by the TdA-TLP after the lapse of the relief program.

Notwithstanding the very broad scope provided under Art. 2 lit. b) TdA-TLP, ad-hoc arbitral panels used it several times to claim the existence of a general principle of free trade among Mercosur member states.[282] They sustained the prohibition of any measure that 'unilaterally prevents or impedes reciprocal trade'. In this vein, the first ad-hoc arbitral panel found that Mercosur member states have the duty to eliminate all restrictions on trade within the ambit of Art. 2 lit. b) TdA-TLP with the lapse of the aforementioned date,[283] reconfirming the validity of the provision and its operability as of 31 December 1999.

The sixth ad-hoc arbitral panel added precision to the concept of non-fiscal trade-restrictive measures by showing awareness of the distinction between QRs and

---

[279] Ibid., para. 85(x).

[280] Cf. Art. 5 in CMC Restricciones no arancelarias Dec. 27/07.

[281] Original wording of Art. 10 TdA-TLP: Los Estados Partes sólo podrán aplicar hasta el 31 de diciembre de 1994, a los productos comprendidos en el programa de desgravación, las restricciones no arancelarias expresamente declaradas en las Notas Complementarias al acuerdo de complementación que los Estados Partes celebrarán en el marco del Tratado de Montevideo de 1980. Al 31 de diciembre de 1994 y en el ámbito del Mercado Común, quedarán eliminadas todas las restricciones no arancelarias.

[282] Original wording: "el principio de la libertad de comercio". Cf. Mercosur ad hoc arbitral panel (Brasília), Laudo "Aplicación De Medidas De Salvaguardia Sobre Productos Textiles (Res. 861/99) Del Ministerio De Economia Y Obras Y Servicios Publicos", Judgment of 2 March 2000, sec. H3, p. 28.

[283] Mercosur ad hoc arbitral panel (Brasília), Laudo Arbitral "Controversia sobre Comunicados N° 37 del 17 de diciembre de 1997 y N° 7 del 20 de febrero de 1998 del Departamento de Operaciones de Comercio Exterior (DECEX) de la Secretaría de Comercio Exterior (SECEX): Aplicación de Medidas Restrictivas al Comercio Recíproco", Judgment of 28 April 1999, para. 81.

MEQRs as developed in the doctrine of the CJEU.[284] Yet, this did not give rise to the ad-hoc arbitral panel to delve further into the doctrinal consequences resulting from this distinction, especially the application of the concept of *mandatory requirements*. Rather, the reference to both types of measures were used to underline the trade-restrictive character of the disputed measures in question, which was a plain import ban.[285] Equally, the trade-restrictive character of the measures and their qualification, as prohibited under the several provisions establishing the duty to eliminate restrictions in general, were predominantly the result of the ad-hoc arbitral panel's assessment, which refrained from categorizing the measures within a specific concept under the general notion of Art. 2 lit. b) TdA-TLP. The first ad-hoc arbitral panel issuing a decision on non-automatic import licenses,[286] the seventh ad-hoc arbitral panel dealing with import-registration duties for phytosanitary products,[287] the eleventh ad-hoc arbitral panel assessing an import ban on remolded tires from Uruguay,[288] and the twelfth ad-hoc arbitral panel dealing with a claim for omission to protect international routes from roadblocks by protestors in Argentina[289] did not find it necessary to distinguish further between the different types of restrictions

---

[284]Mercosur ad hoc arbitral panel (Brasília), Laudo "Prohibición de Importación de Neumáticos Remoldeados (Remolded) Procedentes de Uruguay", Judgment of 9 January 2002, pt. 3.1.b): "The time of the courts, the arbitrariness and unpredictability of the same, the alternatives in the presentation, and the duration of their practice have been so variable and of such an entity that the Ad-hoc Arbitration Court cannot fail to assess as an infringement of the provisions of Article 1 of the Treaty of Asunción the effectiveness of the restrictions resulting from all this for the freedom of movement of goods and services." Original wording: "El tiempo de los cortes; la arbitrariedad e imprevisibilidad de los mismos, las alternativas en la presentación y duración de su práctica han sido tan variables y del tal entidad que el Tribunal Arbitral Ad Hoc no puede dejar de valorar como infracción a lo establecido en el artículo 1 del Tratado de Asunción la efectividad de las restricciones resultantes de todo ello para la libertad de circulación de mercancías y servicios."

[285]Mercosur ad hoc arbitral panel (Brasília), Laudo "Prohibición de Importación de Neumáticos Remoldeados (Remolded) Procedentes de Uruguay", Judgment of 9 January 2002; TPR, Laudo N° 01/2005, Judgment of 20 December 2005; TPR, Laudo N°01/2006, Judgment of 13 January 2006; TPR, Laudo N°01/2007, Judgment of 8 July 2007; TPR, Laudo N°01/2008, Judgment of 25 April 2008.

[286]Mercosur ad hoc arbitral panel (Brasília), Laudo Arbitral "Controversia sobre Comunicados N° 37 del 17 de diciembre de 1997 y N° 7 del 20 de febrero de 1998 del Departamento de Operaciones de Comercio Exterior (DECEX) de la Secretaría de Comercio Exterior (SECEX): Aplicación de Medidas Restrictivas al Comercio Recíproco", Judgment of 28 April 1999, para. 21.

[287]Mercosur ad hoc arbitral panel (Brasília), Laudo "Obstáculos al ingreso de productos fitosanitarios argentinos en el mercado brasileño. No incorporación de las Resoluciones GMC N° 48/96, 87/96, 149/96, 156/96 y 71/98 lo que impide su entrada en vigencia en el MERCOSUR", Judgment of 19 April 2002, para. 9.4.

[288]Mercosur ad hoc arbitral panel (Brasília), Laudo "Prohibición de importación de neumáticos remodelados", Judgment of 25 October 2005, p. 53.

[289]Mercosur ad hoc arbitral panel (Olivos), Laudo "Omisión del Estado Argentino en adoptar medidas aprobadas para prevenir y/o hacer cesar los impedimentos a la libre circulación derivados de los cortes en territorio argentino de vías de acceso a los puentes internacionales GRAL. San Martín y GRAL. Artigas que unen la República Argentia con la República Oriental del Uruguay", Judgment of 6 September 2006; TPR, Laudo N°02/2006, Judgment of 6 July 2006.

encompassed under Art. 2 lit. b) TdA-TLP. Equally, the finding of the first ad-hoc arbitral panel that a mere transition to a computational system for the handling of import formalities was not a non-fiscal restriction on trade was delivered without any further legal argument.[290] Likewise, neither the twelfth ad-hoc arbitral panel nor the TPR tried to classify the trade-restrictive measures in question, instead holding that it amounted to a breach of the most general provision of Art. 1 TdA.[291]

5.4.2.4.2   Second Element: General Exception Clause Under Art. 50 TdM

The doctrine of Art. 50 TdM, which serves as a justification for measures falling within the scope of Art. 2 lit. b) TdM-TLP, remains mostly obscure, due to its relatively scarce use in front of the PTA-DSM of the Mercosur. Nonetheless, some general observations were made by several ad-hoc arbitral panels and the TPR, which help to identify the basic requirements for successfully relying on the justification.

In this regard, the appeal award by the TPR in the dispute concerning the *Argentine Importation Ban of Remolded Tires from Uruguay* is highly distinct from the first and seventh ad-hoc arbitral panel decisions, which equally dealt with the analysis of the General Exception Clause under Art. 50 TdM. Whereas the first and seventh ad-hoc arbitral panel decisions remained predominantly vague concerning a specific test on the legality of trade-restrictive measures under Art. 50 TdM, the TPR provided for an extensive and definite test under this provision, which explored all its requirements, even when the TPR found that the disputed measure in any case would not comply with the respective requirement under analysis. The TPR assumed an almost educational role and tried to lay the ground-work for the correct use of Art. 50 TdM in future Mercosur disputes.[292]

---

[290] Mercosur ad hoc arbitral panel (Brasília), Laudo Arbitral "Controversia sobre Comunicados N° 37 del 17 de diciembre de 1997 y N° 7 del 20 de febrero de 1998 del Departamento de Operaciones de Comercio Exterior (DECEX) de la Secretaría de Comercio Exterior (SECEX): Aplicación de Medidas Restrictivas al Comercio Recíproco", Judgment of 28 April 1999, para. 82.

[291] Mercosur ad hoc arbitral panel (Olivos), Laudo "Omisión del Estado Argentino en adoptar medidas aprobadas para prevenir y/o hacer cesar los impedimentos a la libre circulación derivados de los cortes en territorio argentino de vías de acceso a los puentes internacionales GRAL. San Martín y GRAL. Artigas que unen la República Argentia con la República Oriental del Uruguay", Judgment of 6 September 2006, para. 113.

[292] Cf. TPR, Laudo N°01/2005, Judgment of 20 December 2005, para. 10: "Unfortunately, the arbitral award under review does not contain any statement to that effect, much less fulfill its institutional role, which clearly consists, in such circumstances and in the face of a normative vacuum, of establishing a clear and concise jurisprudential criterion for such rigorous criteria and then applying them to the specific case."
Original wording: "El laudo arbitral en revisión no contiene lamentablemente ninguna aseveración en tal sentido, y mucho menos cumple su rol institucional que consiste claramente en tales circunstancias, ante un vacío normativo, en establecer un criterio jurisprudencia) claro y conciso de tales criterios de rigor para luego aplicarlos al caso concreto."

The first ad-hoc arbitral tribunal confirmed that the General Exception Clause under Art. 50 TdM, is available as a justification if a Mercosur Member State wishes to introduce or maintain trade-restrictive measures falling within the ambit of Art. 2 lit. b) TdA-TLP. Against the practice of Mercosur member states prescribed under Decision 03/94 above, the first ad-hoc arbitral panel stated that the inscription of non-fiscal trade-restrictive measures does not have a legitimizing effect for the existence of this admittedly trade-restrictive instrument. It held that the lists serve to establish whether Mercosur member states have committed to the elimination or harmonization of a specific trade-restrictive measure, thereby upholding the author- ity of the CMG to decide on its further administration.[293] Notwithstanding the inscription of a trade-restrictive measure in this list, the ad-hoc arbitral panel equally held that any trade-restrictive measure, whether listed therein or not, would still have to fulfill the requirements under Art. 50 TdM and would eventually have to be harmonized among the Mercosur member states.[294] In this vein, regarding secondary Mercosur legislation harmonizing specific policy areas between Mercosur member states, the seventh ad-hoc arbitral panel implied that Art. 50 TdM would most probably not be available as a justification if the harmonizing legislation was properly implemented by the respondent.[295]

Moreover, the dispute on *Argentine Importation Ban of Remolded Tires from Uruguay* brought further clarity on the dichotomy of the rule to liberalize trade and the exception to it, which emerges from the coexistence of Arts. 1 and 2 lit. b) TdA-TLP and Art. 50 TdM in the TLP. The eleventh ad-hoc arbitral panel held, in this dispute, that Mercosur's legal framework accommodated, on the one hand, the principle to liberalize trade due to the respective provisions and, on the other hand, a principle of environmental protection due to the availability of Art. 50 TdM.[296] Upon appeal, the TPR held that the eleventh ad-hoc arbitral panel erred in assuming

---

[293] Mercosur ad hoc arbitral panel (Brasília), Laudo Arbitral "Controversia sobre Comunicados N° 37 del 17 de diciembre de 1997 y N° 7 del 20 de febrero de 1998 del Departamento de Operaciones de Comercio Exterior (DECEX) de la Secretaría de Comercio Exterior (SECEX): Aplicación de Medidas Restrictivas al Comercio Recíproco", Judgment of 28 April 1999, para. 38.

[294] Ibid., para. 85(x).

[295] Mercosur ad hoc arbitral panel (Brasília), Laudo "Obstáculos al ingreso de productos fitosanitarios argentinos en el mercado brasileño. No incorporación de las Resoluciones GMC N° 48/96, 87/96, 149/96, 156/96 y 71/98 lo que impide su entrada en vigencia en el MERCOSUR", Judgment of 19 April 2002, para. 9.7: "Finally, the Tribunal fails to find the congruence between the invocation of the exception derived from the 1980 Treaty of Montevideo, with the prior acknowl- edgment by the Respondent of its obligation of incorporation and the assertion that Decree 4074/02 represents a first stage in the process of incorporation of the aforementioned regulations." Original wording: "Finalmente, el Tribunal no logra apreciar la congruencia existente entre la invocación de la excepción derivada del Tratado de Montevideo de 1980, con el previo reconocimiento por la Parte reclamada de su obligación de incorporación y con la afirmación que el decreto 4074/02 representa una primera etapa en el proceso de incorporación de la referida normativa."

[296] Mercosur ad hoc arbitral panel (Brasília), Laudo "Prohibición de importación de neumáticos remodelados", Judgment of 25 October 2005, para. 55.

a *general principle* of environmental protection provided by the Mercosur rules and also held that

> "There is only one principle (of free trade), to which certain exceptions can be put (such as the environmental exception mentioned above)."[297]

The TPR underlined that the provisions under Arts. 1 and 2 lit. b) TdA-TLP and Art. 50 TdM would not require weighing both allegedly existing principles against each other, but instead would have to assess whether recourse to the exception would be possible.[298]

Despite the decision of the first ad-hoc arbitral panel, which confirmed that Art. 50 TdM is available as a justification for trade-restrictive measures, this finding remained abstract, since it did not provide any precise legal analysis on how to assess the disputed non-automatic import licenses in question. Instead, the ad-hoc arbitral panel held in a general manner that Art. 50 TdM could be available as a justification, subject to the condition that the disputed non-automatic import licenses fulfilled the requirements set out in Art. 50 TdM.[299] Shortly after the installation of the TPR, on appeal of the eleventh ad-hoc arbitral panel assessing an import ban on remolded tires from Uruguay in *Uruguay v Argentina (11)*,[300] the TPR aimed at introducing precise requirements that needed to be fulfilled successfully in order for CAN member states to invoke Art. 50 TdM.

For this purpose, the TPR stressed the independent and restrictive character of the General Exception Clause under Art. 50 TdM.[301] In view of the ad-hoc arbitral-panel decision issued by the eleventh arbitral tribunal, which combined the analysis of the justification of the ban on tires in question by making reference not only to Art.

---

[297] TPR, Laudo N°01/2005, Judgment of 20 December 2005, para. 9. Original wording: "Existe un solo principio (el libre comercio), al cual se le pueden anteponer ciertas excepciones (como por ejemplo la excepción medio-ambiental aludida)."

[298] Ibid., para. 9. "Also, this TPR disagrees with the last part of the award under review of Number 55, where it stipulates that the Court will weigh the application of the mentioned principles in confrontation (free trade and environmental protection) defining the prevalence of one over the other [. . .]. This TPR understands that the issue discussed in question is whether or not the environmental exception is feasible under Mercosur law [. . .]."

Orignal wording: "Asimismo, este TPR no concuerda en cuanto a lo sostenido por el laudo en revisión en su última parte del Numeral 55 donde estipula que el Tribunal ponderará la aplicación de los mencionados principios en confrontación (libre comercio y protección de medioambiente) definiendo la prevalencia de uno sobre otro, [. . .]. Este TPR entiende que la cuestión debatida en autos es la viabilidad o no de la excepción medio-ambiental a tenor de la normativa mercosureña [. . .]."

[299] Mercosur ad hoc arbitral panel (Brasília), Laudo Arbitral "Controversia sobre Comunicados N° 37 del 17 de diciembre de 1997 y N° 7 del 20 de febrero de 1998 del Departamento de Operaciones de Comercio Exterior (DECEX) de la Secretaría de Comercio Exterior (SECEX): Aplicación de Medidas Restrictivas al Comercio Recíproco", Judgment of 28 April 1999, no. 85(x).

[300] Mercosur ad hoc arbitral panel (Brasília), Laudo "Prohibición de importación de neumáticos remodelados", Judgment of 25 October 2005, p. 53.

[301] TPR, Laudo N°01/2005, Judgment of 20 December 2005, paras 10; 17.

50 TdM, but also to the more general environmental agreement under the Rio Declaration, the TPR held that it

> "understands that the issue discussed in the question is whether or not the environmental exception is feasible under Mercosur and not under international law. In making this assertion the TPR is aware that notwithstanding the principles and provisions of international law are included in the Protocol of Olivos as one of the references (Art. 34), its application must always be only in the form of a legal subsidiarity (or at best complementarity) and only when applicable to the case. [It should be never applied] [. . .] directly and first, as it certainly corresponds to integration law (which Mercosur already has) as well as to a community law to which we aspire (which Mercosur does not yet have) due to the absence of the so longed for supranationality. In short, the law of integration has and must have sufficient autonomy from the other branches of law. Not considering this will always contribute in a negative way to the development of Mercosur's institutionality and regulations."[302]

Concerning the principle of restrictive reading of the General Exception Clause, the TPR defined that in

> "[. . .] the invocation of the exception in particular, first of all in integration law as well as in community law, whoever invokes an exception to free trade must prove it. Normatively, there is no legal body in Mercosur that clearly and concretely establishes the criteria of strictness to be analyzed for the invocation of such exceptions, which must always be interpreted with restrictive criteria. In this respect, we do not share the view of the Uruguayan representation granting them the status of authorizing legislation. Unfortunately, the arbitral award under review does not contain any assertion in this sense, much less does it fulfill its institutional role, which clearly consists in such circumstances, in the face of a normative vacuum, in establishing a clear and concise jurisprudence of such criteria of strictness and then apply them to the specific case."[303]

In the following, the TPR provided that a trade-restrictive measure would have to fulfill four specific requirements under Art. 50 TdM for a Mercosur Member State to rely on it successfully.[304]

---

[302] Ibid., para. 9. Original wording: "Este TPR entiende que la cuestión debatida en autos es la viabilidad o no de la excepción medio-ambiental a tenor de la normativa mercosureña y no a tenor del derecho internacional. Al hacer esta aseveración el TPR es conciente de que no obstante de que los principios y disposiciones del derecho internacional están incluidos en el Protocolo de Olivos como uno de los referentes jurídicos a ser aplicados (Art. 34), su aplicación siempre debe ser solo en forma subsidiaria (o en el mejor de los casos complementaria) y solo cuando fueren aplicables al caso. Nunca de manera directa y primera, como desde luego corresponde en un derecho de integración (que ya lo tiene el Mercosur) y en un derecho comunitario al cual se aspira (que todavía no lo tiene el Mercosur) por la ausencia de la tan anhelada supranacionalidad. En suma, el derecho de integración tiene y debe tener suficiente autonomía de las otras ramas del Derecho. El no considerar ello contribuirá siempre de manera negativa al desarrollo de la institucionalidad y normativa mercosureña."

[303] Ibid., para. 10.

[304] Note that the TPR speaks of *five* requirements in total, the first one being the legal analysis whether a measure constitutes a trade-restrictive measure. Cf. ibid., para. 14.

5.4.2.4.2.1 Non-Discriminatory Character of a Measure

According to the TPR, the initial requirement for a measure to be justified under Art. 50 TdM is its non-discriminatory character. By referring to the jurisprudence of the CJEU, the TPR used the case of *Commission v Austria*[305] to illustrate the importance of the criterion of non-discrimination for the invocation of a justification. In this referenced case, the CJEU did not find the measure to be discriminatory and classified it as an MEQR. On the other hand, the measure assessed by the TPR was a QR, because it established an import ban on remolded tires.[306] The TPR remained with this decision of the CJEU to demonstrate how to carry out a complete proportionality analysis under the respective General Exception Clause. It maintained that, even if the CJEU had decided that the measure was discriminatory, it would have had proceeded to the next requirement of the analysis.[307] In the case at hand, the TPR found the import ban of remolded tires to be directly discriminatory, as it affected only foreign products. Moreover, the TPR was inclined to underline that the discriminatory character of the measure certainly existed, in the words: "irrespectively of the fact that it affects not only Uruguay, but the whole world".[308] Finally, the TPR, stressing its strict understanding of the incompatibility of discriminatory measures with Art. 50 TdM, noted that:

> "[. . .] by deciding that the measure is discriminatory, this does also mean that the measure will not sustain."[309]

The introduction of the preliminary requirement for a measure to be non-discriminatory in order to be justified under Art. 50 TdM resulted in a very rigorous approach towards the design of measures that can be indeed justified under this provision.

---

[305] CJEU, *Commission v Austria*, C-28/09; ECLI:EU:C:2011:854, Judgment of 21 December 2011.

[306] The TPR left aside the differentiation between QRs and MEQRs under the legal framework and doctrine of the EU and disregarded that Art. 36 TFEU hypothetically would still be available even for import restrictions; cf. Reyes Tagle (2014), pp. 16–19.

[307] Cf. TPR, Laudo N°01/2005, Judgment of 20 December 2005, para. 15: "[. . .] but assuming that the CJEC agreed on the point in a different way, it would be appropriate to enter into an analysis of the following criterion of strictness". Original wording: "[. . .] pero aseveraba que si la TJCE concluía sobre el punto de manera diferente, correspondería entrar a analizar el siguiente criterio de rigor."

[308] Ibid., para. 15: "In our case, this TPR understands that the measure is directly discriminatory in that it affects only foreign products, irrespectively of the fact that it affects not only Uruguay, but the whole world."

Original wording: "En nuestro caso este TPR entiende que la medida es directamente discriminatoria por cuanto que afecta solo a productos extranjeros, no importando que no solo afecte al Uruguay sino a todo el mundo."

[309] Ibid., para. 15. Original wording: "Nótese que al decidir este TPR que la medida es discriminatoria, ello tampoco significa desde ya que tal medida no va a tener viabilidad."

5.4.2.4.2.2 Legitimate Objective Pursued by the Measure

As a second requirement, the TPR analyzed the availability of a "justification or not of the measure".[310] Under this point, it essentially asked whether the trade-restrictive measure aimed at one of the legitimate objectives enumerated under Art. 50 TdM. By citing the aforementioned jurisprudence by the CJEU which dealt with an MEQR, the TPR recognized that *mandatory requirements* could serve as a justification for a trade-restrictive measure.[311] Nevertheless, it did not further delve into the question of *mandatory requirements*, limiting itself to Argentina's argumentation that the measure was introduced to protect the environment—a concept that the TPR saw as "globally"[312] encompassed within the legitimate aim of protecting human, animal, and plant life and health under Art. Lit. d) 50 TdM.

To ascertain whether the import ban at issue was in fact aimed at these legitimate objectives, the TPR chose to examine the legislative background of the measure. It considered the genesis of the domestic law specifying the import ban, concluding that the measure was exclusively created to protect the national industry based on the considerations of the legislative process,[313] and holding that the measure would therefore not satisfy this second requirement.

5.4.2.4.2.3 Proportionality Analysis on the Invocation of Art. 50 TdM

The TPR continued to elaborate on the third criterion of the analysis under Art. 50 TdM, namely the proportionality of the measure "considering that any measure that obstructs free trade must always be evaluated with restrictive criteria".[314] In line with the doctrine available on the rules under the legal framework of the EU, it saw three criteria encompassed within the proportionality analysis, i.e., the analysis on the necessity of the measure, its proportionality, and the question whether less trade-restrictive measures existed, although it analyzed only the first and third criteria at this point.[315]

5.4.2.4.2.4 Necessity of the Measure

The TPR understood the necessity criterion as requiring an analysis on the measure's contribution to the pursued aim. This included an analysis of the actual impact of the measure on the protection of the alleged legitimate objective pursued. Accordingly,

---

[310] Ibid., para. 16.
[311] Ibid., para. 16, p. 8.
[312] Ibid., para. 8.
[313] Ibid., para. 16.
[314] Ibid., para. 17.
[315] Ibid., para. 17, p. 9.

the TPR found the measure not to satisfy the criterion of necessity: The specific ban on imported remolded tires did not reduce the actual negative impact on the environment, as waste tires remained allowed for import. In this context, the TPR found that the measure did not contribute to the reduction of environmental damage, given that it did not encompass both categories of waste and used tires, and therefore did not contribute to the actual protection of the environment. Moreover, the TPR held that, even if the precautionary principle was applicable, the measure still would not be proportionate, as "[. . .] the threat [resulting from the importation of remolded tires] is not serious or irreversible [. . .], assumptions that must be made for the application of the precautionary principle [. . .]".[316]

5.4.2.4.2.5   Least Trade-restrictive Measure Available for the Protection of the Legitimate Objective Invoked

Finally, under the third criterion on the choice of the least trade-restrictive measure to protect the legitimate objective invoked, the TPR carried out an analysis of its impact on intra-Mercosur trade and suggested alternative less trade-restrictive measures. At the initiative of Uruguay, the TPR was asked to consider at this point the AB report in *Korea – Beef*, which contained a balancing test, stating that "[. . .] the greater the contribution, the easier it will be to consider that the measure is necessary."[317] It concluded that the prohibition of imports of remolded tires was not the only measure for the protection of the environment available to Argentina. For this purpose, it considered the negative effects on the environment, resulting from the access of remolded tires to the domestic market of Argentina, by comparing the equivalence of imported domestic tires. The TPR held that foreign remolded tires were generally as safe as domestic tires, not leading to a greater negative impact on the environment than domestic ones. Based on this analysis, it suggested that both imported and domestic remolded tires were equally prone to turn into waste tires over time, which served as an argument to demonstrate the low contribution of the measure to the protection of the environment. The TPR suggested that Argentina's policy "should rather be oriented towards limiting and eliminating tires in waste",[318] in order truly to protect the environment, implying that such a design of the measure would have a lesser impact on intra-Mercosur trade. Confronted with Argentina's argument concerning a domestic constitutional duty that would only allow the prohibition of the importation of remolded tires, the TPR acknowledged that decision-makers are obliged "to implement the measures of the case responsibly, but from there to conclude that there is a constitutional duty to directly prohibit importation is too

---

[316] Ibid., para. 17. Original wording: "El daño no es grave ni irreversible (presupuestos éstos que se deben dar para la aplicación del principio precautorio)."

[317] Ibid., para. 17.

[318] Ibid., para. 17. Original wording: "Deberían estar más bien orientadas a la limitación y eliminación de los neumáticos en desecho."

great and insurmountable a discrepancy."[319] The TPR concluded that "national rules or practices do not fall within the scope of the exception specified in Art. 36 (now Art. 30) [annotation: of the Treaty Establishing the European Community, now Art. 36 TFEU] if the health and life of people can be protected equally effectively BY MEASURES THAT DO NOT RESTRICT INTRA-COMMUNITY TRADE' (capital letters are ours)[sic].", upholding the CJEU's stance on assessing the proportionality of a trade-restrictive measure under Art. 36 TFEU.[320]

5.4.2.5 Confirming the Equivalence of Doctrines Developed by PTA-DSMS on General Exception Clauses

Despite the differences in the wording of the provisions on the obligation to implement trade liberalization and the respective General Exception Clauses in the different PTAs, the reviewed PTA-DSMs have developed, in large parts, equivalent doctrines on their use and invocation. The reoccurrence of similar understandings and concepts on both elements of the rule to liberalize trade, and the exception to them in all relevant PTA-DSM decisions, confirms that all active PTA-DSMs have generally developed an equivalent understanding concerning the content of the respective General Exception Clauses. This equivalence allows us to identify diverging decisions in a setting of commonalities concerning the PTA-DSMs' legal reasoning on the General Exception Clauses.[321]

Although the PTA-DSMs' understandings of the respective General Exception Clauses overlap in great parts, they have not developed an *identical* doctrine on their content. This calls for a more profound analysis of their equivalence: All reviewed PTA-DSMs have developed and applied equivalent doctrines on non-fiscal trade-restrictive measures that reflect broadly the differentiation between QRs and MEQRs as developed and applied in the doctrine of the CJEU. However, more refined concepts involving MEQRs, such as the distinction concerning Certain Selling Arrangements, have not been echoed by all PTA-DSMs within the obligation of PTA partners to liberalize trade. Equally, the concept of *mandatory requirements* in the context of measures having a negative impact on intra-PTA trade, and those measures allowing their exemption from the scope of the obligation to liberalize trade, was completely omitted by the PTA-DSM of the CAN and accepted by the PTA-DSM of the Mercosur, but never put to practice by both of them.

---

[319]Ibid., para. 17. Original wording: "El deber constitucional resaltado por la representación argentina obviamente obliga a los tomadores de decisión a disponer responsablemente las medidas del caso, pero de ahí a pretender concluir que existe un deber constitucional de directamente prohibir la importación hay demasiada e insalvable distancia."

[320]Ibid., para. 18. Original wording: "'[. . .]Las normas o prácticas nacionales no entran en el ámbito de aplicación de la excepción que se especifica en el Art. 36 (actualmente Art. 30) si la salud y la vida de las personas pueden protegerse de forma igualmente efectiva CON MEDIDAS QUE NO RESTRINJAN EL COMERCIO INTRACOMUNITARIO' (las mayúsculas son nuestras)."

[321]*Supra* Sect. 4.1.

Simultaneously, the PTA-DSMs of the EU, the EFTA, the CAN, and the Mercosur have developed similar doctrines concerning the invocation of the respective General Exception Clauses by PTA partners. All reviewed PTA-DSMs developed a doctrine containing the concept of a proportionality analysis, which allowed further scrutiny of trade-restrictive measures installed by PTA partners. Equally, the proportionality analysis developed by the CJEU in the context of Art. 36 TFEU appears to have served in several instances as a blueprint for the doctrine developed by all other PTA-DSMs. Aspects restricting the successful invocation of the respective General Exception Clauses, such as assessing a trade-restrictive measure's causality for the prevention of a risk to a legitimate objective, the analysis of alternatives, less onerous measures, and the prohibition of excessive trade-restrictive measures, have been integrated in the doctrines of all PTA-DSMs under review. Yet, different orders of analysis and different emphases on the element of non-discrimination instead of the element of anti-protectionism have been adopted by them, equally calling for a more profound analysis of the equivalent understanding of these provisions by the reviewed PTA-DSMs.

In this context, the legal doctrines on the invocation of Art. 73 AdC, as developed by the PTA-DSM, of the CAN, and of Art. 50 TdM by the PTA-DSM of the Mercosur, have effectively narrowed down the scopes of the General Exception Clauses contained in these provisions for justifying trade-restrictive measures. This strong focus on the existence of non-discriminatory trade-restrictive measure appears to reflect a similar requirement established by the CJEU of *indistinctly* applicable measures necessary for the invocation of *mandatory requirements*. Equally, the restrictive understanding of the invocation of the General Exception Clause under the PTA-DSMs of the CAN and the Mercosur can be aligned with the requirements established under Art. 36, second sentence TFEU, which prohibits arbitrary and unjustifiable discrimination as a general principle of proportionality.

Ultimately, the different concepts involving aspects of non-discriminatory treatment under the respective General Exception Clauses demonstrate the different PTA-DSMs' efforts to define a *default level* of trade liberalization between PTA partners which does not lead to a complete deregulation of intra-PTA trade. These concepts involve aspects of non-discriminatory treatment of goods, while at the same time also containing elements that strive for granting market access for imported goods. This effort over the definition of a *default level* of trade liberalization is best understood by focusing on the costs resulting from domestic legislation having an impact on intra-PTA trade. Arguably, all the aforementioned elements depart from the aim of ensuring that the PTA partners' domestic legislation results in the *lowest possible costs* for intra-PTA trade.[322] In applying this standard of *lowest possible costs*, PTA-DSMs seem to have been balancing between an increasing

---

[322] On the difficulty of the exact determination of the market-access approach under the doctrine of the CJEU, cf. Barnard (2019), pp. 26–28; confirming the deregulatory pressure on domestic legislation under the concept of MEQRs, cf. Poiares Maduro (1998a), pp. 304–306; Snell (2010), p. 468.

deregulatory pressure on domestic legislation of PTA partners and the safeguarding of a certain margin of their regulatory autonomy. On the one hand, the broad concept of MEQRs established a *zero-cost* threshold for intra-PTA trade, since, "[i]f the law were to prohibit each and every hindrance to market access, it would as a matter of logic have to ban all rules limiting the commercial freedom of traders."[323] On the other hand, along with the realization that regulating economic activity always comes at some cost for intra-PTA trade, PTA-DSMs aimed at ensuring that only *reasonable costs* of domestic legislation on intra-PTA trade would be allowed under the obligation to liberalize trade. This is best exemplified in the doctrinal turn of the CJEU from *Dassonville* to *Cassis de Dijon* to *Keck*: It modified the benchmark on the negative impact of domestic regulation of intra-EU trade from *zero costs* to *reasonable costs* with the introduction of the concept of *mandatory requirements*, as well as a further differentiation of the *reasonable costs* with the introduction of a distinguishing factor for Certain Selling Arrangements. Apart from acknowledging that EU member states may have important non-economic, sociocultural values required by EU member states to maintain some regulation of the economic activity on their markets, a core element under the concept of *mandatory requirements* was to allow only domestic regulation to have an impact on intra-PTA trade if trade-restrictive measures applied *indistinctly*. The regulatory impact of domestic regulation was tied to the maximum effect on the PTA partners' domestic goods. Consequently, domestic regulation denying market access by establishing certain characteristics of imported goods was less likely to profit from the derogation established under the concept of *mandatory requirements* and would have to satisfy the criteria under the more restrictive General Exception Clause of Art. 36 TFEU. The CJEU created an incentive to adopt a domestic regulation focusing primarily on characteristics for market access, while at the same time creating an assumption that such a type of regulation would result in *reasonable costs* on intra-PTA trade. Therefore, indistinctly applicable trade-restrictive measures that generated *costs* on intra-EU trade were presumed to create *reasonable costs* and were not deemed to constitute MEQRs. To ensure that this was the case, the test for the effective protection of *mandatory requirements* contained rationality and proportionality criteria to allow the CJEU to decide effectively on the appropriate level of trade-restiveness of these indistinctly applicable measures, and consequently on the appropriate level of reasonable costs on intra-EU trade.

In light of these considerations on *reasonable costs* resulting from domestic regulation having a native impact on intra-PTA trade, the approach taken by the PTA-DSMS of the CAN and Mercosur appears equally understandable. It may have been developed to require from CAN and Mercosur member states the adoption of legislation that had an effect on intra-PTA trade, focusing primarily on market access, instead of denial thereof in equally encompassing characteristics necessary for the market access of domestic goods. The goal behind such a reading of the respective General Exception Clauses can ultimately be seen as allowing a

---

[323] Snell (2010), p. 468.

justification of trade-restrictive measures which only applies *indistinctly* to imported and domestic goods alike. This reflects the development of legal tests for *mandatory requirements* in the context of MEQRs by the CJEU on reasonable costs for intra-PTA trade. The preliminary requirement that a measure applies on a non-discriminatory basis necessarily includes a broader notion of its *indistinct* application. Parallel to the TJCAN and SGCAN, the Mercosur ad-hoc arbitral tribunals and the TPR have equally opted for such an understanding of the General Exception Clause under the invocation of Art. 50 TdM, effectively barring Mercosur member states from justifying distinctly applicable measures from the invocation of Art. 50 TdM.

Notwithstanding the equivalent rationale of both approaches towards the definition of *reasonable costs* resulting from domestic regulation having an impact on intra-PTA trade, the practices of the different PTA-DSMs on the invocation of specific legitimate objectives for the justification of trade-restrictive measures by PTA partners calls for another profound analysis of their equivalent understanding of the respective General Exception Clauses. In particular, the development of an unevenly permissive practice on the invocation of specific legitimate objectives could give rise to assume that the understandings of the PTA-DSMs on the invocation of the General Exception Clauses could not in fact be equivalent. The acceptance of *additional* legitimate objectives by PTA-DSMs in the context of the invocation of the respective General Exception Clauses could indicate their justification of trade-restrictive measures. PTA-DSMs allowing the invocation of a broader array of *additional* legitimate objectives may do this with the aim of weakening their obligation to liberalize trade. Such a fundamental difference in the understanding of the obligation to liberalize trade and the use of General Exception Clauses could speak for a lack of systemic operation of the seemingly equivalent rules. Facing the availability of *additional* legitimate objectives in the practice of the reviewed PTA-DSMs calls into question their uniform understanding of justifications within the adjudication of trade-restrictive measures.

Conversely, the development of a doctrine by different PTA-DSMs, which allows the invocation of *additional* legitimate objectives, confirms that certain policy objectives that are not formally covered by the original legitimate objectives under the respective General Exception Clauses are available for the justification of trade-restrictive measures. In this regard, the practice of the CJEU on the invocation of the generally open-ended *mandatory requirement*, in the same manner as a legitimate objective under the General Exception Clause, could indicate that it has become more lenient towards the spectrum of purposes for which trade-restrictive measures can be adopted by EU member states. It could have resulted in the general availability of *additional* legitimate objectives to justify trade-restrictive measures for EU member states in front of the CJEU, which would exist in addition to the original legitimate objectives enumerated under Art. 36 TFEU.

In contrast, it appears that the PTA-DSMs of the CAN and Mercosur have not integrated the doctrine of *mandatory requirements* within the concept of MEQRs; nor have they dissolved the differentiation between the different purposes of their use. Consequently, *additional* legitimate objectives should have remained less available to the CAN and Mercosur member states when litigating in front of their respective PTA-DSMs. Although both PTA-DSMs recognized the broad concept of MEQRs despite the lack of a textual basis under their PTA rules, they have not replicated the same openness for the concept of *mandatory requirements* as the CJEU or the EFTA Court. The PTA-DSM of the CAN reiterated several times that all domestic legislation making intra-CAN trade costlier required a justification under the General Exception Clause of Art. 73 AdC, maintaining a demanding standard of trade liberalization. At the same time, the SGCAN and the TJCAN have only allowed for a minimal broadening of the legitimate objectives under Art. 73 AdC, allowing only consumer protection to constitute a reason that could justify trade-restrictive measures.

At the backdrop of these difficulties of assuming the equivalent understanding of the respective General Exception Clauses of the reviewed PTA-DSMs, the analysis of all PTA-DSM decisions regarding the invocation of such *additional* legitimate objectives shows nevertheless that their respective understandings of the justification of trade-restrictive measures have not diverged for several reasons.

5.4.2.5.1   Effects of PTA-DSM Decisions on the Economies of PTA Partners, and Their Need to Rely on Justifications for the Existence of Trade-Restrictive Measures

The PTA-DSMs' understanding concerning the scope of the obligation to implement trade liberalization can compel PTA partners to rely on justifications to maintain trade-restrictive measures more frequently and/or for a broader array of policy reasons than provided under the respective General Exception Clauses. This may influence the PTA partners' frequency of invoking, *inter alia*, *additional* legitimate objectives in front of PTA-DSMs.

With more domestic regulation falling under the purview of judicial scrutiny of PTA-DSMs, which may be declared by them as unlawful, the PTA partners are required to terminate these trade-restrictive measures to comply with their obligation to liberalize trade and the corresponding PTA-DSM decisions. Successfully challenged domestic regulation in front of the respective PTA-DSM, which results in the duty to eliminate the trade-restrictive measures in dispute, reduces the existing economic protection of specific industries within the market of the PTA partners that have introduced them. After the termination of these trade-restrictive measures, the most effective producers of a specific industry among *all* PTA partners are given the opportunity fully to exploit their comparative advantage vis-à-vis the previously protected ones. As a result, the most effective producers offering goods at the most competitive conditions can gain market shares that were held by the producers of the formerly protected specific industries, through the existence of the subsequently terminated trade-restrictive measure within the market of a PTA-partner. In line with economic theory, unproductive producers of a specific industry would then become redundant, while the productive producers would prevail in this market. Given that this process releases labor as well as capital, the PTA-DSM decisions in which the invocation of the General Exception Clause becomes relevant can be regarded as having the potential to produce direct adjustment costs of trade liberalization for PTA partners. Unproductive producers become especially affected by the duty to terminate trade-restrictive measures, since their unproductive industries lose their former economic protection from the withdrawal of trade-restrictive measures, as required by the provisions on the effective implementation of trade liberalization.

Against this backdrop, a broad judicial purview of PTA-DSMs over domestic regulation ultimately translates into far-reaching economic effects for the PTA partners. A broader concept of the obligation to liberalize trade pursued by the PTA-DSMs generates their increased potential to generate adjustment costs due to the effective implementation of the trade liberalization process among the PTA partners in the aftermath of their decisions. Therefore, the PTA partners may have an increased interest in preventing adjustment costs from materializing,[324] and for this reason could try to justify the existence of trade-restrictive measures in their economies in front of the PTA-DSMs.[325] In judicial proceedings in front of the PTA-DSMs, this may result in the PTA partners relying more frequently on justifications to prevent the termination of the disputed trade-restrictive measures. Successfully justified, these measures would not have to be terminated and could therefore continue to grant economic protection to unproductive domestic industries.

This increased demand by PTA partners to justify trade-restrictive measures can manifest itself either in the use of General Exception Clauses, and consequently the invocation of the legitimate objectives contained therein. However, considering the limited number of legitimate objectives contained under the respective General Exception Clauses and the far-reaching economic consequences arising from the process of trade liberalization, the content of these provisions may prove to be insufficient for PTA partners to justify trade-restrictive measures they regard as essential for their economic well-being. Therefore, PTA partners may turn to advocating that PTA-DSMs equally accept supplementary policy objectives to justify the existence of the disputed trade-restrictive measures—alternatively to the ones contained under the respective General Exception Clauses.

Where PTA-DSMs find that trade-restrictive measures can be maintained because they aim at certain reasonable policy objectives, and where these policy objectives are supplementary to the policy objectives already contained in the respective General Exception Clauses, they can be classified as *additional* legitimate objectives. Reliance on these *additional* legitimate objectives by PTA partners effectively broadens the range of the justification for trade-restrictive measures beyond the policy objectives already contained under the respective General Exception Clauses. The invocation of these *additional* legitimate objectives equally prevents adjustment

---

[324]Cf. de Córdoba et al. (2006), pp. 68–69, concerning the different motives of policy-makers to prevent adjustment costs from materializing. This would correspond to relying on justifications of trade-restrictive measures in proceedings in front of PTA-DSMs.

[325] *Supra*, Sect. 2.3.1.2.

costs from materializing analogously to the effect resulting from the invocation of original legitimate objectives.

Ultimately, the broader a PTA-DSM's understanding of the concept of trade-restrictive measures is in a given case, the more important its understanding of the coverage of the respective General Exception Clause will become for PTA partners. Consequently, in response to the PTA partners' needs to maintain domestic regulations that have a negative impact on intra-PTA trade, PTA-DSMs may facilitate this and adjust their legal reasoning. Either they may simply confirm the successful invocation of the respective General Exception Clause by PTA partners, without an elaborate legal reasoning, or they may effectively broaden the scope of the respective General Exception Clause by means of interpretation, which results in the availability of *additional* legitimate objectives in a given case.

Depending on the type of the adjudicated measure, PTA-DSM decisions on the inconsistency of domestic policy with the obligation to liberalize trade in a PTA differ with regard to their potential to generate adjustment costs for PTA partners. In particular, the differentiation between QRs and MEQRs corresponds with a gradually increasing impact on a PTA-partner's economy, once the respective trade-restrictive measures are terminated: While QRs are easily identifiable as they limit the importation or exportation of goods to a specific numerical threshold onto a market, the economic impact resulting from their removal equally remains limited to the entry or exit of goods to and from their market. In particular, the removal of QRs does not interfere with domestic economic policy, which determines the specific structure and legal design of the domestic market, resulting in a certain protection of selected industries. Consequently, in terms of adjustment costs, the removal of QRs is easily calculable and already contemplated by PTA partners when negotiating a PTA.

By contrast, the removal of MEQRs has a greater economic impact on the structure and legal design of a PTA-partner's domestic market. Given that MEQRs go beyond the regulation of the importation or exportation of goods, but also include the organization of the domestic market, as well as the standards that apply therein, the elimination of MEQRs can have a qualitatively and quantitatively amplified economic impact due to the resulting high adjustment costs for PTA partners. The removal of MEQRs is typically equally agreed on in PTAs. However, the exact method leading to the removal of MEQRs is a matter of ongoing negotiation, for which PTA-DSMs play an important role.[326] As the identification of MEQRs is a predominantly normative undertaking, PTA-DSMs need to differentiate between trade-restrictive and trade-regulating measures, making MEQRs much less calculable concerning the adjustment costs they will generate once they are eliminated. The process of administrating this financial burden for the PTA partners requires the

---

[326]For the ongoing and steadily changing understanding of the market structure that is to be accomplished in the context of the EU and the role of the CJEU for this process, cf. Poiares Maduro (1998b). For an example of a more formalist process of the removal of MEQRs in the Mercosur context, *supra* Sect. 5.4.2.4.1.

PTA-DSMs to create an equally complex doctrine on the availability of *additional* legitimate objectives, which permits case-by-case decisions concerning the economic and political feasibility of cost distribution onto PTA partners.

The circumstance that PTA partners in some PTA-DSMs can successfully rely on *additional* legitimate objectives than in front of other PTA-DSMs therefore may not be a result of a respective PTA-DSM's permissive—and hence fundamentally different—understanding of the use of the General Exception Clause in the process of trade liberalization.[327] Rather, *additional* legitimate objectives become increasingly important within the legal reasoning in the context of the respective General Exception Clauses, the more frequently PTA-DSMs adjudicate MEQRs and therefore have the potential to generate high adjustment costs for PTA partners once they issue decisions demanding their termination. PTA-DSMs dealing more frequently with the adjudication of MEQRs may have an influence on the development of a practice accommodating the PTA partners' requests to maintain domestic regulation to strike a sensitive balance between their regulatory autonomy for certain policy objectives and the implementation of trade liberalization. The actual frequency and proportion of adjudication of measures with the potential of creating high adjustment costs in front of the reviewed PTA-DSMs may explain the general availability and the broader range of *additional* legitimate objectives for the PTA-DSMs when the PTA-DSMs have dealt with such measures on a large scale in the context of the respective General Exception Clauses. The range of available *additional* legitimate objectives possibly becomes broader once the PTA-DSMs deal more frequently with measures potentially generating high adjustment costs on a large scale.

To understand the invocation of the specific legitimate objectives better in the context of disputes involving the legal reasoning on the respective General Exception Clauses, every measure identified by the PTA-DSMs as being trade-restrictive can be classified according to its potential to generate high adjustment costs. Consequently, QRs are all those measures that restrict market access of goods numerically by providing an import ban or quotas. MEQRs are all those measures that do not possess these characteristics, but which nonetheless have been considered by the PTA-DSMs as trade-restrictive and generally required to be justified by the responsible PTA-partner. Given the different scopes of application of the reviewed PTAs, the invocation of each legitimate objective requires it to be counted for each specific good that was affected by a trade-restrictive measure. The actual frequency of PTA-DSMs dealing with *additional* legitimate objectives invoked for trade-restrictive measures and their potential impact on the respective PTA partners' economies can thus be better understood.

---

[327] See *supra*, at Sect. 2.2.2.

5.4.2.5.2   Analyzing the Availability of *Additional* Legitimate Objectives for PTA Partners in Decisions Regarding General Exception Clauses

The analysis of all PTA-DSM decisions containing a legal reasoning on the respective General Exception Clauses confirms that PTA-DSMs that were facing a high caseload of measures potentially generating high adjustment costs, namely falling into the category of MEQRs, have also dealt more frequently with the invocation of *additional* legitimate objectives. Considering that not all PTA-DSMs have dealt in the same frequency with measures potentially generating high adjustment costs, this has resulted in PTA-DSMs being less exposed to the invocation of *additional* legitimate objectives by PTA partners. Equally, due to the low activity concerning the adjudication of cases in which *additional* legitimate objects were invoked, these PTA-DSMs were less occupied with developing a legal doctrine on their successful use.

Beyond the PTA-DSMs' adjudicative performance regarding different types of trade-restrictive measures, the review of all successfully invoked *additional* legitimate objectives shows that their majority is thematically closely related to the original legitimate objectives already contained in the respective General Exception Clauses. Only few successfully invoked *additional* legitimate objectives have a truly novel character that could broaden the scope of the justification of trade-restrictive measures.

Furthermore, the analysis of the PTA-DSMs' legal reasoning on *additional* legitimate objectives confirms that they have generally been handling their invocation and successful use by PTA partners restrictively. In this regard, all PTA-DSMs dealing with *additional* legitimate objectives invoked in the context of General Exception Clauses have developed different mechanisms to limit the PTA partners' reliance on them.

5.4.2.5.2.1   *Varying Availability of* Additional *Legitimate Objectives in the Decisions of the Different PTA-DSMs*

On the one hand, the analysis of the PTA-DSM decisions shows that PTA partners in front of *all* reviewed PTA-DSMs have tried to rely on *additional* legitimate objectives in the context of the invocation of General Exception Clauses. PTA partners in front of all PTA-DSMs have attempted to argue that *additional* legitimate objectives could justify *a priori* trade-restrictive measures. Consequently, as Table 8.3 shows, all PTA-DSMs were confronted with attempts by the PTA partners to invoke *additional* legitimate objectives that were not explicitly contained in the respective General Exception Clauses.[328]

On the other hand, the data clarify that PTA-DSMs provided PTA partners with the opportunity to rely on *additional* legitimate objectives differently: Although the

---

[328] Cf. *infra* Sect. 8.2.4, Table 8.3.

PTA-DSMs of the EU, EFTA, and CAN allowed PTA partners to rely successfully on *additional* legitimate objectives, the distribution of successful invocations of *additional* legitimate objectives varies across the different PTA-DSMs, see Table 8.4.[329] While the CJEU has decided 61 times that EU member states could successfully rely on a total of twelve *additional* legitimate objectives, under the PTA-DSM of the CAN this was only possible three times—only for a total of two *additional* legitimate objectives, and only four times concerning one *additional* legitimate objective in front of the EFTA Court. The data demonstrate that, in general, EU member states have a broader array of *additional* objectives they can theoretically rely on when justifying trade-restrictive measures in front of the CJEU and, conversely, that the CJEU accepts more *additional* legitimate objectives to justify trade-restrictive measures *a priori*, compared to other PTA-DSMs.

5.4.2.5.2.2 Considering the Adjudication Record of PTA-DSMs Concerning Trade-restrictive Measures Generating High Adjustment Costs

Although it appears that there is a varying availability of *additional* legitimate objectives for PTA partners in front of the different PTA-DSMs, a closer look at the data clarifies that this varying availability depends on the individual PTA-DSMs' frequency in adjudicating trade-restrictive measures that have the potential to generate high adjustment costs for the respective PTA partners. The data at hand confirm the hypothesis, made above, on the importance of the invocation of *additional* legitimate objectives by PTA partners for justifying trade-restrictive measures in front of PTA-DSMs, given that their termination would generate high adjustment costs.

Consequently, the PTA-DSMs allow the successful recourse to *additional* legitimate objectives when their record on the adjudication of trade-restrictive measures shows a high frequency and proportion of such trade-restrictive measures. In line with this understanding, the frequency and portion of QRs and MEQRs of cases in which a justification was attempted to be invoked by PTA partners represents a good indicator for the adjudicative record of PTA-DSMs concerning trade-restrictive measures that potentially create high adjustment costs for PTA partners. Considering this indication, the overall frequency of PTA-DSMs adjudicating MEQRs vis-à-vis QRs, for which a justification was invoked by the respective PTA partners, is distributed unevenly. Equally, the overall proportion of MEQRs vis-à-vis QRs and the overall adjudication record of PTA-DSMs for which justifications were pleaded by a PTA-partner vary considerably:

Among all reviewed PTA-DSMs, the CJEU has the highest record of adjudicating invoked justifications for trade-restrictive measures. It adjudicated justifications for MEQRs 328 times and justifications for QRs 66 times. This amounts to a proportion of roughly 82.8% of justifications dealing with MEQRs, and 16.7% of justifications dealing with QRs (the remaining 0.5% accounting for measures that had no effect on

---

[329] Cf. *infra* Sect. 8.2.5, Table 8.4.

trade) in the adjudication record of the CJEU on the respective General Exception Clause. The PTA-DSM of the CAN adjudicated justifications for MEQRs 25 times, and justifications for QRs 12 times. This amounts to a proportion of roughly 68% of justifications dealing with MEQRs, and 32% of justifications dealing with QRs, in the adjudication record of the PTA-DSM of the CAN on the respective General Exception Clause. The PTA-DSM of the Mercosur adjudicated justifications for MEQRs three times and justifications for QRs twice. This amounts to a proportion of 60% in which the PTA-DSM of the Mercosur dealt with justifications for MEQRs, and 40% in which it dealt with QRs. Finally, the EFTA Court adjudicated justifications for MEQRs 16 times, and one justification for QRs. As Table 8.5 shows, this amounts to a proportion of 94% in which the EFTA Court dealt with justifications for MEQRs, and 6% of justifications for QRs.[330]

The uneven distribution in the frequency of the adjudication of justifications concerning MEQRs, as well as the proportion of justifications concerning MEQRs in the adjudication record of the reviewed PTA-DSMs, may serve as an explanatory backdrop towards understanding why the availability of *additional* legitimate objectives varies depending on the individual PTA-DSM under review. It shows that PTA-DSMs, specifically the CJEU, that were frequently facing the adjudication of justifications for trade-restrictive measures, whose elimination has a greater potential to generate high adjustment costs for PTA partners, have allowed for the successful recourse to *additional* legitimate objectives, as well as a broader range of the individual *additional* legitimate objectives. The performance of the reviewed PTA-DSMs regarding the adjudication of justifications for MEQR, as well as the potential of these measures to create particularly high adjustment costs, puts the development of doctrines permitting the invocation of *additional* legitimate objectives into perspective: While the CJEU developed its doctrine on *mandatory requirements* because it was confronted more often with the adjudication of justifications for MEQRs,[331] so far, this type of trade-restrictive measure simply has not appeared as frequently on the agenda of the PTA-DSMs of the CAN[332] and Mercosur.[333]

Bearing in mind the economic and political implications of adjudicating measures with the potential to create high adjustment costs, the data show that the PTA-DSMs' turning towards allowing the successful invocation of *additional* legitimate objectives in the context of General Exception Clauses did not happen inadvertently. Rather, the experience of a certain pressure to provide PTA partners with additional

---

[330]Cf. *infra* Sect. 8.2.6, Table 8.5.

[331]Originally, the doctrine of *mandatory requirements* did not technically allow a justification under Art. 36 TFEU regarding indistinctly applicable MEQRs that had a negative impact on intra-EU trade. The rising number of cases involving such trade-restrictive measures might have influenced the CJEU to elaborate and remain with its doctrine of *mandatory requirements*. On the other hand, a rising number of cases involving such trade-restrictive measures might have also contributed to the dilution of the differentiation between mandatory requirements and the legitimate objectives under the Art. 36 TFEU. Cf. also *supra* 5.4.2.1.1.2.

[332]Cf. *supra* Sect. 5.4.2.3.1.

[333]Cf. *supra* Sect. 5.4.2.4.2.2.

regulatory autonomy, especially in the domain of sociocultural reasons, for which a negative reasoning could provoke questions on the legitimacy of the decision by a non-domestic adjudicative body, adds an additional layer of information to the development allowing the parallel use of *mandatory requirements* by EU member states next to the original legitimate objectives under Art. 36 TFEU at the CJEU.[334]

Moreover, this link between the adjudication record on trade-restrictive measures, with the potential of creating high adjustment costs, and PTA-DSMs successfully allowing PTA partners to have recourse to *additional* legitimate objectives is confirmed by the data on the type of measure for successfully invoked *additional* legitimate objectives: Although the reviewed PTA-DSMs have also allowed the successful recourse to *additional* legitimate objectives in the context of General Exception Clauses for QRs, this remains rather a marginal phenomenon. In the practice of the CJEU, *additional* legitimate objectives could be invoked successfully for the justification of 54 MEQRs, while this was only the case for seven QRs. For the PTA-DSM of the CAN, successful invocation of *additional* legitimate objectives was possible for the justification of ten MEQRs, and none for QRs. For the EFTA Court, a successful invocation of *additional* legitimate objectives was available for the justification of three MEQRs, and none for QRs, see Table 8.6.[335]

5.4.2.5.2.3   Confirming a Restrictive Handling of Successfully Invoked Additional Legitimate Objectives by PTA-DSMs

Notwithstanding the development of a practice of some PTA-DSMs to allow PTA partners to rely successfully on *additional* legitimate objectives, the low availability of individual successfully invoked legitimate objectives, the restrictive legal reasoning, the PTA-DSMs' findings on *faux additional* legitimate objectives, and the few genuine *additional* legitimate objectives taking their novel character into account speak for an equivalent restrictive understanding of their invocation and the general purpose of justifications for trade-restrictive measures within the process of trade liberalization by all reviewed PTA-DSMs. These findings may discard the claim that some PTA-DSMs have developed a different understanding of the use of the respective General Exception Clauses indicated by accepting an increasing number of *additional* legitimate objectives that would correspond to a weakening of the obligation PTA partners to liberalize trade.

5.4.2.5.2.3.1   Low Total Amount of Successfully Invoked Additional Legitimate Objectives

The data on the successful invocation of *additional* legitimate objectives by PTA partners show that the number of successfully invoked individual *additional* legitimate objectives is much smaller than the number of those *additional* legitimate

---

[334] Cf. *supra* Sect. 5.4.2.1.2.
[335] Cf. *infra* Sect. 8.2.7, Table 8.6.

objectives PTA partners attempted to invoke PTA partners. The general list of *additional* legitimate objectives that PTA partners could successfully rely on in disputes involving the invocation of the respective General Exception Clause in front of the respective PTA-DSMs is substantially shorter[336] than the list of *additional* legitimate objectives they attempted to invoke.[337] While PTA partners attempted to invoke a total of 33 *additional* legitimate objectives, only twelve could be successfully relied on. The overview of all successfully invoked *additional* legitimate objectives confirms that PTA partners try to invoke a broader variety of

---

[336] The list contains twelve additional legitimate objectives in total that were pleaded successfully in front of the reviewed PTA-DSMs. They are classified for purposes of clarity, namely: justification on the grounds of **animal health** including the protection of animal welfare and conservation of biodiversity; **antitrust and fair competition reasons**, including the necessity of combating fraud/smuggling/tax evasion, ensuring the fairness of commercial transactions/fair trade/preventing excessive competitive advantages; justification of the protection of the **conformity of community rules**; justification of **protection of the culture**, including the necessity to protect the cinema as a cultural good; justification on the grounds of **protecting the environment and sustainability**; justification on the grounds of **specific health protection**, including the necessity of a measure for the protection of general health, public-health protection, and protection of roads or traffic safety; the justification of measures on the grounds of the **protection of fundamental rights**; the justification of measures on the grounds of **consumer protection**; as well as **non-specified reasons**.

[337] The list contains in total 33 additional legitimate objectives which are classified for purposes of clarity in certain thematical subfields (in bold), namely: justifications required due to the **administrative burden** resulting from the implementation of alternative measures; justification required for the **protection of the agricultural sector**, namely by safeguarding a common agricultural trade policy or the pasta sector, or by giving full effect to the common organization of the market in the cereals sector; justification due to **animal health**, namely on the grounds of the protection of animal welfare and the conservation of biodiversity and wild birds; justification due to **antitrust and fair competition reasons**, such as the necessity of combating fraud/smuggling/tax evasion, ensuring fiscal supervision and the fairness of commercial transactions/fair trade/preventing excessive competitive advantages; justification for the protection of the **conformity of community rules**; justification of **protection of the culture**, such as the necessity to protect the cinema as a cultural good, securing cultural expression and diversity; justification on the grounds of **economic interest**, such as the necessity to ensure the viability of an undertaking or securing the electrical supply of a country; justification on the grounds of **protecting the environment and sustainability**, such as the protection of animal welfare, the conservation of biodiversity, the protection of the environment, the prevention of pollution, and the protection of wild birds; justification on grounds of **specific health protection**, such as the necessity of a measure of the protection of consumer health, ensuring the quality of medicinal products, the protection of general health and public health, and the necessity to safeguard the public-health system; justification on the grounds of the **measurement of trade flows**, such as the necessity of a measure for statistical purposes or the measurement of trade flows; justification on the grounds of **specific protection of morality**, such as the necessity of a measure for the protection of minors; justification on the grounds of **observation of other obligations under public international law**, such as the necessity of a measure for the observation of other international agreements; justification of measures on the grounds of the **protection of fundamental rights**; justification of measures on the grounds of **consumer protection**, such as the necessity of a measure for the designation of the quality of a product; justification of a measure on the grounds of the protection of **road or traffic safety**; justification of a measure on the grounds of **safety considerations**, such as the necessity of a measure for combating crime; justification of a measure on the grounds of the **securing supply chains,** such as the necessity of a measure for securing the supply of goods at short distance, as well as **non-specified reasons**.

additional legitimate objectives than they can successfully rely on due to a restrictive handling of PTA-DSMs.

5.4.2.5.2.3.2 Restrictive Reasoning of PTA-DSMs Concerning the Availability of Additional *Legitimate Objectives*

PTA-DSMs do not accept lightly the invocation of *additional* legitimate objectives by PTA partners in the context of the respective General Exception Clauses. The data confirm that, in almost all decisions in which *additional* legitimate objectives were invoked by PTA partners, PTA-DSMs have employed methods entailing a restrictive reasoning to constrain their successful invocation. These restrictive methods have been either applied by PTA-DSMs in their legal reasoning regarding the availability of *additional* legitimate objectives, i.e., by clarifying whether a certain *additional* legitimate objective can be generally relied on by a PTA-partner, or regarding the assessment of the consequences, should an *additional* legitimate objective be available, i.e., by analyzing its impact on intra-PTA trade.

At the level of the availability of *additional* legitimate objectives, PTA-DSMs have resorted to additional reasoning or the reference to existing case law to confirm that PTA partners could rely on them as a justification for certain trade-restrictive measures.

While for some *additional* legitimate objectives PTA-DSMs have allowed their straightforward invocation and did not engage in an additional reasoning on their availability for PTA partners, for other *additional* legitimate objectives PTA-DSMs have resorted to a profound reasoning. In those instances in which the availability of the *additional* legitimate was discussed by PTA-DSMs, the quality of the reasoning varies regarding the argumentative effort that is carried out by PTA-DSMs to allow PTA partners to rely on them successfully. While PTA-DSMs occasionally resort to *additional* legal sources, international-law doctrine, or fundamental values contained in respective PTAs, other PTA-DSMs refer to the existence of case law which mandates their invocation by PTA partners.

Notwithstanding the different qualities of the reasoning concerning the availability of *additional* legitimate objectives, the apparent need for PTA-DSM to justify the existence of *additional* legitimate objectives speaks for a predominantly restrictive understanding of PTA-DSMs concerning their use by PTA partners.

For the most successfully invoked legitimate objectives, PTA-DSMs have carried out some reasoning on the *availability* of PTA-DSMs. In roughly 35% of the times of successfully invoked *additional* legitimate objectives, PTA-DSMs have argued that these were already covered by the wording of the respective General Exception Clause, see Table 8.8.[338] This practice, and its proportion among the successfully invoked *additional* legitimate objectives, testifies to the circumstance that the individual General Exception Clauses in PTAs contain general wording that can encompass a multitude of concepts concerning the legitimate objectives already contained

---

[338]Cf. Sect. 8.2.9, Table 8.8.

within. It demonstrates that the existing General Exception Clauses provide PTA partners and PTA-DSMs with generous flexibility to adapt their argumentation and reasoning to new factual developments echoed by a development of nuanced subdivisions already existing from the very outset of the original legitimate objectives.

The remainder of the times in which *additional* legitimate objectives were successfully invoked, PTA-DSMs engaged in a legal discussion on their availability for PTA partners outside the margins of the respective General Exception Clauses. In roughly 30% of the justifications involving the successful invocation of *additional* legitimate objectives, PTA-DSMs referenced case law to confirm their availability for PTA partners. This practice legitimizes the availability of *additional* legitimate objectives in the context of General Exception Clauses by indicating cases where such a necessity was already found to exist—in this context, the establishment of a practice of referencing cases in which the availability of a certain *additional* legitimate objective has already been confirmed. It increases the pressure on PTA-DSMs to resort equally to this method of referencing case law. Ultimately, it acts as another restrictive layer for PTA-DSMs to confirm the availability of *additional* legitimate objectives for PTA partners and testifies to the fact that PTA-DSMs remain particularly constrained when allowing their invocation. Consequently, the argumentative effort that is carried out by PTA-DSMs already at the level of the availability of *additional* legitimate objective results in another restrictive requirement that makes their successful use by PTA partners more difficult. Moreover, roughly 13% of the time PTA-DSMs engaged in a profound reasoning on the availability of the *additional* legitimate objective in question. By contrast, in roughly 21% of the justifications involving the successful invocation of *additional* legitimate objectives, PTA-DSMs did not engage in an additional argumentation for their availability.

Despite the considerable share of successful invocations of *additional* legitimate objectives for which PTA-DSMs did not engage in any additional argumentation on their availability, overall, the numbers above demonstrate that the PTA-DSMs do not automatically accept the availability of *additional* legitimate objectives in the context of the respective General Exception Clauses. If the instances in which the PTA-DSMs held that a successfully invoked *additional* legitimate objective was already covered by the respective General Exception Clause are disregarded, the PTA-DSMs have rather proven to entail at least some sort of reasoning for its availability over 69% of the times it was invoked by PTA partners.

Nevertheless, the comparison reveals that some PTA-DSMs have engaged in a profound legal reasoning to confirm the availability of *additional* legitimate objectives for PTA partners, while other PTA-DSMs have not. This is most apparent for the case of consumer protection in the practice of the PTA-DSMs of the CAN and the EU. The finding demonstrates that the PTA-DSM of the CAN made more argumentative efforts to arrive at the availability of consumer protection as a valid justification for trade-restrictive measures compared with the CJEU: At the request of Colombia and Peru, the SGCAN initiated investigations under *Resolution 759* on a Venezuelan labelling requirement that entailed minimum information on textile products that were to be permitted for marketing in Venezuela.[339] The label in textile products was required to contain minimum information on the Venezuelan national registration number of textile manufacturers and importers and the composition of fibers used for the labelled textile products as a percentage of the whole product. Moreover, the label was supposed to be affixed directly to the product in case of footwear, as well as during the manufacturing process. Moreover, it had to conform with a minimum size to ensure its legibility.

As Venezuela claimed to have introduced these measures for the purpose of protecting consumers, the SGCAN confirmed the availability of this *additional* legitimate objective with a view to the Venezuelan constitution (VenCon), which contained, in Art. 117 VenCon, a guarantee of the state to provide access to citizens for quality goods, as well as consumer information to ensure fair and decent execution of freedom of choice, but not under the General Exception Clause of Art. 73 AdC.[340] Moreover, the SGCAN reviewed the treaties establishing the CAN on its potential for the protection of consumers. It cited an array of different legal sources that would allow recourse to the *additional* legitimate objective of consumer protection by holding

> "that [...], as long as there is no Community norm on the matter, the Member Countries maintain their competence to issue regulations that affect imported and national products without distinction, to the extent that such internal regulations have the purpose of guaranteeing objectives of general interest worthy of protection in the light of Community Law, such as consumer protection, which, in addition to being recognized by the *constitutional traditions* of the countries of the Community, is also congruent with the *purpose* of 'procuring a persistent improvement in the standard of living of the citizens of the Subregion' *pursued by the Cartagena Agreement*, as well as with the *objectives of the Cartagena Agreement*, as well as with the *objectives of the Andean System of Standardization, Accreditation, Testing, Certification, Technical Regulations and Metrology*, among which is to promote 'the progressive improvement of the quality of products and services exchanged in international trade, and for the protection of health, safety, the environment and consumer protection' (third recital)." (emphasis added)[341]

---

[339] SGCAN, *Resolución 759*, Judgment of 29 August 2003.

[340] Translation of Art. 113 of the Venezuelan Constitution as cited by the SGCAN: "All persons shall have the right to have access to quality goods and services, as well as to adequate and non-deceptive information on the content and characteristics of consumer products and services, to freedom of choice, and to fair and decent treatment."

Original wording of Art. 113 of the Venezuelan Constitution, as cited by the SGCAN: "Todas las personas tendrán derecho a disponer de bienes y servicios de calidad, así como a una información adecuada y no engañosa sobre el contenido y características de los productos y servicios de consumo, a la libertad de elección y a un trato equitativo y digno, see ibid., p. 4.

[341] Original wording: "Que la Secretaría General considera que, siempre que no exista norma comunitaria en la materia, los Países Miembros mantienen su competencia para expedir reglamentaciones que afecten sin distinción a productos importados y nacionales, en la medida que tales reglamentaciones internas tengan por finalidad garantizar objetivos de interés general dignos de protección a la luz del Derecho comunitario, como lo es la protección del consumidor, la cual, además de ser reconocida por las tradiciones constitucionales de los países de la Comunidad, también resulta congruente con la finalidad de 'procurar un mejoramiento persistente en el nivel de vida de los habitantes de la Subregión' que persigue el Acuerdo de Cartagena, así como con los

Based on these considerations, the SGCAN proceeded with a proportionality analysis of the measures in question and found that, in general, a labelling requirement containing information on the producer of the textile product by means of a national registration number, subject to the condition of being automatically obtained and renewed by importing traders, could contribute to the goal of consumer protection.[342] In the consecutive non-compliance case against Venezuela, the TJCAN upheld the reasoning of the SGCAN. It did not call into question the elaborate argumentation of the SGCAN on the availability of consumer protection as an *additional* legitimate objective.[343]

By contrast, among the successfully invoked *additional* legitimate objectives of consumer protection in front of the CJEU, an equally elaborate argumentation for its availability is missing. As opposed to the reasoning provided by the SGCAN, the CJEU did not explain on which basis consumer protection would be applicable in the cases at hand, nor whether overarching values for its invocation were available. On several occasions, the CJEU did not engage at all in a profound argumentation on the availability of consumer protection as an *additional* legitimate objective.[344] Alternatively, the CJEU referred to case law establishing the availability of consumer protection.[345] The reference to *Cassis de Dijon* played a major role in four out of five cases for confirming the availability of consumer protection as a *mandatory requirement* that could act as a justification in the same sense as Art. 36 TFEU.[346] Yet, the argumentative efforts of both PTA-DSMs to confirm the availability of the *additional* legitimate objectives differ concerning the depth and extent.

The comparison of the CJEU decisions referencing *Cassis de Dijon,* as well as its decisions in *Cassis de Dijon* itself, with the mentioned CAN case shows that the

---

objetivos del Sistema Andino de Normalización, Acreditación, Ensayos, Certificación, Reglamentos Técnicos y Metrología, entre los cuales se encuentra propiciar 'la mejora progresiva de la calidad de los productos y servicios que se intercambian en el comercio internacional, y para la protección de la salud, la seguridad, el medio ambiente y la protección al consumidor' (tercer considerando)." Ibid., p. 4.

[342] Ibid., pp. 5–6.

[343] TCJAN, *125-AI-2004*, Judgment of 13 July 2006, para. 2.4(a).

[344] CJEU, *Criminal Proceedings v Wurmser and Others*, C-25/88; ECLI:EU:C:1989:187, Judgment of 11 May 1989; CJEU, *Spain v Council*, C-350/92; ECLI:EU:C:1995:237, Judgment of 13 July 1995; CJEU, *A-Punkt Schmuckhandels GmbH*, C-441/04; ECLI:EU:C:2006:141, Judgment of 23 February 2006.

[345] CJEU, *Denkavit Futtermittel*, C-39/90; ECLI:EU:C:1991:267, Judgment of 20 June 1991; CJEU, *Graffione*, C-313/94; ECLI:EU:C:1996:450, Judgment of 26 November 1996; CJEU, *Ko v De Agostini and TV-Shop*, C-34/95; ECLI:EU:C:1997:344, Judgment of 9 July 1997; CJEU, *ATRAL SA*, C-14/02; ECLI:EU:C:2003:265, Judgment of 8 May 2003.

[346] Regarding decision C-25/88, the reference is contained in para. 10 to decision C-120/78; regarding decision C-39/90, the reference is contained in para. 20 to decision C-73/84; regarding decision C-313/94 the reference is contained in para. 17 to decisions C-120/78, C-238/89, C-126/91, C-470/93; regarding decision C-34/95 the reference is contained in para. 46 to decision C-120/78; regarding decision C-14/02, reference is contained in para. 64 to decisions C-120/78, C-388/00, C-429/00.

CJEU did not engage in a profound argumentation on its availability. The decision in *Cassis de Dijon* does not contain any legal basis or superseding value that would allow confirmation of the availability of consumer protection as a *mandatory requirement* to be relied on before the CJEU.[347] The variation on the argumentative effort in the decisions of the two PTA-DSMs regarding consumer protection is noteworthy, considering that the CJEU developed an elaborate doctrine on *mandatory requirements* that gradually permitted their invocation as *additional* legitimate objectives. It reveals that the PTA-DSM of the CAN rather applies a very restrictive approach to the availability of *additional* legitimate objectives by refusing to introduce a general doctrine that could take the same permissive development as the concept of *mandatory requirements* developed by the CJEU. Instead by resorting to a profound argumentation on the availability of consumer protection as a justification, it has thereby signaled that its openness towards *additional* legitimate objectives would generally remain limited. Conversely, the PTA-DSM of the CAN provided much more information on the concept of consumer protection and the precise effects it would require from trade-restrictive measures to have to be successfully justified under this *additional* legitimate objective, namely the improvement of the quality and goods exchanged among CAN member states. The concept of consumer protection of the CJEU has remained much vaguer at the outset in *Cassis de Dijon*, and has only been refined over time, with more EU member states invoking it as a justification for trade-restrictive measures.

This comparison reveals the dimension of the PTA-DSMs' role as focal points for the discourse on available legislative and procedural action for PTA partners throughout the process of trade liberalization. The variations in the depth of legal reasoning of PTA-DSMs on the availability of *additional* legitimate objectives demonstrate that, even though identical *additional* legitimate objectives might be available under multiple PTA-DSMs, their adjudication can be used for different purposes even when the PTA partners can invoke them to justify trade-restrictive measures. While the PTA-DSMs might use their authority to introduce innovative concepts that are beneficial for the growth of the economies of PTA partners as a justification requirement in the context of the respective General Exception Clause,[348] they might equally use it when a general concept is readily disseminated among PTA partners, but different understandings on it exist that could subsequently hamper the process of trade liberalization. Accordingly, scholarly literature on the concept of consumer protection in the CAN member states suggests that it is not widely dispersed among CAN member states.[349] It might explain why the SGCAN felt urged to develop a profound argumentation on its availability. On the other hand, scholarly literature on the concept of consumer protection in the EU indicates that it

---

[347] CJEU, *Rewe v Bundesmonopolverwaltung für Branntwein*, 120/78; ECLI:EU:C:1979:42, Judgment of 20 February 1979, para. 8.

[348] Haupt (2003), pt. A, on the general economic beneficial effects of consumer protection; specifically on the role of consumer information for consumer protection, cf. Wein (2001).

[349] Rejanovinschi (2017), p. 266.

benefits from high acceptance in EU member states, but the understandings on its scope vary. It might explain why the CJEU did not have to contemplate on its availability, but rather on its application, which benefits the process of trade liberalization among EU member states the most by emphasizing the proportionality analysis for this purpose.[350]

5.4.2.5.2.3.3   Restrictive Reasoning by Means of Proportionality Analyses for Successfully Invoked Additional Legitimate Objectives

In complement to the general restrictive handling of PTA-DSMs on the availability of *additional* legitimate objectives, the PTA-DSMs have resorted to proportionality analyses to constrain their use by PTA partners when assessing the effects of their invocation for intra-PTA trade. Even in instances in which the PTA-DSMs have not resorted to a profound argumentation for the availability of *additional* legitimate objectives, in any case the PTA-DSMs have always additionally scrutinized their invocation.

The review of all successfully invoked *additional* legitimate objectives shows that all PTA-DSMs have introduced proportionality analyses to curtail further their use by PTA partners. Within the course of the proportionality analyses, PTA partners are required to substantiate the reasons why disputed trade-restrictive measures fulfil certain criteria on the protection of the invoked *additional* legitimate objective. In this regard, the argumentative requirements that PTA-DSMs have established to allow PTA partners to rely successfully on *additional* legitimate objectives vary, however, concerning their strictness and quality. The fact that such requirements are generally in place nevertheless confirms that the PTA partners are generally limited in relying on *additional* legitimate objectives in front of all PTA-DSMs, even in successful cases:

In roughly 77% of successfully invoked *additional* legitimate objectives, the PTA-DSMs have scrutinized one of the elements on the proportionality analysis, see Table 8.10.[351] Within this group, for roughly 77% of successfully invoked *additional* legitimate objectives the PTA-DSMs carried out an elaborate proportionality analysis and found that the disputed measure was proportionate and not excessive. This significant share of PTA-DSMs carrying out a profound proportionality test speaks again for their restrictive handling on the invocation of *additional* legitimate objectives.

For the remaining 23% of adjudication of trade-restrictive measures for which no proportionality analysis was carried out, the PTA partners could only rely successfully on the *additional* legitimate objective in question, because the measure was not

---

[350] Howells and Straetmans (2017).

[351] *Infra* Sect. 8.2.10, Table 8.9: Reasons for Success in Cases where Additional Legitimate Objectives, namely the data under the following reasons for the success: Measure proportionate/ not excessive; measure is necessary; measure does not discriminate arbitrarily and unjustifiably; measure does attain legitimate goal.

found to constitute insufficient action by the EU Council,[352] or for procedural reasons as the complainant had not produced sufficient information on the reasons why the measure would not be justified, thereby not satisfying its burden of proof.[353] The principal share of roughly 63% of adjudication for which no proportionality analysis took place contains legal reasoning of trade-restrictive measures in three cases adjudicated by the CJEU, for which the domestic courts had not provided sufficient information either on the violation of the rule to liberalize trade or on the justification of it.[354] In these three cases, which were brought to the CJEU in the context of preliminary proceedings, it held that generally the trade-restrictive measures could be justified only if certain factual assumptions about them were true. Consequently, domestic courts were mandated by the CJEU to reassess the cases, as laid out by it, in order to come to a genuine finding on their legality.

---

[352] CJEU, *Spain v Council*, C-350/92; ECLI:EU:C:1995:237, Judgment of 13 July 1995, para. 39. In this specific case, the CJEU assessed whether the EU Council had sufficiently taken into account consumer protection by adopting EU legislation that extended the patent protection on medicinal products, thereby making it more difficult for Spanish citizens to obtain generics at a more affordable price.

[353] Concerning Italian legislation that could have resulted in an import ban on cheese, because the EC did not provide information that the provision containing the ban was indeed set in motion by Italian authorities, cf. CJEU, *Commission v Italy*, C-95/89; ECLI:EU:C:1992:323, Judgment of 16 July 1992, para. 15; concerning a testing method for salmonella, as the EC could not provide information that a more lenient testing method was required to be prioritized based on scientific evidence, cf. CJEU, *Commission v Greece*, C-375/90; ECLI:EU:C:1993:154, Judgment of 27 April 1993, paras 22–25; concerning additional legitimate objectives, not further specified, as Colombia could not demonstrate that the Venezuelan measure was disproportionate, cf. SGCAN, *Resolución 453*, Judgment of 20 November 2000; concerning a ban on beverages containing caffeine, as the EC could not provide any contrary evidence to an opinion issued by a domestic health institute confirming such a risk, cf. CJEU, *Commission v France*, C-24/00; ECLI:EU:C:2004:70, Judgment of 5 February 2004, para. 70.

[354] Concerning an advertising ban on toys in Swedish television to protect minors from undue advertising, CJEU, *Ko v De Agostini and TV-Shop*, C-34/95; ECLI:EU:C:1997:344, Judgment of 9 July 1997, paras 46-47. Note, however, that the CJEU charged the domestic court with conducting a proportionality analysis on the ban; concerning the requirement to subject alarm systems to an analysis by a Belgian technical committee in order to be allowed for marketing in Belgium, CJEU, *ATRAL SA*, C-14/02; ECLI:EU:C:2003:265, Judgment of 8 May 2003. Note that the CJEU held that the testing requirement violated Art. 30 of the Treaty Establishing the European Community, now Art. 34 TFEU. It laid out to the domestic court that the EU Member State claiming the violation to be justified bears the burden of proof to demonstrate the existence of such a legitimate objective, which needed to be ascertained by it in the domestic proceedings; concerning the requirement to affix a temporary license for a car for being imported from Germany to Italy, CJEU, *Grilli*, C-12/02; ECLI:EU:C:2003:538, Judgment of 2 October 2003. Note that the CJEU mandated the domestic court to carry out an assessment on whether this measure affected exports negatively and therefore could contradict Art. 34 TFEU. Moreover, the CJEU held that such a measure could be justified under Art. 36 TFEU, but did not specify under which legitimate objective.

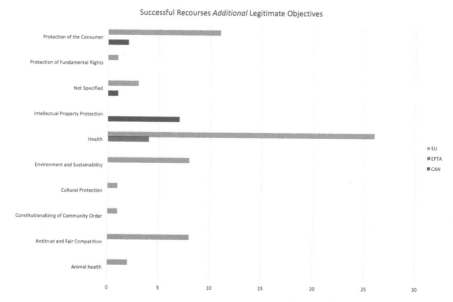

Fig. 5.8 Overview of Successful Recourses of PTA partners Concerning Individual Additional Legitimate Objectives. *Source*: Author's novel dataset

5.4.2.5.2.3.4   Low Success Rates for Invoked Legitimate Objectives

Considering the different adjudicative records on the invocation of *additional* legitimate objectives for the justification of trade-restrictive measures, the issue on whether PTA-DSMs have a different understanding concerning *all* legitimate objectives, i.e., those explicitly contained and those recognized over time, available under the respective General Exception Clauses again becomes relevant. The data on the successful invocation of legitimate objectives can serve again to confirm the general trend of restrictive handling of justifications by PTA-DSMs. They reflect he restrictive handling regarding *additional* legitimate objectives by PTA-DSMs. Considering *all* legitimate objectives, the reviewed PTA-DSMs have only restrictively allowed the PTA partners to rely successfully on justifications: Of the 347 occasions where legitimate objectives were invoked, their invocation was successful only 118 times. This average success rate of roughly 34% is approximately reflected in the adjudicative practice by each of the reviewed PTA-DSMs.

As Fig. 5.8 shows, the distribution of successfully invoked *additional* legitimate objectives, as we have already seen above for the general distribution of invoked legitimate objectives, varies depending on the reviewed PTA-DSM: Given that the CJEU has been the most active PTA-DSM in terms of its existence and overall adjudicative activity, successful cases can be found concerning all *additional* legitimate objectives. Due to the much lower adjudication records, and the much shorter time of being operational, the remaining two successful PTA-DSMs cases in these categories are equally less available, see Table 8.12.[355]

5.4.2.5.2.3.5 Findings on Faux Additional Legitimate Objectives as an Indicator for PTA-DSM Awareness of the Restrictive Handling of Justifications

Additionally, the findings of the PTA-DSMs on specific *additional* legitimate objectives that concluded that these are covered by the respective General Exception Clauses display their awareness to remain restrictive overall concerning the invocation of justifications for trade-restrictive measures. Concerning the awareness of a restrictive handling at the level of the availability of *additional* legitimate objectives, the CJEU and the EFTA Court have found that several formally different legitimate objectives were already covered by the respective General Exception Clauses.

Accordingly, the CJEU has held that the protection of biodiversity is encompassed under protection of animal life under Art. 36 TFEU, as the life of animals would be endangered if protected species were not saved.[356] Moreover, the view was that road safety falls under Art. 36 TFEU, most probably protecting human life and health.[357] Equally, the CJEU held that the designation of origin violated Art. 30 TFEU, but since it aimed at preventing fraudulent practices, it could not amount to an infringement of this provision, implicitly maintaining that this legitimate objective fell under Art. 36 TFEU, most probably protecting public safety.[358] Likewise, the CJEU held that the protection of the environment was encompassed by Art. 36 TFEU most probably protecting the life and health of humans and animals, considering the consequences resulting from its pollution.[359] Equally, the CJEU held on several occasions that the protection of public health was synonymous

---

[355] *Infra* 8.2.13, Table 8.12.

[356] CJEU, *Bluhme*, C-67/97; ECLI:EU:C:1998:584, Judgment of 3 December 1998, para. 33.

[357] CJEU, *Procureur De La République v Gofette and Gilliard*, C-406/85; ECLI:EU:C:1987:274, Judgment of 11 June 1987, para. 7.

[358] CJEU, *Commission v Belgium*, C-2/78; ECLI:EU:C:1979:128, Judgment of 16 May 1979, para. 45.

[359] CJEU, *Schreiber*, C-443/02; ECLI:EU:C:2004:453, Judgment of 15 July 2004, para. 47.

with the protection of human health under Art. 36 TFEU.[360] Conversely, the EFTA Court held that public-health protection is an aspect covered under Art. 13 EEA.[361]

5.4.2.5.2.3.6 *Few Genuine* Additional *Legitimate Objectives*

Finally, the comparison of the remaining *additional* legitimate objectives with the original ones contained in the respective General Exception Clauses shows that these are thematically closely related to the original legitimate objectives available under the respective General Exception Clauses. Only a marginal number of *additional* legitimate objectives can therefore be seen as innovative, and therefore as constituting *genuine additional* legitimate objectives.

The findings of PTA-DSMs on the *faux additional* legitimate objectives already indicates a general trend which suggests that most of the successfully invoked *additional* legitimate objectives are not novel. Rather, they constitute variations of original legitimate objectives. Consequently, the protection of animal welfare and conservation of biodiversity can be regarded as a variation of the protection of animal life and health. Equally, protection of road or traffic safety can be understood as a variation of the protection of human life and health. Approaching the individual, successfully invoked, *additional* legitimate objectives based on their content-related

---

[360] CJEU, *Solgar Vitamin's France and Others*, C-446/08; ECLI:EU:C:2010:233, Judgment of 29 April 2010, para. 55; CJEU, *Commission v Germany*, C-141/07; ECLI:EU:C:2008:492, Judgment of 11 September 2008, para. 46; CJEU, *Ahokainen and Leppik*, C-434/04; ECLI:EU:C:2006: 609, Judgment of 28 September 2006, para. 33; CJEU, *Schwarz*, C-366/04, Judgment of 24 November 2005, para. 32 although in this case the CJEU made a distinction between human health and public health but applied the same standard; CJEU, *Schreiber*, C-443/02; ECLI:EU: C:2004:453, Judgment of 15 July 2004, para. 47; CJEU, *Greenham and Abel*, C-95/01; ECLI:EU: C:2004:71, Judgment of 5 February 2004, para. 38; CJEU, *Commission v France*, C-24/00; ECLI: EU:C:2004:70, Judgment of 5 February 2004, para. 70; CJEU, *Gourmet International Products*, C-405/98; ECLI:EU:C:2001:135, Judgment of 8 March 2001, para. 34; CJEU, *Brandsma*, C-293/ 94; ECLI:EU:C:1996:254, Judgment of 27 June 1996, paras 9–10; CJEU, *LPO*, C-271/92; ECLI: EU:C:1993:214, Judgment of 25 May 1993, para. 10; CJEU, *Commission v Italy*, C-228/91; ECLI: EU:C:1993:206, Judgment of 25 May 1993, para. 17; CJEU, *Bellon*, C-42/90; ECLI:EU:C:1990: 475, Judgment of 13 December 1990, paras 13–14; CJEU, *Aragonesa De Publicidad Exterior and Publivía*, C-1/90; ECLI:EU:C:1991:327, Judgment of 25 July 1991, para. 13; CJEU, *Ministère Public v Mirepoix*, C-54/85; ECLI:EU:C:1986:123, Judgment of 13 March 1986, para. 6; CJEU, *Ministère Public v Muller*, C-304/84; ECLI:EU:C:1986:194, Judgment of 6 May 1986, para. 25; CJEU, *Heijn*, C-94/83, ECLI:EU:C:1984:285, Judgment of 25 April 1983, para. 8; CJEU, *Frans-Nederlandse Maatschappij Voor Biologische Producten*, C-272/80; ECLI:EU:C:1981:312, Judgment of 17 December 1981, para. 13; CJEU, *United Foods and Van Den Abeele v Belgium*, C-132/ 80; ECLI:EU:C:1981:87, Judgment of 7 April 1981, para. 25; CJEU, *Commission v Denmark*, C-158/82; ECLI:EU:C:1983:317, Judgment of 9 November 1983, para. 3.

[361] EFTA Court, *Tore Wilhelmsen AS and Oslo kommune*, E-6/96, Judgment of 27 June 1997, para. 111; EFTA Court, *Pedicel AS and Sosial- og helsedirektoratet (Directorate for Health and Social Affairs)*, E-4/04, Judgment of 25 February 2005, para. 55; indirectly EFTA Court, *Philip Morris Norway AS and The Norwegian State, represented by the Ministry of Health and Care Services*, E-16/10, Judgment of 12 September 2011, para. 85; EFTA Court, *Vín Tríó ehf. and the Icelandic State*, E-19/11, Judgment of 30 November 2012, p. 54.

proximity, this leaves a total of six types of novel *additional* legitimate objectives, namely measures introduced for antitrust and fair competition purposes encompassing the combating of fraud, smuggling, tax evasion, the ensuring of the fairness of commercial transactions, fair trading, and preventing excessive competitive advantages; measures constitutionalizing a PTA's legal order, which encompass the protection of the conformity of PTA rules; measures introduced for the protection of the culture encompassing the protection of the cinema as a cultural public good; measures introduced for the measurement of trade flows, which include the introduction of measures for statistical purposes; measures introduced for the protection of fundamental rights, which encompass the direct protection of specific fundamental rights and the protection of the diversity of the press as an outflow of the freedom of expression; measures introduced for the protection of the consumer; as well as measures introduced for unspecified purposes. Especially the last type of novel *additional* legitimate objectives surfaced mainly due to procedural reasons or constraints of PTA-DSMs to ascertain factually the disputes about trade-restrictive measures.[362] Equally, the protection of the environment is treated here as an additional and novel legitimate objective due to the variety of specific goods it might be invoked for, ranging from the protection of human health to the protection of animal health.

5.4.2.5.2.3.7 Overall Restrictive Handling of Remaining Legitimate Objectives

Finally, as already confirmed regarding successfully invoked *additional* legitimate objectives, the PTA-DSMs generally handle successfully invoked original legitimate objectives restrictively. Their legal reasoning covered aspects of the proportionality analysis for nearly all successfully invoked legitimate objectives. The CJEU in particular conducted a profound proportionality test in roughly 82% of all times that legitimate objectives were invoked by EU member states.

The practice of the PTA-DSM of the CAN is slightly less evident due to a much lower frequency of adjudication. For 62.5% of times when legitimate objectives were successfully invoked, the PTA-DSM of the CAN carried out a proportionality analysis. Nevertheless, this constitutes the majority of the times legitimate objectives have been successfully relied on by PTA partners and equally sustains the restrictive handling of legitimate objectives by this PTA-DSM.

As already found above in the context of *additional* legitimate objectives, only in rare instances have PTA-DSMs decided that PTA partners can invoke original legitimate objectives successfully without any further analysis: It is mainly due to procedural reasons that the complaining party has not produced enough evidence that a measure would in fact be trade-restrictive,[363] or that a measure would not

---

[362] *Supra* Sect. 5.4.2.5.2.3.3.

[363] CJEU, *Commission v Italy*, C-95/89; ECLI:EU:C:1992:323, Judgment of 16 July 1992; CJEU, *Commission v Greece*, C-293/89; ECLI:EU:C:1992:324, Judgment of 16 July 1992; CJEU, *Commission v France*, C-344/90, Judgment of 16 July 1992.

protect the legitimate objective as effectively as it was claimed by the responding party.[364] In this context, the generally broad regulatory autonomy of PTA partners concerning the protection of human and animal health, which included their right to determine the appropriate level of protection, as reiterated by PTA-DSMs on several occasions, was essential for the CJEU to abstain from conducting a proportionality analysis in one instance.[365]

Another reason for PTA-DSMs not to engage in any kind of proportionality analysis for successfully invoked legitimate objectives appears to be the restricted availability of information on the disputed measure in question. In this context, the decisions on the successful invocation of a legitimate objective are very broad. They generally confirm that a justification of a measure would be possible, but only under the condition that the measure be designed in fact as assumed by the PTA-DSM.[366]

5.5 Conclusion

The general activity of all PTA-DSMs that have issued decisions on the respective General Exception Clauses of the different PTAs has remained very low. Only four PTA-DSMs have been active in this legal domain so far, namely the PTA-DSMs of the EU, EFTA, CAN, and Mercosur. Moreover, the review of the activity of PTA-DSMs issuing decisions on the respective General Exception Clauses shows that the distribution of cases on these provisions varies to a great extent and speaks

---

[364] Concerning an Ecuadorian import ban on disassembled automobiles, which the TJCAN found to protect the environment, as the ban would contribute to a general lower number of cars being available and driven in Ecuador. The SGCAN did not provide sufficient alternative measures that could have proven the measure as not attaining the legitimate objective as effectively, TJCAN, *02-AN-2015*, Judgment of 26 August 2016, para. 3.4.25–3.4.35.

[365] Cf. a French regulation concerning safety requirements for wood-working machines, establishing a de-facto obligation to equip these with a high level of automation devices. France argued that this requirement ensured a low level of manual interaction and resulted in the protection of human health by reducing bodily injuries to persons operating these machines. The EC could not demonstrate that other less automated approaches to the operation of wood-working machines would be equally capable of attaining the level of health protection chosen by French legislation, CJEU, *Commission v France*, C-188/84; ECLI:EU:C:1986:43, Judgment of 28 January 1986, paras 10–23.

[366] Concerning a Dutch measure introducing minimum requirements for raising and keeping breeding calves, according to the TJEU, the measure already did not constitute an export restriction. The TJEU nevertheless held that it would be allowed under Art. 36 TFEU for the protection of animal life and health, encompassed by this provision, CJEU, *Holdijk*, C-141/81; ECLI:EU:C:1982:122, Judgment of 1 April 1982; in the case of Colombian restrictions on the importation of vehicles for public transport, the TJCAN held that whether the measure was a restriction needed to be declared by the SGCAN, upholding the procedural authority of the agency in this regard. Moreover, it held that a justification based on the grounds of protecting human health was generally possible, but provided only general remarks, TJCAN, *241-IP-2015*, Judgment of 12 June 2017, para. 3.5-3.8.

for a different development of their adjudication within the different PTA contexts. A comparison of the ordinary meaning of the respective General Exception Clauses, including the obligation to liberalize trade among the PTA partners, as well as the doctrines established by the PTA-DSMs in response to the PTA partners' invocation of the respective General Exception Clauses, confirms the equivalence of these provisions. The acceptance of *additional* legitimate objectives for the justification of trade-restrictive measures by PTA-DSMs does not call into question the equivalence of these provisions. On the contrary, PTA-DSMs that have experienced a high frequency of litigation involving trade-restrictive measures with a potential to generate high adjustment costs from trade liberalization correspondingly have allowed the PTA partners to rely on these *additional* legitimate objectives. Nevertheless, this has not given rise to a more permissive approach of the PTA-DSMs concerning the obligation to liberalize trade due to the availability of *additional* legitimate objectives for their justification. Instead, most of the successfully invoked *additional* legitimate objectives have been understood by PTA-DSMs as falling within the ambit of the original legitimate objectives under the respective General Exception Clauses. This testifies to the broad language used in these provisions, which can encompass a multitude of concepts under the original legitimate objectives contained therein. More specifically, this has resulted in only very few genuine *additional* legitimate objectives to be available for the justification of trade-restrictive measures in front of the reviewed PTA-DSMs, supporting the general observation of the PTA-DSMs' restrictive handling of the respective General Exception Clauses. Moreover, the PTA-DSMs have demonstrated a restrictive practice in the adjudication of these *additional* legitimate objectives, given their low success rates and the inclusion of various elements of a proportionality analysis for their invocation. As a result, the PTA-DSMs' equivalent understandings of the respective General Exception Clauses successfully serve to establish a setting of commonalities for the analysis of their decisions regarding their *incommensurability* by identifying *recurring case groups*.

References

Abellán Honrubia V, García de Enterría E, García EA (1986) Tratado de derecho comunitario europeo : (estudio sistematico desde el derecho espanol). Ed. Civitas, Madrid

Alter KJ, Helfer LR (2017) Transplanting international courts: the law and politics of the Andean Tribunal of Justice, 1st edn. Oxford University Press, Oxford

Alter KJ, Meunier-Aitsahalia S (1994) Judicial politics in the European Community: European Integration and the Pathbreaking Cassis de Dijon Decision. Comp Polit Stud 26:535–561. https://doi.org/10.1177/0010414094026004007

Alter KJ, Helfer L, McAllister JR (2013) A new international human rights court for West Africa: the ECOWAS community Court of Justice. Ame J Int Law 107:737–779. https://doi.org/10.5305/amerjintelaw.107.4.0737

Appleton AE (1997) GATT Article XX's Chapeau: A Disguised Necessary Test: The WTO Appellate Body's Ruling in United States -Standards for Reformulated and Conventional Gasoline. Rev Eur Comp Int Environ Law 6:131–138

Armingeon K, Milewicz K, Peter S, Peters A (2011) The constitutionalisation of international trade law. In: Cottier T, Delimatsis P (eds) The prospects of international trade regulation. Cambridge University Press, Cambridge, pp 69–102

Barents R (1981) New development in measures having equivalent effect. Common Mark Law Rev:271–308

Barnard C (2019) The substantive law of the EU. Oxford University Press, Oxford

Barnard C, Peers S (eds) (2020) Table of equivalences. In: European Union Law, 3rd edn. Oxford University Press, Oxford

Bartels L, Paddeu F (eds) (2020) Exceptions in international law, 1st edn. Oxford University Press, Oxford

Baudenbacher C (2005) The implementation of decisions of the ECJ and of the EFTA Court in Member States' domestic legal orders. Tex Int Law J 40:383–416

Baur G (2020) The European Free Trade Association: an intergovernmental platform for trade relations. Intersentia, Cambridge

Baur G, Rydelski MS, Zatschler C (2018) European Free Trade Association (EFTA) and the European Economic Area (EEA), 2nd edn. Kluwer Law International B.V., Den Haag

Berry DS (2014) Caribbean integration law, 1st edn. Oxford University Press, Oxford

Björnsson T (2013) Inside and outside the EFTA Court: evaluating the effectiveness of the EFTA court through its structures. Israel Law Rev 46:61–93. https://doi.org/10.1017/S0021223712000295

Castro Bernieri J (2003) El Comercio Intracomunitario y el Mercado Común Andino. In: Derecho comunitario andino. Fondo Editorial PUCP, Cercado de Lima, pp 117–141

Craig PP (2011) Institutions, power and institutional balance. In: Craig P, de Búrca G (eds) The evolution of EU law. Oxford University Press, Oxford, pp 41–84

Craig PP, De Búrca G (2015) EU law: text, cases, and materials, 6th edn. Oxford University Press, Oxford

Danilenko GM (1998) The economic court of the commonwealth of independent states symposium issue: the proliferation of international tribunals: piecing together the Puzzle. New York Univ J Int Law Polit 31:893–918

de Córdoba SF, Laird S, Maur J-C, Serena JM (2006) Adjustment costs and trade liberalization. In: Laird S, de Córdoba SF (eds) Coping with trade reforms: a developing country perspective on the WTO industrial tariff negotiations. Palgrave Macmillan UK, London, pp 66–85

Dolcetti A, Ratti GB (2020) Derogation and defeasibility in international law. In: Bartels L, Paddeu F (eds) Exceptions in international law. Oxford University Press, Oxford, pp 108–124

Dragneva R (2018) The case of the economic court of the CIS. In: Ulfstein G, Ruiz-Fabri H, Zang MQ, Howse R (eds) The legitimacy of international trade courts and tribunals. Cambridge University Press, Cambridge, pp 286–313

Franch VB (2006) Los procedimientos para la solución de controversias en el Mercosur. Agenda Internacional XII:261–294

Fredriksen HH (2010) One market, two courts: legal pluralism vs. homogeneity in the European economic area. Nordic J Int Law 76:481–500

Fuders F (2010) Economic Freedoms in MERCOSUR. In: Franca Filho MT, Lixinski L, Olmos Giupponi MB, Toscana M (eds) The law of Mercosur. Hart, Oxford

Gathii JT (2018) The COMESA Court of Justice. In: Ulfstein G, Ruiz-Fabri H, Zang MQ, Howse R (eds) The legitimacy of international trade courts and tribunals. Cambridge University Press, Cambridge, pp 314–348

Haupt S (2003) An economic analysis of consumer protection in contract law. German Law J 4:1137–1164. https://doi.org/10.1017/S2071832200012013

Howells G, Straetmans G (2017) The interpretive function of the CJEU and the interrelationship of EU and national levels of consumer protection. Persp Federalism 9:E-180–E-215. https://doi.org/10.1515/pof-2017-0014

Howse R (2012) 20. Regulatory Measures. In: Narlikar A, Daunton MJ, Stern RM (eds) The Oxford handbook on the World Trade Organization. Oxford University Press, Oxford, pp 441–457

Kanellakis M, Martinopoulos G, Zachariadis T (2013) European energy policy—a review. Energy Policy 62:1020–1030. https://doi.org/10.1016/j.enpol.2013.08.008

Klumpp M (2013) Schiedsgerichtsbarkeit und Ständiges Revisionsgericht des Mercosur: Integrationsförderung durch zwischenstaatliche Streitbeilegung und Rechtsprechung im Mercosur. Springer, Berlin

Kurtz J (ed) (2016) Common exceptions and derogations. In: The WTO and international investment law: converging systems. Cambridge University Press, Cambridge, pp 168–228

Lazo RP, Sauvé P (2018) The treatment of regulatory convergence in preferential trade agreements. World Trade Rev 17:575–607. https://doi.org/10.1017/S1474745617000519

Lenaerts K, Maselis I, Gutman K, Nowak JT (2014) EU procedural law, 1st edn. Oxford University Press, Oxford

Malamud A (2010) Theories of regional integration and the origins of MERCOSUR. In: Filho MTF, Lixinski L, Olmos Giupponi MB (eds) The law of MERCOSUR. Hart, Oxford, pp 9–27

Maletić I (2013) The law and policy of harmonisation in Europe's internal market. Edward Elgar Publishing, Cheltenham

O'Keefe TA (2000) The Central American Integration System (SICA) at the Dawn of a New Century: will the Central American Isthmus finally be able to achieve economic and political unity? Florida J Int Law 13:243–262

Pauwelyn J (2005) Rien ne Va Plus – distinguishing domestic regulation from market access in GATT and GATS. World Trade Rev 4:131–170

Pelc KJ (2016) Making and bending international rules: the design of exceptions and escape clauses in trade law. Cambridge University Press, Cambridge

Perišin T (2008) Free movement of goods and limits of regulatory autonomy in the EU and WTO. T.M.C. Asser Press, Den Haag

Pétursson GT (2018) Article 11 [Quantitative restrictions on imports and measures having equivalent effect] Quantitative restrictions on imports. In: Agreement on the European Economic Area, A Commentary. Nomos Verlagsgesellschaft mbH & Co. KG, München, pp 289–299

Piérola Castro NFN (2006) Solución de diferencias ante la OMC: presente y perspectivas. Cameron May, London

Pizzolo C (2010) Derecho e integración regional: Comunidad Andina, Mercosur, SICA, Unión Europea, 1st edn. EDIAR, Buenos Aires

Poiares Maduro M (1998a) The Saga of Article 30 EC treaty: to be continued. Maastricht J Eur Comp Law 5:298–316

Poiares Maduro M (1998b) We the court: the European Court of Justice and The European economic constitution. Hart Publishing, Oxford

Possi A (2018) An appraisal of the functioning and effectiveness of the East African Court of Justice. PER 21:1–42. https://doi.org/10.17159/1727-3781/2018/v21i0a2311

Raygada PSL (2003) Libre comercio de bienes en la Comunidad Andina - Eliminación de gravámenes y restricciones. Derecho & Sociedad 302–311

Reich N (2017) Francovich enforcement analysed and illustrated by German (and English) Law. In: Jakab A, Kochenov D (eds) The enforcement of EU law and values. Oxford University Press, Oxford

Rejanovinschi M (2017) Hacia la protección del consumidor en la comunidad andina. Anuario de Investigación del CICAJ 2016

Reyes Tagle Y (2012) Free movement of goods in the Andean community: how far can Dassonville go? SSRN Electron J. https://doi.org/10.2139/ssrn.2618403

Reyes Tagle Y (2014) The free movement of goods in MERCOSUR: developing a European Court of Justice approach in MERCOSUR? SSRN Electron J. https://doi.org/10.2139/ssrn.2618408

Reyes Tagle Y (2018) El impacto de la jurisprudencia del Tribunal de Justicia de la Unión Europea en la definición del principio de libre circulación de mercancías en la Comunidad Andina y el Mercosur. Agenda Internacional 25:235–256. https://doi.org/10.18800/agenda.201801.012

Roberts A, Stephan PB, Verdier P-H, Versteeg M (2018) Conceptualizing comparative international law. In: Roberts A, Stephan PB, Verdier P-H, Versteeg M (eds) Comparative international law. Oxford University Press, New York, pp 3–31

Rojas Penso P (2004) Nuevas Perspectivas Para La Solución De Controversias En La Asociación Latinoamericana De Integración (ALADI). In: Conference on International Trade Dispute Settlement, Lacarte Muró JA, Granados J (eds) Solución de controversias comerciales intergubernamentales: enfoques multilaterales y regionales. Instituto para la Integración de América Latina y el Caribe (BID-INTAL), Buenos Aires

Sasaki Otani MÁ (2012) El sistema de sanciones por incumplimiento en el ámbito de la Comunidad Andina. Anuario Mexicano de Derecho Internacional 1. https://doi.org/10.22201/iij.24487872e. 2012.12.400

Sauvé P (2019) To fuse, not to fuse, or simply confuse? Assessing the case for normative convergence between goods and services trade law. J Int Econ Law 22:355–371. https://doi. org/10.1093/jiel/jgz022

Siems M (2018) The comparative legal method. In: Comparative law. Cambridge University Press, Cambridge, pp 15–49

Skouris V (2005) The ECJ and the EFTA Court under the EEA agreement: a paradigm for international cooperation between judicial institutions. In: The EFTA court: ten years on. Hart Publishing, Oxford, pp 123–129

Snell J (2002) Goods and services in EC law: a study of the relationship between the freedoms, 1st edn. Oxford University Press, Oxford

Snell J (2010) The notion of market access: a concept or a slogan? Common Mark Law Rev 47: 437–472

Susani N (2010) Dispute settlement. In: Filho MTF, Lixinski L, Olmos Giupponi MB (eds) The law of MERCOSUR. Hart, Oxford

Talavera FN, Carias ARB, Bernieri JC et al (2003) Derecho comunitario andino. Fondo Editorial - Pontificia Universidad Católica del Perú - Instituto de Estudios Internacionales, Cercado de Lima

Waltermann A, Arosemena G, Hage J (2020) Exceptions in international law. In: Bartels L, Paddeu F (eds) Exceptions in international law. Oxford University Press, Oxford, pp 11–34

Weiler JHH (ed) (2001a) Cain and Abel—convergence and divergence in international trade law. In: The EU, the WTO, and the NAFTA: towards a common law of international trade? Oxford University Press, Oxford, pp 1–4

Weiler JHH (ed) (2001b) Epilogue: towards a common law of international trade. In: The EU, the WTO, and the NAFTA: towards a common law of international trade? Oxford University Press, Oxford, pp 201–222

Wein T (2001) Chapter 4. Consumer information problems – causes and consequences. In: Grundmann S, Kerber W, Weatherill S (eds) Party autonomy and the role of information in the internal market, 1st edn. De Gruyter, Berlin

Wennerås P (2017) Making effective use of Article 260 TFEU. In: Jakab A, Kochenov D (eds) The enforcement of EU law and values. Oxford University Press, Oxford

Chapter 6
Results on the Role of PTA-DSMs for the Fragmentation of International Trade Law

Held against the claims presented under the *predominantly formalist* approach to international trade law, the review of PTA-DSMs decisions issued in the context of the respective General Exception Clauses paints a counterintuitive picture of the fragmentation of international trade law. Already at the outset, an inquiry into the *incommensurability* of PTA-DSMs decisions on the respective General Exception Clauses proves very difficult, due to the scarcity of *recurring case groups* adjudicated by more than one of them. This finding speaks for a highly particularized development of trade liberalization within PTAs and a corresponding varying activity of PTA-DSMs, which adjudicate selected trade matters only. So far, this has generally prevented the assumed normative tensions on equivalent rules on international trade to emerge because of PTA-DSMs activity.

Beyond this observation, the very few *recurring case groups* that have been dealt with by more than one PTA-DSM do not allow us to conclude that they are *incommensurable*. On the one hand, different procedural practices of the reviewed PTA-DSMs preclude us from finding precise information on the disputed trade-restrictive measures, as well as on the factual backdrop leading to the invocation of the General Exception Clauses in the issued decisions. The remaining few decisions that contain a sufficient quality of information allowing an inquiry into their *incommensurability* show that PTA-DSMs mostly have arrived at the same conclusions when scrutinizing the same trade-restrictive measures in the light of the same legitimate objectives. Yet, differences in their legal reasonings exist and reflect their different standings in the institutional structure established by the respective PTAs.

Finally, to ascertain the future of the fragmentations of international trade law, a review of the PTA-DSMs' referencing practices suggests that the decisions of the CJEU have exerted a considerable influence on the reasoning of all other PTA-DSMs so far. Even if eventually the activity of all active PTA-DSMs should converge, meaning that they would adjudicate uniformly the same types of trade-restrictive measures in the context of the same legitimate objectives, the referencing

© The Author(s), under exclusive license to Springer Nature Switzerland AG 2023
P. Wasilczyk, *Fragmentation of International Trade Law Reassessed*, EYIEL
Monographs - Studies in European and International Economic Law 32,
https://doi.org/10.1007/978-3-031-40601-0_6

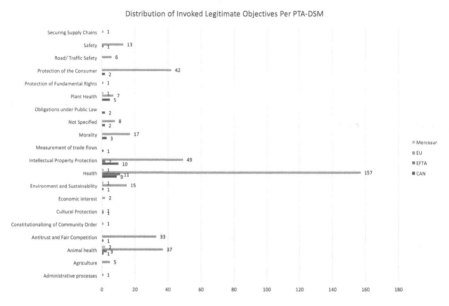

Fig. 6.1 Distribution of Invoked Legitimate Objectives Per PTA-DSM. Source: Author's novel dataset

practice of all PTA-DSMs has made the CJEU a focal point for the development of their legal reasoning in cases involving the invocation of the respective General Exception Clauses. It can be assumed that the establishment of the legal reasoning of the CJEU as a reference point for other PTA-DSMs will act to a certain extent as a bulwark against their issuing of *incommensurable* decisions in the future.

6.1   Scarcity of *Recurring Case Groups* Indicating the Absence of Any Systemic Operation of Substantively Equivalent PTA Provisions

There are only very few *recurring case groups* which have been adjudicated across multiple PTA-DSMs. Their existence is rather the exception than the rule. These few *recurring case groups* have been adjudicated by the PTA-DSMs generally regarding highly invoked legitimate objectives by PTA partners, namely health protection, the measurement of trade flows, the protection of public morality, and consumer protection and safety, see Fig. 6.1. Concerning all other legitimate objectives, only certain PTA-DSMs have been adjudicating corresponding cases to a varying extent. Therefore, the remaining adjudicative records of PTA-DSMs do not contain cases that share globally common characteristics. This prevents us from making an assessment on the *incommensurability* of the corresponding PTA-DSM decisions.

6.2 Analysis of Incommensurability of PTA-DSM Decisions on *Recurring Case Groups*

A more detailed analysis of the caseload of the reviewed PTA-DSMs shows that the lack of *recurring case groups* indeed has partially been caused by the practice of PTA-DSMs to permit PTA partners to invoke *additional* legitimate objectives successfully in the context of the General Exception Clause, i.e., for policy objectives that are formally not contained under the legitimate objectives of the respective General Exception Clauses.

The PTA-DSMs' practice allowing the PTA partners to invoke a justification for trade-restrictive measures due to a broader range of policy objectives in the form of *additional* legitimate objectives can therefore serve as explanation for the overall scarcity of *recurring case groups*. Given the development to allow the successful invocation of *additional* legitimate objectives in several of the reviewed PTA-DSMs, it becomes less probable to find *recurring case groups* that have been adjudicated across several PTA-DSMs in their overall adjudicative record. The larger choice of specific legitimate objectives available to PTA partners for the justification of trade-restrictive measures makes it less likely for PTA-DSMs to issue decisions in which they have scrutinized the same type of trade-restrictive measures that affected the same goods and for which the respective PTA partners have invoked the same specific legitimate objective for its justification. Consequently, a diverse range of legitimate objectives prevents an inquiry into the *incommensurability* of PTA-DSM decisions.

However, if only the general thematic categories of all invoked legitimate objectives in front of the reviewed PTA-DSMs are considered, disregarding their classification as *additional* or original legitimate objectives, the PTA-DSMs have uniformly become highly active concerning the adjudication of trade-restrictive measures justified on the grounds of human health protection, see Table 8.11.[1] The PTA-DSMs of the CAN, EFTA, and the EU have been adjudicating primarily trade-restrictive measures that were claimed by the PTA partners to protect human health. The PTA-DSM of the Mercosur has mostly dealt with trade-restrictive measures that were claimed to be introduced for the protection of animal health by the PTA partners. This also constituted the second-highest invoked legitimate objectives in front of the PTA-DSMs of EFTA and the EU.

Apart from this uniform development in PTA-DSM activity concerning the adjudication of General Exception Clauses, clear variations on the scrutinized specific legitimate objectives exist. They speak for the different dynamics of

---

[1] *Infra* Sect. 8.2.12, Table 8.11.

PTA-DSMs concerning the adjudication of trade-restrictive measures in the context of the respective General Exception Clauses. While the PTA-DSM of the CAN has been predominantly occupied with adjudicating trade-restrictive measures that were invoked for the protection of plant health, other PTA-DSMs have not seen such a high invocation of this legitimate objective. Equally, the protection of public morality played an important part in the justification of trade-restrictive measures in front of the PTA-DSM of the CAN, while it was only of minor importance in the practice of other PTA-DSMs.

Despite these similarities in the general trends of adjudication within the individual PTA-DSMs, the variations in their activity result in different adjudicative records regarding the justification of trade-restrictive measures, see Table 8.10.[2] These variations in the adjudicative records have an extremely significant impact on the low occurrence of *recurring case groups* adjudicated by multiple PTA-DSMs, which prevents finding *incommensurable* PTA-DSM decisions. Considering the current composition of the adjudicative records of the PTA-DSMs, the contribution of PTA-DSMs to the diversity of regulation of international trade is already difficult to argue, given that no uniform and similar development of adjudicative activity of PTA-DSMs has taken place so far.

In this context, the diversification of legitimate objectives available to PTA partners in front of the different PTA-DSMs appears to be a rather inevitable development. The data on the adjudicated specific types of trade-restrictive measures by PTA-DSMs suggest that diversification occurs when PTA-DSMs deal more frequently with trade-restrictive measures that can generate high adjustment costs for PTA partners. On this point, the reviewed PTA-DSMs have not unfolded a similar adjudicative activity in this regard, which has prevented them from developing a practice pursuant to which PTA partners have equally resorted to the same *additional* legitimate objectives across all reviewed PTA-DSMs.

Given the observation that PTA-DSMs generally handle the invocation of General Exception Clauses, including original and *additional* legitimate objectives, restrictively, *recurring case groups* can be found concerning highly invoked legitimate objectives despite the highly diversified practice of PTA-DSMs in this matter. Nonetheless, an inquiry into the *incommensurability* of these decisions remains difficult for several reasons.

Firstly, *recurring case groups* remain very scarce due to the diverse composition of cases adjudicated by the reviewed PTA-DSMs. The PTA-DSMs have not assessed the same type of trade-restrictive measures that affected the same goods in light of the same legitimate objective under the respective General Exception Clause. PTA-DSM decisions fulfilling this preliminary requirement to qualify as *recurring case groups* are rare. As has already become manifest in the different dynamics of PTA partners to invoke different legitimate objectives, the PTA-DSMs have equally adjudicated different types of trade-restrictive measures at a different frequency. These varying dynamics equally exist concerning the goods these

---

[2] *Infra* Sect. 8.2.11, Table 8.10.

trade-restrictive measures have been affecting. This varying composition of cases adjudicated by PTA-DSMs makes it more difficult to identify *recurring case groups*. Only in the adjudicative record of the different PTA-DSMs do variations in the case composition indicate different litigation dynamics concerning the trade-restrictive measures affecting specific goods. The data on PTA-DSM decisions, which addressed the same specific goods affected by the same trade-restrictive measures, testify to the individually different development of PTA-DSM activity.

Secondly, the differences in the PTAs' general scopes of application have precluded the PTA-DSMs from dealing with *recurring case groups*. The reviewed PTA-DSMs have a different jurisdiction and a different legal mandate to assess trade-restrictive measures, as well as potential justifications for their existence, given the varying scope of goods the corresponding PTAs encompass. Consequently, the reviewed PTA-DSMs' legal reasonings have encompassed *recurring case groups* because they were precluded from hearing them at a substantive PTA level.

Thirdly, even where PTAs have the same scopes and encompass the same section of goods, the varying compositions of the PTA partners' economies implementing the respective PTAs have contributed to the condition that PTA-DSMs have been called upon to adjudicate only very few *recurring case groups*. Considering the obligations to liberalize trade by PTA partners, these differences in the composition of the individual PTA partners' economies result in a different impact on their domestic industries experienced in the course of effective trade liberalization. In this regard, the data on the composition of the cases adjudicated by the different PTA-DSMs suggest that, in certain PTAs, it is more probable that PTA-DSMs are called upon to adjudicate trade-restrictive measures affecting specific goods from certain industries compared to other PTAs. This is a plausible development for the adjudicative activity of PTA-DSMs, which corresponds to political and economic theory drawing on the distribution of transformation costs incurred through trade liberalization. Consequently, trade-restrictive measures protecting uncompetitive industries in the individual PTA partners' economies can be expected to be in place more frequently concerning certain industries and depending on the individual PTA in question. Therefore, it can be expected that trade-restrictive measures affecting certain goods will be challenged more frequently in front of the PTA-DSMs by PTA partners seeking to exploit their comparative advantage if they comprise certain competitive industries. The different distribution and composition of competitive as well as uncompetitive industries in the individual PTA partners across the different PTAs explain the varying adjudicative records of PTA-DSMs.

6.2.1   Scarcity of Recurring Case Groups Due to Different Case Compositions

PTAs are negotiated between PTA partners whose economies are composed differently. Accordingly, the PTA partners' domestic industries are affected to different degrees by the trade liberalization that takes place due to implementation of PTAs. Against the adjustment costs emerging throughout effective trade liberalization in PTAs, the PTA partners attempt to delineate the scopes of application of PTAs by choosing the goods to which they apply. They aim to reduce the adjustment costs, or at least to attempt to control their emergence by means of, e.g., implementation phases, already at the outset of a PTA's execution.[3] This also explains why countries engage in lengthy negotiations over the content of PTA and their treaty provisions.

The data on the PTA-DSMs' adjudication of trade-restrictive measures, for which the respective General Exception Clauses were invoked by PTA partners, exhibit the different scopes of application of PTAs which at the outset limit the potential for the fragmentation of international trade law at the substantive level. These different scopes of application are reflected by the adjudicative practice of respective PTA-DSMs. Although the data at hand on the adjudication of General Exception Clauses by PTA-DSMs do not contain information on the precise scope of goods covered by the individual PTAs, nonetheless they suggest that the adjudication of trade-restrictive measures by the PTA-DSMs is subject to different dynamics. Consequently, the PTA-DSMs have issued decisions on trade-restrictive measures that affect only certain selected goods. There are two reasons for this focus on adjudication of selected goods, which has developed for the different PTA-DSMs. Firstly, PTAs can have different scopes of application and simply do not cover the same range of goods compared to other PTAs. Secondly, even where the same range of goods is covered by different PTAs, varying dynamics in the adjudication of specific goods have emerged throughout the different PTAs. These varying dynamics have precluded PTA-DSMs from issuing decisions on *recurring case groups* and limit the inquiring into their *incommensurability*.

6.2.1.1   The Adjudicative Record of PTA-DSM Concerning the Goods Affected by Trade-restrictive Measures

The data on the adjudication of trade-restrictive measures in the context of the respective General Exception Clauses show that the goods affected by these measures vary depending on the PTA-DSM in question. Generally, more active PTA-DSMs have adjudicated trade-restrictive measures that affect a more diverse range of goods, while less active PTA-DSMs have issued decisions on trade-restrictive measure that encompass a much narrower selection of goods, see

---

[3] *Supra*, Sect. 4.4.

Table 8.13.[4] In comparing the variety of goods subject to adjudication by the PTA-DSMs in the context of the respective General Exception Clauses, trends for a certain specialization can be identified for some PTA-DSMs. Consequently, as Fig. 8.13 shows, for the highly active CJEU, a certain regular adjudication practice concerning trade-restrictive measures affecting HS section IV can be found, covering prepared foodstuffs, beverages, spirits, vinegar, tobacco, and manufactured tobacco substitutes. A total number of 94 adjudicated trade-restrictive measures have affected goods under this HS section. Conversely, for other PTA-DSMs with a lower activity in adjudication, such a clear trend of specialization on the adjudication of trade-restrictive measures affecting only predominantly goods from under one HS code cannot be confirmed, see Figs. 8.1, 8.2 and 8.4.[5]

The variety of goods subject to adjudication is especially high for the justification of trade-restrictive measures in front of the CJEU. In total, goods falling within 17 out of 21 different HS sections were adjudicated by this PTA-DSM. Moreover, measures that affected trade between EU member states more broadly and could not be classified within one of the HS sections were also subject to adjudication by the CJEU. Among these 17 HS sections, roughly 27% of the measures affected goods falling under HS Section IV, namely "prepared foodstuffs, beverages, spirits, vinegar, tobacco, and manufactured tobacco substitutes". This was followed by roughly 21% of the measures affecting goods falling under HS Section I, namely "live animals and animal products"; and roughly 20% of the measures affected goods falling under HS Section VI, namely "products of the chemical or allied industries", encompassing, *inter alia*, medical and pharmaceutical products.

The PTA-DSM of the CAN, as the second-most active PTA-DSM under review, has adjudicated trade-restrictive measures that in total affected goods falling within 11 out of 21 different HS sections. Moreover, measures were adjudicated that affected the trade between CAN Member States more broadly and therefore could not be classified within one of the HS sections. Out of these 11 HS sections, roughly 15% of the measures adjudicated affected goods falling under HS Section I, namely "live animals, animal products". They were followed by measures affecting goods falling under HS Section VI, namely "products of the chemical or allied industries", encompassing, *inter alia*, medical and pharmaceutical products. Measures affecting goods under HS Section XI, "textiles and textile articles"; HS Section II "vegetable products"; and HS Section V "mineral products", as well as those affecting trade in general, accounted for 11% each of measures adjudicated under the respective General Exception Clause.

The EFTA Court, as the third-most active PTA-DSM under review, has adjudicated trade-restrictive measures affecting goods falling within five out of 21 different HS sections. Among these five HS sections, roughly 50% of the adjudicated measures affected goods falling under HS Section IV, namely "prepared foodstuffs, beverages, spirits and vinegar, tobacco, and manufactured tobacco substitutes".

---

[4] *Infra* Sect. 8.2.14, Table 8.13.
[5] *Infra* Sect. 8.2.16.

They were followed by roughly 19% of measures affecting goods under HS Section I, live animals; animal products" and roughly 13% falling under HS Section XIII articles of stone, plaster, cement, asbestos, mica, or similar materials; ceramic products; glass and glassware".

Finally, the PTA-DSM of the Mercosur, as the least active PTA-DSM under review, adjudicated trade-restrictive measures affecting only three out of 21 HS Code sections. Of these three HS sections, 60% of the adjudicated measures affected goods falling under HS section II, "vegetable products". They were followed by adjudicated measures that affected goods under HS section VII, "plastics and articles thereof; rubber and articles thereof"; as well as HS section I, "live animals; animal products", which each amounted to 20% of all adjudicated measures.

6.2.1.2   Reasons for the Development of Different Dynamics in Adjudication of Trade-restrictive Measures Affecting Only Certain Goods

The development of different adjudication practices of PTA-DSMs concerning trade-restrictive measures is a plausible and foreseeable circumstance for several reasons. It corresponds with assumptions available under economic and political theory, namely the distribution of adjustment costs on a regularly small group of unproductive producers, as well as their reactions when facing these costs, pursuant to the logic of collective action.

On the one hand, the variety of goods affected by the adjudication of PTA-DSMs can be explained by considering the varying scopes of applications of PTAs. As not all PTAs encompass all imaginable goods from the outset, naturally PTA-DSMs will not develop an adjudicative practice that encompasses the whole spectrum of goods.

Conversely, even where PTAs cover the same range of goods, not all PTA partners' economies necessarily have the same composition. While certain PTA partners of one PTA are home to different industries, other PTA partners of another PTA are not. Consequently, adjudication dynamics will vary among the different PTAs, with the result that a PTA-DSM of one PTA will not adjudicate the same selection of trade-restrictive measures affecting certain goods of the HS sections, compared to the PTA-DSM of another PTA.

The composition of the PTA partners' economies matters concerning the actual adjudication practice of PTA-DSMs, even when several PTAs cover the same scope of goods. Given that different compositions of PTA partners' economies necessarily entail some industries that are more and less productive with regard to manufacturing certain goods in one PTA compared to other PTAs, these different allocations of (un)productive industries will result in different litigation incentives and the development of different dynamics in the adjudication of trade-restrictive measures by PTA-DSMs affecting only certain goods. More specifically, according to economic and political theory, these different adjudication dynamics should even be expected: The different allocation of (un)productive industries within specific PTAs causes adjustment costs resulting from trade liberalization to be borne by different individual industries. In this context, *Santiago de Córdoba* refers to *Mancur Olson* in considering the effects of the implementation of a PTA, which generate so-called transformation costs, since

"[. . .] [a]ny policy change generates winners and losers. The benefits from liberalization are diffused among many (mainly consumers), while the losses affect a small number of producers, which thus are more likely to organize themselves against the policy change [. . .]."[6]

Olson's postulate on *The Logic of Collective Action* therefore provides the reason why it is highly probable that the small groups of producers of unproductive industries will aim at preventing the implementation of such policies.[7] This in turn is expected to generate more protective domestic legislation for these industries, which would subsequently be challenged in front of PTA-DSMs. It is for these two reasons—firstly, that losses from trade liberalization are borne directly by a small number of producers and, secondly, that small groups are more efficient in advocating their collective good, allowing domestic producers to mobilize efficiently against the policy changes resulting from the implementation of a PTA – that individual adjudication dynamics of PTA-DSMs can be expected. In economic terms, unproductive producers put pressure on the domestic legislature to save them from adjustment costs. Therefore, domestic legislators will maintain or implement regulations that especially protect industries of unproductive producers, causing adjudication to take place more frequently for trade-restrictive measures affecting these goods, in correspondence with the composition of the respective PTA partners' economies.

Despite the explanatory background for the development of different adjudication dynamics of PTA-DSMs, certain similarities in the dynamics of adjudication in front of PTA-DSMs can be equally identified. All the reviewed PTA-DSMs have adjudicated trade-restrictive measures affecting goods falling under HS section I, namely live animals; animal products", and II, namely vegetable products. Further commonly adjudicated trade-restrictive measures affected the goods of the HS sections IV–namely, "prepared foodstuffs; beverages, spirits and vinegar; tobacco and manufactured tobacco substitutes" and VI–namely, "products of the chemical or allied industries" encompassing, *inter alia*, medical and pharmaceutical products. They play an important role in the adjudication of trade-restrictive measures in front of the CJEU, the EFTA Court, and the PTA-DSM of the CAN.

The similarities concerning the most affected goods under the HS sections in the adjudication of trade-restrictive measures confirm that the scopes of application of the PTAs under review have the same coverage, given that adjudication was available for these goods. Moreover, the similarities concerning the goods most affected by adjudication testify to the presence of strongly regulated industries within the individual PTAs.[8] They confirm the general purpose of PTA-DSMs to

---

[6]de Córdoba et al. (2006), pp. 68–69.

[7]Olson (2012), p. 36.

[8]Awasthi et al. (2019).

decide on the appropriateness of the existing regulation of these industries, which are generally said to be introduced for socioeconomic reasons, such as securing the provision of public goods, or the protection of these domestic industries from foreign competition.[9] This characterization of the purposes for the existence of regulated industries corresponds with the data suggesting that trade-restrictive measures affecting foodstuffs and luxury foods were particularly central to the adjudication practice of PTA-DSMs.

6.2.2   Conditions Not Permitting an Assessment of Incommensurability of PTA-DSM Decisions Issued for Recurring Case Groups

Furthermore, the inquiry into the incommensurability of the few PTA-DSM decisions on *recurring case groups* is partially prevented due to the different practice and reasoning of the individual PTA-DSMs. For the decisions available on the few *recurring case groups*, their juxtaposition shows that circumstances exist which, on the one hand, prevent PTA-DSMs from engaging in a legal analysis of the disputed measure. On the other hand, PTA-DSM decisions contain legal reasonings that are not always comparable. This is due to the different aspects PTA-DSMs can focus on due to the complex design of the obligation to liberalize trade and the corresponding respective General Exception Clauses. Consequently, the quality and density of information in PTA-DSM decisions vary and make only a few decisions on *recurring case groups* available for an inquiry into their *incommensurability*.

6.2.2.1   PTA-DSMs Issuing Decisions in Which They Refrain From Making a Complete Legal Assessment

The review of PTA-DSM decisions on *recurring case groups* reveals that the practice pursuant to which PTA-DSMs refrain from making a legal assessment of the trade-restrictive measure or of the respective General Exception Clause poses a significant obstacle to the analysis of incommensurable decisions. There are two reasons for this practice of issuing decisions without a legal assessment: firstly, a substantive reason and, secondly, an institutional reason.

6.2.2.1.1   Substantive Reason: The Principle of Harmonization of Laws

A substantive reason for PTA-DSMs to refrain completely from carrying out a legal analysis in *recurring case groups* is their reference to the *principle of harmonization*

---

[9]Ibid., p. 309.

of laws. The use of the *principle of harmonization of laws* can be identified to some degree at all reviewed PTA-DSMs. Those PTA-DSMs having recourse to this principle usually argue that the General Exception Clause is not available to PTA partners due to existing harmonizing PTA legislation, which exhaustively regulates the use of specific means to counter a specific risk encompassed by one of the legitimate objectives thereunder. Even though, in the context of the *principle of harmonization of laws*, the PTA-DSMs may arrive at findings that a measure is illegal, technically this decision is not based on the respective General Exception Clause. Instead, the PTA-DSMs resort to the *principle of harmonization of laws* to establish and enforce a normative order within the different rules arising under the different PTA contexts. This precludes PTA partners from having recourse to the more generic respective General Exception Clauses. Decisions of the EFTA Court and the CJEU on the invocation of animal-health protection for the introduction of additional phytosanitary inspections for the meat and edible meat offal illustrate this practice. Neither of the PTA-DSMs engaged in a legal analysis of the justification put forward by the defending PTA-partner under the respective General Exception Clauses. In line with the *principle of harmonization of laws*, they held the respective General Exception Clauses to be inapplicable due to the existence of subsequent PTA legislation, which prevented PTA partners from having recourse to the more general reasons for justification thereunder. Having found the General Exception Clause unavailable to the PTA partners for the justification of the trade-restrictive measures, the PTA-DSMs found the measures to be illegal.[10] Among all reviewed PTA-DSM decisions, the *principle of harmonization of laws* is a rather nominal phenomenon regarding the invocation of the General Exception Clause.

Nevertheless, it has proven significant for the analysis of the incommensurability of decisions in *recurring case groups*.[11] Concerning the *recurring case group* on phytosanitary measures for live trees and other plants for the protection of plant

---

[10] CJEU, *Simmenthal v Italian Minister for Finance*, C-35/76; ECLI:EU:C:1976:180, Judgment of 15 December 1976, para. 19; CJEU, *Commission v Germany*, C-102/96; ECLI:EU:C:1998:529, Judgment of 12 November 1998, para. 22; EFTA Court, *EFTA Surveillance Authority V. Iceland*, E-2/17, Judgment of 14 November 2017, para. 67; EFTA Court, *Ferskar kjötvörur ehf. and The Icelandic State*, E-17/15, Judgment of 1 February 2016, para. 52.

[11] CJEU, *Simmenthal v Italian Minister for Finance*, C-35/76; ECLI:EU:C:1976:180, Judgment of 15 December 1976, para. 19; CJEU, *Dansk Denkavit v Danish Ministry of Agriculture*, C-29/87; ECLI:EU:C:1988:299, Judgment of 14 June 1988, para. 18; CJEU, *Oberkreisdirektor des Kreises Borken and Another v Moormann*, C-190/87; ECLI:EU:C:1988:424, Judgment of 20 September 1988, paras 11–13; CJEU, *Commission v Italy*, C-249/92; ECLI:EU:C:1994:335, Judgment of 20 September 1994, para. 20; CJEU, *R v Maff, Ex Parte Compassion in World Farming*, C-1/96; ECLI:EU:C:1998:113, Judgment of 19 March 1998, para. 47; CJEU, *Commission v Germany*, C-102/96; ECLI:EU:C:1998:529, Judgment of 12 November 1998, para. 23; CJEU, *Nilsson and Others*, C-162/97; ECLI:EU:C:1998:554, Judgment of 19 November 1998, para. 41; CJEU, *Commission v Italy*, C-112/97; ECLI:EU:C:1999:168, Judgment of 25 March 1999, para. 5; CJEU, *National Farmers' Union*, C-241/01; ECLI:EU:C:2002:604, Judgment of 22 October 2002, para. 62; EFTA Court, *Ferskar kjötvörur ehf. and The Icelandic State*, E-17/15, Judgment of 1 February 2016, para. 52; EFTA Court, *EFTA Surveillance Authority V. Iceland*, E-2/17, Judgment of 14 November 2017, para. 67.

health, in *Commission v Italy* the CJEU did not accept the recourse to Art. 36 TFEU, given that a harmonized procedure for phytosanitary checks among EU member states already existed.[12] In the case *Argentina v Brazil – Productos fitosanitarios (07)*, the seventh Mercosur ad-hoc arbitral panel dealt with plant registration procedures that were necessary for the importation of these products and were supposed to take place on basis of a harmonized procedure. This procedure remained unadopted under Brazilian domestic law. Brazil continued to carry out the registration process according to its own domestic policy. In this regard, it argued that it could still rely on this domestically defined procedure on the grounds of protecting plant health, enshrined under Art. 50 TdM. The ad-hoc arbitral panel refused this argument and held that Brazil could still invoke Art. 50 TdM for the protection of the legitimate objectives specified thereunder, but not "to oppose the whole regime of incorporation of the rules on the whole regime on the registration of plant products previously agreed upon."[13] It clarified that, beyond the registration regime, Brazil retained the right to invoke Art. 50 TdM "to solve specific and concrete problems that may arise on the occasion of specific imports of plant products, carried out within the [registration] framework".[14] Without explicitly mentioning it, thus, it applied a legal reasoning in line with the *principle of harmonization of laws*, which prevented Brazil from having recourse to the General Exception Clause for the specific phytosanitary checks that had already been prescribed with sufficient precision under Mercosur rules.

6.2.2.1.2   Institutional Reason: Delegation of Fact-Finding to Domestic courts

Moreover, the comparison of PTA-DSM decisions on *recurring case groups* shows that they do not always carry out a *complete* legal analysis of either the trade-restrictive measure or the respective General Exception Clauses, or both. Instead, by means of their decisions, the PTA-DSMs delegate fact-finding tasks to the domestic courts to confirm or reject their legal reasoning on the trade-restrictive measure in question should it in fact be designed as assumed. The delegation of fact-finding to the domestic courts appears to be a widespread phenomenon for all PTA-DSMs. Decisions entailing the delegation of fact-finding to the domestic courts consequently require the domestic courts to take these decisions themselves on the successful justification of a trade-restrictive measure under the respective General Exception Clauses. Although such decisions contain a general tendency whether a

---

[12] CJEU, *Commission v Italy*, C-249/92; ECLI:EU:C:1994:335, Judgment of 20 September 1994, para. 7.

[13] Mercosur ad hoc arbitral panel (Brasília), Laudo "Obstáculos al ingreso de productos fitosanitarios argentinos en el mercado brasileño. No incorporación de las Resoluciones GMC N° 48/96, 87/96, 149/96, 156/96 y 71/98 lo que impide su entrada en vigencia en el MERCOSUR", Judgment of 19 April 2002, para. 9.5.

[14] Ibid., para. 9.6.

hypothetical measure would be justified, they do not preclude domestic courts from nonetheless reaching an opposing conclusion.[15] It is noteworthy that these decisions technically only contain information on a hypothetical trade-restrictive measure. The practice of delegating fact-finding to the domestic courts shows that the PTA-DSMs resort to practices that are related to *direct and soft forms of governance*,[16] by allowing the domestic courts to make a final analysis on the legality of a measure

---

[15]The delegation of fact-finding to domestic courts has become relevant concerning 73 invocations of legitimate objectives under the respective General Exception Clauses in 36 cases: CJEU, *Rewe-Zentralfinanz v Landwirtschaftskammer*, C-4/75; ECLI:EU:C:1975:98, Judgment of 8 July 1975, para. 8; CJEU, *De Peijper*, C-104/75; ECLI:EU:C:1976:67, Judgment of 20 May 1976, para. 32; CJEU, *Denkavit Futtermittel v Minister für Ernährung, Landwirtschaft und Forsten*, C-251/78; ECLI:EU:C:1979:252, Judgment of 8 November 1979, para. 28; CJEU, *United Foods and Van Den Abeele v Belgium*, C-132/80; ECLI:EU:C:1981:87, Judgment of 7 April 1981, para. 30; CJEU, *Van Bennekom*, C-227/82; ECLI:EU:C:1983:354, Judgment of 30 November 1983, para. 25; CJEU, *Ministère Public v Muller*, C-304/84; ECLI:EU:C:1986:194, Judgment of 6 May 1986, para. 26; CJEU, *Schloh v Auto Contrôle Technique*, C-50/85; ECLI:EU:C:1986:244, Judgment of 12 June 1986, para. 15; CJEU, *Torfaen Borough Council v B & Q Plc*, C-145/88; ECLI:EU:C:1989: 593, Judgment of 23 November 1989, para. 16; CJEU, *Delattre*, C-369/88; ECLI:EU:C:1991:137, Judgment of 21 March 1991, para. 59; CJEU, *Monteil and Samanni*, C-60/89; ECLI:EU:C:1991: 138, Judgment of 21 March 1991, para. 45; CJEU, *Richardt and 'Les Accessoires Scientifiques'*, C-367/89; ECLI:EU:C:1991:376, Judgment of 4 October 1991, para. 25; CJEU, *Cacchiarelli and Stanghellini*, C-54/94; ECLI:EU:C:1995:56, Judgment of 23 February 1995, para. 14; CJEU, *Graffione*, C-313/94; ECLI:EU:C:1996:450, Judgment of 26 November 1996, para. 25; CJEU, *Celestini v Saar-Sektkellerei Faber*, C-105/94; ECLI:EU:C:1997:277, Judgment of 5 June 1997, para. 39; EFTA Court, *Tore Wilhelmsen AS and Oslo kommune*, E-6/96, Judgment of 27 June 1997, para. 66; CJEU, *Harpegnies*, C-400/96; ECLI:EU:C:1998:414, Judgment of 17 September 1998, para. 36; Mercosur ad hoc arbitral panel (Brasília), Laudo Arbitral "Controversia sobre Comunicados N° 37 del 17 de diciembre de 1997 y N° 7 del 20 de febrero de 1998 del Departamento de Operaciones de Comercio Exterior (DECEX) de la Secretaría de Comercio Exterior (SECEX): Aplicación de Medidas Restrictivas al Comercio Recíproco", Judgment of 28 April 1999, paras 80–82; CJEU, *Gourmet International Products*, C-405/98; ECLI:EU: C:2001:135, Judgment of 8 March 2001, para. 33; CJEU, *Tridon*, C-510/99; ECLI:EU:C:2001: 559, Judgment of 23 October 2001, para. 40; CJEU, *Grilli*, C-12/02; ECLI:EU:C:2003:538, Judgment of 2 October 2003, para. 45; CJEU, *Greenham and Abel*, C-95/01; ECLI:EU:C:2004: 71, Judgment of 5 February 2004, para. 33; EFTA Court, *Pedicel AS and Sosial- og helsedirektoratet (Directorate for Health and Social Affairs)*, E-4/04, Judgment of 25 February 2005, para. 57; CJEU, *Burmanier and Others*, C-20/03; ECLI:EU:C:2005:307, Judgment of 26 May 2005, paras 31–32; CJEU, *A-Punkt Schmuckhandels GmbH*, C-441/04; ECLI:EU: C:2006:141, Judgment of 23 February 2006, para. 25; CJEU, *Lidl Magyarország*, C-132/08; ECLI:EU:C:2009:281, Judgment of 30 April 2009, para. 46; CJEU, *Sandström*, C-433/05; ECLI:EU:C:2010:184, Judgment of 15 April 2010, para. 38; CJEU, *Solgar Vitamin's France and Others*, C-446/08; ECLI:EU:C:2010:233, Judgment of 29 April 2010, para. 57; CJEU, *Lahousse and Lavichy*, C-142/09; ECLI:EU:C:2010:694, Judgment of 18 November 2010, para. 47; EFTA Court, *Philip Morris Norway AS and The Norwegian State, represented by the Ministry of Health and Care Services*, E-16/10, Judgment of 12 September 2011, para. 86; CJEU, *Ascafor and Asidac*, C-484/10; ECLI:EU:C:2012:113, Judgment of 1 March 2012, para. 66; CJEU, *Ålands Vindkraft Ab v Energimyndigheten*, C-573/12; ECLI:EU:C:2014:2037, Judgment of 1 July 2014, para. 132; CJEU, *Visnapuu*, C-198/14; ECLI:EU:C:2015:751, Judgment of 12 November 2015, para. 119; TJCAN, *241-IP-2015*, Judgment of 12 June 2017, para. 3.8.

[16]Abbott et al. (2014), p. 9.

within the legal margins set out for them. However, such decisions do contain only limited information on whether the trade-restrictive measures will be found to be compatible with the respective PTA rule or not. Therefore, decisions containing the delegation of fact- finding to the domestic courts are only of limited use for an analysis of their *incommensurability*, as the exact design of the disputed trade-restrictive measure remains unknown, and consequently the identification of *recurring case groups* remains impossible.

This type of PTA-DSM decision-making has become very apparent concerning the aforementioned *recurring case* of the protection of animal health for additional phytosanitary inspection for meat and edible meat offal in front of the CJEU. Although the CJEU found that the *systematic* additional phytosanitary inspections could not be justified under Art. 36 TFEU due to the *principle of harmonization of laws*, it held that *occasional* additional phytosanitary inspections could still be justified under the General Exception Clause. The finding, however, was not as straightforward as it may appear, since the CJEU gave its conclusion subject to the compliance of the inspections with the last requirement under Art. 36 TFEU, i.e., they should not constitute a disguised restriction of trade among EU member states. To ascertain this, the CJEU charged the national Italian court, which addressed it in the Preliminary Judgments Proceedings, to carry out a factual assessment on this matter by stating:

> "It is for the national courts, before which such cases may be brought, to determine, in the event of a dispute, whether the procedures adopted for the inspections, on which they are asked to give a ruling, are incompatible with the requirements of Article 36."[17]

In the same vein, this type of reasoning could be observed in decisions by the CJEU and the EFTA Court on the *recurring case groups* of bans on advertisements for alcoholic beverages in order to protect human health. In *Pedicel AS and Sosial- og helsedirektoratet*, the EFTA Court – and the CJEU in *Gourmet International Products*–did not carry out a final analysis of the measure in question. Both found that the domestic courts were more competent to carry out a factual assessment of the effects resulting in the ban on advertisements for alcoholic beverages. In this regard, the CJEU as well as the EFTA Court even used the same wording for their reasoning by stating that the "national court is in a better position than the Court [. . .] to carry out [. . .] an analysis of the circumstances of law and of fact which characterize the situation in the [PTA partners' jurisdictions]".[18]

Similarly, the PTA-DSMs refrain from making a *complete* legal assessment on a trade-restrictive measure and its justification under a General Exception Clause to safeguard a specific procedure for this purpose established in a respective PTA. Regarding the practice of the PTA-DSM of the CAN, although the TJCAN has

---

[17] CJEU, *Simmenthal v Italian Minister for Finance*, C-35/76; ECLI:EU:C:1976:180, Judgment of 15 December 1976, para. 20.

[18] CJEU, *Gourmet International Products*, C-405/98; ECLI:EU:C:2001:135, Judgment of 8 March 2001, para. 33; EFTA Court, *Pedicel AS and Sosial- og helsedirektoratet (Directorate for Health and Social Affairs)*, E-4/04, Judgment of 25 February 2005, para. 57.

regularly signaled having broad judicial scrutiny over the assessment of trade-restrictive measures and the respective General Exception Clauses, it delegated fact-finding to the SGCAN to safeguard the specialized procedure established within this PTA. This becomes most apparent concerning the *recurring case group* on import restrictions for vehicles with the purpose of protecting human health. In the decision on the adoption of a Colombian import ban on public-transport vehicles, the TJCAN carried out a vague legal analysis, only confirming the general availability of a justification under Art. 73 AdC for trade-restrictive measures. However, it did not carry out a complete assessment of the disputed measure –let alone its justification. Instead, it provided criteria that should be observed when carrying out a legal analysis for the successful justification of a trade-restrictive measure. This happened most probably to prevent any interference of the TJCAN with the competence of the authority of the SGCAN granted to it under its specific proceedings.[19]

6.2.2.2   Varying Content and Quality of the Legal Analysis within PTA-DSM Decisions

In addition to the difficulty of considering all PTA-DSM decisions on *recurring case groups* for the assessment concerning their *incommensurability* because of the lack of a complete legal analysis contained therein, further difficulties exist even for decisions in which the PTA-DSMs have carried out a full legal analysis. These difficulties arise from the different aspects of a trade-restrictive measure or justification under the General Exception Clause, which the PTA-DSMs addressed, and result in a different quality of the respective decisions. These variations in the quality of the legal reasoning in PTA-DSM decisions appear due to the complex legal design of the obligation to liberalize trade among PTA partners and the respective General Exception Clauses, as well as the varying designs of the adjudicated trade-restrictive measures. PTA-DSM decisions vary regarding the specific aspect they address within the legal analysis on the justification of a trade-restrictive measure. Regarding the risk to the legitimate objective invoked by the PTA partners, the PTA-DSM decisions can differ regarding the analysis of the proximity of the risk that is aimed at being prevented.

  PTA-DSM decisions containing a legal reasoning on the legality of a trade-restrictive measure that aims to prevent a risk, in proximity to the legitimate objective invoked by a PTA partners, are difficult to compare with PTA-DSM decisions dealing with trade-restrictive measures that aim to prevent such a risk at a distance. Given that PTA partners have the discretion to choose the level of causal proximity of a risk to an invoked legitimate objective for which a trade-restrictive measure is put in place, the PTA-DSMs may adjudicate different dimensions of trade-restrictive measures introduced for the same risk to a legitimate objective. For instance, a certain good may be banned, e.g., explosives due to their risk of causing

---

[19] TJCAN, *241-IP-2015*, Judgment of 12 June 2017, para. 3.5-3.8.

injuries (protection of human health), or a product that contributes to this risk materializing, e.g., matches which are necessary to light the fuse of an explosive. Although both measures aim at mitigating the risks to human health stemming from the availability of explosives, the trade-restrictive measures in question aim at preventing these risks from materializing at different levels of causal proximity.

Consequently, several PTA-DSM decisions have proven incomparable and not suitable for an assessment of their *incommensurability* due to the different levels of causal proximity of trade-restrictive measures aiming at the protection of a legitimate objective. This becomes especially visible in the *recurring case group* dealing with trade-restrictive measures affecting vehicles for the protection of human health: In one case, the TJCAN was called upon to decide on an import ban in Colombia on CKDs (disassembled vehicles), which strove towards an overall reduction of the fleet in the country to counteract the consequences for human health due to its contribution to climate change.[20] In several other cases, the CJEU dealt with certain requirements to ascertain the roadworthiness of used and imported vehicles to prevent unsuitable vehicles from posing a risk to human health.[21] Besides the fact that both measures differed qualitatively, as one imposed an import ban, while the other still allowed the importation of the goods in question, and that both measures were protecting the same legitimate objectives of human health for risks arising from the same goods, their proximity to the risk they were preventing varies. In the case of the Colombian import ban on vehicles, the risk to human life due to their contribution to climate change is much more distant compared to the risk resulting from the use of a vehicle that has not passed a roadworthiness test and can cause a more instant and direct injury to (the legitimate aim of) human health. Consequently, although the measures affected the same goods and the same legitimate objective was invoked, the difference in their proximity to the risk makes the decision unsuitable for assessing their *incommensurability*.

Moreover, the inherently broad concepts on legitimate objectives encompassed by the respective General Exception Clauses has led the PTA-DSMs to adjudicate trade-restrictive measures under the same legitimate objective concerning the prevention of qualitatively distinct risks. The corresponding PTA-DSM decisions on trade-restrictive measures that were introduced to mitigate qualitatively the different risks under the same legitimate objectives make them equally unsuitable for assessing their *incommensurability*. This becomes apparent in the *recurring case group* on trade-restrictive measures affecting toys introduced on the grounds of protecting public morals. While the SGCAN dealt with an Ecuadorian import ban on slot machines that were claimed to pose a threat to public morals,[22] the CJEU

---

[20]TJCAN, *241-IP-2015*, Judgment of 12 June 2017.

[21]CJEU, *Schloh v Auto Contrôle Technique*, C-50/85; ECLI:EU:C:1986:244, Judgment of 12 June 1986; CJEU, *Procureur De La République v Gofette and Gilliard*, C-406/85; ECLI:EU:C:1987:274, Judgment of 11 June 1987; CJEU, *Lahousse and Lavichy*, C-142/09; ECLI:EU:C:2010:694, Judgment of 18 November 2010.

[22]SGCAN, *Resolución 966*, Judgment of 20 October 2005.

dealt with the confiscation of adult toys that were equally claimed to pose a risk to public morals in the United Kingdom.[23] Considering the different purposes of the affected toys in question, it is questionable whether the PTA partners as well as the PTA-DSMs departed from the same quality of risk to public morals that the trade-restrictive measure designed to protect. Even though the trade-restrictive measures in both cases were introduced to reduce the risk to the same legitimate objective, they attempted this at different proximities to the risk. Given that the notion of public morals is so extensive and allows PTA partners to avert the risks for this legitimate objective at different proximities, the decisions appear unsuitable for a comparison concerning their *incommensurability*.

6.2.3 Comparable Decisions Suitable for the Inquiry Into Their Incommensurability

Despite the varying content and quality of the PTA-DSM decisions for *recurring case groups*, a handful of decisions is suitable for the analysis of their *incommensurability*. The analysis of these decisions demonstrates that the PTA-DSMs have issued decisions containing legal reasoning which indeed differ concerning the employed legal test. Yet, they cannot be found to be *incommensurable* given that most of them arrived at the same legal evaluation of the trade-restrictive measures in dispute, or because of their different regulatory backdrop.

6.2.3.1 The Recurring Case Group of Decisions Dealing with Phytosanitary Import Bans on Dairy Produce and Birds' Eggs for the Protection of Animal Health

Both the CJEU and the PTA-DSM of Mercosur dealt with a *recurring case group* involving the adoption of import licenses on animal-based products, namely dairy produce and birds' eggs, for phytosanitary purposes to prevent their risk to animal health.

In *Commission v United Kingdom,* the CJEU dealt with an import-licensing regime for UHT milk which applied to all EU member states to prevent the spread of foot-and-mouth disease. The CJEU held that an import-licensing regime would generally not be compatible under Art. 34 TFEU. It held that it constituted a trade-restrictive measure; even if the granting of import licenses was automatic and prompt, the CJEU considered the remaining degree of discretion of national authorities as causing legal uncertainty for traders over their ability to export UHT milk

---

[23] CJEU, *Conegate v HM Customs & Excise*, C-121/85; ECLI:EU:C:1986:114, Judgment of 11 March 1986.

into the United Kingdom.[24] The CJEU saw the measures as generally justifiable for the protection of animal health and recognized the need of the national authorities of the United Kingdom to obtain centralized information on the origin of the product, so as to remain able to react in case of an outbreak of the disease by tracing the consignments and banning them from the market.[25] Nevertheless, the CJEU found the licensing regime to be excessive and suggested the use of import declarations, if necessary accompanied by health certificates, as this would provide the same amount of protection, but at the same time the restriction on trade would only be small.[26]

In *Commission v Ireland*, the CJEU was charged with assessing an Irish import-licensing regime that applied, *inter alia*, to bird's eggs and was introduced to prevent the spread of the Newcastle disease. In distinguishing between open and non-open licenses, the CJEU held that non-open licenses would automatically contradict Art. 34 TFEU.[27] Non-open licenses, which were used by Ireland, required a justification under Art. 36 TFEU. The CJEU established that the licensing regime encompassing non-open licenses was not disproportionate and that Ireland could successfully invoke the justification for it. [28] It added that whether the introduction of a non-open licensing regime was admissible could not be answered uniformly, but required a case-by-case analysis of the inconvenience and financial burdens it caused to trade among EU member states, in addition to the dangers and risks for animal health resulting from the imports of products. In the case at hand, the CJEU found the risks to animal health to outweigh the inconveniences for trade among EU member states.[29]

The first Mercosur ad-hoc arbitral panel *Argentina v Brazil (01)* dealt with the Brazilian import-licensing regime for, *inter alia*, dairy products for the protection of animal health. The exact reason for the risk to animal health deriving from dairy products was not further specified in the proceedings. The panel rejected the claim that the WTO Agreement on import-licensing constituted a sufficient source to introduce a licensing regime. Making a reference to scholarly literature on EU law and the jurisprudence of the CJEU, it found that the prohibition of all trade-restrictive measures encompassed all formalities for imports,[30] and consequently also all licensing regimes for imports. It clarified in the operational part of its decision that automatic licensing would be compatible if the issuing of the licenses

---

[24] CJEU, *Commission v United Kingdom*, C-124/81; ECLI:EU:C:1983:30, Judgment of 8 February 1983, para. 18.

[25] Ibid., para. 17.

[26] Ibid., para. 18.

[27] CJEU, *Commission v Ireland*, C-74/82; ECLI:EU:C:1984:34, Judgment of 31 January 1984, para. 47.

[28] Ibid., para. 50.

[29] Ibid., para. 51.

[30] Mercosur ad hoc arbitral panel (Brasília), Laudo Arbitral "Controversia sobre Comunicados N° 37 del 17 de diciembre de 1997 y N° 7 del 20 de febrero de 1998 del Departamento de Operaciones de Comercio Exterior (DECEX) de la Secretaría de Comercio Exterior (SECEX): Aplicación de Medidas Restrictivas al Comercio Recíproco", Judgment of 28 April 1999, para. 81.

did not require the fulfilment of any conditions or procedures for their granting and remained limited to the registration procedure throughout the clearing by customs. By contrast, non-automatic licensing would only be available under the conditions set out under the General Exception Clause of Art. 50 TdM.[31]

The review of all three decisions on this *recurring case group* shows that the respective PTA-DSMs followed an equivalent approach for the trade-restrictiveness of licensing regimes for imports. Although technical and linguistic differences in the decisions exist, they can nevertheless be found commensurable given that they ultimately address different concepts for the role of national authorities within the process of trade liberalization among PTA partners.

Pursuant to the reasoning of the CJEU in *Commission v United Kingdom*, all licensing regimes, even automatic ones, were regarded as trade-restrictive and as violating Art. 34 TFEU. The most crucial characteristic in this finding for the CJEU to consider the licensing regime to be trade-restrictive was the remainder of a national authority's discretion for the granting of the actual import license. This characteristic of the measure could not even be remedied by the *automatic* granting of the license, since a "system requiring the issue of an administrative authorization necessarily involves the exercise of a certain degree of discretion [which] creates legal uncertainty for traders".[32] Compared to this understanding, the approach taken by the CJEU in *Commission v Ireland* is much more permissive, as can be inferred from the differentiation between import licenses and open general licenses. In this case, the CJEU completely abstained from a differentiation between the automatic and non-automatic granting of licenses, probably because already in *Commission v United Kingdom* it did not serve to identify an administrative practice of EU member states under which the national authorities retained some degree of discretion for the granting of a license. Instead, it resorted to the concept of open general licenses to define an importation procedure that would not be captured by the prohibition of Art. 34 TFEU. In this context, *Argentina v Brazil (01)* reads like a synthesis of both aforementioned decisions of the CJEU: The ad-hoc arbitral panel clarified that only "[a]utomatic licences are compatible with the MERCOSUR regulatory system as long as they do not contain conditions or procedures and are limited to a registration operated without delay during the customs procedure."[33] This definition incorporates both elements concerning the remainder of discretion of national authorities, as developed in both decisions of the CJEU, given that licenses need to be granted

---

[31] Ibid., para. 85(x).

[32] CJEU, *Commission v United Kingdom*, C-124/81; ECLI:EU:C:1983:30, Judgment of 8 February 1983, para. 18.

[33] Mercosur ad hoc arbitral panel (Brasília), Laudo Arbitral "Controversia sobre Comunicados N° 37 del 17 de diciembre de 1997 y N° 7 del 20 de febrero de 1998 del Departamento de Operaciones de Comercio Exterior (DECEX) de la Secretaría de Comercio Exterior (SECEX): Aplicación de Medidas Restrictivas al Comercio Recíproco", Judgment of 28 April 1999, para. 81. Original wording: "Las licencias automáticas son compatibles con el sistema normativo del MERCOSUR en tanto no contengan condiciones o procedimientos y se limiten a un registro operado sin demora durante el trámite aduanero."

automatically upon application and without delay and should not be any different from the customs procedure that takes place in any case. Under these conditions, pursuant to the concept of the Mercosur ad-hoc arbitral panel on import licensing, the national authorities would be not allowed to retain any discretion regarding the granting of the permission to import.

The conclusions of the CJEU and the Mercosur ad-hoc arbitral panel that were reached in order to justify the import-licensing regimes nonetheless differ regarding the *default level* of trade liberalization that should be attained under the rules of the respective PTAs. However, they are not *incommensurable*. According to *Commission v Ireland* and *Argentina v Brazil (01)*, a discretionary licensing regime could still be justified under the respective General Exception Clauses if a risk to animal health existed. In contrast, *Commission v United Kingdom* found the automatic import regime to be excessive despite a present risk to animal health. The alternative put forward by the CJEU in *Commission v United Kingdom*, namely import decla- rations, was the only trade-restrictive measure it could regard as potentially *justified*, since it would result in EU member states "confin[ing] themselves to obtaining the information which is of use to them".[34] This very demanding understanding of *Commission v United Kingdom*, as opposed to the more lenient approach under *Commission v Ireland* for the liberalization of trade between EU member states, which subsequently was also applied in *Argentina v Brazil (01)* regarding the liberalization of trade between Mercosur member states, exemplifies the different concepts of the minimum degree of domestic regulation having an impact on intra- PTA trade which the PTA-DSMs may envisage. In the case of *Commission v United Kingdom,* the CJEU departed from an understanding of domestic regulation resulting in *zero cost* on the intra-EU trade which could be accomplished by well- informed national authorities that could remove infectious goods even after reaching the domestic market of a PTA-partner. By contrast, the legal reasonings in *Commis- sion v Ireland* and *Argentina v Brazil (01)* rather speak for an understanding in which, either because of the lack of resources of the PTA-partner or due to the specific risk of the disease, PTA partners would be allowed to deny import autho- rization to potentially harmful goods, barring them from accessing the domestic market of a PTA-partner. Ultimately, both concepts are merely nuances apart, given that all three decisions confirm a PTA-partner's right to act against potentially harmful goods by preventing them from entering their domestic market. Neverthe- less, both concepts entail different actual and potential costs on traders and con- sumers. On the one hand, the concept of declarations proposed in *Commission v United Kingdom* results in much lower administration costs for traders, given that the importation of the concerned goods remains guaranteed. On the other hand, the opposite is the case for discretionary licensing regimes, as suggested under *Com- mission v Ireland* and *Argentina v Brazil (01)*. Here, traders are still required to apply for a license if their products are potentially harmful to animal health and are

---

[34]CJEU, *Commission v United Kingdom*, C-124/81; ECLI:EU:C:1983:30, Judgment of 8 February 1983, para. 18.

dependent from the national authority's decision over their importation. Conversely, import declarations increase the probability of consumers being exposed to a risk, as the harmful products can access the market straightaway, whereas the probability is lower with discretionary licensing. Whether one of the approaches is preferable remains unclear, as can be seen from the ongoing debate on the precautionary versus the aftercare principle.[35]

6.2.3.2   The Recurring Case Group of Decisions Dealing with the Prohibitions of Enriched Foodstuffs for the Protection of Human Health

In *EFTA Surveillance Authority v. Norway,* the EFTA Court dealt with a Norwegian refusal to grant marketing authorization for cornflakes enriched with vitamins and iron. It relied on the protection of human health for this purpose. Norway argued that the intake of enriched foodstuffs could result in damages to the health of persons consuming them and that, as a general rule, foodstuffs should be produced without additional enrichment except in the case of the competent authorities recommending its addition because of a nutritional deficiency in the population.[36] In referencing jurisprudence by the CJEU, the EFTA Court confirmed that states retain their authority to limit the marketing of enriched foodstuffs, given that "the Community legislature has shown considerable prudence regarding the potential harmfulness of additives, and, where uncertainty persists, a wide discretion has been left to the Member States."[37] In the specific case of the enrichment in question, the scientific uncertainty about its effect even allowed Norway to rely on the precautionary principle.[38] Nevertheless, it could not successfully rely on the General Exception Clause, because a procedure in which the dangers of the enrichment of the foodstuffs to human health were assessed was not established. Instead, the national authority relied on the lack of a nutritional need of the population to justify their refusal to grant marketing authorization. Consequently, the Norwegian authorities did not carry out any risk assessment when the marketing authorization was lodged and therefore could not rely on Art. 13 EEAA.[39] Moreover, the EFTA Court underlined the fact that enriched whey cheese was allowed to be sold on the Norwegian market at the time of the application for marketing authorization of cornflakes, and that this circumstance could not be reconciled either with the requirements under Art. 13 EEA.[40]

---

[35] Schroeder (2016), pp. 497–498.

[36] EFTA Court, *EFTA Surveillance Authority V. Norway*, E-3/00, Judgment of 5 April 2001, para. 2.

[37] Ibid., para. 26.

[38] Ibid., para. 33.

[39] Ibid., para. 38.

[40] Ibid., para. 41.

In *Commission v Netherlands*, the CJEU assessed a very similar practice of a refusal of marketing authorizations by Dutch authorities of enriched foodstuffs. It remained in place unless the enriched foodstuffs satisfied a nutritional need of the population. Moreover, the procedure for the granting of the marketing authorization took into account the nutritional need of the population of the Netherlands by reviewing the overall presence of enriched foodstuffs on the domestic market. Like the EFTA Court, the CJEU confirmed that the Dutch authorities could rely on the precautionary principle if uncertainties regarding the damage to human health from the enriched foodstuffs existed because the exact threshold for the toxicological margins was still scientifically disputed.[41] In parallel to Norway, the Netherlands could not rely successfully on Art. 36 TFEU because it did not provide evidence that could have had confirmed a harmful level of enrichment of foodstuff to human health.[42] Concerning the actual assessment of the nutritional need of the population and notwithstanding the failure to carry out a risk assessment, the CJEU held that the authorities did not consider which enriched foodstuffs already available on the market would be substituted if the products in question were granted a marketing authorization. The national authorities did not satisfy the requirements under the General Exception Clause.[43]

Both decisions are almost identical concerning their outcome and the availability of the precautionary principle. On the one hand, both PTA-DSMs found that the lack of a nutritional need in a population cannot be the only criterion for national authorities to refuse the permission for being marketed. On the other hand, both PTA-DSMs confirmed that the PTA partners could rely on the precautionary principle under the respective General Exception Clauses if scientific uncertainties on the degree of risk to human health exist. Despite these similarities, the legal reasonings of both PTA-DSMs as to why precisely the national procedure did not satisfy the requirements under the respective General Exception Clauses are very distinct. At the level of assessing the existence of a risk, the EFTA Court did not require Norway to provide it with scientific evidence for the harmfulness of enriched foodstuffs. Instead, it based its decision on the incongruence of the domestic practice in light of the invoked legitimate objective and criticized the lack of risk assessment on a case-by-case basis. By contrast, the CJEU applied a much more thorough approach at the level of verifying the existence of a risk, as well as the application of the trade-restrictive measure, as it criticized the Netherlands that its national authorities did not provide any scientific evidence for the existence of a risk nor give precise instructions on detailed conduct of the procedure.

The comparison of both PTA-DSM decisions demonstrates that, in general, they can take different approaches towards the review of the margin of appreciation of PTA partners. Requesting scientific evidence can expose the lack of a risk perceived

---

[41] CJEU, *Commission v Netherlands*, C-41/02; ECLI:EU:C:2004:762, Judgment of 2 December 2004, paras 51–54.

[42] Ibid., para. 59.

[43] Ibid., para. 70.

by PTA partners. It can be a very effective method to strike down trade-restrictive measures resulting from domestic policies not being based entirely or only partially on facts. Such an approach can lead to a diminished margin of appreciation of PTA partners in assessing risk and designing policies to counteract them. For the feasibility of such a thorough review of domestic measures, the PTA-DSMs nevertheless require strong political support by domestic policy-makers. A thorough review of domestic measures may expose them to criticism over the legitimacy of their actions and eventually even give rise to different PTA partners' domestic entities to block their collaboration with a PTA-DSM.[44]

6.2.3.3 The Recurring Case Group of Decisions Dealing with Standard Setting for Medicinal Products for the Protection of Human Health

In *Resolutions 576* and *757*, the SGCAN was called upon to decide whether the requirement to obtain a so-called Certificate of Compliance with Good Manufacturing Practice for domestically produced or imported medicinal products from the Colombian Food and Drug Surveillance Institute (Instituto de Vigilancia de Medicamentos y Alimentos, INVIMA) was justified on the grounds of preventing health risks in Colombia. The certificates for imported goods needed to be issued by the competent authorities of the manufacturing countries, namely the United States, Canada, Germany, Switzerland, France, the United Kingdom, Denmark, Holland, Sweden, Japan, and Norway. Equally, a certificate from the European Medicines Agency (now EMA) or national authorities that signed mutual recognition agreements with the EMA were also accepted to put the medicinal products on the market. Peru complained in the proceedings that the acceptance of the certificates issued by non-CAN partners constituted an advantage that was not extended to other CAN member states and violated the MFN principle inscribed in Art. 155 AdC. Concerning the violation of the MFN principle, the SGCAN held that the claim was not appropriate, since the recognition of the certificates did not constitute any favor or advantage. Instead, it continued with the assessment whether the measure needed to be considered as trade-restrictive, since it "[. . .] prohibits the entry of products that do not obtain the Certificate issued by INVIMA, a measure that in fact hinders imports of medicines from other [CAN] Member Countries. However, Article 72 of the Cartagena Agreement exempts from the concept of 'restrictions of any kind' for the purposes of the *Liberalization Program* those measures that, although they prevent or hinder imports, are intended, among other reasons, to protect the life and health of people".[45] Consequently, the SGCAN found the measure to be justified, because it effectively protected human life and health, as set out under Art. 73 lit. d) AdC. *Resolution 757* rejected the appeal of Peru, because

---

[44] Cf. Kuijper (2018), pp. 121–122.
[45] SGCAN, *Resolución 576*, Judgment of 12 December 2001, p. 4.

it could not demonstrate that its standards and evaluation procedures on the manufacture of medicinal products were equivalent with those established under the Certificate of Compliance with Good Manufacturing Practice requirement.[46]

In *Commission v Belgium*, the CJEU dealt with the permission to market medicinal products only upon completion of a conformity examination, which attested that the products were consistent with the relevant laws and regulations of Belgium for the protection of human health. Products that were not subject to such a conformity assessment had to be monitored by a laboratory approved by Belgian authorities. The CJEU briefly held that the requirement of an examination of sterile medical supplies constituted an obstacle to the free movement of goods violating Art. 34 TFEU. Moreover, it found that the trade-restrictive measure could not be justified on the grounds of public health for products that were already subject to a conformity assessment in the exporting EU Member State, and where the results of this assessment had already been presented to the national authorities.[47]

In *Commission v France*, a measure prescribing prior registration of medicinal products included the obligation to adduce extensive documentation on the medicinal products in question to the competent Agence du Médicament (Medicinal Products Agency) of France, as well as the placement of a registration number onto the outer packaging of the product for admission on the French market. Regarding the registration requirement, the CJEU rejected the claim of the EC, as it did not produce any evidence that would confirm that it was unnecessary in light of the protection of public health. Although the CJEU noted the extensive documentation requirement for the registration procedure at the Medical Products Agency, it could not make any conclusions on its unnecessary character because the EC did not present any substantial arguments that would prove this.[48]

In *Humanplasma*, the CJEU assessed the Austrian requirement for human blood products to be obtained from persons who had not received any remuneration for their blood donation to receive a marketing permission. Austria claimed that this requirement was justified on the grounds of human health protection, since only unpaid blood donors could contribute to improving the overall quality of blood donations. The CJEU accepted this argument and confirmed that, in general, voluntary and unpaid blood donations contributed to high safety standards for blood donors and blood donations.[49] Moreover, it added that, under Art. 36 TFEU, the EU member states retained their power to determine the degree of protection of human health which they considered appropriate.[50] However, it found the

---

[46] SGCAN, *Resolución 757*, Judgment of 29 August 2003, pp. 3–4.

[47] CJEU, *Commission v Belgium*, C-373/92; ECLI:EU:C:1993:227, Judgment of 8 June 1993, para. 9.

[48] CJEU, *Commission v France*, C-55/99; ECLI:EU:C:2000:693, Judgment of 14 December 2000, paras 30–39.

[49] CJEU, *Humanplasma*, C-421/09; ECLI:EU:C:2010:760, Judgment of 9 December 2010, para. 35.

[50] Ibid., para. 39.

requirement to be excessive, since the EU directives and international standards on blood donations did not establish any obligation to obtain blood donations from voluntary and unpaid donors to secure its high-level quality. By contrast, the CJEU found that the rationale of EU directives and international standards on blood donations aimed at protecting the well-being of the donors themselves. Consequently, these regulations did not completely prohibit all payments to blood donors, allowing for, e.g., the reimbursement of a donor's travel costs, refreshments, and other small gifts.[51]

Finally, in *Medisanus*, the CJEU assessed another measure relating to human-blood products. In this case, human-blood products needed to be obtained from Slovenian donors as a priority to conclude successfully a public contract on the supply of a hospital in Slovenia with human-blood products. Slovenia tried to justify the measure on the grounds of protection of public health, by stating that the national-origin requirement for human-blood products encouraged voluntary blood donations by the Slovenian public, thus contributing to attaining national self-sufficiency in human-blood products.[52] The CJEU rejected this argumentation and deemed the national-origin requirement not necessary for the attainment of national self-sufficiency in human-blood products. Rather, this goal could have been accomplished by equally allowing imports from other EU member states of voluntary blood donations.[53]

The review of all five cases exposes that the decisions issued by the respective PTA-DSMs contain multiple commonalities regarding the justification of the marketing requirements of medicinal products for the protection of human health. All PTA-DSMs have issued decisions that generally confirmed the regulatory autonomy of the concerned PTA partners to decide on their appropriate level of protection of human health, in the absence of any harmonizing PTA rules. Consequently, restrictive effects on trade among PTA partners were generally accepted if they contributed to the prevention of the risks arising from medicinal products to human health. The choice of the appropriate level of protection provides PTA partners with large room for maneuver to adopt domestic legislation as they deem appropriate. It appears that, at the level of suitability of the adopted measures, the CJEU employed different standards of review depending on the complexity of the measure at issue. While in *Medisanus* it thoroughly assessed the contribution of the national-origin requirement, in *Commission v France* the lack of substantive arguments by the EC was sufficient for the disputed measure to be sustained. Both measures vary in their degree of complexity, given that *Medisanus* dealt with an obviously discriminatory measure, while such a discriminatory character could not be as easily identified for the measure disputed in *Commission v France*. A higher complexity of the disputed trade-restrictive measure may also explain why the SGCAN, in *Resolution 576*, did not engage either in a deeper analysis of the suitability of the Colombian certification

---

[51] Ibid., para. 44.

[52] CJEU, *Medisanus*, C-296/15; ECLI:EU:C:2017:431, Judgment of 8 June 2017, para. 85.

[53] Ibid., para. 98.

equivalent. In this context, the certification requirements encompassed a wide range of countries in which the regulatory regimes and principles for marketing authorization of national medicinal authorities varied considerably, adding further complexity to assessing the measure's discriminatory nature.[54]

Moreover, in these decisions, the range of deviation of a national standard from an international standard on medicinal products played an important role for the PTA-DSMs to confirm the necessity of a measure regarding its contribution to the invoked legitimate objective. While the SGCAN in *Resolution 576* was assessing a measure that did not deviate at all from, *inter alia*, the different international standards for the Certificate of Compliance with Good Manufacturing Practice, in *Humanplasma* the CJEU had to deal with domestic legislation that deviated considerably from the relevant international standard on blood donations. This deviation allowed the CJEU to identify the excessiveness of the measure in light of the General Exception Clause.

Nevertheless, a considerable difference between the approach taken in by the CJEU and the SGCAN is apparent regarding the principle of mutual recognition among PTA partners. It establishes the duty of PTA partners to accept that goods are in compliance with the PTA-partner's own domestic regulations on the sale and distribution of the goods if they were placed on another PTA-partner's market, namely with its own relevant domestic regulations. The SGCAN signaled its awareness concerning this principle by explaining extensively the foundations of the principle of mutual recognition:

> "That recognition is given to the conformity assessment practice in the exporting country and not to the requirements, since these are of the importer. This conformity assessment practice of the exporting country must be supported by a certain technical and physical infrastructure and a certain *minimum degree of confidence* to the other importing party, so that when it evaluates the product to be exported (in this case, the manufacturing system of the pharmaceutical laboratory) with the requirements of the importer, it yields reliable results, which are the ones that would be reflected in the certificate."[55] (emphasis added)

Pursuant to this argument, Colombia was not required to accept medicinal products imported from Peru which had been legally placed on the Peruvian market. Without elaborating on the reason for this finding, the SGCAN most probably assumed that the degree of confidence in the technical and physical infrastructure between CAN member states was not considered as given at that time.

The decision of the SGCAN shows that the adjudication took place in awareness of the different economic and regulatory pitfalls that can arise from the transposition of the principle of mutual recognition into the jurisprudence of the PTA-DSM of the CAN. The SGCAN chose to keep the middle ground between a *negative* and *positive* approach to integration.[56] While negative integration of domestic markets within an PTA requires PTA partners to adhere to a more rigorous non-discrimination

---

[54]Dalla Torre Di Sanguinetto et al. (2019).

[55]SGCAN, *Resolución 576*, Judgment of 12 December 2001, p. 6.

[56]Perišin (2008), p. 9; Heiskanen (2004), p. 14.

principle of imports,[57] which limits the recourse to domestic regulation for the distinction between goods for policy purposes and therefore initiates partial dereg-ulation,[58] *positive* integration involves the adoption of common rules or the creation of a uniform international regulatory infrastructure.[59] Consequently, positive inte-gration gives way to common policies in the different domestic markets of PTA partners.[60] Most probably the SGCAN had to square a circle between the potential of negative and positive integration. On the one hand, it most probably wanted to prevent the initiation of a regulatory *race to the bottom*[61] between CAN member states, as would have been the case had it advocated the application of the principle of mutual recognition. Given that some of the PTA partners' economies are consid-ered as poor, classifying them in the group of so-called developing countries, this status usually entails weaknesses regarding the administrative infrastructure which favor such a development. These weaknesses are very likely to result in a poor observation of domestic regulations on medicinal products and effectively imply a higher risk to human health should such goods be imported freely into the markets of all CAN member states. On the other hand, the SGCAN was most probably constrained in promoting a fully positive integrationist approach, considering that poor CAN member states in particular would have only limited financial and administrative resources to fulfill common standards applicable across the whole CAN member states. Considering the lack of harmonized rules for the admission of medicinal products among the CAN member states, the SGCAN confirmed a partially positive integrationist approach by allowing Colombia to adhere to princi-ples of several other states with a high regulatory power and a good reputation on standard settings from medicinal products to ensure effective human-health protection.

Considering that the infrastructural differences between the CAN member states as the decisive criterion most likely informed the SGCAN's legal reasoning and prevented it from encouraging a fully positive integrationist approach among CAN member states, the CJEU was confronted with this criterion in *Commission v Belgium* to a minimal extent. In contrast to the *Resolutions 576* and *757* of the SGCAN, the comparable standard of administrative processes of the national medic-inal authorities, as well as comparable preferences for the quality of medicinal products in the EU member states, allowed the CJEU to rely fully on the principle of mutual recognition. However, in a setting of almost identical administrative standards and security controls in the individual EU member states, the CJEU expressed a minor reservation to the full application of the principle of mutual recognition. It made its finding subject to the condition that "[. . .] the results of

---

[57] Heiskanen (2004), n. 50.

[58] Perišin (2008), p. 9.

[59] Heiskanen (2004), p. 14.

[60] Ibid., n. 50.

[61] Majone (2006), p. 623.

that examination [carried out in another EU Member State] may be made available to the national authorities".[62]

Ultimately, *Resolutions 576* and *757* of the SGCAN and the decision of the CJEU in *Commission v Belgium* contributed to the same result: They ordered the dismantling of non-fiscal trade-restrictive measures by resorting, on the one hand, to the principle of mutual recognition and, on the other hand, to limiting the potential for the development of new trade-restrictive measures in allowing Colombia to retain its regulation of equivalence informed by a predominantly international standard.

6.2.3.4   The Recurring Case Group of Decisions Dealing with Different Commercial Bans Concerning Live Animals for the Protection of Animal Health

In the *recurring case group* containing decisions which deal with different commercial bans concerning live animals for the protection of animal health, both the SGCAN and the CJEU have issued decisions in which the PTA-DSMs criticized the respective PTA partners' trade-restrictive measures for not being sufficiently demanding in light of this legitimate objective.

In *Resolution 986*, the SGAN assessed a ban on landing vessels fishing for tuna in Ecuadorian ports, the importation of tuna products into Ecuador, and the prohibition of all other commercial transactions if the tuna was not fished in accordance with the requirements set out under the Inter-American Tropical Tuna Commission (IATTC). The IATTC provides an international legal framework on the conservation of yellowfin tuna, bonitos, and other fish species. The SGCAN assumed that the ban was supposed to protect the life and health of these animals, because it made commercial transactions relating to tuna that was not fished in accordance with the requirements under the IATTC impossible. Therefore, the SGCAN supposed that Ecuador would invoke the justification under Art. 73 AdC because of the ban aimed at protecting this fish species. The SGCAN refused this argument by highlighting the qualitatively and quantitatively minor contribution to the conservation of tuna by the Ecuadorian trade-restrictive measure. It found that the measure could not contribute to the conservation of the species-firstly, because it was in place only for several months of the year and, secondly, because it contained only a prohibition of vessels that fished for tuna landing in Ecuadorian ports.[63]

In *Commission v Belgium*, the CJEU analyzed a regulation dealing with the importation and sale of birds, kept and raised in captivity, birds that were lawfully placed on the market in other EU member states. These birds needed to be equipped with a specific marking defined by the Belgian authorities. Belgium claimed that the requirement to equip these birds with the specific marking prevented traders from

---

[62] CJEU, *Commission v Belgium*, C-373/92; ECLI:EU:C:1993:227, Judgment of 8 June 1993, para. 9.

[63] SGCAN, *Resolución 986*, Judgment of 15 December 2005, p. 3.

selling them as specimens kept and raised in captivity, although in fact they had grown up in the wilderness. Accordingly, the requirement was argued to allow the sale of birds that were equipped with the specific marking and contributed to the protection of biodiversity by keeping the indigenous Belgian bird population from being sold as farm animals.[64] The CJEU rejected the justification for two reasons and found the measure to be excessive: Firstly, the Belgian regulation did not contain sufficiently clear information on the indigenous Belgian bird population that needed to be protected by it despite the availability of clearly defined standards in the Convention on International Trade in Endangered Species of Wild Fauna and Flora (CITES), which specified endangered species of birds. Secondly, the CJEU found that only the Belgian marking requirement and not the so-called CITES certificates, which also attested to the safety of sold birds, were recognized legally in Belgium. Equally, the CJEU found that only the Belgian marking requirement was legally recognized and did not extend to other methods allowed in other EU member states for the marking of birds bred in captivity. Moreover, the Belgian requirement did not provide for an objective procedure pursuant to which the equivalence of markings allowed in other EU member states could be certified by the national authorities.[65]

Both decisions effectively declared the two individual trade-restrictive measures as unjustified under the respective General Exception Clauses, although in principle both PTA-DSM decisions contained indications that the measures generally had the potential to contribute to the protection of biodiversity, and consequently of animal health. Although the two measures were considered by the PTA-DSMs as being motivated and roughly covered by overarching international agreements for the conservation of certain animal species, their poor design did not allow the CJEU or the SGCAN to conclude that they contributed substantially to this goal. Therefore, the PTA-DSMs found that the measures did not suffice under the proportionality analyses in the respective General Exception Clauses. Again, different approaches in the PTA-DSM decisions can be identified: While the SGCAN merely found that the commercial and fishing ban on tuna did not contribute to the legitimate objective aimed at by Ecuador, the CJEU provided precise instructions to the Belgian national authorities on how to improve the measure to bring it into conformity with the international standard for wildlife conservation as well as with the requirements under EU rules. In this context, it should be borne in mind that the EU itself is a signatory of the CITES convention,[66] while the SGCAN needed to decide on the IATTC to which only Ecuador is a party. This circumstance can explain why the CJEU not only stuck to the finding that the measure was inconsistent with requirements under Art. 36 TFEU, but provided additional guidance beyond it. Conversely,

---

[64] CJEU, *Commission v Belgium*, C-100/08; ECLI:EU:C:2009:537, Judgment of 10 September 2009, para. 90.

[65] Ibid., paras 96–103.

[66] (1996) Council Regulation (EC) No 338/97 of 9 December 1996 on the Protection of Species of Wild Fauna and Flora by Regulating Trade Therein.

the CAN, not a signatory of the IATTC, and therefore the SGCAN had no legal mandate to provide additional assistance to Ecuador on the modalities that would have brought its measure into conformity with this agreement.

6.2.3.5 The Recurring Case Group of Decisions Dealing with Product Requirements for Machinery and Mechanical Appliances as Well as Electrical Equipment for the Protection of Human Health

In the *recurring case group* concerning product requirements for machinery and mechanical appliances, as well as electrical equipment for the protection of human health, the CJEU and the SGCAN were called upon to assess whether technical requirements indeed contributed to the protection of this legitimate objective.

In *Resolution 1289*, the SGCAN issued a decision on the admissibility of a Peruvian technical requirement for a specific metallic cover on zinc-carbon batteries. Peru claimed that it aimed at preventing the leaking of batteries and consequently any bodily injuries. Moreover, it argued that the metallic cover would help to prevent such leakage and consequently would have to be regarded as justified under Art. 73 AdC.[67] The SGCAN rejected this argument and found that its introduction was not backed by scientific evidence, which Peru did not furnish either in the SGCAN proceedings.[68] Moreover, the SGCAN found the technical requirement to be excessive in light of the lack of scientific evidence, as well as not irreplaceable, given that a relevant international standard for the cover of batteries existed which permitted different materials to be used for this purpose.[69]

In *Commission v France*, the CJEU issued a decision on a French regulation of safety requirements of woodworking machines establishing a de facto obligation to equip these with a high level of automation devices for the protection of human health. France argued that the disputed automation devices minimized manual interaction of the woodworking machine for the purpose of reducing injuries to their users. The CJEU found the measure to be justified under Art. 36 TFEU, because the EC could not demonstrate that other less automated approaches to the operation of woodworking machines would be equally capable of attaining the level of health protection chosen by the French legislator.[70]

Both decisions contain entirely opposing outcomes and provoke the question on their *incommensurability* given the different treatment of the regulatory autonomy regarding the protection of human health by both PTA-DSMs. On the one hand, the SGCAN did not allow Peru to invoke successfully the General Exception Clause to

---

[67] SGCAN, *Resolución 1289*, Judgment of 11 November 2009, p. 19.

[68] Ibid., pt. D.1.

[69] Ibid., pt. D.2 and D.3.

[70] CJEU, *Commission v France*, C-188/84; ECLI:EU:C:1986:43, Judgment of 28 January 1986, paras 10–23.

justify a-in Peru's view-necessarily trade-restrictive measure for the protection of human health. On the other hand, the CJEU allowed the successful recourse to the justification solely based on the reason that the EC could not produce scientific evidence that could have confirmed the contribution of the measure for the legitimate objective aimed at by France. Consequently, France was allowed to leave its technical regulation in place.

Nevertheless, it should be kept in mind that the two technical regulations were different from a point of view of international standardization: Whereas for the Peruvian requirement to equip batteries with a metal coating an international standard existed that led to the presumption by the SGCAN that the measure was not necessary, it appears that at the time of the dispute no corresponding standard existed for the French automation requirement.[71]

The influence of the design of the proceedings may constitute another noteworthy aspect that becomes apparent when both decisions are compared. According to the architecture for dispute settlement, the SGCAN is assigned the simultaneous role of an investigating and adjudicating agency, while the proceedings before the CJEU are predominantly of an adversarial nature with corresponding procedural rights and obligations for the EC and the responding EU Member State. The existence of these procedural rights and obligations for the EC before the CJEU allowed the CJEU to issue a decision on the legality of the disputed trade-restrictive measure without fully investigating its regulatory backdrop.

6.3   No Incommensurability of PTA-DSM Decisions

The review of all PTA-DSM decisions in the few *recurring case groups* demonstrates that the outcome reached by the individual PTA-DSMs were not *incommensurable*: In each of the *recurring case groups*, the PTA-DSMs have issued decisions containing equal assessments on the trade-restrictive measures' legality or illegality, except for the decisions in the *recurring case group* on product requirements for machinery and mechanical appliances, as well as electrical equipment for the protection of human health. Nevertheless, even for these deviating decisions, the differences in the individual measures adjudicated and their international regulatory backdrop explain the different outcomes reached in the PTA-DSM decisions.

The comparison of the PTA-DSM decisions concerning all *recurring case groups* uncovers a variety of methods they have employed to come to the same outcomes. As could already be seen from the variety of the procedural rules on the resolution of disputes for the underlying PTAs, the PTA-DSMs are not created as a monolithic entity. Instead, they are embedded in different institutional settings with functions

---

[71] Guide 75 on Strategic principles for future IEC and ISO standardization in industrial automation was only published in November 2006, cf., ISO (2006) ISO IEC Guide 75 2006(E) – Strategic principles for future IEC and ISO standardization in industrial automation.

adapted to these structures. Correspondingly, the methods they use in their legal reasoning for evaluating a trade-restrictive measure's legality reflect the different fundamental aspects of the process of trade liberalization in each PTA for which PTA-DSMs are called upon to contribute to this goal. These aspects are worth considering when dealing with the debate on the fragmentation of international trade law. At least within the dimension of the *predominantly formalist* approach of the debate they have been insufficiently considered because the existing framework of the WTO does not address these aspects.

6.3.1   Different Models and Default Levels of Trade Liberalization

The choice among the different economic and political models of trade liberalization is boundless. The welfare policy of trade liberalization allows an accomplishing of welfare gains through diverse regulatory choices. Ultimately, the actual choice observed and applied by PTA-DSMs in their legal reasoning is influenced by various factors pertaining to the political, cultural, and societal preferences of the members of the individual PTA-DSM. Differences on the concepts of administrative practices and the role of the of state within the process of trade liberalization explain the marginal variances in the outcomes reached by the PTA-DSMs of the EU and Mercosur in the decisions in the *recurring case group* of phytosanitary import bans on dairy produce and bird's eggs for the protection of animal health. They demonstrate that the role of the state depends on the different economic preferences engrained in the legal and political culture of the adjudicators. In this context, neither the application of the aftercare nor the precautionary principles lead to different effects for the liberalization of trade among PTA partners at a general level. Under both principles, the PTA partners ultimately retain their regulatory autonomy for risk regulation, since they prevent dangerous goods from entering their domestic markets. For the individual trading partners in the economies of the PTA partners, however, they result in a significantly different impact for their business activity.[72]

The implementation of the aftercare principle results in a substantially lower burden for trading partners from administrative practices at the beginning of the trading lifecycle. The aftercare principle is characterized by administrative practices reduced to a minimum, in which considerable leeway is secured for the activity of business operators for the extension of cross-border business. These minimal administrative practices result in lower opportunity costs to start cross-border business and therefore to access other PTA partners' markets. Consequently, business operators from one PTA-partner dispose over more capital to develop markets in other PTA partners. By contrast, the precautionary principle entails a much higher administrative burden on business operators and consequently creates relatively higher

---

[72] For a critical economic analysis of both principles, cf. Sachs (2011).

opportunity costs for business operators at the beginning of the trading lifecycle. Due to the existing administrative requirements, business operators from one PTA-partner generally dispose of less capital to enter the market of other PTA partners. Depending on the exact opportunity costs of these administrative practices under the precautionary principle, this can constitute a barrier to business operations that do not have adequate financial resources.

Nevertheless, the application of both principles can have a very different impact on the activity of business operators, when considering the whole trading lifecycle. In view of the dangers for the public goods protected by the legitimate objectives contained under the respective General Exception Clauses, the application of the aftercare principle usually involves more stringent administrative practices to be in place to mitigate or compensate the risk once it has materialized from the importation of dangerous goods. Even if national authorities still have the possibility of acting after potentially dangerous goods have entered the domestic market, thus preventing their inherent risk from materializing, this may become a costlier and less efficient endeavor compared to a security screening before these goods are imported on the market, depending on the individual goods and the specific risks involved in question. In the same vein, regulatory systems relying on the aftercare principle often not only require trading partners to compensate the damage that has materialized due to the risk originating from these goods, but also entail costly disciplinary measure to incentivize good regulatory practices. The costs resulting from these disciplinary measures may turn out to be prohibitive for some business operators after initiation of the business lifecycle, forcing them to end their activity. In this context, the aftercare principle may be less sustainable for the securing of a *long-term* market presence of business partners depending on the level of risks that arise from imported goods. Opposed to this concept under the precautionary principle, usually additional costs from compensatory and disciplinary measures do not arise for business partners throughout their business lifecycle and prevent them from incurring the said prohibitive costs.

The actual principle to which preference is given depends essentially on the general level of risk PTA-DSMs are willing to attribute throughout the business lifecycle onto business operators, as well on the general public. It is ultimately a multifactorial choice that PTA-DSMs have, which depends on economic considerations such as the general level of financial resilience of business operators to the opportunity costs arising from administrative practices, as well as the political preferences involving the level of risk the public is willing to accept. Administrative considerations also play a role, reflecting the ability of the individual PTA partners to remove potential risks originating from imported goods after they have entered the domestic market. On the other hand, the PTA-DSMs' willingness to promote practices of the aftercare principle fundamentally depends on whether they believe that national authorities will be successfully compensated by business operators responsible for the importation of harmful goods in case risks should materialize.

These different choices on the exact mode of trade liberalization are reflected in the reasoning of the different PTA-DSMs. They are subject to constant changes resulting from a constant evaluation of the risks of goods for the legitimate objectives encompassed under the General Exception Clauses, independently of their status of being either imported or produced domestically.[73]

6.3.2 General Exception Clauses used to Promote Methods of Negative and Positive Integration Instead of Sustaining National Preferences

The PTA-DSMs resort to doctrines encompassing the proportionality analyses for the successful invocation of General Exception Clauses to measure the performance of trade-restrictive measures in remedying the risk which they are said to prevent. Where the PTA-DSMs find a trade-restrictive measure to contribute to the general prevention of a risk to a legitimate objective, doctrines encompassing the proportionality analyses of trade-restrictive measures entail two further important aspects concerning the measurement of the *actual* performance in this regard. On the one hand, trade-restrictive measures cannot be overly burdensome for the trade among PTA partners to prevent unnecessary general impediments to their trade. On the other hand, trade-restrictive measures must prevent the risk effectively by identifying and terminating any unnecessary disturbances on intra-PTA trade.

The differences in the approaches of the PTA-DSMs concerning their doctrines encompassing the proportionality analyses exemplify the different degrees of judicial review for which PTA-DSM can opt concerning the two important aspects of the measurement of the *actual* performance of trade-restrictive measures for remedying a risk. The elements can be assessed at different stringencies, having different impacts on the *negative* and *positive* integration of the PTA partners' economies, but nevertheless generally contributing to integration. Negative legal integration of the PTA partners does not allow the PTA partners to resort to the respective General Exception Clauses and to block market access of imported goods, because imported goods are presumed to be equivalent concerning the protection of a said legitimate objective. Under a *negative* integrationist approach, this amounts to a factual guarantee for business operators from importing PTA partners that their goods will have unrestricted market access. Under a *positive* integrationist approach, the PTA partners create common standards on the quality of goods entering their markets, thereby establishing a regulatory playing field in defining methods and regulations that prevent goods from being regarded as harmful. Also under a *positive* integrationist approach, business operators in PTA partners profit equally, as the fulfillment of the common PTA standard for imported goods equally ensures that these goods will have unrestricted market access in any other PTA partners' market. Yet, both methods of integration require the allocation of resources by PTA partners to a different degree. While *negative* integration does not require the allocation of any resources, as imported goods are regarded as produced under equivalent rules to

---

[73] Arguing for a complex variety of reasons, see Vogel (2012).

those in place at the domestic market, *positive* integration requires human, administrative, political, and scientific resources to be available for the negotiation of a common standard among PTA partners. To establish a common standard, the PTA partners require the exchange of information on the different procedures and risk assessments in the different PTA partners' jurisdictions in place; ultimately, negotiations should be guided by scientific evidence on the outcome of the common standard acceptable to all PTA partners. Trade liberalization by means of a *negative* integration approach thus constitutes a much faster method for arriving at lower trade barriers among PTA partners, which in turn requires only a low use of resources compared to the *positive* integration approach. On the other hand, especially in the field of regulatory diversity, this entails the risk of a regulatory race-to-the-bottom, which may hamper economic growth due to the potential of market failures.

Against this backdrop of economic theory, the PTA-DSMs can promote legal integration by using different methods fostering *negative* and *positive* integration within their legal reasoning. The review of the decisions in the *recurring case groups* shows that the PTA-DSMs have employed the principle of proportionality to promote different elements of *negative* and *positive* integration. In the context of the necessity analysis of a disputed trade-restrictive measure, they partially went beyond the simple assessment of the performance of a trade-restrictive measure for the protection of the legitimate objective under the respective General Exception Clause.

Although the PTA-DSMs easily could have encouraged the principle of mutual recognition within the necessity analyses as a method that stimulates *negative* integration and efficiently quashes trade-restrictive measures, the review of the decisions in the *recurring case group* of standard-setting for medicinal products for the protection of human health demonstrates that this depends on the economic parameters present in the individual PTA partners. The decisions show that the PTA-DSMs most probably resort to the principle of mutual recognition if economic disparities between PTA partners are minimal. Consequently, the CJEU found the requirement for a conformity assessment of sterile chirurgical equipment unnecessary in light of the principle of mutual recognition. It presupposed that the assessment of technical requirements is equally carried out mainly due to the same economic and administrative situations present in all EU member states. Under such conditions, it is very likely that their regulatory preferences align and that their administrative infrastructure admits the effective protection of the legitimate objective invoked. By contrast, the SGCAN did not find the conformity assessment for cosmetic products to be unnecessary on the basis of the principle of mutual recognition among CAN member states, most probably because different economic and administrative disparities prevailed between these CAN member states at the time of issuing the decision.

Considering a limited use of the principle of mutual recognition, the PTA-DSMs still arrived at a reasoning in which they encouraged methods that are able to secure at least future *positive* integration of PTA partners. Again, the decision on the *recurring case group* of standard setting for medicinal products for the protection of human health shows that the PTA-DSMs may mandate the use of third-party standards by PTA partners, thereby laying the foundation for the establishment of a common standard within a PTA, even if the PTA partners have not harmonized certain regulations yet. Most probably, mandating the use of third-party standards by a PTA-DSM can contribute to laying the groundwork for a development of common rules for the protection of certain legitimate objectives.

Equally, the decisions in the *recurring case group* of the prohibition of enriched foodstuffs for the protection of human health shows that, even if the PTA-DSMs find PTA partners to retain regulatory autonomy to enforce their domestic standards for the protection of legitimate goods, they may oblige the PTA partners to do this in a way that allows *positive* integration to happen in the future. Consequently, the PTA-DSMs may allow the PTA partners to rely on their domestic standards for the protection of legitimate objectives, while at the same time requesting them to be transparent and congruent in its application. These two latter elements constitute the precondition for the PTA partners to engage in a dialog on their harmonization of rules in the future.

In this context, the PTA-DSMs have shown a wide margin of judicial scrutiny to discuss further the necessity of trade-restrictive measures for the protection of a legitimate objective. A thorough judicial review of a trade-restrictive measure can ultimately provide key data for PTA partners for the future harmonization of a regulation. The PTA-DSMs' thoroughness in the review of trade-restrictive measures varies from PTA-DSMs choosing merely to stipulate general requirements of transparency, on the one hand, and congruent application of a detailed prescription of the different aspects of these criteria, on the other. Consequently, the PTA-DSMs can require the PTA partners to produce scientific evidence in the proceedings or PTA partners to apply a certain administrative practice that will ensure its congruent application. Requesting scientific evidence is able to sustain or refute the necessity for the adoption of a trade-restrictive measure and provides the matrix for a detailed analysis of the different aspects of the implementation of a trade-restrictive measure. It most likely constitutes a starting point for the harmonization of a regulation between PTA partners.

The decisions in the *recurring case group* of prohibition of enriched foodstuffs for the protection of human health demonstrates that the choice of PTA-DSMs to engage in a more profound analysis on the existence of the risk to the legitimate objective, as well as the congruent application of the trade-restrictive measure, is not merely a stylistic choice. Instead, depending on the regulatory infrastructure that the PTA offers for PTA partners to engage in harmonization, it can serve to pave the way towards harmonization of rules and regulations concerning the protection of the legitimate objective invoked. Consequently, given that the EFTA or the CAN have agreements under which fewer possibilities exist to exert pressure on PTA partners to bring legislation on its way towards harmonization, it becomes clear why their

PTA-DSMs have less incentives to engage in an exigent analysis of the measures.[74] By contrast, within the EU, the EC can use its power of initiative for legislative proposals and try to achieve harmonization in tandem with the considerations set out by the CJEU. Consequently, the CJEU requiring PTA partners to produce scientific evidence for the protection of legitimate objectives within the analysis of the justification not only ensures that the administrative processes are evidence-based, but they also enable the EC to use them for the preparation of common standards and signal to the PTA partners the need for their development.[75]

6.3.3   PTA-DSMs and Their Embeddedness in the International Regulatory Architecture

The reasoning of the PTA-DSMs with regard to the decisions in the *recurring case group* concerning commercial bans on live animals for the protection of animal health reveals the importance of embeddedness of PTAs, as well as PTA-DSMs within other international obligations or regulatory structures, for a PTA-DSM to include them in their legal reasoning. Ultimately, whether PTA-DSMs will apply other international rules or regulations and how they will give meaning to them depends on the status of the PTA partners as parties to the international agreements in question. PTA-DSM decisions that include a reasoning on the direct application of obligations under other international agreements are much less probable to be exposed to criticism if all PTA partners, or the PTA itself, are parties to this treaty. PTA-DSMs resorting to international rules, regulations, or legal principles do not have to deal with the problematic question on the legitimacy surrounding its use. On the other hand, where international obligations under other treaties are not as evident due to a low participation in such an agreement among PTA partners, this may explain why the PTA-DSMs are more reluctant to give direct meaning to other international obligations and use it in the context of the legal reasoning on General Exception Clauses. The dynamic pursuant to which the interpretation and application of international norms generally needs to be justified by the PTA-DSMs was already experienced in several instances for multiple international adjudicative bodies.[76]

On the other hand, the legal reasoning in the *recurring case group* of product requirements for machinery and mechanical appliances, as well as electrical equipment for the protection of human health, shows that the outcomes reached by the PTA-DSMs depend on the density of international standards and other regulations

---

[74] It should be added that the CJEU was traditionally regarded as prioritizing a negative integration approach. A more stringent judicial review, while at the same time holding that a measure could be generally justified, speaks against such an understanding. Cf. Scharpf (1998), pp. 169–171.

[75] Alter and Meunier-Aitsahalia (1994), p. 553.

[76] Lindroos (2005).

on the aspects in which the trade-restrictive measure itself appears. The choice of PTA-DSMs to give meaning to other international obligations can be assumed to be dynamic, considering the current state of corresponding international regulation and the economic effects such a decision would produce.

Consequently, it appears reasonable that the SGCAN in *Resolution 1289* decided that the Peruvian requirement on metal covers for batteries could not be sustained due to the availability of a long-standing and well-observed international standards already existing at the time of the decision. Any other reasoning would have probably contributed to the partitioning of the market of batteries within the CAN member states and could have made Peru's supply with batteries more difficult at the global level.

On the other hand, the decision of the CJEU in *Commission v France* reads very differently, as the relatively new requirement to use machines at a high level of automation was not subject to standardization at the international level back when the decision was issued. The choice of the CJEU to accept the measure can be expected to have had a lower economic impact on France, as there was no dominant international regulatory regime in place concerning this aspect. Although the CJEU allowed the French measure to remain in place, which certainly had an impact on the producers of wood-working machines in the EU, the risk of a partitioning of the market was probably smaller, given that there was no established standard available at the global level.

6.4 Probability of Incommensurable PTA-DSM Decisions in the Future

The retrospective on the adjudication of trade-restrictive measures in light of the respective General Exception Clauses shows that PTA-DSMs have so far not issued *incommensurable* decisions. This finding, however, is only momentary. It does not guarantee that the identified dynamics for the adjudication of General Exception Clauses by PTA-DSMs will remain ever unchanged, which prevents *incommensurable* decisions concerning *recurring case groups* from being issued. In this context, the insecurities over the development of the WTO-DSM may increase the activity of PTA-DSMs. The prospects of a new reality of appealing WTO cases "into the void",[77] which would result in a less efficient adjudication of trade-restrictive measures at the multilateral level, may create an impetus for WTO Members to turn to their existing PTA-DSMs for which the use is not compulsory, but which were in deep sleep until now.

Equally, in the search for opportunities for economic growth, the PTA partners may want to advance trade liberalization by relying more heavily on existing compulsory PTA-DSMs for measures that have the potential to create more

---

[77]Pauwelyn (2019).

adjustment costs. This could equally contribute to a rise in the activity of PTA-DSMs, potentially issuing more decisions on *recurring case groups*. Such a scenario would increase the probability of PTA-DSMs issuing *incommensurable* decisions, given that more decisions on *recurring case groups* would be issued overall.

In any case, the aforementioned findings do not exclude the possibility of PTA-DSMs reaching *incommensurable* results, thus contributing to the fragmentation of international trade law one day. Despite these uncertainties over the future development of the adjudication practices of PTA-DSMs on the General Exception Clauses, a look at the referencing practices of the reviewed PTA-DSMs can serve to make an informed speculation on their future contribution to the fragmentation of international trade law.

Referencing practices of the reviewed PTA-DSMs concerning non-PTA sources can serve to understand, on the one hand, whether PTA-DSMs also include in their reasoning references to non-PTA sources in their decisions. The actual use of specific non-PTA sources provides information on whether the PTA-DSMs resort in specific cases to common legal foundations and share an equivalent understanding of the use of specific non-PTA sources for the interpretation of legitimate objectives under the respective General Exception Clauses. Moreover, the specific references to decisions of other PTA-DSMs shed light on the state of transjudicial communication, especially regarding the *horizontal communication* between different PTA-DSMs.[78] Although there are multiple theoretical explanations available to describe such transjudicial communication between international courts, at the most basic level they confirm the awareness of, and relevance to, the practice of other international courts.[79] This awareness may have a limiting effect on the practice of PTA-DSMs to issue incommensurable results. More generally, the review of the *horizontal communication* between different PTA-DSMs is helpful in ascertaining which characterization concerning their activity is most appropriate, namely whether preference is given to engage in a formally independent reasoning to issue their decisions, or whether the PTA-DSMs form part of a *Global Community of Courts*.[80]

Following this understanding, references to non-PTA sources include all direct citations that are formally different from the respective PTA's legal framework. The referencing practices of the reviewed PTA-DSMs show that references to non-PTA sources are overall not widespread. Nevertheless, certain PTA-DSMs appear to have relied more frequently on references to non-PTA sources than others in the context of adjudicating trade-restrictive measures under the respective General Exception Clauses. Moreover, the analysis makes it possible to identify specific non-PTA sources to which PTA-DSMs generally refer concerning the invocation of specific legitimate objectives. This confirms the existence of a common understanding of the

---

[78] Slaughter (1994), p. 103.

[79] Voeten (2010).

[80] Cf. *supra* Sect. 2.3.2.3.

international regulatory architecture of the specific legitimate objectives protected thereunder.[81]

Finally, the account of the references to other PTA-DSMs and the corresponding PTA rules shows that the CJEU exerts a notable influence on the reasoning of other PTA-DSMs. The existence of such an influence increases the probability of other PTA-DSMs possibly finding some guidance in the decisions of the CJEU for upcoming *recurring case groups* in the future. Although a tendency towards the practice of PTA-DSMs to seek guidance in the decisions of the CJEU exists, the overall number of cases in which it played a role remains small, see Table 8.16.[82] Consequently, the influence of the CJEU on the other analyzed PTA-DSMs should not be overestimated.[83]

6.4.1   References to All Non-PTA Sources by PTA-DSMs

Non-PTA sources have been referred to in at least one of the PTA-DSM decisions on trade-restrictive measures concerning the invocation of the respective General Exception Clauses. Generally, referencing practices to non-PTA sources are only a minor phenomenon experienced throughout PTA-DSM activity. However, they are clearly more frequent in the adjudication record of some PTA-DSMs than in others.

As Table 8.15 shows, in total, references to non-PTA sources were contained in 48 cases on the invocation of the respective General Exception Clauses, namely in 17 cases under the PTA-DSM of the CAN, in two cases under the PTA-DSM of the EEA, in 26 cases under the PTA-DSM of the EU, and in three cases under the PTA-DSM of the Mercosur.[84] Compared against the overall numbers of all relevant cases concerning the invocation of General Exception Clauses issued by PTA-DSMs, the proportions of cases containing references to non-PTA sources vary considerably. These variations speak for different degrees of the PTA-DSMs' methodological openness when providing interpretations on the respective General Exception Clauses: While a high methodological openness can be identified for the PTA-DSM of the CAN, where roughly 23% of all adjudicated cases contained direct references to non-PTA sources (18 cases out of 79), and Mercosur, where 60% of the cases contained references to non-PTA sources (three out of five), the methodological openness of the EFTA Court, where roughly 14% of the cases contained references to non-PTA sources (two out of 14), and the CJEU, where roughly 9%

---

[81] *Infra* Sect. 6.4.1.3.

[82] Note that, overall, only seven cases concerning the invocation of General Exception Clauses issued by the PTA-DSMs of the EFTA, Mercosur, and CAN have contained a reference to the jurisprudence of the CJEU and EU rules, cf. infra Sect. 8.2.18 Table 8.16.

[83] *Infra* Sect. 6.4.1.4.

[84] *Infra* Sect. 8.2.17, Table 8.15.

of the cases contained references to non-PTA sources (26 out of 285), can be described as rather moderate to low.

6.4.1.1 Types of Non-PTA Sources and Most Used Non-PTA Sources

Overall, in PTA-DSM decisions, among the references to non-PTA sources, citations of other international agreements and standards can be found (agreements relating to international-biodiversity protection, international environmental law, international food and agriculture regulation, global-health protection, international drug-addiction prevention, human-rights protection, international animal-welfare protection, international regulations on communication services, and international procedure and litigation). Further points include the latest scientific evidence on diverse issues, WTO rules and WTO-DSM decisions, other PTA-DSMs decisions, PTA rules (EU, CAN, and EFTA rules and jurisprudence, as well as other regulations in other regional PTAs), decisions of domestic courts and national agencies, as well as references to scholarly literature.

The top-three non-PTA sources most relied upon in PTA-DSM decisions were WTO rules and WTO-DSM decisions, references to the latest scientific evidence, and international agreements on health protection, see Table 8.15.[85]

6.4.1.2 Varying Degrees of the PTA-DSMs' Methodological Openness

The varying distribution of cases in which specific types of non-PTA sources were referred to by the reviewed PTA-DSMs testifies to the different degrees of openness of the individual PTA-DSMs to use non-PTA sources for their legal reasoning concerning the invocation of the respective General Exception Clauses by PTA partners. Methodological openness can be considered wide where the PTA-DSMs were willing to include different types of non-PTA sources in the context of interpreting the respective General Exception Clauses. It can be considered limited where the PTA-DSMs included only selected types of non-PTA sources in their decisions. The level of methodological openness of the individual PTA-DSMs varies. It reflects their different self-conceptions and their institutional dependencies, which they express through their references to non-PTA sources in their legal reasoning for the adjudication of trade-restrictive measures under the respective General Exception Clauses.

Generally, a stark difference in the methodological openness of PTA-DSMs can be seen from the referencing practices of PTA-DSMs to other PTA rules, PTA-DSM decisions, and corresponding scholarly literature in their decisions, see Fig. 6.2. The PTA-DSM of the CAN, in its decisions, referred to the rules under the legal framework of the EU, as well as decisions of the CJEU and scholarly literature on

---

[85] *Infra* Sect. 8.2.17, Table 8.15.

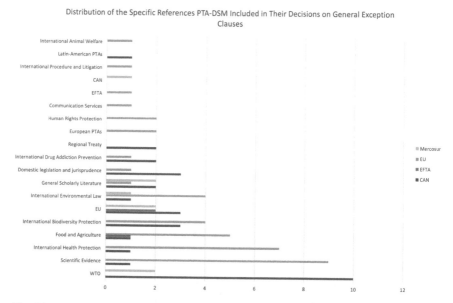

Fig. 6.2 Distribution of the Specific References PTA-DSM Included in Their Decisions on General Exception Clauses. Source: Author's novel dataset

this topic. Likewise, the PTA-DSM of the Mercosur added references to decisions of the PTA-DSM of the CAN, as well as CAN rules. The inclusion of these types of references by the PTA-DSMs of the CAN and the Mercosur stands in contrast to the referencing practices of the CJEU and the EFTA Court in this regard. These PTA-DSMs included only references to each other's decisions.[86] The greatest contrast in the methodological openness can be seen regarding the PTA-DSMs of the CAN and the Mercosur towards WTO rules and decisions of the WTO-DSM, as opposed to the CJEU and the EFFTA Court. While the CJEU and the EFTA Court do not contain a single reference to WTO rules and the decisions of the WTO-DSM for the adjudication of trade-restrictive measures under the respective General Exception Clauses, the PTA-DSMs of the CAN and of the Mercosur have referenced them several times in their decisions.

On the other hand, differing methodological openness is also reflected in referencing practices of PTA-DSMs to domestic legislation and jurisprudence. Concerning this aspect, the PTA-DSM of the CAN made references to the Bolivian Constitution, Mexican law, as well as to decisions of the Spanish Constitutional Court for the adjudication of trade-restrictive measures under the General Exception Clause of Art. 73 AdC. In the same vein, the CJEU referred to domestic legal acts for

---

[86] References of the EFTA Court to rules under the legal framework of the EU were not considered at this point, as they were only made to confirm the Court's obligation to carry out a homologous interpretation of the rules under the EEA and the rules under the legal framework of EU.

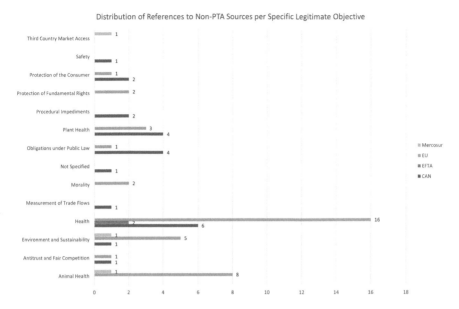

Fig. 6.3 Distribution of References to Non-PTA Sources per Specific Legitimate Objective Included by PTA-DSMs in the Decisions Dealing With General Exception Clauses. Source: Author's novel dataset.

the interpretation of the Art. 36 TFEU, while all other PTA-DSMs did not make any references to domestic legislation and jurisprudence in their decisions.

6.4.1.3   Patterns on the Use of References to Non-PTA Sources for Specific Legitimate Objectives

Apart from the differences in the overall methodological openness of PTA-DSMs, similarities in the use of references to the specific non-PTA sources exist for the individual legitimate objectives under the General Exception Clauses, see Fig. 6.3.

In the context of adjudicating measures under the legitimate objective protecting the environment and sustainability, the PTA-DSMs of the CAN, Mercosur, and the EU have proven to refer generally to non-PTA sources. Equally, in the context of adjudicating measures under the legitimate objective protecting human health, the PTA-DSMs of the CAN, EFTA, and the EU have referred to non-PTA sources in their reasoning. For the aforementioned PTA-DSMs, this means that they refer to non-PTA sources in their legal reasoning, most probably for the purpose of increasing the legitimacy of their decisions. This speaks for the PTA-DSMs' awareness of the developments concerning the protection of the legitimate objectives at the international level. The PTA-DSMs have been signaling that the protection of the environment and sustainable development, as well as the protection of public health as encompassed through various types of different non-PTA sources, is a generally legitimate policy goal capable of justifying disruptions of trade among PTA partners.

6.4.1.4 Assessing the Transjudicial Communication Between PTA-DSMs

The differences in the methodological openness of the PTA-DSMs foretell that a genuine transjudicial communication by means of which the PTA-DSMs establish a *Global Community of Courts* exists only to a limited degree for the adjudication of trade-restrictive measures under the respective General Exception Clauses. The rare references to other PTA-DSMs decisions by only some PTA-DSMs rather speak for a linear process of dissemination of information from the CJEU to the other PTA-DSMs. This development appears plausible regarding one theoretical explanation of the reasons for referencing practices of international courts provided by *Erik Voeten,* namely their usefulness for *learning purposes:* References to other PTA-DSMs have the aim to "improve the quality of [their own PTA-DSMs] decisions".[87] This appears to be the case in the adjudication record of PTA-DSMs in which the legal reasonings of other PTA-DSMs on equivalent PTA rules have been presented and transposed – or at least they tried to transpose them – to the own context of PTA rules, underlining the general process of trade liberalization within PTAs.

Moreover, regarding the referencing practices of the PTA-DSMs of the CAN and Mercosur to WTO rules and the decisions of the WTO-DSM, it appears that these decisions can be best explained as being added for strategic purposes, with the aim to "enhance the institutional authority"[88] of the respective PTA-DSMs. The use of these references to WTO rules and the WTO-DSM contrasts with the distinct nature of PTA rules against the multilateral legal framework and aims to establish an autonomous normative order of the PTA in question.

References to other PTA-DSMs decisions are a rare phenomenon, see Fig. 6.4: This has mainly occurred among the reviewed PTA-DSMs concerning decisions of the CJEU. Accordingly, the PTA-DSM of the CAN has made references to decisions of the CJEU in one case;[89] the PTA-DSM of the Mercosur has referred to decisions of the CJEU in two cases;[90] and the EFTA Court referred to decisions of the CJEU in

---

[87] Voeten (2010), pp. 550–551.

[88] Ibid., p. 553.

[89] SGCAN, *Resolución 1716*, Judgment of 18 August 2014, p. 5.

[90] Mercosur ad hoc arbitral panel (Brasília), Laudo Arbitral "Controversia sobre Comunicados N° 37 del 17 de diciembre de 1997 y N° 7 del 20 de febrero de 1998 del Departamento de Operaciones de Comercio Exterior (DECEX) de la Secretaría de Comercio Exterior (SECEX): Aplicación de Medidas Restrictivas al Comercio Recíproco", Judgment of 28 April 1999, paras 4, 5, 16, 17, 19; TPR, Laudo N°01/2005, Judgment of 20 December 2005, paras 4, 16, 18, 19.

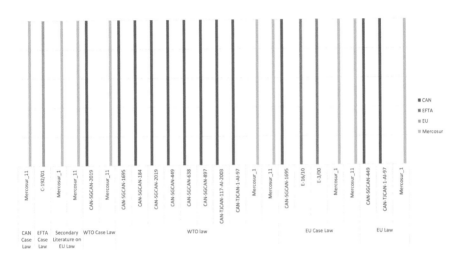

Overview of Decisions Containing References to Other PTA-DSM decisions/law and/or WTO Case Law and/or Case Law

Fig. 6.4 Overview of Decisions Containing References to Other PTA-DSM decisions/law and/or WTO Case Law and/or Case Law. Source: Author's novel dataset

two cases.[91] The referencing practices of these three PTA-DSMs do not allow any identification of important citations to so-called "key" cases of the CJEU. Such a common citation practice by all PTA-DSMs concerning the decisions of the CJEU would indicate a highly systematic understanding of its developed case law by the other PTA-DSMs. As Table 8.15 shows, the referencing practices of the other PTA-DSMs appear rather incidental instead.[92]

Among the reviewed PTA-DSMs, the PTA-DSMs of the CAN and Mercosur stand out regarding their referencing activity to the decisions of the WTO-DSM as well as to the different rules under the legal framework of the WTO. References to the different rules under the legal framework of the WTO are even more frequent than references to the EU. Regarding the PTA-DSM of the CAN, eight decisions contain references to WTO rules, and one decision refers to WTO-DSM decisions. Concerning the PTA-DSM of Mercosur, one case contains references to both WTO-DSM decisions and rules, and one decision contains only references to WTO rules, see Table 8.16.[93]

---

[91] EFTA Court, EFTA Surveillance Authority V. Norway, E-3/00, Judgment of 5 April 2001, paras 24, 26, 35, 39; EFTA Court, Philip Morris Norway AS and The Norwegian State, represented by the Ministry of Health and Care Services, E-16/10, Judgment of 12 September 2011, paras 39–41; 44, 48, 50, 77, 80–81.

[92] Cf. *infra* Sect. 8.2.17 Table 8.15.

[93] Cf. *infra* Sect. 8.2.18 Table 8.16.

6.4.1.4.1   Assessing the Quality of the PTA-DSMs' References
to the Decisions of the CJEU and Rules under the Legal
Framework of the EU

While the references of the EFTA Court to the decisions of the CJEU are not unexpected due to the *principle of judicial homogeneity* under the EEA agreement,[94] references of the PTA-DSMs of the CAN and the Mercosur to the decisions of the CJEU call for an explanation. Generally, such referring practices are not foreseen given the lack of any formal relationship between the PTA-DSMs of the CAN and the Mercosur with the CJEU or EU rules under their corresponding legal frameworks. The review of decisions issued by the PTA-DSM of the CAN shows that both the SGCAN and the TJCAN decided to include the references to the decision of the CJEU and the rules under the EU legal framework, due a perceived shared historical origin between EU and CAN provisions, and to provide technical guidance on the concepts of the rule to liberalize trade and the exception to it.

In this context, Venezuelan import restrictions on garlic originating from Peru constituted the backdrop for the decision issued by TJCAN in the process *1-AI-97*. Peru claimed that the import restrictions were illegal and resulted from the requirement to possess a phytosanitary permit for their importation. The phytosanitary permit was not inscribed in the CAN record of allowed phytosanitary measures, and Peru held Venezuela to be in violation of its obligations to liberalize trade. The TJCAN agreed that the import permits were not justified on the grounds of protection of plant health, given that they were not intended for planting, but for consumption, thus not posing any risk to plant health. Moreover, the TJCAN called in question whether garlic could pose such a risk at all, due to a lack of a scientific evidence.[95] For this purpose, the TJCAN found it necessary to repeat its fundamental finding, issued in the process *3-AI-96*, concerning the historical motives for trade liberalization within the EU member states. It held that:

> "[a] historical account of the evolution of world trade shows how, prior to 1914, the international panorama was characterized by the presence of three freedoms: freedom of movement of persons, freedom of movement of goods and freedom of movement of capital, also protected today in the European Union. These freedoms, deteriorated by the economic consequences of the First World War and by the ravages of the depression of the 1930s, ended up being destroyed on the eve of the Second World War with the appearance of progressive limitations on trade, the increasingly marked presence of protectionist practices, the formation of autarkic tendencies and the establishment of closed economic areas, which led to a frank process of "disintegration of the world economy."[96]

The TJCAN underlined the high importance of the removal of trade restrictions, which led it to the conclusion that Venezuela was still required to respect its obligations to lower the existing trade barriers generally, also regarding trade with

---

[94] Cf. *supra* Sect. 5.3.2.2.

[95] TJCAN, *1-AI-97*, 1-AI-97, Judgment of 11 December 1997, p. 20.

[96] Ibid., p. 15.

Peru, which was temporarily not part of the free-trade zone established between the CAN member states at the time of the decision.[97]

In the subsequent decisions issued by the SGCAN, it provided gradually expanding references to the rules under EU legal framework. In *Resolution 449* and on its appeal in *Resolution 489*, the SGCAN endorsed a rather general and discreet reference to scholarly literature to clarify the purpose of Art. 34 TFEU, which states that "for the purposes of the application of Article 30 EEC [now Art. 34 TFEU], it is sufficient for a measure to have a potential restrictive effect on trade, without it [i.e., the measure] being necessary for it to have an actual restrictive effect, it is enough that it is POTENTIALLY CAPABLE OF RESTRICTING TRADE'. (emphasis ours) [sic]" [98] In contrast, *Resolution 1716*, which was issued on appeal of *Resolution 1695*, reads like a synopsis of all those relevant decisions of the CJEU establishing the concept of free movement of goods under the TFEU. The extensive review of CJEU case law and corresponding rules for the liberalization of goods under the legal framework of the EU demonstrate how the SGCAN aimed at informing, and potentially convincing, the involved CAN member states of an extensive reading of the equivalent provisions under the AdC. The proceedings in front of the SGCAN were initiated on the adoption of an Ecuadorian requirement to furnish so-called certificates of recognition for cosmetic products upon importation into the country, which could only be obtained if an additional conformity-assessment procedure had taken place in laboratories designated by Ecuador. Colombia and Peru claimed that this was against the harmonized procedure on conformity assessments, and therefore against its obligations under Art. 73 AdC. Arguing against this assertion, Ecuador claimed that the harmonized regulation still left sufficient regulatory autonomy to adopt the legislation requiring the certificate of recognition from importers. The SGCAN disagreed and stated that "it is therefore concluded that there are no gaps in the Andean Regulations which, in accordance with those indicated in Process 118-AI-2003 [...] cited by Ecuador, allow "[...] recourse to the General Principles of Community Law, the substantive law of the Member Countries, and the principles of international law, and in addition to the provisions emanating from the World Trade Organization, provided that they are consistent with the principles and rules of the Andean Integration Agreement."[99] Against this finding, and on the basis of the *complemento indispensable* doctrine,

---

[97] Cf. Ibid., p. 17.

[98] Original wording: "consideran suficiente, a los efectos de la aplicación del artículo 30° CEE, que una medida comporte efectos restrictivos potenciales sobre los intercambios, sin que sea necesario que tenga una incidencia restrictiva real, bastando que sea POTENCIALMENTE CAPAZ DE RESTRINGIRLOS' (Enfasis nuestro).", SGCAN, *Resolución 449*, Judgment of 2 November 2000b, p. 6; SGCAN, *Resolución 489*, Judgment of 9 March 2001, p. 16.

[99] Original wording: "[...] acudir a los Principios Generales del Derecho Comunitario, al derecho sustantivo de los Países Miembros, y a los principios del Derecho Internacional, y en forma complementaria, a las disposiciones emanadas de la Organización Mundial del Comercio, siempre que sean compatibles con los principios y normas del Acuerdo de Integración Andina", SGCAN, *Resolución 1695*, Judgment of 6 June 2014, p. 14.

Ecuador claimed to be authorized to adopt the disputed measure.[100] Accordingly, although the SGAN had already determined that the Ecuadorian measure was subject to harmonization, making the invocation of the General Exception Clause impossible, it nevertheless assessed the measure under the requirements established by Arts. 72 and 73 AdC. The SGCAN found that the certificate of recognition could not be justified on the grounds of the protection of human health, because less trade-restrictive alternatives existed, namely the automatic recognition of the goods pursuant to another legislation harmonizing this procedure among CAN member states.[101] On appeal, the SGCAN cited an abundance of CJEU decisions, despite the fact that Ecuador *conceded* the measure was in violation of Art. 72 AdC and therefore constituted a restriction on trade. The SGCAN used the opportunity to clarify the content of Art. 34 TFEU and to carry out an in-depth analysis on the trade-restrictiveness of the measure.[102] Moreover, the SGCAN reexamined the justification of the measure under Art. 73 lit. d) AdC to find that it does not fulfil the requirements under the proportionality analysis. Moreover, the SGAN carried out an in-depth analysis of the non-discrimination resulting from the application of the requirement to furnish a certificate of recognition, encompassing the NT and MFN obligations under the AdC, although such a legal analysis is not common in the practice of the CJEU.[103]

Formal dispute settlement in front of the PTA-DSM of the Mercosur contained in its starting phase references to the rules under the legal framework of the EU. The first Mercosur ad-hoc arbitral panel in *Argentina v Brazil (01)* included indirect references to decisions of the CJEU by citing scholarly works on EU rules. Being faced with Mercosur member states' ACE 18 decision, by which the date for the removal of trade-restrictive measures was effectively postponed, and which introduced the method of enlisting non-fiscal trade-restrictive measures by Mercosur member states without removing them, the arbitral panel seemingly searched for a method to make the provisions under the TdA operable nonetheless. To prevent a substantial carve-out from the obligations on trade liberalization under the TdA, the first Mercosur ad-hoc arbitral panel reached out to the fundamental principles of *effet utile* developed by the CJEU to deliver a teleological interpretation of the legal

---

[100]The *complemento indispensable* doctrine allows CAN member states to adopt regulation of trade in areas that are not encompassed by CAN legislation, subject to the condition that it does not conflict directly with the rules under the CAN legal framework. Cf. Alter and Helfer (2017), p. 19, who claim that the doctrine was established by the TJCAN to give more deference to CAN member states in adjusting the pace of trade liberalization and to avoid the TJCAN from being confronted with controversial human-rights issues.

[101]SGCAN, *Resolución 1695*, Judgment of 6 June 2014, p. 23.

[102]Note, however, that such an analysis of the trade-restrictive measure would have never been carried out in a comparable technical manner by the CJEU. See SGCAN, *Resolución 1716*, Judgment of 18 August 2014, pp. 4–10.

[103]Ibid., pp. 10–26, cf. *supra* at Sect. 5.4.2.3.2.1.

framework of the Mercosur.[104] Pursuant to this understanding, the arbitral panel held that

"A logical conclusion since, as Gustavo Magariños says (Comercio e Integración, fcu, Montevideo, 1994, volume III, p. 169), 'Non-tariff restrictions are included in the liberalization programs of integration systems and their elimination is compulsory'. The author points out that the variety of these measures and the difficulty in identifying them 'have turned them into one of the main trade weapons of today'. Regarding this characterization Soldatos (op. cit. p. 125 to 126) compares these measures to the mythological Hydra of Lerna, due to their capacity to regenerate and multiply. It is for this reason that they must necessarily be part of the liberalization program and must have the same destiny as tariff restrictions. It would be impossible to have a regime with total tariff dismantling in which NTMs [note: non-tariff measures] would remain and could even be placed or expanded ad libitum, by unilateral decision of any of the Parties."[105]

The ad-hoc arbitral panel was in a position to conclude that non-fiscal measures would have to be generally eliminated under Mercosur rules. Where this was not the case, they would have to be justified under Art. 50 TdM, notwithstanding the ACE 18 decision of the Mercosur member states.[106] Being called upon to issue its first appellate decision in 2005, the TPR resumed this programmatic approach to the provisions under the Mercosur legal framework. It referred several times to the decisions of the CJEU in its reasoning on appealing the eleventh ad-hoc arbitral panel decision in *Uruguay v Argentina (11)*. The original proceedings in *Uruguay v Argentina (11)* dealt with an Argentine prohibition on the importation of used tires that could be utilized subsequently to produce remolded tires within a refurbishing process. The eleventh arbitral panel found the measure to be justified on the grounds of environmental protection, as it accepted the argument that the importation of used tires would lead to more accumulation of waste in Argentina, which would result in greater harm to the environment.[107] The TPR overturned this finding by holding that the ad-hoc arbitral panel erred in law in assuming equivalent principles of free trade

---

[104] Mercosur ad hoc arbitral panel (Brasília), Laudo Arbitral "Controversia sobre Comunicados N° 37 del 17 de diciembre de 1997 y N° 7 del 20 de febrero de 1998 del Departamento de Operaciones de Comercio Exterior (DECEX) de la Secretaría de Comercio Exterior (SECEX): Aplicación de Medidas Restrictivas al Comercio Recíproco", Judgment of 28 April 1999, para. 61.

[105] Original wording: "Conclusión lógica pues, como dice Gustavo Magariños (Comercio e Integración, fcu, Montevideo, 1994, tomo III, p. 169), 'Las restricciones no arancelarias están comprendidas en los programas de liberación de los sistemas de integración y su eliminación es forzosamente obligatoria.' Señalando el autor que la variedad de esas medidas y la dificultad para identificarlas las 'han convertido en una de las principales armas comerciales de la actualidad'. Al punto que Soldatos (Op. cit. p. 125 a 126) compara dichas medidas con la mitológica Hidra de Lerna, por su capacidad de regenerarse y de multiplicarse. Es por ese motivo que necesariamente han de integrar los programas de liberación y han de correr la misma suerte que las restricciones arancelarias. Sería imposible un régimen con desmantelamiento arancelario total en el cual las RNA permanezcan y, aún, pudieran ser colocadas u ampliadas ad libitum, por decisión unilateral de cualquiera de las Partes." Ibid., para. 69.

[106] Ibid., para. 85 (viii).

[107] Mercosur ad hoc arbitral panel (Brasília), Laudo "Prohibición de importación de neumáticos remodelados", Judgment of 25 October 2005, paras 97–99.

and environmental protection under the legal framework of the Mercosur, disregarding the criteria of the proportionality analysis under Art. 50 TdM.[108] The TPR referred to the decision of the CJEU in *Commission v Austria* to indicate the criteria of the proportionality analysis under Art. 36 TFEU.[109] It acknowledged that *mandatory requirements* could be generally available to Mercosur member states to justify trade-restrictive measures. Still, it found that Argentina's import ban on used tires could not constitute such a requirement, given that the domestic legislative process was explicitly aimed at the protection of the domestic tire-supplying industry.[110]

6.4.1.4.2   PTA-DSMs Referring to WTO-DSM Decisions and Rules Under the Legal Framework of the WTO

It is striking that almost all the decisions issued by the PTA-DSMs of the CAN and Mercosur, cited above, which contain references to decisions of the CJEU and rules under the legal framework of the EU, equally contain references to WTO rules. These references are much more general and rather of anecdotal character to support the understanding of the rules on trade liberalization within the respective PTAs.

Concerning the decision issued by the TJCAN for the process *1-AI-97*, the shared experiences from unsuccessful trade liberalization until World War Two have resulted in a general

> "[...] movement towards trade liberalization [which] emerged in the post-war period as a formula to counteract the prevailing trends and proceed with the reconstruction of economies devastated by the world wars. It is a movement based on the commercial expansion of the industrialized countries as a formula to ensure the balanced development of the contemporary world. Thus, financial, monetary and trade organizations emerged, molded within the scheme of free exchange and open trade, such as the World Bank, the International Monetary Fund and the General Agreement on Tariffs and Trade (GATT), which, on the basis of free trade, established instruments of international cooperation for the liberalization of world trade. The developing world is involved in this process through its adhesion to the respective international agreements and, more recently, through its incorporation into economic integration processes which, like the Andean area, are inspired by trade liberalization."[111]

Based on these considerations, the TJCAN further explained the existence and origin of the SPS Agreement by stating that

---

[108] TPR, Laudo N°01/2005, Judgment of 20 December 2005, para. C.3.9.

[109] It needs to be noted that the choice of the CJEU decision in *Commission v Austria* appears questionable considering the character of the measure as an MEQR, while the import ban on tires constituted a QR originally making the doctrine of *mandatory requirements* not applicable in such a case. Referring to CJEU, *Commission v Austria*, C-320/03; ECLI:EU:C:2005:684, Judgment of 15 November 2005; TPR, Laudo N°01/2005, Judgment of 20 December 2005, para. C.3.14.

[110] TPR, Laudo N°01/2005, Judgment of 20 December 2005, para. C.3.16.

[111] TJCAN, *1-AI-97*, 1-AI-97, Judgment of 11 December 1997, p. 15.

"[t]he SPS Agreement supports plant disease prevention measures on the basis that once the level of risk has been determined, appropriate alternative measures (such as treatment, quarantine or enhanced inspection) should be taken, choosing among them those most appropriate to achieve sanitary protection with the least restrictive effect on trade."[112]

The TJCAN did this to rely on the SPS Agreement as a basis allowing harmonization of the content of the disputed measure, to which Venezuela had not applied the harmonized procedure on phytosanitary inspections in the case at hand.[113] Moreover, the TJCAN addressed the SPS Agreement under the necessity analysis of the import restrictions on garlic for the protection of plant health to hold that import restrictions were no available alternative measures for protection from the plant disease, as alleged by Venezuela.

In the same vein, in *Resolution 489*, by citing the earlier *Resolution 049*, the SGCAN merely underlined its competence to identify the existence of trade restrictions. It indicated that a corresponding practice already existed within the context of the WTO and as well as in the EU, in this case carried out by the EC. [114]

Equally, the references to WTO rules in *Resolutions 1695* and *1716* were added by the SGCAN in the context of the existence of the General Exception Clause under Art. XX GATT 1994. The SGCAN maintained that this provision would only be available within the WTO context and, additionally, only in case a trade-restrictive measure was able to protect the legitimate objective and not used for protectionist purposes. Although Art. XX GATT 1994 was found by the SGCAN to be only available within the WTO context, the reference to the criteria contained within the proportionality analysis under this provision served to reconfirm the SGCAN's restrictive legal assessment under Art. 73 AdC.[115]

In addition to these general references to WTO rules and WTO-DSM decisions, the SGCAN used similar references either when they were advanced by CAN member states defending their trade-restrictive measures within a proceeding, or *proprio motu* to establish the autonomy of the Andean legal order. In *Resolution 184,* the SGCAN referred to Art. XXIV GATT 1994 to "contain[...] the principle of the coexistence of regional integration and trade regimes with the multilateral GATT/WTO regime."[116] In *Resolution 638*, facing the contention of Bolivia that its system of import licenses was in line with WTO rules, the SGCAN briefly held that, "with regard to Bolivia's argument justifying the imposition of licenses under WTO rules, it should be noted that this regime is not binding on the Andean Community".[117] In the same vein, in *117-AI-2003*, the TJCAN cited its previous

---

[112] Ibid., p. 16.

[113] Ibid., p. 17.

[114] SGCAN, *Resolución 449*, Judgment of 2 November 2000b, p. 6; SGCAN, *Resolución 489*, Judgment of 9 March 2001, p. 16.

[115] SGCAN, *Resolución 1716*, Judgment of 18 August 2014, p. 9.

[116] SGCAN, *Resolución 184*, Judgment of 29 January 1999, pp. 7–8.

[117] SGCAN, *Resolución 638*, Judgment of 3 July 2002, p. 4.

decision *7-AI-98*, confronted by the claim of Ecuador that it implemented an import-licensing scheme in accordance with WTO rules, by holding that

> "[i]n particular, with regard to the Member States' dual link with the Community's legal system and with the Marrakech Agreement establishing the World Trade Organization, the Court's criterion has been that the fact that the Member Countries of the Andean Community are themselves members of the World Trade Organization does not exempt them from obeying Andean Community rules on the pretext that they are complying with the organization's rules or that they intend to comply with their commitments to the organization. This would be no more and no less than a denial of the supremacy of the Andean Community system which, as has been said, is predominant not only over the internal legal systems of the Member Countries, but also over the other international legal systems to which they belong. In this respect, the case law of this Court has clearly expressed the nature of the principle of supremacy of Community law."[118]

In *5-AI-2007*, the TJCAN did not even further address the claim of Ecuador that the import ban on table salt was equally justified under Art. XX lit. b) GATT 1994. The SGCAN proceeded in the same way in *Resolution 784* and merely reproduced the claim put forward by Ecuador that its measures concerning the pre-authorization of different products were justified under WTO rules, but did not address them in its analysis.[119] Also, the SGCAN did not further assess Peru's claim in *Resolution 1289* that its requirement of a metal coating for batteries was justified under WTO rules.[120]

Moreover, *Resolution 2019* is noteworthy regarding the SGCAN's awareness of its impact within the multilateral trading system. It had to assess the conformity of a Colombian special-import procedure for imports of cement and the limitation of ports of entry for this good. Colombia claimed the restrictions to be justified on the grounds of human-health protection, as the controlled import of cement into its territory could prevent the production of cocaine. The SGCAN confirmed the argument of Colombia and referred also to the WTO-DSM decision in *Colombia— Ports of Entry*.[121] In this context, the SGCAN showed awareness that a WTO panel had criticized the unsteady assignments of ports of entry in one of the CAN member states, declaring them an import restriction in the sense of Art. XI GATT 1994. The SGCAN stressed in the corresponding footnote that the reduction of ports of entry itself was not at the heart of the WTO panel's decisions, and therefore was not precluded from taking place.[122]

Concerning the PTA-DSM of the Mercosur, the TPR, on the appeal of the eleventh arbitral panel's decision in *Uruguay v Argentina (11)*, merely reflected on the AB report on *Korea – Beef*, which was advanced by Uruguay concerning the

---

[118] TJCAN, *117-AI-2003*, Judgment of 19 September 2006, p. 14.

[119] SGCAN, *Resolución 784*, Judgment of 6 November 2003.

[120] SGCAN, *Resolución 1289*, Judgment of 11 November 2009.

[121] Cf. WTO Panel, Colombia — Indicative Prices and Restrictions on Ports of Entry (Panel), WT/DS366, Judgment of 27 April 2009, para. 2.274.

[122] SGCAN, *Resolución 2019*, Judgment of 14 August 2018, n. 90.

availability of weighing and balancing tests, but did not use them for its legal analysis.[123]

6.4.1.4.3   PTA-DSM of the Mercosur Citing Decisions of the PTA-DSM of the CAN

In addition to the references to CJEU decisions, the TPR, on appeal of the eleventh ad-hoc arbitral panel's decision in *Uruguay v Argentina (11)*, referred to the practice of the TJCAN concerning a procedural question. Faced with the request of Uruguay assessing the identified trade-restrictive measure on the importation of used tires in its *current* application, the TPR refused to change the terms of reference of the appellate proceedings. It reflected the practice of the TJCAN, which developed the concept of a *continuing violation of the CAN legal order* throughout its activity. According to the TPR, this concept allowed the TJCAN to scrutinize the disputed measure in its most recent application. Although the TPR appreciated this practice, it nevertheless declined to proceed in the same manner due to the differing procedural restraints in place under its procedural statutes.[124]

6.4.2   Effects of the Referencing Practices on the Future Adjudication of **Recurring Case Groups** by **PTA-DSMs**

The review of the referencing practices of PTA-DSMs shows that the already minimal transjudicial communication has remained mostly asymmetrical. On the one hand, this observation appears plausible, given the different states of maturity of the reviewed PTA-DSMs. As some of the reviewed PTA-DSMs have been active for a relatively short period, the development of a profound transjudicial dialog cannot be expected at this point. On the other hand, even if an emerging transjudicial dialog were assumed, significant evidence of an existing influence on the reasoning of PTA-DSMs by other PTA-DSM decisions can already be seen. PTA-DSM decisions on *recurring case groups* in particular contain many references to other PTA-DSM decisions. This is particularly noteworthy, as referencing of non-PTA sources is not generally widespread among PTA-DSMs. This speaks for a high degree of transjudicial dialog within the area of *recurring case groups* among the reviewed PTA-DSMs.

Accordingly, the decision of the first Mercosur ad-hoc arbitral panel in *Argentina v Brazil (01)* contains a reference to decisions of the CJEU and rules under the EU legal framework. This reference stands out, as the PTA-DSM of the Mercosur usually does not contain citations of other PTA-DSM decisions.

---

[123]TPR, Laudo N°01/2005, Judgment of 20 December 2005, para. C.3.17.
[124]Ibid., para. B.5.

Equally, *EFTA Surveillance Authority v Norway* is one of few the decisions that are relevant to the interpretation of the General Exception Clause under Art. 13 EEA, in which the EFTA Court added several references to the decisions of the CJEU, thereby fulfilling the EFTA Court's obligation on the homologous interpretation of EEA rules. Moreover, it is noteworthy that the decision of the *EFTA Surveillance Authority v Norway* is the only PTA-DSM decision that was referred to by the CJEU in the context of the interpretation of the General Exception Clause under Art. 36 TFEU.[125]

Generally, the abundantly available decisions of the CJEU transpired through to the legal reasoning in the decisions of all other PTA-DSMs. Rudimentary horizontal communication may be identified at best between the CJEU and the EFTA Court. At first sight, this might appear as a deception to an approaching development of a *Global Community of Courts* among PTA-DSMs. Nevertheless, for the purpose of assessing the impact of this transjudicial communication on decisions in future *recurring case groups*, a rather significant impact can be assumed.

Whether the current state of transjudicial communication will suffice to prevent PTA-DSMs from issuing *incommensurable* decisions on future *recurring case groups* remains questionable. Certainly, an ordering impact on future decision-making could prevail due to the establishment of the CJEU as a formal and informal focal and anchor point for the reasoning of all other PTA-DSMs. This speaks for the ability of the CJEU to exert some influence on the adjudicative process of other PTA-DSMs and limits the probability of the PTA-DSMs coming to incommensurable results.

Moreover, the references to WTO rules and decisions of the WTO-DSM have remained predominantly general regarding the liberalization of trade among the PTA partners' commitments contained in its legal framework. This reconfirms the limited usefulness of the rules under the WTO's legal framework and corresponding WTO-DSM decisions in providing advice to PTA-DSMs at the substantive level concerning the process of trade liberalization which goes beyond the one mandated by the WTO's own legal framework.

Nonetheless, the referencing practice to other PTA-DSM decisions and PTA rules has remained rather limited, which becomes especially apparent when they are compared with the much higher referencing record of PTA-DSM decisions to the decisions of the WTO-DSM and WTO rules. In no case do referencing practices to other PTA-DSM decisions and PTA rules constitute a *guarantee* against PTA-DSMs issuing *incommensurable* decisions with regard to *recurring case groups* in the future.

---

[125] CJEU, *Commission v Denmark*, C-192/01; ECLI:EU:C:2003:492, Judgment of 23 September 2003, paras 25, 33, 47, 49, 50, 51, 52, 53.

6.5   Conclusion

The analysis of PTA-DSM decisions on *recurring case groups* confirms that they have not issued *incommensurable* decisions. This conclusion draws on three observations:

Firstly, the lack of *incommensurable* PTA-DSM decisions comes from the different and specialized activities of PTA-DSMs concerning the adjudication of trade-restrictive measures under the respective General Exception Clauses. These different and specialized activities have precluded PTA-DSMs from developing a uniform activity that would have led them to adjudicate *recurring case groups*. Varying scopes of application of the different PTAs have allowed PTA-DSMs to issue decisions that contain legal reasonings on the respective General Exception Clauses, pertaining only to selected parts of the trade in goods between PTA partners. This has significantly reduced the probability of PTA-DSMs being called upon to issue decisions in *recurring case groups*, and has contributed to the scarcity of PTA-DSM decisions in *recurring case groups*. Consequently, PTA-DSM decisions affecting different types of trade-restrictive measures that have impacted varying goods, and for which diverse legitimate objectives have been invoked by the PTA partners, constitute a considerable impediment to the inquiry concerning their *incommensurability*.

Secondly, the identification of decisions in *recurring case groups* nevertheless remains an approximation with regard to the equivalence of the factual and legal circumstances surrounding the specific cases at hand. Most notably, the different practices developed by PTA-DSMs, such as their reliance on the principle of harmonization of laws or the delegation of fact-finding to domestic courts, do not allow them to identify *recurring case groups*.

Thirdly, the review of the decisions on *recurring case groups* exposes differences in the quality of PTA-DSM decisions which render them equally unsuitable for an assessment concerning their incommensurability. The decisions on *recurring case groups* do not always contain sufficient information to conduct an inquiry into their incommensurability. Broad concepts of legitimate objectives contained in the respective General Exception Clauses under which the prevention of risks to identical legitimate objectives at different proximities or different concepts remains possible play a decisive role for this obstacle in the analysis of the *incommensurability* of PTA-DSM decisions.

However, the review of the remaining decisions that have proven suitable for the analysis and were issued by the PTA-DSMs on General Exception Clauses shows that the PTA-DSMs indeed have not issued incommensurable decisions in the context of the respective General Exception Clauses. Although the PTA-DSMs have resorted to different *means* within their reasoning, they have arrived at the same *ends* concerning the justifiability of trade-restrictive measures regarding the specific legitimate objectives invoked. These different *means* reveal variations, but no fundamental differences, concerning the concept of trade liberalization among the PTA partners in their legal reasoning on General Exception Clauses. This has been especially visible in the decisions of the PTA-DSMs on one *recurring case* in which decisions from different PTA-DSMs generally allowed the maintaining of a disputed ban on the importation of foodstuffs by PTA partners, while at the same time differing concerning the techniques that the PTA partners were allowed to use for its enforcement to protect the legitimate objective in question. While according to one decision goods posing a risk to the legitimate objective of animal health were allowed access to the market of PTA partners by dismantling all importation formalities in another decision, a risk assessment could stay in place which could be carried out by means of importation formalities, namely import licenses.

Moreover, the PTA-DSMs have proven to apply different levels of thoroughness in the assessment of the trade-restrictive measures, but came to the same conclusion on the justifiability of a trade-restrictive measure. These variations in the legal thoroughness applied by the PTA-DSMs have a different impact on the potential for the legal integration of PTA partners. The different approaches by PTA-DSMs testify to the variance in self-perceptions concerning their role in the process of trade liberalization among PTA partners. Their different exigencies towards disputing PTA partners to provide scientific evidence for verifying whether trade-restrictive measures indeed protect the invoked legitimate objectives speak for the different motivations and legal mandates of PTA-DSMs to encourage legal integration of PTA partners.

Finally, the diverging conclusions of the PTA-DSMs in the *recurring case* on the technical standards for mechanical appliances serving the protection of human health demonstrate the importance of the ongoing and evolving regulation of goods at the international level for the legal reasoning of PTA-DSMs. The diverging conclusions reached on the non-justifiability of a Peruvian requirement for batteries and the justifiability of a French requirement on automation for wood-working machines nevertheless can be considered commensurable. Both decisions need to be read in the different contexts and different stages of international standardization for electronic goods at the time at which they were issued. Whereas batteries were subject to a high degree of international standardization, including the admissible requirements at the time when the SGCAN issued its decision, international standardization of automation requirements in any kind of mechanical appliance were not even contemplated when the CJEU issued its decision. The review of both decisions shows that they appeared economically reasonable when the decisions were issued. They prevented a partitioning of the market in the sale of batteries in the CAN, on the one hand, and, on the other, a corresponding market for automated wood-working machines was not established in the EU at the time.

With these results on hand, the review of the referencing practices of the PTA-DSMs shows that, in their decisions on non-PTA sources, they enclose citations only to a very limited extent. Where citations are contained within their decisions, however, the PTA-DSMs use them to legitimize their legal reasoning on certain legitimate objectives. Consequently, the reviewed PTA-DSMs have engaged in rudimentary transjudicial communication by means of their referencing practice. In particular, decisions of the CJEU have been referenced regularly by all other PTA-DSM throughout their activity. Considering that the concepts of the obligation to liberalize trade in the reviewed PTAs draw heavily from those contained within the legal framework of the EU and interpreted by the CJEU, the referencing practice of the PTA-DSMs to decisions of the CJEU can be best characterized as an attempt to improve the quality of their legal reasoning. It has allowed them to reflect the legal doctrine developed by the CJEU, which has established a rather demanding standard for the liberalization of trade between EU member states, and to transpose it to their own PTA contexts. Simultaneously, the referencing practices of the PTA-DSM of the CAN and Mercosur, in mentioning WTO rules and WTO-DSM decisions concerning the interpretation of the respective General Exception Clauses, have allowed them to underline the distinctiveness of their own PTA rules from the multilateral rules on trade liberalization. Both observations speak for a relatively strong effect of the CJEU on the reasoning of the reviewed PTA-DSMs, acting as a focal point for the development of legal concepts on the liberalization of trade in PTAs. Both the references to WTO rules and decisions of the WTO-DSM testify to an awareness of the PTA-DSMs for the international and multilateral surroundings in which they operate. Whether this systemic awareness is enough to prevent PTA-DSMs from issuing *incommensurable* decisions in the future, once their activity aligns, cannot be guaranteed. Nevertheless, these two observations confirm that the CJEU *de facto* has already taken a guiding role concerning the development of the doctrine of the liberalization of trade in other PTA-DSMs. Despite all this evidence on the influence of the CJEU on the legal reasoning of the other PTA-DSMs, overall references to CJEU decisions have remained scarce. Given the absence of *incommensurable* PTA-DSM decisions, this confirms that PTA-DSMs have resorted to the same logic for the adjudication of trade-restrictive measures in the context of the respective General Exception Clauses. Apparently, the PTA-DSMs' excellent understanding of the principles of trade liberalization has helped them to remain within the same logic of trade liberalization. Most probably, this constitutes another circumstance which so far has made explicit references of PTA-DSMs to other PTA-DSMs largely redundant.

References

Abbott KW, Genschel P, Snidal D, Zangl B (2014) Orchestration. In: Abbott KW, Genschel P, Snidal D, Zangl B (eds) International organizations as orchestrators. Cambridge University Press, Cambridge, pp 3–36

Alter KJ, Helfer LR (2017) Transplanting international courts: the law and politics of the Andean Tribunal of Justice, 1st edn. Oxford University Press, Oxford

Alter KJ, Meunier-Aitsahalia S (1994) Judicial politics in the European community: European integration and the pathbreaking Cassis de Dijon decision. Comp Polit Stud 26:535–561. https://doi.org/10.1177/0010414094026004007

Awasthi K, Yayavaram S, George R, Sastry T (2019) Classification for regulated industries: a new index. IIMB Manage Rev 31:309–315. https://doi.org/10.1016/j.iimb.2019.01.002

Dalla Torre Di Sanguinetto S, Heinonen E, Antonov J, Bolte C (2019) A comparative review of marketing authorization decisions in Switzerland, the EU, and the USA. Therap Innov Regul Sci 53:86–94. https://doi.org/10.1177/2168479018764660

de Córdoba SF, Laird S, Maur J-C, Serena JM (2006) Adjustment costs and trade liberalization. In: Laird S, de Córdoba SF (eds) Coping with trade reforms: a developing country perspective on the WTO industrial tariff negotiations. Palgrave Macmillan UK, London, pp 66–85

Heiskanen V (2004) The regulatory philosophy of international trade law. Journal of World Trade 38:1–36

Kuijper PJ (2018) The Court of Justice of the European Union. In: Ulfstein G, Ruiz-Fabri H, Zang MQ, Howse R (eds) The legitimacy of international trade courts and tribunals. Cambridge University Press, Cambridge, pp 70–137

Lindroos A (2005) Dispelling the Chimera of 'Self-Contained Regimes' international law and the WTO. Eur J Int Law 16:857–877. https://doi.org/10.1093/ejil/chi148

Majone G (2006) The common sense of European integration. J Eur Public Policy 13:607–626. https://doi.org/10.1080/13501760600808212

Olson M (2012) The logic of collective action public goods and the theory of groups. Harvard University Press, Cambridge, Mass

Pauwelyn J (2019) WTO dispute settlement post 2019: what to expect? J Int Econ Law 22:297–321. https://doi.org/10.1093/jiel/jgz024

Perišin T (2008) Free movement of goods and limits of regulatory autonomy in the EU and WTO. T.M.C. Asser Press, Den Haag

Sachs NM (2011) Rescuing the strong precautionary principle from its critics. Univ Ill Law Rev 2011:1285–1338

Scharpf F (1998) Negative and positive integration in the political economy of European welfare states. In: Rhodes M, Mény Y (eds) The future of European welfare: a new social contract? Palgrave Macmillan UK, London, pp 157–177

Schroeder W (2016) Transatlantic Free Trade Agreements and European Food Standards. Eur Food Feed Law Rev (EFFL) 11:494–501

Slaughter A-M (1994) A typology of transjudicial communication symposium: human rights international law. Univ Richmond Law Rev 29:99–138

Voeten E (2010) Borrowing and nonborrowing among international courts. J Leg Stud 39:547–576. https://doi.org/10.1086/652460

Vogel D (2012) Chapter Two. Explaining regulatory policy divergence. In: The politics of precaution. Princeton University Press, Princeton, pp 22–42

Chapter 7
General Conclusion

The findings made throughout this work cast a different vision of the role of PTA-DSMs for the fragmentation of international trade law, compared to one traditionally assumed under the *predominantly formalist* approach to international trade law. The low level of activity in the whole universe of existing PTA-DSMs and, where PTA-DSMs have become active, the lack of incommensurable PTA-DSM decisions prove a different role for the fragmentation of international trade law than predicted under the *predominantly formalist* approach. The analysis of all decisions of PTA-DSMs issued in the context of the adjudication of the respective General Exception Clauses indicates that PTA-DSMs and their function to promote a judicialized process of trade liberalization are of varying significance in the respective PTAs and for the respective PTA partners. This has led to the development of varying dynamics in the adjudication of substantively equivalent PTA rules among the reviewed PTA-DSMs. Until now, these varying dynamics have not given rise to assume that PTA-DSMs would engage in any legal reasoning that would call into question the systemic operation of the rules on international trade. The PTA-DSMs' varying activities preclude us from assessing whether they *generally* resort to the same logic when examining trade-restrictive measures under the General Exception Clauses *on a large scale*. Nevertheless, where PTA-DSMs have developed a record of adjudication in *recurring case groups*, their decisions have proven to be not *incommensurable*. Rather, the comparison of decisions in *recurring case groups* has revealed the broad range of possible multifactorial approaches available for PTA-DSMs to integrate in their legal reasoning in order to arrive at an effective liberalization of trade among PTA partners. These varying specific approaches for the successful implementation of policies that ensure the effective liberalization of trade among PTA partners through the activity of PTA-DSMs has often been neglected in the discussion on the fragmentation of international trade law. An excessively narrow focus on the interplay of PTAs with the multilateral legal framework of the WTO is the main reason why these varying approaches, used in the legal reasoning of the different PTA-DSMs, have remained underexplored. Given that the WTO provisions on PTAs can guide WTO Members only to a very limited extent on how actually to attain trade liberalization beyond their commitments on the multilateral level, this narrow focus on the interplay between the WTO and PTA has proven to be an inadequate projection surface for questions on more ambitious trade liberalization and deeper economic integration of WTO Members choosing to engage in PTAs. Departing from a *predominantly formalist* understanding of international trade law, PTA-DSMs in general have not become as active as predicted and have not developed into an institutional threat to the WTO-DSM. The assumption that the PTA partners would automatically resort to dispute settlement under PTA-DSMs, merely due to their availability under PTAs, has proven inaccurate. The low overall activity of PTA-DSMs and the different dynamics in their activities exist in contrast to the very high activity of litigation under the WTO-DSM experienced so far. This observation speaks for a central characteristic of all adjudicative bodies within the realm of international trade law: Their individual activity and importance builds on the specific and varying institutional settings in which they operate. The findings therefore show that it is imprecise to draw from the experience of litigation on trade matters under the WTO-DSM for the purpose of assessing the role of all PTA-DSMs for the fragmentation of international trade law.

Consequently, it can be held that the systemic dangers voiced over the activity of PTA-DSMs for the fragmentation of international trade law have not materialized yet. This is mostly due to the economic and political complexity of the process of trade liberalization itself, which results from the different economic compositions of PTA partners and their different needs to resort to specific legitimate objectives under the respective General Exception Clauses. The complexity of this process has led PTA-DSMs to develop an uneven, *not uniform*, activity on the adjudication of different types of trade-restrictive measures, which ultimately does not allow us to draw the conclusion that their legal reasoning is harmful to the systemic operation of the rules in international trade law.

What role do the PTA-DSMs then assume for the fragmentation of international trade law? The results of this analysis allow us to observe that only those PTA-DSMs have become active that were intended by the respective PTA partners to lead their way into a long-lasting and profound transformation of their economies in the context of most ambitious obligations to liberalize trade requiring the deep legal integration of their economies. They have catered to the PTA partners' specific needs within a highly legalized process of trade liberalization and have proven to be used in different ways for the attainment of this goal. Through their activity they have been exposed to varying economic and institutional problems arising in their respective PTA contexts. These observations suggest that an alternative understanding of PTA-DSMs for the fragmentation of international trade law is necessary. This would require taking aspects into consideration that go beyond the enforcement of legal obligations among the PTA partners. One proposition would be to characterize the PTA-DSMs as *far less*, but also *far more*, than merely means set up to cause trade diversion or the hampering of a multilateral approach on the liberalization of trade. Departing from the analysis of PTA-DSM activity in this work, PTA-DSMs can be characterized as *far less* a systemic threat if they remain only a signal or guarantee of the PTA partners' conviction to engage in trade liberalization. The analysis of PTA-DSM activity has shown that the vast majority have been set up, without really aiming at developing any activity, let alone a legal doctrine that would break with the general understanding of trade liberalization as developed by the WTO-DSM and other PTA-DSMs. However, PTA-DSMs can be characterized as are *far more* than a systemic threat if they are set up to develop a legal doctrine on trade liberalization in the legal area that surpasses the level of trade liberalization provided under WTO rules. As the WTO-DSM has proven an unsuitable forum for this purpose so far, the activity of PTA-DSMs within this field of international trade law allows PTA partners to moderate the complex economic, political, and societal consequences resulting from effective trade liberalization. It assists them in properly shaping this process by providing the resonating body for a departure into unchartered territory, given the various economic and legal transformations that develop along the process of trade liberalization. Consequently, the findings on the different approaches taken by PTA-DSMs for the review of trade-restrictive measures under the respective General Exception Clauses could not be confirmed as incommensurable, as they focused on different *means* of trade liberalization among the PTA partners to arrive at the same *ends*. At the same time, the analysis of the few active PTA-DSMs exposes them as relatively open regarding other non-PTA law and other PTA-DSM decisions. This again demonstrates that their characterization as a systemic threat is rather inaccurate, given that the reviewed PTA-DSMs have proven to be aware of the international regulatory architecture in which they were operating, and which they regularly integrated in their legal reasoning.

At the micro-level, the range of different methods used by the PTA-DSMs to ensure the effective implementation of the process of trade liberalization calls for additional research. This future research should strive to provide a generalized understanding of the importance of PTA-DSM activity for the successful liberalization of trade in PTAs. As for now, the PTA-DSMs seem only to have had the opportunity to draw from the experience on trade liberalization as conceptualized in the legal framework of the EU and as experienced by the adjudication of the CJEU. This experience, however, appears to be of limited use considering the existing institutional and economic differences in place in the individual PTAs. Conversely, the importance of the decisions of the CJEU for the reasoning of PTA-DSMs can create an awareness that the decisions of the CJEU are received not only by the EU member states and their citizens, but also by a much larger audience beyond the EU. [1] This calls for even more scholarly work on the economic effects of the decisions of the CJEU on the EU member states' economies, in order to develop a generalized understanding of the effects of PTA-DSM decisions on the process of trade liberalization. This would contribute to developing precise knowledge on the economic results of the PTA-DSM decisions, and to better informing the other PTA-DSMs and PTA partners about their policy choices under PTAs. An important

---

[1] In this vein, cf. Bradford (2019).

factor to achieve this aim is the development of a clear and coherent legal doctrine on trade-liberalization PTA-DSMs, most importantly by the CJEU, given its influential role on other PTA-DSMs. It would assist other PTA-DSMs in engaging in a meaningful discussion on the concept of a trade liberalization that is most suited to the specific economic and institutional situation in which they are operating.

At the macro-level, the record and outcome of PTA-DSM activity on the adjudication of General Exception Clauses could assist in shaping a new narrative on the PTA-DSMs' role within the international trading system. Against the backdrop of the low overall activity of PTA-DSMs and the broad range of different means of dispute settlement available to PTA partners, the active PTA-DSMs, operating in a highly legalist mode, can rather be thought of as indications of a shared belief in the general observance of the *rule of law* and a third-party review of executive power by international adjudicative bodies, as already proposed by *Karen Alter* and *Liesbet Hooghe.* [2] Instead of a narrative promoting PTA-DSMs as an *institutional threat* to the WTO, a narrative focusing on their contribution as a general *institutional backup* for the development of the *trade rule of law* [3] could assist us in fostering cooperation among all DSMs that are called upon to adjudicate trade matters. Acknowledgement of the adjudication of trade rules by all DSMs, resulting from such an understanding, could help any of those DSMs to become more aware of their abilities and limitations within the international trading system. With this awareness at hand, DSMs could ensure a future systemic development of international trade law.

References

Alter KJ, Hooghe L (2016) Regional Dispute Settlement. In: Börzel TA, Risse T (eds) The Oxford Handbook of Comparative Regionalism. Oxford University Press, Oxford, pp 538–559. https://doi.org/10.1093/oxfordhb/9780199682300.013.24

Bradford A (2019) The Brussels Effect: how the European Union Rules the World. Oxford University Press, Oxford

Claussen K (2019) Old wine in new bottles? The Trade Rule of law. Yale J Int Law Online 44:61–68

---

[2] Alter and Hooghe (2016), p. 553.

[3] Claussen (2019).

Chapter 8
Annex

8.1 Codebook

8.1.1 Meta Data

[Decision No.] Unique ID for each decision in the database.

[Date of Decision] Date of the decision taken by the respective PTA-DSM.

[DSM] Unique ID for the PTA under which the PTA-DSM was operating.

[Regime] Unique ID for the legal regime from which the PTA-DSM based its substantive reasoning. Moreover, the regime indicates whether the case was overruled by subsequent decisions of the PTA-DSM.

Code	Regime Description
100	TFEU
101	European Communities (Nice)
102	European Communities (Amsterdam)
103	European Communities (Maastricht)
105	European Economic Cooperation. (Rome)
200	TJCAN
220	Junta
230	Secretaría General
250	SGCAN
250-OR	SGCAN overruled
260	JUNAC
260-OR	JUNAC overruled
310	Mercosur ad-hoc Brasilia
310-OR	Mercosur ad-hoc Brasilia overruled
320	Mercosur ad-hoc Olivos

(continued)

The original version of this chapter was revised: The date format of entries in sections 8.2.1.1 and 8.2.1.3 have been changed. The correction to this chapter is available at https://doi.org/10.1007/978-3-031-40601-0_10

Code	Regime Description
320-OR	Mercosur ad-hoc Olivos overruled
330	TPR
330-OR	TPR overruled
600	EFTA

[Compl] ID for the complaining party in a case.

Country_Code	Country_Name
111	Austria
112	Belgium
113	Bulgaria
114	Croatia
115	Cyprus
116	Czech Republic
117	Denmark
118	Estonia
119	Finland
120	France
121	Germany
122	Greece
123	Hungary
124	Ireland
125	Italy
126	Latvia
127	Lithuania
128	Luxembourg
129	Malta
130	Netherlands
131	Poland
132	Portugal
133	Romania
134	Slovakia
135	Slovenia
136	Spain
137	Sweden
138	United Kingdom
140	Commission
145	Council
150	Private
201	Bolivia (1969)
202	Colombia (1969)
203	Ecuador (1969)
204	Peru (1969)

(continued)

Country_Code	Country_Name
205	Venezuela (1973–2006)
206	Chile
301	Argentina (1991)
302	Brazil (1991)
303	Paraguay (1991)
304	Uruguay (1991)
601	Iceland
602	Liechtenstein
603	Norway
604	Switzerland
605	Secretariat/Surveillance Authority

[Resp] ID for the responding party in a case. Where a domestic court initiated the dispute for preliminary proceedings, the space is left blank and instead the origin of the domestic court is inserted under [**Compl**].

[Proceedings] ID for the specific proceedings in which the decision was issued.

Code	Type of proceeding
801	Adversary proceedings (including initiation by agency)
802	Preliminary proceedings
803	Summary proceedings
804	Ad-hoc proceedings
805	Non-court proceedings (SGCAN)
806	Appeal proceedings

[Foregoing Decision] Unique ID for each case in the database is inserted in case of a foregoing decision. This is especially relevant for proceedings under CAN and Mercosur law.

8.1.2   Disputed Measure at Issue

[Type of Measure] Type of disputed measure.

Code	Type of proceeding
1	Non-fiscal measure
2	Fiscal measure

[Measure Specifically Targeted At] Type of trade the disputed measure was targeted at.

Code	Type of proceeding
1	Imports
2	Exports
3	Both

[Characterization of Measure] Characterization that the PTA-DSM ascribed to the disputed measure.

Number—Types of Measure 3	Explanation—Types of Measure 3
0	No effect
1	Customs duty
2	Equivalent effect to customs duty
3	Tax
4	Service fee
5	Quantitative restriction (QR)
6	Measure of equivalent effect as quantitative restriction (MEQR)
7	Too uncertain effect of the measure on trade
8	Financial transaction (Dumping)
9	Minimum prices
10	Subsidies
11	Safeguards
12	Rules of origin
13	Monopoly
14	Refusal to act/legal omission by the PTA partner
15	Referential prices for customs valuation
16	Multiple measures

8.1.3 Goods Affected by the Measure

[Multiple Goods] Indication whether the challenged measure at issue affected more than one type of goods. For very broad measures, the variable was set at 1.

Code	Type of proceeding
0	Only one type of good affected
1	More than one type of good affected

[Type of Goods] Indication for the type of good affected by the challenges measure, expressed by the chapter under which the affected good is categorized according to the Harmonized Tariff Schedule of the WCO. Where a measure affected more than

one chapter, but was limited to one section, the relevant section number was inserted. Where a measure affected goods of more than one section, the variable '0' was inserted.

[Digits After Chapter] Indication of the subheading under the Harmonized Tariff Schedule of the WCO of the good affected by the measure.

8.1.4   Use of the General Exception Clause

[General Exception Clause Relevant] Relevance of the respective General Exception Clause for a PTA-DSM decision. This variable was inserted after the manual keyword search.

Code	Type of proceeding
0	Irrelevant
1	Relevant

[Recourse to Area] Legitimate objective under which the disputed measure was argued as being justified.

Code	Legitimate objective
0	Not specified
10	Public morals
20	Public policy/public order
21	Securing the electrical supply of a country
30	Public security/public safety
40	General health protection (unspecified)
41	Human health protection
42	Animal health protection
43	Plant health protection
50	Trade in gold/silver
60	Customs enforcement
70	Prevention of monopolies/antitrust issues
80	Intellectual property protection
90	Prevention of deceptive practices
100	Prison labor
110	Societal value
111	Artistic value
112	Historic value
113	Archeological value
120	Conservation of natural resources
130	Trade in fissionable materials; arms trade
140	Trade in nuclear materials

(continued)

Code	Legitimate objective
150	Child labor
160	Prevention of food shortages
170	Prevention of double taxation
180	Consumer protection
181	Designation of quality
190	Road traffic safety
200	Environment
201	Conservation of biodiversity
202	Wild birds
203	Prevention of pollution
210	Cultural expression/diversity
211	Printed books as a cultural good
212	Cinema as a cultural good
213	Diversity of the press
220	Animal welfare
230	Working conditions
240	Minors/children
250	Functioning of the social security system
251	Ensuring quality of medicinal products
252	Currency
260	Public-health protection
261	Consumer-health protection
262	Safeguarding the public-health system
263	Ensuring a less costly public-health system
270	Combating fraud/smuggling/tax evasion
280	Combating crime
290	Ensuring fiscal supervision
300	Protection of fundamental rights
400	Supply of goods at short distance
500	Ensuring the fairness of commercial transactions/fair trade/preventing excessive competitive advantages
501	Giving full effect to the common organization of the market in the cereals sector
600	Protecting the conformity of community rules
700	Ensuring the viability of an undertaking (economic measure)
800	Measures introduced for statistical purposes
801	Measures introduced for scientific purposes
802	Measures introduced for reduction of energy consumption
803	Measures introduced for municipal development purposes
900	Administrative burden
1000	Services rendered by national authorities
1050	National legislation
1100	Common agricultural trade policy
1200	Common organization of pasta sector
2000	Other international agreement

[Explicitly Included in General Exception Clause] Indication whether the area is explicitly included in the wording of the provision containing the General Exception Clause in the respective PTA.

Code	Type of proceeding
0	Area is not explicitly included.
1	Area is explicitly included.

[Argumentation for Additional Legitimate Objective] Indication for the arguments that the respective PTA-DSM has relied on to justify the (un)successful recourse to an additional legitimate objective invoked.

Code	Type of proceeding
0	No additional argumentation.
1	Additional profound argumentation.
2	Reference to established case law.
3	Finding of equivalence of legitimate objective under General Exception Clause.

[Multiple Areas] Indication whether the measure was argued under more than one legitimate objective.

Code	Type of proceeding
0	Only one legitimate objective invoked.
1	More than one legitimate objective invoked.

[Category] Indication of the broader category into which the specific legitimate objective fell; e.g., for the legitimate objective "public health", the broader category of "human health" was selected.

Code	Category Title
A	Morality
AA	Economic interest
AAA	Restriction definition
B	Safety
BB	Measurement of trade flows
C	Health
CC	Administrative processes
DD	Agriculture
E	Precious metals
EE	Obligations under public law
FF	Customs management
GG	Automotive sector
H	Intellectual property protection
HH	Exchange rate policy

(continued)

Code	Category Title
I	Antitrust and fair competition
J	Prison labor
JJ	Sanitary and phytosanitary measure
K	Protection of the culture
LL	Rules of origin
M	Trade in fissionable materials/arms trade
MM	Procedural impediments
N	Trade in nuclear materials
NN	Services
NOT	Not specified
O	Unfavorable working conditions
P	Securing supply chains
Q	Services of general interest
R	Protection of the consumer
RR	Arms trade
SS	Export restrictions
T	Road traffic safety
TT	Trade with developing CAN member states
U	Environment and sustainability
UU	Third-country market access
V	Animal health
VV	Infringement of other law
Y	Protection of fundamental rights
Z	Constitutionalizing of community order
W	Plant health

8.1.5 Decision and Type of Decision

[Recourse Successful] Indication whether the recourse to the respective General Exception Clause was successful.

Code	Type of proceeding
0	Recourse not successful
1	Recourse successful

[Reason for (No) Success] Indication of the concrete reason, within the reasoning of the application of the General Exception Clause, why the PTA-DSM finds the measure to be consistent or inconsistent with PTA law. This element indicates the reason as to why the PTA-DSM, at the level of the General Exception Clause, found the measure to be (not) justified. A PTA-DSM may have found that a specific

requirement of the exception clause was not fulfilled, or instead that only that the burden of proof had not been met by one of the parties of the dispute.[1]

Code	Reason for (no) success
0	Measure does (not) attain legitimate goal (i.e., the threat to a legitimate objective is accepted, but the suitability of the measure to attain its protection is denied)
1	Measure (not) necessary
2	Measure (dis)proportionate/excessive (and not necessary)
3	(No) harmonization of laws (esp. in CAN, (no) inscription in SPS catalogue, or not authorized safeguard measure)
4	No threat to the legitimate objectives established by a disputing party (i.e., the threat is denied by the PTA-DSM)
5	Respondent has not given sufficient information on the content of the measure (burden of proof not satisfied)
6	Complainant has not given sufficient information on the contents of the measure (burden of proof not satisfied)
7	Measure has ceased to exist
8	Appeal too late
9	No information
10	Justification should have been used in foregoing prejudicial proceedings (SGCAN vs. TJCAN)
11	Justification not available
12	Violation conceded
13	Measure discriminates arbitrarily and unjustifiably
14	Effect of the measure on trade too uncertain

[Type of Decision Reached] Indication concerning the type of legal conclusion the PTA-DSM made regarding the trade-restrictive measure in question.

Code	Decision Type
1	Measure (in)consistent (no more information)
2	Precise other measure suggested
3	Other measure suggested and referred back to member/court to carry out a proper assessment
4	Mixed content of legal conclusion

8.1.6 Context of the Decision

[Other PTA Law Relevant] Indication whether the PTA-DSM issued the decision solely based on the respective General Exception Clause or whether it also considered other PTA law for the purpose of its interpretation.

---

[1] Waltermann et al. (2020), pp. 31–34.

Code	Other PTA law relevant
0	Decision issued solely based on the respective General Exception Clause.
1	Decision issued in conjunction with other existing PTA law.

[Other Non-PTA Law Relevant] Indication whether other non-PTA law was referenced by the PTA-DSM in its decision on the respective General Exception Clause.

Code	Non-PTA law relevant
0	Non-PTA law not relevant.
1	Non-PTA law relevant.

[Reference to Other Scientific Body] Indication whether the PTA-DSM referred to another scientific body within its decision.

Code	Non-PTA law relevant
0	No reference to other scientific body.
1	Reference to other scientific body.

[Further Proceeding at Body of Higher Instance] Indication whether the case was heard by another body of higher instance of the PTA-DSM, where applicable.

Code	Type of proceeding
0	Case was not heard by a body of higher instance.
1	Case was heard by a body of higher instance.

8.1.7   References in PTA-DSM Decisions

[Non-PTA Reference Sources] Indication concerning the source of non-PTA law, that was referenced by PTA-DSM in the decision.

Code	Name of Source Entity
0	Non-PTA law irrelevant
10	Kyoto Protocol
11	UNFCCC
12	CITES
13	Convention on Biological Diversity (Rio Convention)
14	Stockholm Convention
15	International Environmental Law
16	European Convention on the Protection of Animals Kept for Farming Purposes
17	CITES Conference of Parties
18	IATTC: Inter-American Tropical Tuna Commission

(continued)

Code	Name of Source Entity
19	Rotterdam Convention
20	Basel Convention on hazardous waste;
30	FAO
40	WHO
41	WHO Guideline for Drinking Water
50	Codex Alimentarius
60	Convention on Narcotic Drugs
70	ISO
80	DIN
90	ECHR
91	Other International Treaties on Human Rights
92	Recommendation R (95) 14 Council of Europe
100	Geneva Convention 1923
110	Universal Postal Convention
120	VCLT
130	UN Doc
150	EU Law
151	EU Case Law
160	WTO law
161	WTO Case Law
162	TBT
163	SPS
164	Import Licensing Agreement
200	CAN Case Law
300	Domestic Legal Acts
301	Bolivian Constitution
302	Spanish Constitutional Court
303	Mexican Domestic Law
304	National Authority on Drug Abuse
401	EU Norway PTA
402	EC Sweden PTA
403	Convention of Automotive Sector (between Colombia, Ecuador, Venezuela)
404	International Agreement between Ecuador and USA
500	OEEC List of Trade Liberalization
600	Latest Scientific Data/International Research
700	EC's own Scientific Committee
800	General Scholarly Literature
801	Secondary Literature on EU Law
802	Encyclopedic Dictionary of Law Usual of Guillermo Cabanellas
900	Not explicitly mentioned (implicit reference to preceding case)
1000	EFTA Case Law

[Non-PTA Reference Category] For practical reasons the individual sources of non-PTA law have been grouped in code categories, as follows:

Code	Code Category	Source	Name of Source Entity
0	O	Non-PTA law irrelevant	Non-PTA law irrelevant
10	A	International Environmental Law	Kyoto Protocol
11	A	International Environmental Law	UNFCCC
12	B	International Biodiversity Protection	CITES
13	B	International Biodiversity Protection	Convention on Biological Diversity (Rio Convention)
14	B	International Biodiversity Protection	Stockholm Convention
15	A	International Environmental Law	Intl. Environmental Law
16	T	International Animal Welfare	European Convention on the Protection of Animals Kept for Farming Purposes
17	B	International Biodiversity Protection	CITES Conference of Parties
18	B	International Biodiversity Protection	IATTC: Inter-American Tropical Tuna Commission
19	A	International Environmental Law	Rotterdam Convention
20	A	International Environmental Law	Basel Convention on hazardous waste;
30	H	Food and Agriculture	FAO
40	K	International Health Protection	WHO
41	K	International Health Protection	WHO Guide Line for Drinking Water
50	H	Food and Agriculture	Codex Alimentarius
60	J	International Drug Addiction Prevention	Convention on Narcotic Drugs
70	Q	Standardization	ISO
80	Q	Standardization	DIN
90	I	Human Rights Protection	ECHR
91	I	Human Rights Protection	other intl. Treaties on human rights
92	K	International Health Protection	Recommendation R (95) 14 Council of Europe
100	L	International Procedure and Litigation	Geneva Convention 1923
110	D	Communication	Universal Postal Convention
120	N	International Treaty Interpretation	VCLT

(continued)

Code	Code Category	Source	Name of Source Entity
130	R	United Nations	UN Doc
150	G	EU	EU Law
151	G	EU	EU Case Law
160	S	WTO	WTO law
161	S	WTO	WTO Case Law
162	S	WTO	TBT
163	S	WTO	SPS
164	S	WTO	Import Licensing Agreement
200	C	CAN	CAN Case Law
300	E	Domestic legislation and jurisprudence	Domestic Legal Acts
301	E	Domestic legislation and jurisprudence	BOL constitution
302	E	Domestic legislation and jurisprudence	Spanish Const. Court
303	E	Domestic legislation and jurisprudence	Mexican law
304	J	International Drug Addiction Prevention	National authority on drug abuse
305	E	Domestic legislation and jurisprudence	Mexican law
401	GG	European PTAs	EU Norway PTA
402	GG	European PTAs	EC Sweden PTA
403	CC	Regional Treaty	Convention of Automotive Sector (COL, ECU, VEN)
404	U	CAN PTAs	Intl. Agreement btw ECU + USA
500	M	International Trade Regulation	OEEC list of trade liberalization
600	P	Scientific Evidence	Latest scientific data/international research
700	P	Scientific Evidence	EC's own Scientific Committee;
800	Z	General Scholarly Literature	General Scholarly Literature
801	G	EU	Secondary Literature on EU Law
802	Z	General Scholarly Literature	Encyclopedic Dictionary of Law Usual of Guillermo Cabanellas
900	O	Non-PTA law irrelevant	not mentioned anymore (implicit reference to preceding case)
1000	F	EFTA	EFTA Case Law

[Type of Reference] Explanation of whether the provided reference is explicitly prescribed under PTA law or was intentionally invoked by the PTA-DSM.

Code	Type of Reference
1	Independent reference, i.e., made by PTA-DSM deliberately.
2	Dependent reference, i.e., possible due to explicit link in PTA law.

[Purpose of Reference] Indication for which purpose the PTA-DSM has made the reference to a source other than respective PTA law.

Code	Purpose of reference
1	Interpretation of PTA law.
2	Identification of independent additional obligation, apart from PTA law.

[Level of Use of Reference] Explanation of the role or extent to which non-PTA law references were utilized in the legal analysis of the relevant PTA-DSM.

Code	Level of Use
0	Non-PTA law irrelevant
1	Rule
11	Quantitative restriction
12	MEQR
13	Charges of equivalent effect
2	Exception
21	Identification of legitimate objective
211	Legitimate objective available
212	Legitimate objective not available
22	Proportionality
221	Measure aimed at legitimate objective (making sure that the measure actually aims at an available legitimate objective)
222	Suitable measure (making sure that the measure remedies the threat protected under the available legitimate objective)
223	Necessity (no less trade restrictive measure available)
224	Measure discriminatory or disguised restriction on trade
3	Nullity of a decision
4	Effet utile
5	Estoppel
6	Facts and preliminary judgments

[Multiple Levels of Use of Reference] Clarification regarding whether the PTA-DSM made use of the reference in multiple sections of the legal analysis.

Code	Multiple levels of use of reference
0	The reference was used in only one part of the legal analysis in the legal decision by the PTA-DSM.
1	The reference was used in more than one part of the legal analysis in the legal decision by the PTA-DSM.

8.2   Supplementary Tables and Figures

8.2.1   List of All Analyzed PTA-DSM Decisions

8.2.1.1   Decisions of the CJEU

Date of the decision	Decision No.
19 December 1961	C-7/61
10 December 1968	C-7/68
10 October 1971	C-3/78
14 December 1972	C-29/72
3 July 1974	C-192/73
11 July 1974	C-8/74
31 October 1974	C-16/74
31 October 1974	C-15/74
20 February 1975	C-12/74
8 July 1975	C-4/75
20 May 1976	C-104/75
22 June 1976	C-119/75
15 December 1976	C-35/76
25 January 1977	C-46/76
5 October 1977	C-5/77
23 May 1978	C-102/77
12 October 1978	C-13/78
23 November 1978	C-7/78
5 April 1979	C-148/78
12 July 1979	C-153/78
8 November 1979	C-251/78
14 December 1979	C-34/79
10 July 1980	C-152/78
20 January 1981	C-55/80
22 January 1981	C-58/80
28 January 1981	C-32/80
5 February 1981	C-53/80

(continued)

Date of the decision	Decision No.
7 April 1981	C-132/80
17 June 1981	C-113/80
14 July 1981	C-187/80
3 December 1981	C-1/81
9 December 1981	C-193/80
17 December 1981	C-272/80
9 June 1982	C-95/81
9 June 1982	C-206/80
14 September 1982	C-144/81
8 February 1983	C-124/81
2 March 1983	C-155/82
22 March 1983	C-42/82
14 July 1983	C-174/82
9 November 1983	C-158/82
30 November 1983	C-227/82
31 January 1984	C-74/82
31 January 1984	C-40/82
7 February 1984	C-238/82
28 February 1984	C-247/81
13 March 1984	C-16/83
20 March 1984	C-314/82
27 March 1984	C-50/83
6 June 1984	C-97/83
10 July 1984	C-72/83
19 September 1984	C-94/83
6 November 1984	C-177/83
10 January 1985	C-229/83
29 January 1985	C-231/81
29 January 1985	C-231/83
27 March 1985	C-73/84
25 April 1985	C-207/83
11 June 1985	C-288/83
9 July 1985	C-19/84
11 July 1985	C-60/84
25 September 1985	C-202/84
25 September 1985	C-201/84
25 September 1985	C-149/84
25 September 1985	C-114/84
25 September 1985	C-34/84
26 November 1985	C-182/84
10 December 1985	C-247/84
28 January 1986	C-188/84
11 March 1986	C-121/85

(continued)

Date of the decision	Decision No.
13 March 1986	C-54/85
6 May 1986	C-304/84
27 May 1986	C-87/85
5 June 1986	C-103/84
12 June 1986	C-50/85
10 July 1986	C-95/84
16 December 1986	C-124/85
16 February 1987	C-45/87 R
12 March 1987	C-178/84
12 March 1987	C-176/84
9 April 1987	C-402/85
11 June 1987	C-406/85
17 June 1987	C-154/85
6 October 1987	C-118/86
4 February 1988	C-261/85
4 February 1988	C-261/85
23 February 1988	C-216/84
3 March 1988	C-434/85
17 May 1988	C-158/86
14 June 1988	C-29/87
30 June 1988	C-35/87
14 July 1988	C-407/85
14 July 1988	C-298/87
14 July 1988	C-90/86
20 September 1988	C-190/87
20 September 1988	C-302/86
22 September 1988	C-45/87
5 October 1988	C-53/87
24 January 1989	C-341/87
2 February 1989	C-274/87
7 March 1989	C-215/87
11 May 1989	C-25/88
11 May 1989	C-25/88
11 May 1989	C-76/86
18 May 1989	C-266/87
7 November 1989	C-125/88
23 November 1989	C-145/88
7 March 1990	C-362/88
20 March 1990	C-21/88
2 May 1990	C-111/89
23 May 1990	C-169/89
5 July 1990	C-304/88
12 July 1990	C-128/89

(continued)

Date of the decision	Decision No.
11 October 1990	C-196/89
17 October 1990	C-10/89
13 November 1990	C-269/89
12 December 1990	C-241/89
12 December 1990	C-270/86
13 December 1990	C-42/90
13 December 1990	C-347/88
19 March 1991	C-205/89
21 March 1991	C-60/89
21 March 1991	C-369/88
16 April 1991	C-347/89
30 April 1991	C-239/90
20 June 1991	C-39/90
25 July 1991	C-1/90
4 October 1991	C-367/89
18 February 1992	C-30/90
18 February 1992	C-235/89
8 April 1992	C-62/90
4 June 1992	C-13/91
9 June 1992	C-47/90
9 July 1992	C-2/90
16 July 1992	C-344/90
16 July 1992	C-293/89
16 July 1992	C-95/89
16 July 1992	C-95/89
27 October 1992	C-191/90
10 November 1992	C-3/91
17 November 1992	C-235/91
27 April 1993	C-375/90
18 May 1993	C-126/91
25 May 1993	C-271/92
25 May 1993	C-228/91
8 June 1993	C-373/92
17 November 1993	C-71/92
30 November 1993	C-317/91
2 February 1994	C-315/92
22 June 1994	C-9/93
22 June 1994	C-426/92
13 July 1994	C-131/93
14 July 1994	C-17/93
20 September 1994	C-249/92
5 October 1994	C-323/93
10 November 1994	C-320/93

(continued)

Date of the decision	Decision No.
23 February 1995	C-54/94
28 March 1995	C-324/93
13 July 1995	C-350/92
21 March 1996	C-297/94
27 June 1996	C-240/95
27 June 1996	C-293/94
11 July 1996	C-232/94
11 July 1996	C-71/94
11 July 1996	C-427/93
26 November 1996	C-313/94
5 December 1996	C-267/95
13 March 1997	C-358/95
15 April 1997	C-272/95
7 May 1997	C-321/94
5 June 1997	C-105/94
9 July 1997	C-316/95
9 July 1997	C-34/95
23 October 1997	C-189/95
4 November 1997	C-337/95
11 November 1997	C-349/95
9 December 1997	C-265/95
19 March 1998	C-1/96
28 April 1998	C-120/95
25 June 1998	C-203/96
17 September 1998	C-400/96
22 September 1998	C-61/97
12 November 1998	C-102/96
19 November 1998	C-162/97
3 December 1998	C-67/97
25 March 1999	C-112/97
11 May 1999	C-350/97
12 October 1999	C-379/97
16 December 1999	C-94/98
13 January 2000	C-254/98
16 May 2000	C-388/95
23 May 2000	C-209/98
11 July 2000	C-473/98
26 September 2000	C-23/99
12 October 2000	C-3/99
19 October 2000	C-216/98
16 November 2000	C-217/99
5 December 2000	C-448/98
14 December 2000	C-55/99

(continued)

Date of the decision	Decision No.
8 March 2001	C-405/98
5 April 2001	C-123/00
23 October 2001	C-510/99
25 October 2001	C-398/98
27 February 2002	C-302/00
22 October 2002	C-241/01
24 October 2002	C-121/00
5 November 2002	C-325/00
16 January 2003	C-12/00
8 April 2003	C-244/00
8 May 2003	C-14/02
8 May 2003	C-113/01
8 May 2003	C-15/01
20 May 2003	C-108/01
20 May 2003	C-469/00
19 June 2003	C-420/01
18 September 2003	C-416/00
23 September 2003	C–192/01
2 October 2003	C-12/02
13 November 2003	C-294/01
11 December 2003	C-322/01
5 February 2004	C-270/02
5 February 2004	C-95/01
5 February 2004	C-24/00
1 April 2004	C-112/02
29 April 2004	C-387/99
15 July 2004	C-443/02
15 July 2004	C-239/02
2 December 2004	C-41/02
14 December 2004	C-210/03
26 May 2005	C-20/03
9 June 2005	C-211/03
10 November 2005	C-432/03
24 November 2005	C-366/04
23 February 2006	C-441/04
28 September 2006	C-434/04
15 March 2007	C-54/05
5 June 2007	C-170/04
20 September 2007	C-297/05
4 October 2007	C-186/05
8 November 2007	C-143/06
15 November 2007	C-319/05
13 March 2008	C-227/06

(continued)

Date of the decision	Decision No.
10 April 2008	C-265/06
19 June 2008	C-219/07
11 September 2008	C-141/07
4 December 2008	C-249/07
16 December 2008	C-205/07
5 March 2009	C-88/07
30 April 2009	C-132/08
30 April 2009	C-531/07
4 June 2009	C-142/05
8 September 2009	C-478/07
10 September 2009	C-100/08
15 April 2010	C-433/05
29 April 2010	C-446/08
18 November 2010	C-142/09
2 December 2010	C-108/09
9 December 2010	C-421/09
3 March 2011	C-161/09
6 October 2011	C-443/10
21 December 2011	C-28/09
1 March 2012	C-484/10
26 April 2012	C-456/10
21 June 2012	C-5/11
6 September 2012	C-150/11
18 October 2012	C-385/10
3 April 2014	C-428/12
1 July 2014	C-573/12
10 September 2014	C-423/13
11 September 2014	C-204/12
6 November 2014	C-108/13
6 October 2015	C-354/14
12 November 2015	C-198/14
23 December 2015	C-333/14
17 March 2016	C-472/14
22 September 2016	C-525/14
29 September 2016	C-492/14
19 October 2016	C-148/15
27 October 2016	C-114/15
8 June 2017	C-296/15
25 July 2018	C-528/16
26 September 2018	C-137/17
3 July 2019	C-387/18
17 September 2020	C-648/18
8 October 2020	C-602/19

8.2.1.2   Decisions of the EFTA Court

Date of the decision	Decision No.
16 December 1994	E-1/94
26 February 1997	E-5/96
27 June 1997	E-6/96
12 May 1999	E-5/98
05 April 2001	E-3/00
15 March 2002	E-9/00
25 February 2005	E-4/04
12 September 2011	E-16/10
30 March 2012	E-7/11
01 February 2016	E-17/15
14 November 2017	E-2/17

8.2.1.3   Decisions of the PTA-DSM of the CAN

Date of the decision	Decision No.
11 December 1997	1-AI-97
15 March 1999	201
27 October 1999	308
20 November 2000	452
20 November 2000	453
9 March 2001	489
9 March 2001	490
3 April 2001	498
25 January 2002	43-Al-99-1
26 November 2002	676
29 August 2003	757
20 October 2005	966
15 December 2005	986
13 July 2006	125-AI-2004
19 September 2006	117-AI-2003
25 January 2007	136-AI-2004
15 June 2009	05-AI-2007
11 November 2009	1289
26 August 2016	02-AN-2015
12 June 2017	241-IP-2015
14 August 2018	2019

8.2.1.4 Decisions of the PTA-DSM of the Mercosur

Date of the decision	Decision No.
28 April 1999	1
19 April 2002	7
20 December 2005	11-A

8.2.2 Schematic Overview of the Temporal Obligations of the SGCAN in Proceedings for Which the SGCAN Has Jurisdiction

Actions during the proceedings in front of the SGCAN	Corresponding timeframes for the conclusion of these actions
Initiation of the procedure under Art. 74 AdC, Title V, Chap. I D.425	
Collection of information and evidence	Max. 5 working days from step 1, Art. 48 D.425
Request for corrections, additional information and evidence	Max. 15 working days from step 2, Art. 48 D.425
Feedback on completion of step 3	Max. 3 working days from step 3, Art. 48 D.425
Initiation of investigation	Immediately after completion of step 4, Art. 49 D.425
Communication directed towards the responding CAN Member State	Max. 10 working days after completion of step 5, Art. 50 D.425
Request for response from the CAN Member State concerned	Max. 20 working days after completion of step 6, Art. 50 lit. c D.425
In case of a request by the CAN Member State concerned, extension of timeframe for response	Max. 10 working days additionally to the completion of step 7, Art. 51 D.425
Issuance of the *resolution* by the SGCAN	Max. 10 working days after the lapse of the timeframe specified under steps 7 and 8, Art. 54 D.425
Possibility to petition for review the *resolution* pursuant to Art. 37 ff D.425	Max. 45 days from the date of completion of step 9, Art. 43 D.425
Resolution of the review	Max. 30 days of the completion of step 10, Art. 43 D.425
Overall timeframe for the procedure	**148 days**

Source: Author

8.2.3   Reappearance of the Same Contested Issue Within the Different Stages of the PTA-DSM of the CAN

Case sequence no. (Initial decision concerning the disputed issue)	non-court decision (SGCAN/ Junta)	Decision TJCAN	Appeal Procedure SGCAN/ TJCAN	Number of times the issue reappeared in the PTA-DSM
CAN-SGCAN-438				
438	1	0	0	**1**
CAN-SGCAN-440				
440	1	0	0	**1**
CAN-JUNAC-430				
JUNAC-430	1	0	0	**1**
CAN-SGCAN-453				
453	1	0	0	**1**
CAN-JUNAC-432				
JUNAC-432	1	0	0	**1**
CAN-SGCAN-512				
512	0	0	1	**1**
CAN-SGCAN-1001				
1001	1	0	0	**1**
CAN-SGCAN-681				
681	1	0	0	**1**
CAN-SGCAN-132				
132	1	0	0	**1**
CAN-SGCAN-784				
784	1	0	0	**1**
CAN-SGCAN-229				
229	1	0	0	**1**
CAN-SGCAN-966				
966	1	0	0	**1**
CAN-TJCAN-3-AI-2006				
3-AI-2006	0	1	0	**1**
CAN-SGCAN-986				
986	1	0	0	**1**
CAN-SCGAN-308				
308	1	0	0	**1**
CAN-TJCAN-117-AI-2003				
117-AI-2003	0	1	0	**1**
CAN-SGCAN-2019				
2019	1	0	0	**1**

(continued)

(continued)

Case sequence no. (Initial decision concerning the disputed issue)	non-court decision (SGCAN/ Junta)	Decision TJCAN	Appeal Procedure SGCAN/ TJCAN	Number of times the issue reappeared in the PTA-DSM
CAN-TJCAN-14-AN-2001				
14-AN-2001	0	1	0	**1**
CAN-JUNAC-431				
JUNAC-458	1	0	0	**1**
CAN-TJCAN-1AI-97				
1-AI-97	0	1	0	**1**
CAN-SGCAN-268				
268	1	0	0	**1**
CAN-TJCAN-241-IP-2015				
241-IP-2015	0	1	0	**1**
CAN-SGCAN-1289				
1289	1	0	0	**1**
CAN-TJCAN-2-AI-96				
2-AI-96	0	1	0	**1**
CAN-SGCAN-407				
407	1	0	0	**1**
452	1	0	1	**2**
CAN-SGCAN-201				
201	1	0	0	**1**
250	2	0	0	**2**
CAN-SGCAN-449				
449	1	0	0	**1**
489	1	0	1	**2**
CAN-SGCAN-897				
05-AI-2007	0	1	0	**1**
897	1	1	0	**2**
CAN-SGCAN-1695				
1695	1	0	0	**1**
1716	1	0	1	**2**
CAN-SCGAN-576				
576	1	0	0	**1**
757	1	0	1	**2**
CAN-SGCAN-184				
184	1	0	0	**1**
249	2	0	0	**2**
CAN-JUNAC-397				
JUNAC-397	1	0	0	**1**
JUNAC-438	2	0	0	**2**
CAN-SGCAN-638				

(continued)

(continued)

Case sequence no. (Initial decision concerning the disputed issue)	non-court decision (SGCAN/ Junta)	Decision TJCAN	Appeal Procedure SGCAN/ TJCAN	Number of times the issue reappeared in the PTA-DSM
638	1	0	0	1
676	1	0	1	2
CAN-JUNAC-476				
101	1	0	0	1
220	2	0	0	2
CAN-SGCAN-490				
490	1	0	0	1
498	1	0	1	2
CAN-SGCAN-139				
139	1	0	0	1
179	1	0	1	2
CAN-SGCAN-802				
136-AI-2004	0	1	0	1
839	0	1	1	2
853	0	1	2	3
CAN-SGCAN-1564				
02-AN-2015	0	1	0	1
1564	1	1	0	2
1622	1	1	1	3
CAN-SGCAN-759				
125-AI-2004	0	1	0	1
759	1	1	0	2
823	1	1	1	3
CAN-SGCAN-278				
278	1	0	0	1
325	2	0	0	2
359	2	0	1	3
CAN-SGCAN-710				
710	1	0	0	1
861	1	0	1	2
902	1	0	2	3
CAN-SCGAN-19				
02-AN-98	0	1	0	1
19	1	1	0	2
47	1	1	1	3
CAN-SCGAN-209				
209	1	0	0	1
230	1	0	1	2
248	2	0	1	3
43-AI-99	2	1	1	4
43-Al-99-1	2	2	1	5

Source: Author's novel dataset

8.2.4 Invocation of Additional Legitimate Objectives in front of the Reviewed PTA-DSMs

General and specific topic of legitimate objective invoked/	Case successful	Case unsuccessful	Grand total
CAN			
Obligations under Public Law			
Other international agreement		2	2
Obligations under Public Law Sum		**2**	**2**
Not specified			
Not specified	1	1	2
Not specified Sum	**1**	**1**	**2**
Protection of the Consumer			
Protection of the consumer	2		2
Protection of the Consumer Sum	**2**		**2**
Environment and Sustainability			
Environment		1	1
Environment and Sustainability Sum		**1**	**1**
Antitrust and Fair Competition			
Combating fraud/smuggling/tax evasion		1	1
Antitrust and Fair Competition Sum		**1**	**1**
Health			
General health protection (unspecified)		1	1
Health Sum		**1**	**1**
Measurement of Trade Flows			
Measures introduced for statistical purposes		1	1
Measurement of Trade Flows Sum		**1**	**1**
CAN Sum	**3**	**7**	**10**
EFTA			
Health			
Public health protection	4	4	8
Health Sum	**4**	**4**	**8**
Protection of the Culture			
Cultural expression/ diversity		1	1
Protection of the Culture Sum		**1**	**1**
EFTA Sum	**4**	**5**	**9**
EU			
Health			
Consumer health protection		5	5
Ensuring quality of medicinal products		2	2
General health protection (unspecified)		1	1
Public health protection	23	35	58

(continued)

(continued)

General and specific topic of legitimate objective invoked/	Case successful	Case unsuccessful	Grand total
Road traffic safety	3		3
Safeguarding the public health system		1	1
Health Sum	**26**	**44**	**70**
Protection of the Consumer			
Designation of quality		1	1
Protection of the consumer	11	30	41
Protection of the Consumer Sum	**11**	**31**	**42**
Antitrust and Fair Competition			
Combating fraud/smuggling/tax evasion	1	6	7
Ensuring fiscal supervision		3	3
Ensuring the fairness of commercial transactions/fair trading/preventing excessive competitive advantages	7	16	23
Antitrust and Fair Competition Sum	**8**	**25**	**33**
Environment and Sustainability			
Environment	8	6	14
Prevention of pollution		1	1
Environment and Sustainability Sum	**8**	**7**	**15**
Not specified			
Not specified	3	5	8
Not specified Sum	**3**	**5**	**8**
Road Traffic Safety			
Road traffic safety		6	6
Road Traffic Safety Sum		**6**	**6**
Agriculture			
Common agricultural trade policy		2	2
Common organization of pasta sector		1	1
To give full effect to the common organization of the market in the cereals sector		2	2
Agriculture Sum		**5**	**5**
Animal health			
Animal welfare	1		1
Conservation of biodiversity	1	1	2
Wild birds		1	1
Animal health Sum	**2**	**2**	**4**
Economic interest			
Ensuring the viability of an undertaking (economic measure)		1	1
Securing the electrical supply of a country		1	1
Economic interest Sum		**2**	**2**
Safety			
Combating of crime		2	2
Safety Sum		**2**	**2**
Administrative processes			

(continued)

(continued)

General and specific topic of legitimate objective invoked/	Case successful	Case unsuccessful	Grand total
Administrative burden		1	1
Administrative processes Sum		**1**	**1**
Securing Supply Chains			
Supply of goods at short distance		1	1
Securing Supply Chains Sum		**1**	**1**
Protection of Fundamental Rights			
Protection of fundamental rights	1		1
Protection of Fundamental Rights Sum	**1**		**1**
Protection of the Culture			
Cinema as cultural good	1		1
Protection of the Culture Sum	**1**		**1**
Constitutionalizing of Community Order			
Protecting the conformity of community rules	1		1
Constitutionalizing of Community Order Sum	**1**		**1**
Morality			
Minors/children		1	1
Morality Sum		**1**	**1**
EU Sum	**61**	**132**	**193**
Mercosur			
Environment and Sustainability			
Environment		1	1
Environment and Sustainability Sum		**1**	**1**
Mercosur Sum		**1**	**1**
Grand Total	**68**	**145**	**213**

Source: Author's novel dataset

8.2.5 Successful *Invocation of All Legitimate Objectives in front of the Reviewed PTA-DSMs*

Character of legitimate objective (additional/ original)	CAN	EFTA	EU	Grand Total
Additional legitimate objectives				
Animal Welfare			1	1
Cinema as Cultural Good			1	1
Combating raud/Smuggling/Tax evasion			1	1
Conservation of Biodiversity			1	1
Diversity of the Press			1	1
Ensuring the Fairness of Commercial Transactions/Fair Trading/Preventing Excessive Competitive Advantages			11	11
Environment			11	11
Measures Introduced for Statistical Purposes			1	1
Not Specified	1		3	4
Protecting the Conformity of Community Rules			1	1
Protection of Fundamental Rights			1	1
Protection of the Consumer	2		16	18
Public Health Protection		4	24	28
Road Traffic Safety			4	4
Additional legitimate objectives Total	**3**	**4**	**77**	**84**
Original legitimate objectives				
Animal Health Protection	1		11	12
Human Health Protection	3		33	36
Plant Health Protection			2	2
Public Morals	1		2	3
Public Policy/Public Order			5	5
Public Security/Public Safety			5	5
Original legitimate objectives Total	**5**		**58**	**63**
Grand Total	**8**	**4**	**135**	**147**

Source: Author's novel dataset

8.2.6   Proportion and Overall Case Numbers of All Relevant Cases Dealing with MEQRs, QRs

Type of measure assessed by PTA-DSM	CAN	EFTA	EU	Mercosur	Grand Total
Measure of equivalent effect as quantitative restriction (MEQR)	69,44%	94,12%	84,40%	60,00%	83,40%
Quantitative restriction (QR)	30,56%	5,88%	15,37%	40,00%	16,40%
No effect	0,00%	0,00%	0,23%	0,00%	0,20%
Grand Total	**100,00%**	**100,00%**	**100,00%**	**100,00%**	**100,00%**

Source: Author's novel dataset

8.2.7   Frequency of Adjudicating MEQRs, QRs per Reviewed PTA-DSM

Type of measure assessed	CAN	EFTA	EU	Mercosur	Grand Total
Measure of equivalent effect as quantitative restriction (MEQR)	17	14	287	3	321
Quantitative restriction (QR)	10	1	58	2	71
No effect			2		2
Grand Total	**27**	**15**	**347**	**5**	**394**

Source: Author's novel dataset

8.2.8 Distribution of Successful Cases Regarding MEQRs, QRs considering Additional and Original Legitimate Objectives

Type of measure/Additional legitimate objective	CAN	EFTA	EU	Grand total
Measure of equivalent effect as quantitative restriction (MEQR)				
Animal Health				
Animal welfare			1	1
Conservation of biodiversity			1	1
Animal Health Sum			**2**	**2**
Antitrust and Fair Competition				
Combating fraud/smuggling/tax evasion			1	1
Ensuring the fairness of commercial transactions/fair trading/ preventing excessive competitive advantages			7	7
Antitrust and Fair Competition Sum			**8**	**8**
Constitutionalizing of Community Order				
Protecting the conformity of community rules			1	1
Constitutionalizing of Community Order Sum			**1**	**1**
Protection of the Culture				
Cinema as cultural good			1	1
Protection of the Culture Sum			**1**	**1**
Environment and Sustainability				
Environment			7	7
Environment and Sustainability Sum			**7**	**7**
Health				
Public health protection		3	18	21
Road traffic safety			3	3
Health Sum		**3**	**21**	**24**
Not Specified				
Not specified	1		2	3
Not Specified Sum	**1**		**2**	**3**
Protection of Fundamental Rights				
Protection of fundamental rights			1	1
Protection of Fundamental Rights Sum			**1**	**1**
Protection of the Consumer				
Protection of the consumer	2		11	13
Protection of the Consumer Sum	**2**		**11**	**13**
Measure of equivalent effect as quantitative restriction (MEQR) Sum	**3**	**3**	**54**	**60**
Quantitative restriction (QR)				
Environment and Sustainability				

(continued)

(continued)

Type of measure/Additional legitimate objective	CAN	EFTA	EU	Grand total
Environment			1	1
Environment and Sustainability Sum			**1**	**1**
Health				
Public health protection			5	5
Health Sum			**5**	**5**
Not Specified				
Not specified			1	1
Not Specified Sum			**1**	**1**
Quantitative restriction (QR) Sum			**7**	**7**
Grand total	**3**	**3**	**61**	**67**

Source: Author's novel dataset

8.2.9 Overview of Argumentative Patterns of PTA-DSMs on Successfully Invoked Additional Legitimate Objectives

Type of argumentation/Additional legitimate objective	CAN	EFTA	EU	Grand total
Additional Profound Argumentation				
Animal Health				
Animal welfare	0,00%	0,00%	1,47%	1,47%
Animal Health Sum	**0,00%**	**0,00%**	**1,47%**	**1,47%**
Protection of the Culture				
Cinema as cultural good	0,00%	0,00%	1,47%	1,47%
Protection of the Culture Sum	**0,00%**	**0,00%**	**1,47%**	**1,47%**
Environment and Sustainability				
Environment	0,00%	0,00%	4,41%	4,41%
Environment and Sustainability Sum	**0,00%**	**0,00%**	**4,41%**	**4,41%**
Health				
Public health protection	0,00%	1,47%	0,00%	1,47%
Health Sum	**0,00%**	**1,47%**	**0,00%**	**1,47%**
Protection of Fundamental Rights				
Protection of fundamental rights	0,00%	0,00%	1,47%	1,47%
Protection of Fundamental Rights Sum	**0,00%**	**0,00%**	**1,47%**	**1,47%**
Protection of the Consumer				
Protection of the consumer	2,94%	0,00%	0,00%	2,94%
Protection of the Consumer Sum	**2,94%**	**0,00%**	**0,00%**	**2,94%**
Additional Profound Argumentation Sum	**2,94%**	**1,47%**	**8,82%**	**13,24%**
Finding of Equivalence of Legitimate Objective under General Exception Clause				

(continued)

(continued)

Type of argumentation/Additional legitimate objective	CAN	EFTA	EU	Grand total
Animal Health				
Conservation of biodiversity	0,00%	0,00%	1,47%	1,47%
Animal Health Sum	**0,00%**	**0,00%**	**1,47%**	**1,47%**
Health				
Public health protection	0,00%	4,41%	27,94%	32,35%
Road traffic safety	0,00%	0,00%	1,47%	1,47%
Health Sum	**0,00%**	**4,41%**	**29,41%**	**33,82%**
Finding of Equivalence of Legitimate Objective under General Exception Clause Sum	**0,00%**	**4,41%**	**30,88%**	**35,29%**
No Additional Argumentation				
Antitrust and Fair Competition				
Combating fraud/ smuggling/ tax evasion	0,00%	0,00%	1,47%	1,47%
Antitrust and Fair Competition Sum	**0,00%**	**0,00%**	**1,47%**	**1,47%**
Constitutionalizing of Community Order				
Protecting the conformity of community rules	0,00%	0,00%	1,47%	1,47%
Constitutionalizing of Community Order Sum	**0,00%**	**0,00%**	**1,47%**	**1,47%**
Environment and Sustainability				
Environment	0,00%	0,00%	2,94%	2,94%
Environment and Sustainability Sum	**0,00%**	**0,00%**	**2,94%**	**2,94%**
Health				
Public health protection	0,00%	0,00%	4,41%	4,41%
Health Sum	**0,00%**	**0,00%**	**4,41%**	**4,41%**
Not specified				
Not specified	1,47%	0,00%	4,41%	5,88%
Not specified Sum	**1,47%**	**0,00%**	**4,41%**	**5,88%**
Protection of the Consumer				
Protection of the consumer	0,00%	0,00%	4,41%	4,41%
Protection of the Consumer Sum	**0,00%**	**0,00%**	**4,41%**	**4,41%**
No Additional Argumentation Sum	**1,47%**	**0,00%**	**19,12%**	**20,59%**
Reference to Established Case Law				
Antitrust and Fair Competition				
Ensuring the fairness of commercial transactions/ fair trading/ preventing excessive competitive advantages	0,00%	0,00%	10,29%	10,29%
Antitrust and Fair Competition Sum	**0,00%**	**0,00%**	**10,29%**	**10,29%**
Environment and Sustainability				
Environment	0,00%	0,00%	4,41%	4,41%
Environment and Sustainability Sum	**0,00%**	**0,00%**	**4,41%**	**4,41%**
Health				
Public health protection	0,00%	0,00%	1,47%	1,47%
Road traffic safety	0,00%	0,00%	2,94%	2,94%
Health Sum	**0,00%**	**0,00%**	**4,41%**	**4,41%**
Protection of the Consumer				
Protection of the consumer	0,00%	0,00%	11,76%	11,76%

(continued)

(continued)

Type of argumentation/Additional legitimate objective	CAN	EFTA	EU	Grand total
Protection of the Consumer Sum	**0,00%**	**0,00%**	**11,76%**	**11,76%**
Reference to Established Case Law Sum	**0,00%**	**0,00%**	**30,88%**	**30,88%**
Grand total	**4,41%**	**5,88%**	**89,71%**	**100,00%**

Source: Author's novel dataset

8.2.10 Reasons for Success in Cases where Additional Legitimate Objectives were invoked

Reason for successful invocation of additional legitimate objective/Additional legitimate objective	CAN	EFTA	EU	Grand Total
Complainant has not given sufficient information on the contents of the measure (burden of proof not satisfied)				
Health				
Public health protection	0,00%	0,00%	5,88%	5,88%
Health Sum	**0,00%**	**0,00%**	**5,88%**	**5,88%**
Not specified				
Not specified	1,47%	0,00%	0,00%	1,47%
Not specified Sum	**1,47%**	**0,00%**	**0,00%**	**1,47%**
Complainant has not given sufficient information on the contents of the measure (burden of proof not satisfied) Sum	**1,47%**	**0,00%**	**5,88%**	**7,35%**
Council took into account legitimate objective when deciding on EU legislation (case of prohibition of insufficient action)				
Protection of the Consumer				
Protection of the consumer	0,00%	0,00%	1,47%	1,47%
Protection of the Consumer Sum	**0,00%**	**0,00%**	**1,47%**	**1,47%**
Council took into account legitimate objective when deciding on EU legislation (case of prohibition of insufficient action) Sum	**0,00%**	**0,00%**	**1,47%**	**1,47%**
Measure (dis)proportionate/excessive (and not necessary)				
Animal Health				
Conservation of biodiversity	0,00%	0,00%	1,47%	1,47%
Animal Health Sum	**0,00%**	**0,00%**	**1,47%**	**1,47%**
Antitrust and Fair Competition				
Combating fraud/smuggling/tax evasion	0,00%	0,00%	1,47%	1,47%
Ensuring the fairness of commercial transactions/fair trading/preventing excessive competitive advantages	0,00%	0,00%	2,94%	2,94%
Antitrust and Fair Competition Sum	**0,00%**	**0,00%**	**4,41%**	**4,41%**
Constitutionalizing of Community Order				
Protecting the conformity of community rules	0,00%	0,00%	1,47%	1,47%

(continued)

(continued)

Reason for successful invocation of additional legitimate objective/Additional legitimate objective	CAN	EFTA	EU	Grand Total
Constitutionalizing of Community Order Sum	**0,00%**	**0,00%**	**1,47%**	**1,47%**
Protection of the Culture				
Cinema as cultural good	0,00%	0,00%	1,47%	1,47%
Protection of the Culture Sum	**0,00%**	**0,00%**	**1,47%**	**1,47%**
Environment and Sustainability				
Environment	0,00%	0,00%	10,29%	10,29%
Environment and Sustainability Sum	**0,00%**	**0,00%**	**10,29%**	**10,29%**
Health				
Public health protection	0,00%	4,41%	23,53%	27,94%
Road traffic safety	0,00%	0,00%	2,94%	2,94%
Health Sum	**0,00%**	**4,41%**	**26,47%**	**30,88%**
Not specified				
Not specified	0,00%	0,00%	2,94%	2,94%
Not specified Sum	**0,00%**	**0,00%**	**2,94%**	**2,94%**
Protection of Fundamental Rights				
Protection of fundamental rights	0,00%	0,00%	1,47%	1,47%
Protection of Fundamental Rights Sum	**0,00%**	**0,00%**	**1,47%**	**1,47%**
Protection of the Consumer				
Protection of the consumer	0,00%	0,00%	4,41%	4,41%
Protection of the Consumer Sum	**0,00%**	**0,00%**	**4,41%**	**4,41%**
Measure (dis)proportionate/excessive (and not necessary) Sum	**0,00%**	**4,41%**	**54,41%**	**58,82%**
Measure (not) necessary				
Animal Health				
Animal welfare	0,00%	0,00%	1,47%	1,47%
Animal Health Sum	**0,00%**	**0,00%**	**1,47%**	**1,47%**
Antitrust and Fair Competition				
Ensuring the fairness of commercial transactions/fair trading/preventing excessive competitive advantages	0,00%	0,00%	1,47%	1,47%
Antitrust and Fair Competition Sum	**0,00%**	**0,00%**	**1,47%**	**1,47%**
Health				
Public health protection	0,00%	0,00%	2,94%	2,94%
Health Sum	**0,00%**	**0,00%**	**2,94%**	**2,94%**
Protection of the Consumer				
Protection of the consumer	2,94%	0,00%	2,94%	5,88%
Protection of the Consumer Sum	**2,94%**	**0,00%**	**2,94%**	**5,88%**
Measure (not) necessary Sum	**2,94%**	**0,00%**	**8,82%**	**11,76%**
Measure discriminates arbitrarily and unjustifiably				
Health				
Public health protection	0,00%	1,47%	0,00%	1,47%
Health Sum	**0,00%**	**1,47%**	**0,00%**	**1,47%**
Measure discriminates arbitrarily and unjustifiably Sum	**0,00%**	**1,47%**	**0,00%**	**1,47%**

(continued)

(continued)

Reason for successful invocation of additional legitimate objective/Additional legitimate objective	CAN	EFTA	EU	Grand Total
Measure does (not) attain legitimate goal (i.e., the threat to a legitimate objective is accepted, but the suitability of the measure to attain its protection is denied)				
Environment and Sustainability				
Environment	0,00%	0,00%	1,47%	1,47%
Environment and Sustainability Sum	**0,00%**	**0,00%**	**1,47%**	**1,47%**
Health				
Public health protection	0,00%	0,00%	1,47%	1,47%
Road traffic safety	0,00%	0,00%	1,47%	1,47%
Health Sum	**0,00%**	**0,00%**	**2,94%**	**2,94%**
Measure does (not) attain legitimate goal (i.e., the threat to a legitimate objective is accepted, but the suitability of the measure to attain its protection is denied) Sum	**0,00%**	**0,00%**	**4,41%**	**4,41%**
No information				
Antitrust and Fair Competition				
Ensuring the fairness of commercial transactions/ fair trading/ preventing excessive competitive advantages	0,00%	0,00%	5,88%	5,88%
Antitrust and Fair Competition Sum	**0,00%**	**0,00%**	**5,88%**	**5,88%**
Not specified				
Not specified	0,00%	0,00%	1,47%	1,47%
Not specified Sum	**0,00%**	**0,00%**	**1,47%**	**1,47%**
Protection of the Consumer				
Protection of the consumer	0,00%	0,00%	7,35%	7,35%
Protection of the Consumer Sum	**0,00%**	**0,00%**	**7,35%**	**7,35%**
No Information Sum	**0,00%**	**0,00%**	**14,71%**	**14,71%**
Grand Total	**4,41%**	**5,88%**	**89,71%**	**100,00%**

Source: Author's novel dataset

8.2.11 Adjudication Record of Reviewed PTA-DSMs Concerning All Legitimate Objectives

Legitimate objective assessed	CAN	EFTA	EU	Mercosur	Grand Total
Administrative Processes			1		1
Agriculture			5		5
Animal Health	1	3	37	2	43
Antitrust and Fair Competition	1		33		34
Constitutionalizing of Community Order			1		1
Protection of the Culture		1	1		2
Economic Interest			2		2
Environment and Sustainability	1		15	1	17
Health	9	11	157	1	178
Measurement of Trade Flows	1				1
Morality	3		17		20
Not specified	2		8		10
Obligations under Public Law	2				2
Plant Health	5		7	1	13
Protection of Fundamental Rights			1		1
Protection of the Consumer	2		42		44
Road Traffic Safety			6		6
Safety		1	13		14
Securing Supply Chains			1		1
Grand Total	27	16	347	5	395

Source: Author's novel dataset

8.2.12 Proportion of Invoked Legitimate Objectives in Front of Reviewed PTA-DSMs (Successful/Unsuccessful)

Original legitimate objective/ Success rates	CAN		CAN Overall proportion	EFTA	EFTA Overall proportion	EU		EU Overall proportion	Mercosur	Mercosur Overall proportion	Grand Total
	Case successful	Case unsuccessful		Case unsuccessful		Case successful	Case unsuccessful		Case unsuccessful		
Animal Health	20,00%	0,00%	5,88%	42,86%	42,86%	20,69%	21,88%	21,43%	50,00%	50,00%	21,43%
Health	60,00%	41,67%	47,06%	42,86%	42,86%	55,17%	57,29%	56,49%	25,00%	25,00%	54,40%
Morality	20,00%	16,67%	17,65%	0,00%	0,00%	12,07%	9,38%	10,39%	0,00%	0,00%	10,44%
Plant Health	0,00%	41,67%	29,41%	0,00%	0,00%	3,45%	5,21%	4,55%	25,00%	25,00%	7,14%
Safety	0,00%	0,00%	0,00%	14,29%	14,29%	8,62%	6,25%	7,14%	0,00%	0,00%	6,59%
Grand Total	100,00%	100,00%	100,00%	100,00%	100,00%	100,00%	100,00%	100,00%	100,00%	100,00%	100,00%

Source: Author's novel dataset

8.2.13 Success Rate for the Invocation of All Legitimate Objectives in Front of Reviewed PTA-DSMs

All legitimate objectives	CAN Case successful	CAN Case unsuccessful	CAN overall proportion	EFTA Case successful	EFTA Case unsuccessful	EFTA overall proportion	EU Case successful	EU Case unsuccessful	EU overall proportion	Mercosur Case unsuccessful	Mercosur overall proportion	Grand Total
Administrative Processes												
Administrative burden			0,00%			0,00%	0,00%	100,00%	100,00%		0,00%	100,00%
Administrative Processes Sum			**0,00%**			**0,00%**	**0,00%**	**100,00%**	**100,00%**		**0,00%**	**100,00%**
Agriculture												
Common agricultural trade policy			0,00%			0,00%	0,00%	100,00%	100,00%		0,00%	100,00%
Common organization of pasta sector			0,00%			0,00%	0,00%	100,00%	100,00%		0,00%	100,00%
To give full effect to the common organization of the market in the cereals sector			0,00%			0,00%	0,00%	100,00%	100,00%		0,00%	100,00%
Agriculture Sum			**0,00%**			**0,00%**	**0,00%**	**100,00%**	**100,00%**		**0,00%**	**100,00%**
Animal Health												
Animal health protection	100,00%	0,00%	2,56%	0,00%	100,00%	7,69%	36,36%	63,64%	84,62%	100,00%	5,13%	100,00%
Animal welfare			0,00%			0,00%	100,00%	0,00%	100,00%		0,00%	100,00%
Conservation of biodiversity			0,00%			0,00%	50,00%	50,00%	100,00%		0,00%	100,00%
Wild birds			0,00%			0,00%	0,00%	100,00%	100,00%		0,00%	100,00%
Animal Health Sum	**100,00%**	**0,00%**	**2,33%**	**0,00%**	**100,00%**	**6,98%**	**37,84%**	**62,16%**	**86,05%**	**100,00%**	**4,65%**	**100,00%**
Antitrust and Fair Competition												
Combating fraud/ smuggling/ tax evasion	0,00%	100,00%	12,50%			0,00%	14,29%	85,71%	87,50%		0,00%	100,00%
Ensuring fiscal supervision			0,00%			0,00%	0,00%	100,00%	100,00%		0,00%	100,00%
Ensuring the fairness of commercial transactions/ fair trading/ preventing excessive competitive advantages			0,00%			0,00%	30,43%	69,57%	100,00%		0,00%	100,00%

Antitrust and Fair Competition Sum	0,00%	100,00%	2,94%		0,00%	24,24%	75,76%	97,06%	0,00%	100,00%
Constitutionalizing of Community Order										
Protecting the conformity of community rules			0,00%		0,00%	100,00%	0,00%	100,00%	0,00%	100,00%
Constitutionalizing of Community Order Sum			0,00%		0,00%	100,00%	0,00%	100,00%	0,00%	100,00%
Protection of the Culture										
Cinema as cultural good			0,00%		0,00%	100,00%	0,00%	100,00%	0,00%	100,00%
Cultural expression/diversity			0,00%	100,00%	100,00%		0,00%	0,00%	0,00%	100,00%
Protection of the Culture Cultural Protection Sum			0,00%	100,00%	50,00%	100,00%	0,00%	50,00%	0,00%	100,00%
Economic Interest										
Ensuring the viability of an undertaking (economic measure)			0,00%		0,00%	0,00%	100,00%	100,00%	0,00%	100,00%
Securing the electrical supply of a country			0,00%		0,00%	0,00%	100,00%	100,00%	0,00%	100,00%
Economic Interest Sum			0,00%		0,00%	0,00%	100,00%	100,00%	0,00%	100,00%
Environment and Sustainability										
Environment	0,00%	100,00%	6,25%		0,00%	57,14%	42,86%	87,50%	6,25%	100,00%
Prevention of pollution			0,00%		0,00%	0,00%	100,00%	100,00%	0,00%	100,00%
Environment and Sustainability Sum	0,00%	100,00%	5,88%		0,00%	53,33%	46,67%	88,24%	5,88%	100,00%
Health										
Consumer health protection			0,00%	100,00%	0,00%	0,00%	100,00%	100,00%	0,00%	100,00%
Ensuring quality of medicinal products			0,00%		0,00%	0,00%	100,00%	100,00%	0,00%	100,00%
General health protection (unspecified)	0,00%	100,00%	50,00%	50,00%	0,00%	0,00%	100,00%	50,00%	0,00%	100,00%
Human health protection	37,50%	62,50%	8,08%	0,00%	3,03%	36,78%	63,22%	87,88%	1,01%	100,00%
Public health protection			0,00%	50,00%	12,12%	39,66%	60,34%	87,88%	0,00%	100,00%
Road traffic safety			0,00%		0,00%	100,00%	0,00%	100,00%	0,00%	100,00%

(continued)

(continued)

	CAN			EFTA			EU			Mercosur		Grand Total
	Case successful	Case unsuccessful	CAN overall proportion	Case successful	Case unsuccessful	EFTA overall proportion	Case successful	Case unsuccessful	EU overall proportion	Case unsuccessful	Mercosur overall proportion	Grand Total
All legitimate objectives												
Safeguarding the public health system			0,00%			0,00%	0,00%	100,00%	100,00%		0,00%	100,00%
Health Sum	33,33%	66,67%	5,06%	36,36%	63,64%	6,18%	36,94%	63,06%	88,20%	100,00%	0,56%	100,00%
Measurement of Trade Flows												
Measures introduced for statistical purposes	0,00%	100,00%	100,00%			0,00%	0,00%		0,00%		0,00%	100,00%
Measurement of Trade Flows Sum	0,00%	100,00%	100,00%			0,00%			0,00%		0,00%	100,00%
Morality												
Minors/ Children			0,00%			0,00%	0,00%	100,00%	100,00%		0,00%	100,00%
Public morals	50,00%	50,00%	33,33%			0,00%	50,00%	50,00%	66,67%		0,00%	100,00%
Public policy/ public order	0,00%	100,00%	7,69%			0,00%	41,67%	58,33%	92,31%		0,00%	100,00%
Morality Sum	33,33%	66,67%	15,00%			0,00%	41,18%	58,82%	85,00%		0,00%	100,00%
Not specified	50,00%	50,00%	20,00%			0,00%	37,50%	62,50%	80,00%		0,00%	100,00%
Not specified Sum	50,00%	50,00%	20,00%			0,00%	37,50%	62,50%	80,00%		0,00%	100,00%
Obligations under Public Law												
Other international agreement	0,00%	100,00%	100,00%			0,00%			0,00%		0,00%	100,00%
Obligations under Public Law Sum	0,00%	100,00%	100,00%			0,00%			0,00%		0,00%	100,00%
Plant Health												
Plant health protection	0,00%	100,00%	38,46%			0,00%	28,57%	71,43%	53,85%	100,00%	7,69%	100,00%
Plant Health Sum	0,00%	100,00%	38,46%			0,00%	28,57%	71,43%	53,85%	100,00%	7,69%	100,00%
Protection of Fundamental Rights												
Diversity of the Press												
Protection of fundamental rights			0,00%			0,00%	100,00%	0,00%	100,00%		0,00%	100,00%
Protection of Fundamental Rights Sum			0,00%			0,00%	100,00%	0,00%	100,00%		0,00%	100,00%

Protection of the Consumer											
Designation of quality	100,00%		0,00%			0,00%	0,00%	100,00%	100,00%	0,00%	100,00%
Protection of the consumer	0,00%		4,65%			0,00%	26,83%	73,17%	95,35%	0,00%	100,00%
Protection of the Con-sumer Sum	**100,00%**		**4,55%**			**0,00%**	**26,19%**	**73,81%**	**95,45%**	**0,00%**	**100,00%**
Road Traffic Safety											
Road traffic safety				0,00%	100,00%	0,00%	0,00%	100,00%	100,00%	0,00%	100,00%
Road Traffic Safety Sum				**0,00%**	**100,00%**	**0,00%**	**0,00%**	**100,00%**	**100,00%**	**0,00%**	**100,00%**
Safety											
Combating of crime				0,00%	100,00%	0,00%	0,00%	100,00%	100,00%	0,00%	100,00%
Public security/ public safety				0,00%	100,00%	8,33%	45,45%	54,55%	91,67%	0,00%	100,00%
Safety Sum				**0,00%**	**100,00%**	**7,14%**	**38,46%**	**61,54%**	**92,86%**	**0,00%**	**100,00%**
Securing Supply Chains											
Supply of goods at short distance						0,00%	0,00%	100,00%	100,00%	0,00%	100,00%
Securing Supply Chains Sum						**0,00%**	**0,00%**	**100,00%**	**100,00%**	**0,00%**	**100,00%**
Grand Total	**29,63%**	**70,37%**	**6,84%**	**25,00%**	**75,00%**	**4,05%**	**34,29%**	**65,71%**	**87,85%**	**1,27%**	**100,00%**

Source: Author's novel dataset

8.2.14 Overview of Argumentative Patterns for of PTA-DSMs on All Legitimate Objectives

Reason for successful invocation of legitimate objective	CAN	EFTA	EU	Grand Total
Complainant has not given sufficient information on the contents of the measure (burden of proof not satisfied)				
Animal health	12,50%	0,00%	0,00%	0,76%
Health	0,00%	0,00%	6,72%	6,11%
Not specified	12,50%	0,00%	0,00%	0,76%
Complainant has not given sufficient information on the contents of the measure (burden of proof not satisfied) Sum	**25,00%**	**0,00%**	**6,72%**	**7,63%**
Council took into account legitimate objective when deciding on EU legislation (case of prohibition of insufficient action)				
Protection of the consumer	0,00%	0,00%	0,84%	0,76%
Council took into account legitimate objective when deciding on EU legislation (case of prohibition of insufficient action) Sum	**0,00%**	**0,00%**	**0,84%**	**0,76%**
measure (dis)proportionate/excessive (and not necessary)				
Animal health	0,00%	0,00%	7,56%	6,87%
Antitrust and fair competition	0,00%	0,00%	2,52%	2,29%
Constitutionalizing of community order	0,00%	0,00%	0,84%	0,76%
Protection of the culture	0,00%	0,00%	0,84%	0,76%
Environment and sustainability	0,00%	0,00%	5,88%	5,34%
Health	12,50%	75,00%	34,45%	34,35%
Morality	12,50%	0,00%	5,04%	5,34%
Not specified	0,00%	0,00%	1,68%	1,53%
Plant health	0,00%	0,00%	1,68%	1,53%
Protection of fundamental rights	0,00%	0,00%	0,84%	0,76%
Protection of the consumer	0,00%	0,00%	2,52%	2,29%
Safety	0,00%	0,00%	2,52%	2,29%
Measure (dis)proportionate/excessive (and not necessary) Sum	**25,00%**	**75,00%**	**66,39%**	**64,12%**
Measure (not) necessary				
Animal health	0,00%	0,00%	2,52%	2,29%
Antitrust and fair competition	0,00%	0,00%	0,84%	0,76%
Health	0,00%	0,00%	4,20%	3,82%
Protection of the consumer	25,00%	0,00%	1,68%	3,05%
Safety	0,00%	0,00%	1,68%	1,53%
Measure (not) necessary Sum	**25,00%**	**0,00%**	**10,92%**	**11,45%**

(continued)

(continued)

Reason for successful invocation of legitimate objective	CAN	EFTA	EU	Grand Total
Measure discriminates arbitrarily and unjustifiably				
Health	0,00%	25,00%	0,00%	0,76%
Measure discriminates arbitrarily and unjustifiably Sum	**0,00%**	**25,00%**	**0,00%**	**0,76%**
Measure does (not) attain legitimate goal (i.e., the threat to a legitimate objective is accepted, but the suitability of the measure to attain its protection is denied)				
Animal health	0,00%	0,00%	0,84%	0,76%
Environment and sustainability	0,00%	0,00%	0,84%	0,76%
Health	12,50%	0,00%	3,36%	3,82%
Measure does (not) attain legitimate goal (i.e., the threat to a legitimate objective is accepted, but the suitability of the measure to attain its protection is denied) Sum	**12,50%**	**0,00%**	**5,04%**	**5,34%**
No information				
Animal health	0,00%	0,00%	0,84%	0,76%
Antitrust and fair competition	0,00%	0,00%	3,36%	3,05%
Health	12,50%	0,00%	0,00%	0,76%
Morality	0,00%	0,00%	0,84%	0,76%
Not specified	0,00%	0,00%	0,84%	0,76%
Protection of the consumer	0,00%	0,00%	4,20%	3,82%
No information Sum	**12,50%**	**0,00%**	**10,08%**	**9,92%**
Grand Total	**100,00%**	**100,00%**	**100,00%**	**100,00%**

Source: Author's novel dataset

8.2.15 Distribution of Goods Adjudicated in the Context of Justifications for Trade-restrictive Measures in front of reviewed PTA-DSMs

HS Chapter Code	CAN	EFTA	EU	Mercosur	Grand Total
00. General Trade (not specified).	3		6		9
01. Live animals; Animal products.	4	3	74	1	82
02. Vegetable Products.	3		13	3	19
03. Animal or Vegetable Fats and Oils and their Cleavage Products; Prepared Edible Fats; Animal or Vegetable Waxes.	1				1
04. Prepared Foodstuffs; Beverages, Spirits and Vinegar; Tobacco and Manufactured Tobacco Substitutes.	1	8	94		103
05. Mineral Products.	3		21		24
06. Products of the Chemical or Allied Industries.	3	1	70		74
07. Plastics and Articles thereof; Rubber and Articles thereof.			3	1	4
08. Raw Hides and Skins, Leather, Furskins and Articles thereof; Saddlery and Harness; Travel Goods, Handbags and Similar Containers; Articles of Animal Gut (Other Than Silk-Worm-Gut).			2		2
09. Wood and Articles of Wood; Wood Charcoal; Cork and Articles of Cork; Manufactures of Straw, of Esparto or of Other Plaiting Materials; Basketware and Wickerwork.			1		1
10. Pulp of Wood or of Other Fibrous Cellulosic Material; Recovered (Waste and Scrap) Paper or Paperboard; Paper and Paperboard and Articles Thereof.			4		4
11. Textiles and Textile Articles.	2		4		6
12. Footwear, Headgear, Umbrellas, Sun Umbrellas, Walking-Sticks, Seat-Sticks, Whips, Riding-Crops and Parts Thereof; Prepared Feathers and Articles Made Therewith; Artificial Flowers; Articles of Human Hair.	1				1
13. Articles of Stone, Plaster, Cement, Asbestos, Mica or Similar Materials; Ceramic Products; Glass and Glassware.		2	3		5
14. Natural or Cultured Pearls, Precious or Semi-Precious Stones, Precious Metals, Metals Clad With Precious Metal and Articles Thereof; Imitation Jewellery; Coin.			5		5
15. Base Metals and Articles of Base Metal.			4		4
	2	2	10		14

(continued)

(continued)

HS Chapter Code	CAN	EFTA	EU	Mercosur	Grand Total
16. Machinery and Mechanical Appliances; Electrical Equipment; Parts Thereof; Sound Recorders and Reproducers, Television Image and Sound Recorders and Reproducers, and Parts and Accessories of such Articles.					
17. Vehicles, Aircraft, Vessels and Associated Transport Equipment.	2		25		27
18. Optical, Photographic, Cinematographic, Measuring, Checking, Precision, Medical or Surgical Instruments and Apparatus; Clocks and Watches; Musical Instruments; Parts and Accessories Thereof.			7		7
20. Miscellaneous Manufactured Articles.	2		1		3
Grand Total	**27**	**16**	**347**	**5**	**395**

Source: Designation as provided by the HS, data author's novel dataset

8.2.16   *Figures on the Proportion of Goods Adjudicated in the Context of Justifications for Trade-Restrictive Measures Per Reviewed PTA-DSM (Figs. 8.1, 8.2, 8.3 and 8.4)*

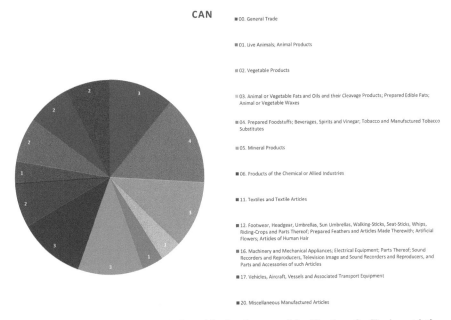

Fig. 8.1 Proportion of Goods Adjudicated in the Context of Justifications for Trade-restrictive Measures Regarding the PTA-DSM of the CAN (*Source* Author's novel dataset)

EFTA

■ 01. Live Animals; Animal Products

■ 04. Prepared Foodstuffs; Beverages, Spirits and Vinegar; Tobacco and Manufactured Tobacco Substitutes

■ 06. Products of the Chemical or Allied Industries

■ 13. Articles of Stone, Plaster, Cement, Asbestos, Mica or Similar Materials; Ceramic Products; Glass and Glassware

■ 16. Machinery and Mechanical Appliances; Electrical Equipment; Parts Thereof; Sound Recorders and Reproducers, Television Image and Sound Recorders and Reproducers, and Parts and Accessories of such Articles

Fig. 8.2 Proportion of Goods Adjudicated in the Context of Justifications for Trade-restrictive Measures Regarding the PTA-DSM of the EEA (*Source* Author's novel dataset)

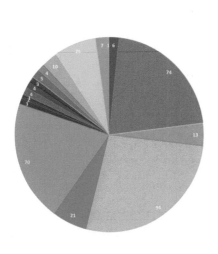

EU

■ 00. General Trade

■ 01. Live Animals; Animal Products

■ 02. Vegetable Products

■ 04. Prepared Foodstuffs; Beverages, Spirits and Vinegar; Tobacco and Manufactured Tobacco Substitutes

■ 05. Mineral Products

■ 06. Products of the Chemical or Allied Industries

■ 07. Plastics and Articles thereof; Rubber and Articles thereof

■ 08. Raw Hides and Skins, Leather, Furskins and Articles thereof; Saddlery and Harness; Travel Goods, Handbags and Similar Containers; Articles of Animal Gut (Other Than Silk-Worm Gut)

■ 09. Wood and Articles of Wood; Wood Charcoal; Cork and Articles of Cork; Manufactures of Straw, of Esparto or of Other Plaiting Materials; Basketware and Wickerwork

■ 10. Pulp of Wood or of Other Fibrous Cellulosic Material; Recovered (Waste and Scrap) Paper or Paperboard; Paper and Paperboard and Articles Thereof

■ 11. Textiles and Textile Articles

■ 13. Articles of Stone, Plaster, Cement, Asbestos, Mica or Similar Materials; Ceramic Products; Glass and Glassware

■ 14. Natural or Cultured Pearls, Precious or Semi-Precious Stones, Precious Metals, Metals Clad With Precious Metal and Articles Thereof; Imitation Jewellery; Coin

■ 15. Base Metals and Articles of Base Metal

■ 16. Machinery and Mechanical Appliances; Electrical Equipment; Parts Thereof; Sound Recorders and Reproducers, Television Image and Sound Recorders and Reproducers, and Parts and Accessories of such Articles
■ 17. Vehicles, Aircraft, Vessels and Associated Transport Equipment

■ 18. Optical, Photographic, Cinematographic, Measuring, Checking, Precision, Medical or Surgical Instruments and Apparatus; Clocks and Watches; Musical Instruments; Parts and Accessories Thereof

Fig. 8.3 Proportion of Goods Adjudicated in the Context of Justifications for Trade-restrictive Measures Regarding the PTA-DSM of the EU (*Source* Author's novel dataset)

MERCOSUR

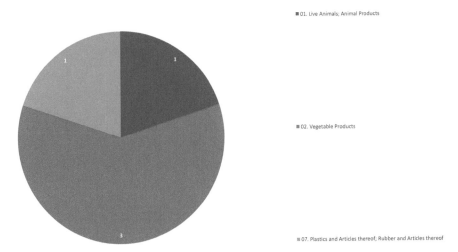

Fig. 8.4 Proportion of Goods Adjudicated in the Context of Justifications for Trade-restrictive Measures Regarding the PTA-DSM of the Mercosur (*Source* Author's novel dataset)

8.2.17   Referencing Practice of Reviewed PTA-DSMs

Case Sequence No.					
Source of reference/Case sequence no.	CAN	EFTA	EU	Mercosur	Grand Total
WTO	**10**			**1**	**11**
CAN-SGCAN-1289	1				1
CAN-SGCAN-1695	1				1
CAN-SGCAN-184	1				1
CAN-SGCAN-2019	1				1
CAN-SGCAN-449	1				1
CAN-SGCAN-638	1				1
CAN-SGCAN-784	1				1
CAN-SGCAN-897	1				1
CAN-TJCAN-117-AI-2003	1				1
CAN-TJCAN-1-AI-97	1				1
Mercosur_11				1	1
Scientific Evidence	**1**		**9**		**10**
C-13/91			1		1
C-176/84			1		1
C-178/84			1		1
C-192/01			1		1
C-24/00			1		1
C-298/87			1		1
C-304/84			1		1
C-387/99			1		1
C-42/90			1		1
CAN-SGCAN-1289	1				1
International Health Protection	**1**		**7**		**8**
C-13/91			1		1
C-176/84			1		1
C-178/84			1		1
C-298/87			1		1
C-42/90			1		1
C-421/09			1		1
C-446/08			1		1
CAN-SGCAN-576	1				1
Food and Agriculture	**1**	**1**	**5**		**7**
C-13/91			1		1
C-176/84			1		1
C-178/84			1		1
C-298/87			1		1
C-42/90			1		1

(continued)

(continued)

| Case Sequence No. | | | | | |
Source of reference/Case sequence no.	CAN	EFTA	EU	Mercosur	Grand Total
CAN-JUNAC-432	1				1
E-3/00		1			1
International Biodiversity Protection	**3**		**4**		**7**
C-100/08			1		1
C-169/89			1		1
C-219/07			1		1
C-510/99			1		1
CAN-SGCAN-784	1				1
CAN-SGCAN-802	1				1
CAN-SGCAN-986	1				1
EU	**3**	**2**		**2**	**7**
CAN-SGCAN-1695	1				1
CAN-SGCAN-449	1				1
CAN-TJCAN-1-AI-97	1				1
E-16/10		1			1
E-3/00		1			1
Mercosur_1				1	1
Mercosur_11				1	1
International Environmental Law	**1**		**4**	**1**	**6**
C-2/90			1		1
C-204/12			1		1
C-573/12			1		1
CAN-SGCAN-784	1				1
Mercosur_11				1	1
General Scholarly Literature	**2**		**1**	**2**	**5**
C-2/90			1		1
CAN-SGCAN-638	1				1
CAN-TJCAN-1-AI-97	1				1
Mercosur_11				1	1
Mercosur_7				1	1
Domestic legislation and jurisprudence	**3**		**1**		**4**
C-24/00			1		1
CAN-SGCAN-1695	1				1
CAN-SGCAN-2019	1				1
CAN-SGCAN-759	1				1
International Drug Addiction Prevention	**2**		**1**		**3**
C-324/93			1		1
CAN-SGCAN-308	1				1
CAN-SGCAN-2019	1				1
Regional Treaty	**2**				**2**
CAN-SGCAN-784	1				1
CAN-SGCAN-802	1				1

(continued)

(continued)

Case Sequence No.					
Source of reference/Case sequence no.	CAN	EFTA	EU	Mercosur	Grand Total
European PTAs			**2**		**2**
C-125/88			1		1
C-228/91			1		1
Human Rights Protection			**2**		**2**
C-112/00			1		1
Communication Services			**1**		**1**
C-121/85			1		1
EFTA			**1**		**1**
C-192/01			1		1
CAN				**1**	**1**
Mercosur_11				1	1
International Procedure and Litigation			**1**		**1**
C-121/85			1		1
Latin-American PTAs	**1**				**1**
CAN-SGCAN-490	1				1
International Animal Welfare			**1**		**1**
C-1/96			1		1
Grand Total	**17**	**2**	**26**	**3**	**46**

Source: Author's novel dataset

8.2.18 References of PTA-DSMs to Other Decisions of Other PTA-DSMs and PTA rules

Case Sequence No.						
Source of reference/Case sequence no.	CAN	EFTA	EU	Mercosur	Overview citations	Grand Total
WTO	7			1		9
WTO Case Law				1		1
Mercosur_11				1	11/A –TPR: Korea – Various Measures on Beef (WTDS/161/AB/R)	1
CAN-SGCAN-2019					Colombia – Ports of Entry (WT/DS366/R)	1
WTO rules	7			1		9
CAN-SGCAN-1695	1				Decisión 1695: General reference to WTO rules 1716: Art. XX GATT	1
CAN-SGCAN-184	1				Decisión 184: Art. XXIV GATT 1994	1
CAN-SGCAN-2019	1				General reference to the NT and MFN principle	1
CAN-SGCAN-449	1				Decisión 489: General reference to WTO rules	1
CAN-SGCAN-638	1				Decisión 638: WTO Licensing Agreement	1
CAN-SGCAN-897	1				5-AI-2007: General reference to WTO rules	1
CAN-TJCAN-117-AI-2003	1				117-AI-2003: WTO Import licensing agreement	1
CAN-1-AI-97				1	GATT SPS Agreement TBT Agreement	1
Mercosur_11				1	General reference through citation of WTO case law (p. 9)	1
Mercosur_1				1	Import Licensing Agreement	1
EU	3	2	2			7
EU Case Law	1	2	1			4
CAN-SGCAN-1695	1				Deutsche Milch Kontor II; C-272/95 Commission v. France; C-21/84	1

(continued)

(continued)

Case Sequence No.						
Source of reference/Case sequence no.	CAN	EFTA	EU	Mercosur	Overview citations	Grand Total
					Denkavit ; C-251/78 Webb; C-279/80 Commission v. Germany; C-205/84 Commission v. Italy; C-455/01 Commission v. Portugal; C-432/03 Digital Satellite Channel; C-390/99 Commission v. Italy; C-270/02 Commission v. Germany; C-319/05 Simmenthal; C-106/77	
E-16/10		1			Commission v. Greece; C-321/92 Commission v. Italy; C-110/05 Keck and Mithouard; C-267/91; C-268/91 Ker-Optika; C-108/09 Commission v. Germany; C-141/07 Guarneri & Cie; C-291/09 Apothekerkammer; C-171/07; C-172/07 Humanplasma; C-421/09 Ahokainen and Leppik; C-434/04	1
E-3/00		1			Sandoz BV ; C-174/82 Ministère public v Muller; C-304/84 Commission v Belgium; C-355/98	1
Mercosur_11			1		Cassis de Dijon; C-120/78 Commission v Austria; C-320/03 Commission v Germany; C-463/01 Radlberger Getränkegesellschaft and S. Spitz; C-309/02 De Peijper C-104/75	1
Mercosur_1			1		General reference to case law of CJEU	

(continued)

(continued)

Case Sequence No.						
Source of reference/Case sequence no.	CAN	EFTA	EU	Mercosur	Overview citations	Grand Total
EU Law	**2**			**1**		**3**
CAN-SGCAN-449	1				Decisión 449: Art. 30 EEC Decisión 489: General reference to EU rules Art. 30 EEC	1
CAN-TJCAN-1-AI-97	1				Art. 30 EEC	1
Mercosur_1				1	*Principle of effet utile*	1
CAN			**1**			**1**
CAN Case Law			**1**			**1**
Mercosur_11				1	30-IP-99	1
EFTA		**1**				**1**
EFTA Case Law		**1**				**1**
C-192/01			1		E-3/00 EFTA Surveillance Authority v. Norway	1
Grand Total	**8**	**2**	**1**	**2**		**13**

Source: Author based on the author's novel dataset

Reference

Waltermann A, Arosemena G, Hage J (2020) Exceptions in International Law. In: Bartels L, Paddeu F (eds) Exceptions in international law. Oxford University Press, Oxford, pp 11–34

Chapter 9
Bibliography

9.1 General Literature

Abbott KW, Genschel P, Snidal D, Zangl B (2014) Orchestration. In: Abbott KW, Genschel P, Snidal D, Zangl B (eds) International organizations as orchestrators. Cambridge University Press, Cambridge, pp 3–36

Abellán Honrubia V, Eduardo GdE, García EA (1986) Tratado de derecho comunitario europeo: (estudio sistematico desde el derecho espanol). Ed. Civitas, Madrid

Acharya R (2016) Some conclusions. In: Acharya R (ed) Regional trade agreements and the multilateral trading system, 1st edn. Cambridge University Press, Cambridge, pp 703–706

Acharya R, Crawford J-A, Maliszewska M, Renard C (2011) Landscape. In: Preferential trade agreement policies for development. World Bank Publications, Washington D.C., pp 37–76

Allee T, Elsig M (2016a) Are the contents of international treaties copied-and-pasted? Evidence from preferential trade agreements. World Trade Institute working papers working paper no. 8

Allee T, Elsig M (2016b) Why do some international institutions contain strong dispute settlement provisions? New evidence from preferential trade agreements. Rev Int Organ 11:89–120. https://doi.org/10.1007/s11558-015-9223-y

Allee T, Elsig M, Lugg A (2017) The ties between the World Trade Organization and preferential trade agreements: a textual analysis. J Int Econ Law 20:333–363. https://doi.org/10.1093/jiel/jgx009

Alter KJ, Helfer L, McAllister JR (2013) A new international human rights court for West Africa: the ECOWAS Community Court of Justice. Am J Int Law 107:737–779. https://doi.org/10.5305/amerjintelaw.107.4.0737

Alter KJ, Helfer LR (2017) Transplanting international courts: the law and politics of the Andean Tribunal of Justice, 1st edn. Oxford University Press, Oxford

© The Author(s), under exclusive license to Springer Nature Switzerland AG 2023
P. Wasilczyk, *Fragmentation of International Trade Law Reassessed*, EYIEL Monographs - Studies in European and International Economic Law 32, https://doi.org/10.1007/978-3-031-40601-0_9

Alter KJ, Hooghe L (2016) Regional dispute settlement. In: Börzel TA, Risse T (eds) The Oxford handbook of comparative regionalism. Oxford University Press, Oxford, pp 538–559

Alter KJ, Meunier-Aitsahalia S (1994) Judicial politics in the European Community: European integration and the pathbreaking Cassis de Dijon decision. Comp Polit Stud 26:535–561. https://doi.org/10.1177/0010414094026004007

Appleton AE (1997) GATT Article XX's Chapeau: a disguised necessary test: the WTO Appellate Body's ruling in United States – standards for reformulated and conventional gasoline. Rev Eur Comp Int Environ Law 6:131–138

Armingeon K, Milewicz K, Peter S, Peters A (2011) The constitutionalisation of international trade law. In: Cottier T, Delimatsis P (eds) The prospects of international trade regulation. Cambridge University Press, Cambridge, pp 69–102

Awasthi K, Yayavaram S, George R, Sastry T (2019) Classification for regulated industries: a new index. IIMB Manag Rev 31:309–315. https://doi.org/10.1016/j.iimb.2019.01.002

Bagwell KW, Mavroidis PC (eds) (2011) Preferential trade agreements: a law and economics analysis. Cambridge University Press, Cambridge

Baier SL, Yotov YV, Zylkin T (2019) On the widely differing effects of free trade agreements: lessons from twenty years of trade integration. J Int Econ 116:206–226. https://doi.org/10.1016/j.jinteco.2018.11.002

Baldwin R, Carpenter T (2011) Regionalism: moving from fragmentation towards coherence. In: Delimatsis P, Cottier T (eds) The prospects of international trade regulation: from fragmentation to coherence. Cambridge University Press, Cambridge, pp 136–166

Baldwin RE, Robert-Nicoud F (2000) Free trade agreements without delocation. Can J Econ/Revue Canadienne d'Economique 33:766–786. https://doi.org/10.1111/0008-4085.00040

Barents R (1981) New development in measures having equivalent effect. Common Mark Law Rev 271–308

Barnard C (2019) The substantive law of the EU. Oxford University Press, Oxford

Barnard C, Peers S (eds) (2020) Table of equivalences. In: European Union law, 3rd edn. Oxford University Press, Oxford

Bartels L (2008) The trade and development policy of the European Union. Oxford University Press, Oxford

Bartels L, Paddeu F (eds) (2020) Exceptions in international law, 1st edn. Oxford University Press, Oxford

Baudenbacher C (2005) The implementation of decisions of the ECJ and of the EFTA Court in Member States' domestic legal orders. Tex Int Law J 40:383–416

Baur G (2020) The European Free Trade Association: an intergovernmental platform for trade relations. Intersentia, Cambridge

Baur G, Rydelski MS, Zatschler C (2018) European Free Trade Association (EFTA) and the European Economic Area (EEA), 2nd edn. Kluwer Law International B. V., Den Haag

Berry DS (2014) Caribbean integration law, 1st edn. Oxford University Press, Oxford

Bhagwati JN (2008) Termites in the trading system: how preferential agreements undermine free trade. Oxford University Press, Oxford

Björnsson T (2013) Inside and outside the EFTA Court: evaluating the effectiveness of the EFTA Court through its structures. Israel Law Rev 46:61–93. https://doi.org/10.1017/S0021223712000295

Bradford A (2019) The Brussels effect: how the European Union rules the world. Oxford University Press, Oxford

Broude T (2008) Fragmentation(s) of international law: on normative integration as authority allocation. In: The shifting allocation of authority in international law: considering sovereignty, supremacy and subsidiarity, 1st edn. Hart, Oxford

Bruns V, Hestermeyer H (2008) Where unity is at risk: when international tribunals proliferate. In: König D, Stoll P-T, Röben V, Matz-Lück N (eds) International law today: new challenges and the need for reform? Springer, Heidelberg, pp 123–140

Bureau J-C, Guimbard H, Jean S (2019) Competing liberalizations: tariffs and trade in the twenty-first century. Rev World Econ. https://doi.org/10.1007/s10290-019-00346-1

Burri M, Polanco R (2020) Digital trade provisions in preferential trade agreements: introducing a new dataset. J Int Econ Law 23:187–220. https://doi.org/10.1093/jiel/jgz044

Busch ML (2007) Overlapping institutions, forum shopping, and dispute settlement in international trade. Int Organ 61:735–761. https://doi.org/10.1017/S0020818307070257

Carmody C (2008) A theory of WTO law. J Int Econ Law 11:527–557. https://doi.org/10.1093/jiel/jgn017

Castro Bernieri J (2003) El Comercio Intracomunitario y el Mercado Común Andino. In: Derecho comunitario andino. Fondo Editorial PUCP, Cercado de Lima, pp 117–141

Cattaneo O (2009) The political economy of PTAs. In: Lester S, Mercurio B (eds) Bilateral and regional trade agreements. Cambridge University Press, Cambridge, pp 28–51

Chafer C, Gil-Pareja S, Llorca-Vivero R (2021) Warning: bilateral trade agreements do not create trade. Bull Econ Res 2021:1–10. https://doi.org/10.1111/boer.12281

Chase C, Yanovich A, Crawford J-A, Ugaz P (2016) Mapping of dispute settlement mechanisms in regional trade agreements–innovative or variations on a theme? In: Acharya R (ed) Regional trade agreements and the multilateral trading system. Cambridge University Press, Cambridge, pp 608–702

Claussen K (2019) Old wine in new bottles? The trade rule of law. Yale J Int Law Online 44:61–68

Cottier T (2008) Challenges ahead in international economic law. J Int Econ Law 12:3–15. https://doi.org/10.1093/jiel/jgp005

Cottier T, Delimatsis P, Gehne K, Payosova T (2011) Introduction: fragmentation and coherence in international trade regulation: analysis and conceptual foundations. In: Cottier T, Delimatsis P (eds) The prospects of international trade regulation. Cambridge University Press, Cambridge, pp 1–66

Cottier T, Foltea M (2006) Constitutional functions of the WTO and regional trade agreements. In: Regional trade agreements and the WTO legal system. Oxford University Press, Oxford

Craig PP (2011) Institutions, power and institutional balance. In: Craig P, de Búrca G (eds) The evolution of EU law. Oxford University Press, Oxford, pp 41–84

Craig PP, De Búrca G (2015) EU law: text, cases, and materials, 6th edn. Oxford University Press, Oxford

Crawford J-A, Fiorentino RV (2005) The changing landscape of regional trade agreements. World Trade Organization, Geneva

Crawford J-A, Laird S (2001) Regional trade agreements and the WTO. N Am J Econ Financ 12:193–211. https://doi.org/10.1016/S1062-9408(01)00047-X

Dalla Torre Di Sanguinetto S, Heinonen E, Antonov J, Bolte C (2019) A comparative review of marketing authorization decisions in Switzerland, the EU, and the USA. Ther Innov Regul Sci 53:86–94. https://doi.org/10.1177/2168479018764660

Damro C (2006) The political economy of regional trade agreements. In: Bartels L, Ortino F (eds) Regional trade agreements and the WTO legal system. Oxford University Press, Oxford

Danilenko GM (1998) The Economic Court of the Commonwealth of Independent States symposium issue: the proliferation of international tribunals: piecing together the puzzle. N Y Univ J Int Law Polit 31:893–918

de Córdoba SF, Laird S, Maur J-C, Serena JM (2006) Adjustment costs and trade liberalization. In: Laird S, de Córdoba SF (eds) Coping with trade reforms: a developing country perspective on the WTO industrial tariff negotiations. Palgrave Macmillan, London, pp 66–85

de Mestral ACM (2013) Dispute settlement under the WTO and RTAs: an uneasy relationship. J Int Econ Law 16:777–825. https://doi.org/10.1093/jiel/jgt032

Devuyst Y, Serdarevic A (2007) The World Trade Organization and regional trade agreements: bridging the constitutional credibility gap. Duke J Comp Int Law 18: 1–76

Do VD, Watson W (2006) Economic analysis of regional trade agreements. In: Bartels L, Ortino F (eds) Regional trade agreements and the WTO legal system. Oxford University Press, Oxford

Dolcetti A, Ratti GB (2020) Derogation and defeasibility in international law. In: Bartels L, Paddeu F (eds) Exceptions in international law. Oxford University Press, Oxford, pp 108–124

Dragneva R (2018) The case of the economic court of the CIS. In: Ulfstein G, Ruiz-Fabri H, Zang MQ, Howse R (eds) The legitimacy of international trade courts and tribunals. Cambridge University Press, Cambridge, pp 286–313

Drahos P (2007) Weaving webs of influence; the United States; free trade agreements and dispute resolution. J World Trade 41:191–210

Drezner DW (2013) The tragedy of the global institutional commons. In: Finnemore M, Goldstein J (eds) Back to basics: state power in a contemporary world. Oxford University Press, New York

Dür A, Baccini L, Elsig M (2014) The design of international trade agreements: introducing a new dataset. Rev Int Organ 9:353–375. https://doi.org/10.1007/s11558-013-9179-8

Dür A, Elsig M (eds) (2015) Trade cooperation: the purpose, design and effects of preferential trade agreements. Cambridge University Press, Cambridge

Franch VB (2006) Los procedimientos para la solución de controversias en el Mercosur. Agenda Internacional XII:261–294

Fredriksen HH (2010) One market, two courts: legal pluralism vs. homogeneity in the European economic area. Nordic J Int Law 76:481–500

Froese MD (2016) Mapping the scope of dispute settlement in regional trade agreements: implications for the multilateral governance of trade. World Trade Rev 15:563–585. https://doi.org/10.1017/S1474745616000057

Fuders F (2010) Economic freedoms in MERCOSUR. In: Franca Filho MT, Lixinski L, Olmos Giupponi MB, Toscana M (eds) The law of Mercosur. Hart, Oxford

Gantz DA (2016) Assessing the impact of WTO and regional dispute resolution mechanisms on the world trading system. In: Jemielniak J, Nielsen L, Olsen HP (eds) Establishing judicial authority in international economic law. Cambridge University Press, Cambridge, pp 31–77

Gathii JT (2018) The COMESA Court of Justice. In: Ulfstein G, Ruiz-Fabri H, Zang MQ, Howse R (eds) The legitimacy of international trade courts and tribunals. Cambridge University Press, Cambridge, pp 314–348

Gobbi Estrella AT, Horlick GN (2006) Mandatory abolition of anti-dumping, countervailing duties and safeguards in customs unions and free-trade areas constituted between World Trade Organization members: revisiting a long-standing discussion in light of the Appellate Body's Turkey — Textiles ruling. J World Trade 40:909–944

Grossman GM, Horn H (2013) Why the WTO? An introduction to the economics of trade agreements. In: Horn H, Mavroidis PC (eds) Legal and economic principles of world trade law: economics of trade agreements, border instruments, and national treasures. Cambridge University Press, Cambridge, pp 9–67

Hamanaka S (2012) Unexpected usage of enabling clause? Proliferation of bilateral trade agreements in Asia. J World Trade 6:1239–1260

Harrison J (2014) The case for investigative legal pluralism in international economic law linkage debates: a strategy for enhancing the value of international legal discourse. London Rev Int Law 2:115–145. https://doi.org/10.1093/lril/lru002

Hart HLA (2012) The concept of law, 3rd edn. Oxford University Press, Oxford

Hart HLA (1983) Kelsen's doctrine of the unity of law. In: Essays in jurisprudence and philosophy. Oxford University Press, Oxford

Haupt S (2003) An economic analysis of consumer protection in contract law. German Law J 4:1137–1164. https://doi.org/10.1017/S2071832200012013

Hauser H, Roitinger A (2004) Two perspectives on international trade agreements. Zeitschrift für ausländisches öffentliches Recht und Völkerrecht 64:641–658

Heiskanen V (2004) The regulatory philosophy of international trade law. J World Trade 38:1–36

Hinton EF (1998) Strengthening the effectiveness of community law: direct effect, Article 5 EC, and the European Court of Justice. N Y Univ J Int Law Polit 31: 307–348

Hoekman B, Sabel C (2019) Open plurilateral agreements, International Regulatory Cooperation and the WTO. Glob Policy 10:297–312. https://doi.org/10.1111/1758-5899.12694

Hoekman BM, Mavroidis PC (2015) WTO 'à la carte' or 'menu du jour'? Assessing the case for more plurilateral agreements. Eur J Int Law 26:319–343. https://doi.org/10.1093/ejil/chv025

Horn H, Mavroidis PC, Sapir A (2010) Beyond the WTO? An anatomy of EU and US preferential trade agreements. World economy 33:1565–1588. https://doi.org/10.1111/j.1467-9701.2010.01273.x

Howells G, Straetmans G (2017) The interpretive function of the CJEU and the interrelationship of EU and national levels of consumer protection. Perspect Federalism 9:E-180–E-215. https://doi.org/10.1515/pof-2017-0014

Howse R (2012) 20. Regulatory measures. In: Narlikar A, Daunton MJ, Stern RM (eds) The Oxford handbook on the World Trade Organization. Oxford University Press, Oxford, pp 441–457

Islam MdR, Alam S (2009) Preferential trade agreements and the scope of GATT Article XXIV, GATS Article V and the enabling clause: an appraisal of GATT/WTO jurisprudence. Netherlands Int Law Rev 56:1. https://doi.org/10.1017/S0165070X09000011

Jemielniak J, Nielsen L, Olsen HP (2016) Introduction. In: Jemielniak J, Nielsen L, Olsen HP (eds) Establishing judicial authority in international economic law. Cambridge University Press, Cambridge, pp 1–28

Jensen T (2012) The role of dispute settlement mechanisms in the constitutionalization of regional trade agreements. Library and Archives Canada = Bibliothèque et Archives Canada, Ottawa

Jo H, Namgung H (2012) Dispute settlement mechanisms in preferential trade agreements: democracy, boilerplates, and the multilateral trade regime. J Confl Resolut 56:1041–1068

Kanellakis M, Martinopoulos G, Zachariadis T (2013) European energy policy—a review. Energy Policy 62:1020–1030. https://doi.org/10.1016/j.enpol.2013.08.008

Kelsen H (2003) Principles of international law, 5th edn. The Lawbook Exchange, Ltd., Clark

Kelsen H (2017) Reine Rechtslehre, 1st edn. Mohr Siebeck, Tübingen

Kim JB (2011) WTO legality of discriminatory liberalization of internal regulations: role of RTA national treatment. World Trade Rev 10:473–496

Kim JB (2018) Adaptation of internal trade requirements in RTAs: substandard internal trade liberalization. J World Trade 375–392

Kim JB (2014) Entrenchment of regionalism: WTO legality of MFN clauses in preferential trade agreements for goods and services. World Trade Rev 13:443–470. https://doi.org/10.1017/S1474745613000311

Kimura F (2021) International production networks and required new global governance: mega-FTAs and the WTO. In: Ogawa E, Raube K, Vanoverbeke D et al (eds) Japan, the European Union and global governance. Edward Elgar, Cheltenham

Klumpp M (2013) Schiedsgerichtsbarkeit und Ständiges Revisionsgericht des Mercosur: Integrationsförderung durch zwischenstaatliche Streitbeilegung und Rechtsprechung im Mercosur. Springer, Heidelberg

Koskenniemi M (2014) What is international law for? In: Evans MD (ed) International law. Oxford University Press, Oxford, pp 28–50

Kreuder-Sonnen C, Zürn M (2020) After fragmentation: norm collisions, interface conflicts, and conflict management. Glob Con 9:241–267. https://doi.org/10.1017/S2045381719000315

Kuijper PJ (2018) The Court of Justice of the European Union. In: Ulfstein G, Ruiz-Fabri H, Zang MQ, Howse R (eds) The legitimacy of international trade courts and tribunals. Cambridge University Press, Cambridge, pp 70–137

Kurtz J (ed) (2016) Common exceptions and derogations. In: The WTO and international investment law: converging systems. Cambridge University Press, Cambridge, pp 168–228

Kwak K, Marceau G (2003) Overlaps and conflicts of jurisdiction between the World Trade Organization and regional trade agreements. Can Yearb Int Law 41:83–152

Lazo RP, Sauvé P (2018) The treatment of regulatory convergence in preferential trade agreements. World Trade Rev 17:575–607. https://doi.org/10.1017/S1474745617000519

Lenaerts K, Maselis I, Gutman K, Nowak JT (2014) EU procedural law, 1st edn. Oxford University Press, Oxford

Lindroos A (2005) Dispelling the chimera of 'self-contained regimes' international law and the WTO. Eur J Int Law 16:857–877. https://doi.org/10.1093/ejil/chi148

Lugg A, Lund N, Allee T, Elsig M (2019) Determining the authorship of preferential trade agreements: a new technique using a supervised author topic model v2.0. In: The political economy of international organization. Salzburg

Majone G (2006) The common sense of European integration. J Eur Public Policy 13:607–626. https://doi.org/10.1080/13501760600808212

Malamud A (2010) Theories of regional integration and the origins of MERCOSUR. In: Filho MTF, Lixinski L, Olmos Giupponi MB (eds) The law of MERCOSUR. Hart, Oxford, pp 9–27

Maletić I (2013) The law and policy of harmonisation in Europe's internal market. Edward Elgar, Cheltenham

Marceau G (1999) A call for coherence in international law—praises for the prohibition against 'clinical isolation' in WTO dispute settlement. J World Trade 87–152

Marceau G, Izaguerri A, Lanovoy V (2013) The WTO's influence on other dispute settlement mechanisms: a lighthouse in the storm of fragmentation. J World Trade 47:481–574

Marceau G, Wyatt J (2010) Dispute settlement regimes intermingled: regional trade agreements and the WTO. J Int Dispute Settlement 1:67–95. https://doi.org/10.1093/jnlids/idp009

Mathis JH (2001) Regional trade agreements in the GATT/WTO: Article XXIV and the internal trade requirement. T.M.C. Asser Press, Den Haag

Mavroidis P (2007) Trade in goods: an analysis of international trade agreements. Oxford University Press, Incorporated, Oxford

Mavroidis PC (2005) The general agreement on tariffs and trade: a commentary. Oxford University Press, Oxford

Mavroidis PC, Sapir A (2015) Dial PTAs for peace: the influence of preferential trade agreements on litigation between trading partners. J World Trade 49:351–372

Mbengue MM (2016) The settlement of trade disputes: is there a monopoly for the WTO? Law Pract Int Courts Tribunals 15:207–248. https://doi.org/10.1163/15718034-12341320

Meissner KL, McKenzie L (2019) The paradox of human rights conditionality in EU trade policy: when strategic interests drive policy outcomes. J Eur Public Policy 26:1273–1291. https://doi.org/10.1080/13501763.2018.1526203

Melillo M (2019) Informal dispute resolution in preferential trade agreements. J World Trade 53:95–127

Mitchell AD (2008) Legal principles in WTO disputes. Cambridge University Press, Cambridge

Morin J-F, Jinnah S (2018) The untapped potential of preferential trade agreements for climate governance. Environ Polit 27:541–565. https://doi.org/10.1080/09644016.2017.1421399

Navarro PE, Rodríguez JL (2014) Deontic logic and legal systems. Cambridge University Press, Cambridge

Nken M, Yildiz HM (2021) Implications of multilateral tariff bindings on the extent of preferential trade agreement formation. Econ Theory. https://doi.org/10.1007/s00199-020-01338-1

Nwobike C (2008) The WTO compatible ACP-EU trade partnership: interpreting the reciprocity requirement to further development. Asper Rev Int Bus Trade Law 8:87–124

Ochieng CMO (2007) The EU–ACP economic partnership agreements and the 'development question': constraints and opportunities posed by Article XXIV and special and differential treatment provisions of the WTO. J Int Econ Law 10:363–395. https://doi.org/10.1093/jiel/jgm009

O'Keefe TA (2000) The Central American Integration System (SICA) at the dawn of a new century: will the Central American Isthmus finally be able to achieve economic and political unity? Florida J Int Law 13:243–262

Olson M (2012) The logic of collective action public goods and the theory of groups. Harvard University Press, Cambridge

Organisation for Economic Co-operation and Development (2003) Regionalism and the multilateral trading system. OECD Publishing, Paris

Ortino F (2004) Basic legal instruments for the liberalisation of trade: a comparative analysis of EC and WTO law. Hart, Oxford

Panagariya A (2000) Preferential trade liberalization: the traditional theory and new developments. J Econ Lit 38:287–331. https://doi.org/10.1257/jel.38.2.287

Pauwelyn J (2003) Conflict of norms in public international law: how WTO law relates to other rules of international law. Cambridge University Press, Cambridge

Pauwelyn J (2004) The puzzle of WTO safeguards and regional trade agreements. J Int Econ Law 7:109–142. https://doi.org/10.1093/jiel/7.1.109

Pauwelyn J (2019) WTO Dispute Settlement Post 2019: what to expect? J Int Econ Law 22:297–321. https://doi.org/10.1093/jiel/jgz024

Pauwelyn J (2005) Rien ne Va Plus – distinguishing domestic regulation from market access in GATT and GATS. World Trade Rev 4:131–170

Pauwelyn J, Alschner W (2014) Forget about the WTO: The network of relations between PTAs and 'Double PTAs'. SSRN Electron J 39. https://doi.org/10.2139/ssrn.2391124

Pelc KJ (2016) Making and bending international rules: the design of exceptions and escape clauses in trade law. Cambridge University Press, Cambridge

Perišin T (2008) Free movement of goods and limits of regulatory autonomy in the EU and WTO. T.M.C. Asser Press, Den Haag

Peters A (2017) The refinement of international law: from fragmentation to regime interaction and politicization. Int J Constitutional Law 15:671–704. https://doi.org/10.1093/icon/mox056

Petersen J (2009) Max Webers Rechtssoziologie und die juristische Methodenlehre. De Gruyter, Berlin

Pétursson GT (2018) Article 11 [Quantitative restrictions on imports and measures having equivalent effect] Quantitative restrictions on imports. In: Agreement on the European economic area, a commentary. Nomos Verlagsgesellschaft mbH & Co. KG, München, pp 289–299

Piérola Castro NFN (2006) Solución de diferencias ante la OMC: presente y perspectivas. Cameron May, London

Pizzolo C (2010) Derecho e integración regional: Comunidad Andina, Mercosur, SICA, Unión Europea, 1st edn. EDIAR, Buenos Aires

Poiares Maduro M (1998a) The saga of Article 30 EC Treaty: to be continued. Maastricht J Eur Comp Law 5:298–316

Poiares Maduro M (1998b) We the court: The European Court of Justice and The European Economic Constitution. Hart, Oxford

Porges A (2011) Dispute settlement. In: Preferential trade agreement policies for development. The World Bank, pp 467–501

Posner RA (2004) Legal pragmatism. Metaphilosophy 35:147–159. https://doi.org/10.1111/j.1467-9973.2004.00310.x

Possi A (2018) An appraisal of the functioning and effectiveness of the East African Court of Justice. PER 21:1–42. https://doi.org/10.17159/1727-3781/2018/v21i0a2311

Prost M (2012) The concept of unity in public international law. Hart, Oxford

Raiser T (2008) Max Weber und die Rationalität des Rechts. JuristenZeitung 63: 853–859. https://doi.org/10.1628/002268808785849654

Raygada PSL (2003) Libre comercio de bienes en la Comunidad Andina – Eliminación de gravámenes y restricciones. Derecho & Sociedad 302–311

Reich N (2017) Francovich enforcement analysed and illustrated by German (and English) law. In: Jakab A, Kochenov D (eds) The enforcement of EU law and values. Oxford University Press, Oxford

Rejanovinschi M (2017) Hacia la protección del consumidor en la comunidad andina. Anuario de Investigación del CICAJ 2016

Reyes Tagle Y (2018) El impacto de la jurisprudencia del Tribunal de Justicia de la Unión Europea en la definición del principio de libre circulación de mercancías en la Comunidad Andina y el Mercosur. Agenda Internacional 25:235–256. https://doi.org/10.18800/agenda.201801.012

Reyes Tagle Y (2012) Free movement of goods in the Andean Community: how far can Dassonville go? SSRN Electron J. https://doi.org/10.2139/ssrn.2618403

Reyes Tagle Y (2014) The free movement of goods in MERCOSUR: developing a European Court of Justice approach in MERCOSUR? SSRN Electron J. https://doi.org/10.2139/ssrn.2618408

Rigod B (2013) Enforcement of the WTO 'regional exceptions': a comparative institutional analysis. In: Cremona M, Hilpold P, Lavranos N et al (eds) Reflections on the constitutionalisation of international economic law: Liber Amicorum for Ernst-Ulrich Petersmann. Nijhoff, Leiden, pp 425–439

Roberts A, Stephan PB, Verdier P-H, Versteeg M (2018) Conceptualizing comparative international law. In: Roberts A, Stephan PB, Verdier P-H, Versteeg M (eds) Comparative international law. Oxford University Press, New York, pp 3–31

Rodríguez Mendoza M, Low P, Kotschwar B (eds) (1999) Trade rules in the making: challenges in regional and multilateral negotiations. Organization of American States. Brookings Institution Press, Washington, D.C.

Rojas Penso P (2004) Nuevas Perspectivas Para La Solución De Controversias En La Asociación Latinoamericana De Integración (ALADI). In: Conference on International Trade Dispute Settlement, Lacarte Muró JA, Granados J (eds) Solución de controversias comerciales inter-gubernamentales: enfoques multilaterales y regionales. Instituto para la Integración de América Latina y el Caribe (BID-INTAL), Buenos Aires

Rosen H (2004) Ch 3, Free trade agreements as foreign policy tools: the US-Israel and US-Jordan FTAs. In: Schott JJ (ed) Free trade agreements: US strategies and priorities. Peterson Institute for International Economics, Washington, DC, pp 51–78

Rosenstock J, Singelnstein T, Boulanger C (2019) Versuch über das Sein und Sollen der Rechtsforschung: Bestandsaufnahme eines interdisziplinären Forschungsfeldes. In: Boulanger C, Rosenstock J, Singelnstein T (eds)

Interdisziplinäre Rechtsforschung. Springer Fachmedien Wiesbaden, Wiesbaden, pp 3–29

Sacerdoti G (2008) WTO law and the 'fragmentation' of international law: specificity, integration, conflicts. In: Janow ME, Donaldson V, Yanovich A (eds) The WTO: governance, dispute settlement and developing countries. Juris Publishing, Huntington, NY, pp 595–609

Sacerdoti G (2015) Resolution of international trade disputes in the WTO and other Fora. J Int Trade Law Policy 14:147–156. https://doi.org/10.1108/JITLP-11-2015-0036

Sachs NM (2011) Rescuing the strong precautionary principle from its critics. Univ Illinois Law Rev 2011:1285–1338

Saluste M, Hoekman BM (2021) Informing WTO reform: dispute settlement performance, 1995–2020. J World Trade 55

Sasaki Otani MÁ (2012) El sistema de sanciones por incumplimiento en el ámbito de la Comunidad Andina. Anuario Mexicano de Derecho Internacional 1. https://doi.org/10.22201/iij.24487872e.2012.12.400

Sauvé P (2019) To fuse, not to fuse, or simply confuse? Assessing the case for normative convergence between goods and services trade law. J Int Econ Law 22:355–371. https://doi.org/10.1093/jiel/jgz022

Scharpf F (1998) Negative and positive integration in the political economy of European welfare states. In: Rhodes M, Mény Y (eds) The future of European welfare: a new social contract? Palgrave Macmillan, London, pp 157–177

Schroeder W (2016) Transatlantic free trade agreements and European food standards. Eur Food Feed Law Rev (EFFL) 11:494–501

Schwartz WF, Sykes AO (1996) Toward a positive theory of the most favored nation obligation and its exceptions in the WTO/GATT system. Int Rev Law Econ 16:27–51. https://doi.org/10.1016/0144-8188(95)00053-4

Seinecke R (2015) Das Recht des Rechtspluralismus. Mohr Siebeck, Tübingen

Siems M (2018) The comparative legal method. In: Comparative law. Cambridge University Press, Cambridge, pp 15–49

Skouris V (2005) The ECJ and the EFTA Court under the EEA Agreement: a paradigm for international cooperation between judicial institutions. In: The EFTA Court: ten years on. Hart, Oxford, pp 123–129

Slaughter A-M (2003) A global community of courts focus: emerging fora for international litigation (part 2). Harv Int Law J 191–220

Slaughter A-M (1994) A typology of transjudicial communication symposium: human rights international law. Univ Richmond Law Rev 29:99–138

Smith JM (2000) The politics of dispute settlement design: explaining legalism in regional trade pacts. Int Organ 54:137–180

Snell J (2002) Goods and services in EC law: a study of the relationship between the freedoms, 1st edn. Oxford University Press, Oxford

Snell J (2010) The notion of market access: a concept or a slogan? Common Mark Law Rev 47:437–472

Sopranzetti S (2018) Overlapping free trade agreements and international trade: a network approach. World Econ 41:1549–1566. https://doi.org/10.1111/twec.12599

Stephenson SM (2010) Services trade in the western hemisphere: liberalization, integration, and reform. Brookings Institution Press, Washington D.C.

Sunstein CR (1993) Incommensurability and valuation in law. Mich Law Rev 92: 779–861

Susani N (2010) Dispute settlement. In: Filho MTF, Lixinski L, Olmos Giupponi MB (eds) The law of MERCOSUR. Hart, Oxford

Sweet AS, Mathews J (2008) Proportionality balancing and global constitutionalism. Columbia J Transnatl Law 47:72–164

Talavera FN, Carias ARB, Bernieri JC et al (2003) Derecho comunitario andino. Fondo Editorial – Pontificia Universidad Católica del Perú – Instituto de Estudios Internacionales, Cercado de Lima

Tamanaha BZ (2004) On the rule of law: history, politics, theory. Cambridge University Press, Cambridge

Trachtman JP (2003) Toward open recognition? Standardization and regional Integration under Article XXIV of GATT. J Int Econ Law 6:459–492

Trachtman JP (2011) The limits of PTAs. In: Bagwell KW, Mavroidis PC (eds) Preferential trade agreements. Cambridge University Press, Cambridge, pp 115–149

United Nations Conference on Trade and Development (2019) The shifting contours of trade under hyperglobalization. In: Trade and Development Report 2018. UN, pp 35–67

Valcke C (2018) Comparing law: comparative law as reconstruction of collective commitments, 1st edn. Cambridge University Press

Van den Bossche P (2005) The law and policy of the World Trade Organization: text, cases and materials. Cambridge University Press, Cambridge

Vidigal G (2017) Why is there so little litigation under free trade agreements? Retaliation and adjudication in international dispute settlement. J Int Econ Law 20:927–950. https://doi.org/10.1093/jiel/jgx037

Viner J (1924) The most-favored-nation clause in American Commercial Treaties. J Polit Econ 32:101–129. https://doi.org/10.1086/253580

Viner J (2014) The customs union issue. Oxford University Press, New York

Voeten E (2010) Borrowing and nonborrowing among international courts. J Leg Stud 39:547–576. https://doi.org/10.1086/652460

Vogel D (2012) Chapter Two. Explaining regulatory policy divergence. In: The politics of precaution. Princeton University Press, Princeton, pp 22–42

Walker N (2008) Beyond boundary disputes and basic grids: mapping the global disorder of normative orders. Int J Constitutional Law 6:373–396. https://doi.org/10.1093/icon/mon016

Walker N (2002) The idea of constitutional pluralism. Mod Law Rev 65:317–359. https://doi.org/10.1111/1468-2230.00383

Waltermann A, Arosemena G, Hage J (2020) Exceptions in international law. In: Bartels L, Paddeu F (eds) Exceptions in international law. Oxford University Press, Oxford, pp 11–34

Weber M (2010) Max Weber-Gesamtausgabe, 1st edn. Mohr Siebeck, Tübingen

Weber M, Rheinstein M, Shils E (1954) Max Weber on law in economy and society. Harvard University Press, Cambridge

Weiler JHH (ed) (2001a) Cain and Abel—convergence and divergence in international trade law. In: The EU, the WTO, and the NAFTA: towards a common law of international trade? Oxford University Press, Oxford, pp 1–4

Weiler JHH (ed) (2001b) Epilogue: towards a common law of international trade. In: The EU, the WTO, and the NAFTA: towards a common law of international trade? Oxford University Press, Oxford, pp 201–222

Wein T (2001) Chapter 4. Consumer information problems – causes and consequences. In: Grundmann S, Kerber W, Weatherill S (eds) Party autonomy and the role of information in the internal market, 1st edn. De Gruyter, Berlin

Wennerås P (2017) Making effective use of Article 260 TFEU. In: Jakab A, Kochenov D (eds) The enforcement of EU law and values. Oxford University Press, Oxford

Winters LA (2017) The WTO and regional trading agreements: is it all over for multilateralism? In: Elsig M, Hoekman B, Pauwelyn J (eds) Assessing the World Trade Organization. Cambridge University Press, Cambridge, pp 344–375

World Trade Organization (ed) (2011) The WTO and preferential trade agreements: from co-existence to coherence. WTO, Geneva

Wüthrich S, Elsig M (2021) Challenged in Geneva: WTO litigation experience and the design of preferential trade agreements. Bus Polit 23:1–20. https://doi.org/10.1017/bap.2020.20

Yang S (2012) The key role of the WTO in settling its jurisdictional conflicts with RTAs. Chin J Int Law 11:281–319. https://doi.org/10.1093/chinesejil/jms036

Yang S (2014) The solution for jurisdictional conflicts between the WTO and RTAs: the forum choice clause. Mich State Int Law Rev 23:107–152

Zeng L (2021) New tendency of the regional trade agreements and its negative impacts on the Doha round. In: Contemporary international law and China's peaceful development. Springer, Singapore, pp 455–473

9.2   EU Materials and Decisions of the PTA-DSM of the EU

9.2.1   Materials

Complaint Form for Breach of EU Law – European Commission, available at https://ec.europa.eu/assets/sg/report-a-breach/complaints_en/ (last visited 3 September 2023).

Consolidated Version of the Treaty Establishing the European Atomic Energy Community, ECLI:12012A, vol. 2012/C 327/01.

Consolidated Version of the Treaty on the Functioning of the European Union, vol. 12016E/TXT, 1 March 2020.

Council Regulation (EC) No 338/97 of 9 December 1996 on the Protection of Species of Wild Fauna and Flora by Regulating Trade Therein, http://data. europa.eu/eli/reg/1997/338/2020-01-01, Council Regulation (EC), vol. No 338/97, 9 December 1996.

EU Pilot – European Commission, available at https://single-market-scoreboard.ec. europa.eu/enforcement-tools/eu-pilot_en (last visited 3 September 2023).

Treaty of Lisbon Amending the Treaty on European Union and the Treaty Establishing the European Community, 12007L/TXT, vol. 2007/C 306/01, 17 December 2007.

9.2.2 Decisions

CJEU, *Ahokainen and Leppik*, C-434/04; ECLI:EU:C:2006:609, 28 September 2006.

CJEU, *Ålands Vindkraft Ab v Energimyndigheten*, C-573/12; ECLI:EU:C:2014: 2037, 1 July 2014.

CJEU, *A-Punkt Schmuckhandels GmbH*, C-441/04; ECLI:EU:C:2006:141, 23 February 2006 12.

CJEU, *Aragonesa De Publicidad Exterior and Publivía*, C-1/90; ECLI:EU:C:1991: 327, 25 July 1991.

CJEU, *Ascafor and Asidac*, C-484/10; ECLI:EU:C:2012:113, 1 March 2012.

CJEU, *ATRAL SA*, C-14/02; ECLI:EU:C:2003:265, 8 May 2003.

CJEU, *Bellon*, C-42/90; ECLI:EU:C:1990:475, 13 December 1990.

CJEU, *Bluhme*, C-67/97; ECLI:EU:C:1998:584, 3 December 1998.

CJEU, *Brandsma*, C-293/94; ECLI:EU:C:1996:254, 27 June 1996.

CJEU, *Burmanier and Others*, C-20/03; ECLI:EU:C:2005:307, 26 May 2005.

CJEU, *Cacchiarelli and Stanghellini*, C-54/94; ECLI:EU:C:1995:56, 23 February 1995.

CJEU, *Canadian Oil Company Sweden Und Rantén*, C-472/14; ECLI:EU:C:2016: 171, 17 March 2016.

CJEU, *Celestini v Saar-Sektkellerei Faber*, C-105/94; ECLI:EU:C:1997:277, 5 June 1997.

CJEU, *CIA Security v Signalson and Securitel*, C-194/94; ECLI:EU:C:1996:172, 30 April 1996.

CJEU, *Commission v Austria*, C-28/09; ECLI:EU:C:2011:854, 21 December 2011 46.

CJEU, *Commission v Austria*, C-320/03; ECLI:EU:C:2005:684, 15 November 2005.

CJEU, *Commission v Belgium*, C-100/08; ECLI:EU:C:2009:537, 10 September 2009.

CJEU, *Commission v Belgium*, C-2/78; ECLI:EU:C:1979:128, 16 May 1979 27.

CJEU, *Commission v Belgium*, C-373/92; ECLI:EU:C:1993:227, 8 June 1993.

CJEU, *Commission v Denmark*, C-158/82; ECLI:EU:C:1983:317, 9 November 1983.

CJEU, *Commission v Denmark*, C-192/01; ECLI:EU:C:2003:492, 23 September 2003.

CJEU, *Commission v France*, C-188/84; ECLI:EU:C:1986:43, 28 January 1986.

CJEU, *Commission v France*, C-24/00; ECLI:EU:C:2004:70, 5 February 2004.

CJEU, *Commission v France*, C-344/90, 16 July 1992.

CJEU, *Commission v France*, C-55/99; ECLI:EU:C:2000:693, 14 December 2000.

CJEU, *Commission v Germany*, C-102/96; ECLI:EU:C:1998:529, 12 November 1998.

CJEU, *Commission v Germany*, C-141/07; ECLI:EU:C:2008:492, 11 September 2008.

CJEU, *Commission v Greece*, C-293/89; ECLI:EU:C:1992:324, 16 July 1992.

CJEU, *Commission v Greece*, C-375/90; ECLI:EU:C:1993:154, 27 April 1993.

CJEU, *Commission v Ireland*, C-74/82; ECLI:EU:C:1984:34, 31 January 1984.

CJEU, *Commission v Italy*, C-110/05; ECLI:EU:C:2009:66, 10 February 2009.

CJEU, *Commission v Italy*, C-112/97; ECLI:EU:C:1999:168, 25 March 1999.

CJEU, *Commission v Italy*, C-228/91; ECLI:EU:C:1993:206, 25 May 1993.

CJEU, *Commission v Italy*, C-249/92; ECLI:EU:C:1994:335, 20 September 1994.

CJEU, *Commission v Italy*, C-270/02; ECLI:EU:C:2004:78, 5 February 2004.

CJEU, *Commission v Italy*, C-7/61; ECLI:EU:C:1961:31, 19 December 1961.

CJEU, *Commission v Italy*, C-95/89; ECLI:EU:C:1992:323, 16 July 1992.

CJEU, *Commission v Lithuania*, C-61/12; ECLI:EU:C:2014:172, 20 March 2014.

CJEU, *Commission v Netherlands*, C-41/02; ECLI:EU:C:2004:762, 2 December 2004.

CJEU, *Commission v United Kingdom*, C-124/0; ECLI:EU:C:1983:30, 8 February 1983.

CJEU, *Conegate v HM Customs & Excise*, C-121/85; ECLI:EU:C:1986:114, 11 March 1986.

CJEU, *Criminal Proceedings v Wurmser and Others*, C-25/88; ECLI:EU:C:1989:187, 11 May 1989.

CJEU, *Dansk Denkavit v Danish Ministry of Agriculture*, C-29/87; ECLI:EU:C:1988:299, 14 June 1988.

CJEU, *De Peijper*, C-104/75; ECLI:EU:C:1976:67, 20 May 1976 27.

CJEU, *Delattre*, C-369/88; ECLI:EU:C:1991:137, 21 March 1991.

CJEU, *Denkavit Futtermittel v Minister Für Ernährung, Landwirtschaft Und Forsten*, C-251/78; ECLI:EU:C:1979:252, 8 November 1979.

CJEU, *Denkavit Futtermittel*, C-39/90; ECLI:EU:C:1991:267, 20 June 1991.

CJEU, *Evans Medical and Macfarlan Smith*, C-324/93; ECLI:EU:C:1995:84, 28 March 1995.

CJEU, *Frans-Nederlandse Maatschappij Voor Biologische Producten*, C-272/80; ECLI:EU:C:1981:312, 17 December 1981.

CJEU, *Gourmet International Products*, C-405/98; ECLI:EU:C:2001:135, 8 March 2001.

CJEU, *Graffione*, C-313/94; ECLI:EU:C:1996:450, 26 November 1996.

CJEU, *Greenham and Abel*, C-95/01; ECLI:EU:C:2004:71, 5 February 2004.

CJEU, *Grilli*, C-12/02; ECLI:EU:C:2003:538, 2 October 2003.

CJEU, *Groenveld v Produktschap Voor Vee En Vlees*, 15/79; ECLI:EU:C:1979:253, 8 November 1979.

CJEU, *Harpegnies*, C-400/96; ECLI:EU:C:1998:414, 17 September 1998.

CJEU, *Heijn*, C-94/83, ECLI:EU:C:1984:285, 25 April 1983 19.

CJEU, *Holdijk*, C-141/81; ECLI:EU:C:1982:122, 1 April 1982.

CJEU, *Humanplasma*, C-421/09; ECLI:EU:C:2010:760, 9 December 2010.

CJEU, *Keck and Mithouard*, C-267/91; C-268/91; ECLI:EU:C:1993:905, 24 November 1993.

CJEU, *Ko v De Agostini and TV-Shop*, C-34/95; ECLI:EU:C:1997:344, 9 July 1997.

CJEU, *Lahousse and Lavichy*, C-142/09; ECLI:EU:C:2010:694, 18 November 2010.

CJEU, *Lidl Magyarország*, C-132/08; ECLI:EU:C:2009:281, 30 April 2009.

CJEU, *LPO*, C-271/92; ECLI:EU:C:1993:214, 25 May 1993.

CJEU, *Medisanus*, C-296/15; ECLI:EU:C:2017:431, 8 June 2017.

CJEU, *Ministère Public v Mirepoix*, C-54/85; ECLI:EU:C:1986:123, 13 March 1986.

CJEU, *Ministère Public v Muller*, C-304/84; ECLI:EU:C:1986:194, 6 May 1986.

CJEU, *Monteil and Samanni*, C-60/89; ECLI:EU:C:1991:138, 21 March 1991.

CJEU, *National Farmers Union*, C-241/01; ECLI:EU:C:2002:604, 22 October 2002.

CJEU, *Nilsson and Others*, C-162/97; ECLI:EU:C:1998:554, 19 November 1998.

CJEU, *Oberkreisdirektor Des Kreises Borken and Another v Moormann*, C-190/87; ECLI:EU:C:1988:424, 20 September 1988.

CJEU, *Procureur De La République v Bouhelier*, 53/76; ECLI:EU:C:1977:17, 3 February 1977 10.

CJEU, *Procureur De La République v Gofette and Gilliard*, C-406/85; ECLI:EU:C:1987:274, 11 June 1987.

CJEU, *Procureur Du Roi v Dassonville*, 8/74; ECLI:EU:C:1974:82, 1974 17.

CJEU, *R v Maff, Ex Parte Compassion in World Farming*, C-1/96; ECLI:EU:C:1998:113, 19 March 1998.

CJEU, *Rewe v Bundesmonopolverwaltung Für Branntwein*, 120/78; ECLI:EU:C:1979:42, 20 February 1979.

CJEU, *Rewe-Zentralfinanz v Landwirtschaftskammer*, C-4/75; ECLI:EU:C:1975:98, 8 July 1975.

CJEU, *Richardt and 'Les Accessoires Scientifiques'*, C-367/89; ECLI:EU:C:1991:376, 4 October 1991.

CJEU, *Sandström*, C-433/05; ECLI:EU:C:2010:184, 15 April 2010.

CJEU, *Schloh v Auto Contrôle Technique*, C-50/85; ECLI:EU:C:1986:244, 12 June 1986.

CJEU, *Schreiber*, C-443/02; ECLI:EU:C:2004:453, 15 July 2004.

CJEU, *Schwarz*, C-366/04, 24 November 2005.

CJEU, *Simmenthal v Italian Minister for Finance*, C-35/76; ECLI:EU:C:1976:180, 15 December 1976.

CJEU, *Slovak Republic v Achmea*, C-284/16; ECLI:EU:C:2018:158, 6 March 2018.

CJEU, *Solgar Vitamin's France and Others*, C-446/08; ECLI:EU:C:2010:233, 29 April 2010 31.

CJEU, *Spain v Council*, C-350/92; ECLI:EU:C:1995:237, 13 July 1995.

CJEU, *The Scotch Whisky Association*, C-333/14; ECLI:EU:C:2015:845, 23 December 2015.

CJEU, *Torfaen Borough Council v B & Q Plc*, C-145/88; ECLI:EU:C:1989:593, 23 November 1989.

CJEU, *Tridon*, C-510/99; ECLI:EU:C:2001:559, 23 October 2001.

CJEU, *United Foods and Van Den Abeele v Belgium*, C-132/80; ECLI:EU:C:1981: 87, 7 April 1981.

CJEU, *Van Bennekom*, C-227/82; ECLI:EU:C:1983:354, 30 November 1983.

CJEU, *Visnapuu*, C-198/14; ECLI:EU:C:2015:751, 12 November 2015.

9.3 EEA Materials and Decisions of the PTA-DSM of the EEA

9.3.1 Materials

Agreement Between the Efta States on the Establishment of a Surveillance Authority and a Court of Justice, OJ L 344, 31.1.1994, p. 3, vol. CELELX:E1994A1231 (01).

Agreement on the European Economic Area, OJ L 1, 3.1.1994, p. 3–522, vol. ECLI:21994A0103(74), 1 January 1994.

The Court, EFTA Court, available at https://eftacourt.int/the-court/ (last visited 3 September 2023).

9.3.2 Decisions

EFTA Court, *EFTA Surveillance Authority v. Iceland*, E-2/17, 14 November 2017.

EFTA Court, *EFTA Surveillance Authority v. Norway*, E-3/00, 5 April 2001.

EFTA Court, *Fagtún Ehf. and Byggingarnefnd Borgarholtsskóla, the Government of Iceland, the City of Reykjavík and the Municipality of Mosfellsbær*, E-5/98, 12 May 1999.

EFTA Court, *Ferskar Kjötvörur Ehf. and The Icelandic State*, E-17/15, 1 February 2016.

EFTA Court, *Pedicel AS and Sosial- Og Helsedirektoratet (Directorate for Health and Social Affairs)*, E-4/04, 25 February 2005 16.

EFTA Court, *Philip Morris Norway AS and The Norwegian State, Represented by the Ministry of Health and Care Services*, E-16/10, 12 September 2011.

EFTA Court, *Ravintoloitsijain Liiton Kustannus Oy Restamark*, E-1/94, 16 December 1994 19.

EFTA Court, *Tore Wilhelmsen AS and Oslo Kommune*, E-6/96, 27 June 1997.

EFTA Court, *Ullensaker Kommune and Others v. Nille AS*, E-5/96, 26 February 1997.

EFTA Court, *Vín Tríó Ehf. and the Icelandic State*, E-19/11, 30 November 2012.

9.4   CAN Materials and Decisions of the PTA-DSMs of the CAN

9.4.1   Materials

Acuerdo De Cartagena (Original), vol. Decisión 236, 15 July 1988.

Comisión, Decisión 425, 425, 14 December 1997.

Comisión, Decisión 456, Normas Para Prevenir o Corregir Las Distorsiones En La Competencia Generadas Por Prácticas de Dumping En Importaciones de Productos Originarios de Países Miembros de La Comunidad Andina, vol. Decisión 456, 4 May 1999.

Comunidad Andina, Decisión 563 Codificación del Acuerdo de Integración Subregional Andino (Acuerdo de Cartagena), Decision, vol. 563, 25 June 2003.

Comunidad Andina, Tratado de Creación del Tribunal de Justicia de la Comunidad Andina, 10 March 1996.

Decisión 623 Reglamento De La Fase Prejudicial De La Acción De Incumplimiento, Decisión 623, 16 July 2005.

Estatuto del Tribunal de Justicia de la Comunidad Andina, Decision, vol. 500.

Jurisprudencia, 20 April 2019, Tribunal de Justicia de la Comunidad Andina, available at https://www.tribunalandino.org.ec/index.php/jurisprudencia/ (last visited 3 September 2023).

Normativa Andina – Comunidad Andina, available at https://www.comunidadandina.org/normativa-andina/ (last visited 3 September 2023).

9.4.2   Decisions

JUNAC, *Resolución 379*, 27 September 1995 2.

JUNAC, *Resolución 397*, 18 March 1996.

SGCAN, *Resolución 047*, 23 January 1998.

SGCAN, *Resolución 1289*, 11 November 2009.

SGCAN, *Resolución 1564*, 14 April 2013.

SGCAN, *Resolución 1622*, 15 November 2013.
SGCAN, *Resolución 1695*, 6 June 2014.
SGCAN, *Resolución 1716*, 18 August 2014.
SGCAN, *Resolución 184*, 29 January 1999.
SGCAN, *Resolución 201*, 15 March 1999.
SGCAN, *Resolución 2019*, 14 August 2018.
SGCAN, *Resolución 209*, 24 March 1999.
SGCAN, *Resolución 230*, 21 May 1999.
SGCAN, *Resolución 248*, 8 July 1999.
SGCAN, *Resolución 308*, 27 October 1999.
SGCAN, *Resolución 407*, 22 June 2000.
SGCAN, *Resolución 440*, 9 October 2000.
SGCAN, *Resolución 449*, 2 November 2000.
SGCAN, *Resolución 449*, 2 November 2000.
SGCAN, *Resolución 453*, 20 November 2000.
SGCAN, *Resolución 489*, 9 March 2001.
SGCAN, *Resolución 570*, 30 November 2001.
SGCAN, *Resolución 576*, 12 December 2001.
SGCAN, *Resolución 638*, 3 July 2002.
SGCAN, *Resolución 681*, 20 December 2002.
SGCAN, *Resolución 710*, 21 March 2003.
SGCAN, *Resolución 739*, 7 July 2003.
SGCAN, *Resolución 757*, 29 August 2003.
SGCAN, *Resolución 759*, 29 August 2003.
SGCAN, *Resolución 784*, 6 November 2003.
SGCAN, *Resolución 823*, 5 May 2004.
SGCAN, *Resolución 897*, 4 February 2005.
SGCAN, *Resolución 966*, 20 October 2005.
SGCAN, *Resolución 986*, 15 December 2005.
TCJAN, *125-AI-2004*, 13 July 2006.
TCJAN, *1-IP-90*, 19 September 1990.
TJCAN, *01-AN-2014*, 19 January 2017.
TJCAN, *02-AN-2015*, 26 August 2016.
TJCAN, *117-AI-2003*, 19 September 2006.
TJCAN, *12-AN-99*, 12-AN-99, 24 September 1999.
TJCAN, *1-AI-97*, 1-AI-97, 11 December 1997.
TJCAN, *1-AN-97*, 26 February 1998.
TJCAN, *241-IP-2015*, 12 June 2017 14.
TJCAN, *2-AN-98*, 2 June 2000.
TJCAN, *3-AI-96*, 3-AI-96, 24 March 1997.
TJCAN, *3-AI-97*, 8 December 1998.
TJCAN, *43-AI-99*, 13 October 2000.
TJCAN, *5-AN-97*, 8 June 1998.
TJCAN, *5-IP-90*, 22 July 1994.

9.5   Mercosur Materials and Decisions of the PTA-DSM of the EEA

9.5.1   Materials

Acuerdo de Alcance Parcial – Complementación Económica 18, 18, 29 November 1991.

CMC, Adecuación Regimen Automotriz Dec. 29/94, Resolución 29/94, vol. 26527_DEC_029–1994.

CMC, Arancel Externo Comun Dec. 07/94, Resolución 07/94, vol. 26418_DEC_007–1994.

CMC, Restricciones No Arancelarias Dec. 03/94, 26393_DEC_003–1994, vol. Resolución 03/94.

CMC, Restricciones No Arancelarias Dec. 27/07, vol. Resolución 27/07.

CMC, Sector Azucarero Dec. 19/94, Resolución 19/94, vol. 26498_DEC_019–1994.

Consejo Del Mercado Común, Reglamento Del Protocolo De Olivos Para La Solución De Controversias En El Mercosur, Decisión, vol. 37/03, 16 December 2003.

Laudos, MERCOSUR, available at https://www.mercosur.int/quienes-somos/solucion-controversias/laudos/ (last visited 3 September 2023).

MERCOSUR Countries, 3 September 2023, MERCOSUR, available at https://www.mercosur.int/en/about-mercosur/mercosur-countries/ (last visited 3 September 2023).

Protocolo de Olivos para la Solución de Controversias en el Mercosur, 18 February 2002.

Regimen de Adecuación, CMC 24/94.

Regimen de Adecuación, CMC 4/94.

Suspensión de Venezuela en el MERCOSUR, 5 August 2017.

Tratado De Montevideo, 12 August 1980.

Tratado Para La Constitucion De Un Mercado Común, 26 March 1991.

9.5.2   Decisions

Mercosur ad hoc arbitral panel (Brasília), Laudo "Obstáculos al Ingreso de Productos Fitosanitarios Argentinos En El Mercado Brasileño. No Incorporación de Las Resoluciones GMC Nº 48/96, 87/96, 149/96, 156/96 y 71/98 Lo Que Impide Su Entrada En Vigencia En El MERCOSUR", 19 April 2002.

Mercosur ad hoc arbitral panel (Brasília), Laudo "Aplicación De Medidas Anti-dumping Contra La Exportación De Pollos Enteros, Provenientes De Brasil, Resolución Nº 574/2000 Del Ministerio De Economía De La República Argentina", 21 May 2001.

Mercosur ad hoc arbitral panel (Brasília), Laudo "Aplicación De Medidas De Salvaguardia Sobre Productos Textiles (Res. 861/99) Del Ministerio De Economia Y Obras Y Servicios Publicos", 2 March 2000.

Mercosur ad hoc arbitral panel (Brasília), Laudo "Prohibición de Importación de Neumáticos Remoldeados (Remolded) Procedentes de Uruguay", 9 January 2002.

Mercosur ad hoc arbitral panel (Brasília), Laudo "Subsidios a La Produccion Y Exportacion De Carne De Cerdo", 27 September 1999.

Mercosur ad hoc arbitral panel (Brasília), Laudo "Prohibición de Importación de Neumáticos Remodelados", 25 October 2005.

Mercosur ad hoc arbitral panel (Brasília), Laudo Arbitral "Controversia Sobre Comunicados N° 37 Del 17 de Diciembre de 1997 y N° 7 Del 20 de Febrero de 1998 Del Departamento de Operaciones de Comercio Exterior (DECEX) de La Secretaría de Comercio Exterior (SECEX): Aplicación de Medidas Restrictivas al Comercio Recíproco", 28 April 1999.

Mercosur ad hoc arbitral panel (Olivos), Laudo "Omisión Del Estado Argentino En Adoptar Medidas Aprobadas Para Prevenir y/o Hacer Cesar Los Impedimentos a La Libre Circulación Derivados de Los Cortes En Territorio Argentino de Vías de Acceso a Los Puentes Internacionales GRAL. San Martín y GRAL. Artigas Que Unen La República Argentia Con La República Oriental Del Uruguay", 6 September 2006.

TPR, Laudo N°01/2005, 20 December 2005.

TPR, Laudo N°01/2006, 13 January 2006.

TPR, Laudo N°01/2007, 8 July 2007.

TPR, Laudo N°01/2008, 25 April 2008.

TPR, Laudo N°02/2006, 6 July 2006.

9.6   GATT/WTO Legal Acts and Decisions of GATT Panels of the WTO-DSM

9.6.1   Materials

Committee on Regional Trade Agreements, Factual Presentation – Accession of Panama to the Central American Common Market (CACM) – Goods – Report by the Secretariat – Revision, 12 April 2019.

Marrakesh Agreement Establishing the World Trade Organization, vol. LT/UR/A/2, 15 April 1994.

Understanding on Rules and Procedures Governing the Settlement of Disputes, vol. LT/UR/A-2/DS/U/1.

WTO Secretariat/RTA Section, FACTS&FIGURES Regional Trade Agreements1 July 2020 – 1 January 2021 1 July 2020 – 1 January 2021.

WTO, *Database on Preferential Trade Arrangements*, WTO – Preferential Trade Arrangements, available at http://ptadb.wto.org/default.aspx (last visited 3 September 2023).

WTO, Differential and More Favourable Treatment Reciprocity and Fuller Participation of Developing Countries ('Enabling Clause'), vol. L/4903, 28 November 1979.

WTO, User Guide of the Regional Trade Information System, 23 April 2019.

WTO, *WTO|Regional Trade Agreements Gateway*, Regional Trade Agreements, available at https://www.wto.org/english/tratop_e/region_e/region_e.htm#rules_ita (last visited 3 September 2023).

9.6.2 Decisions

GATT Panel, European Communities — Tariff Treatment on Imports of Citrus Products from Certain Countries in the Mediterranean Region, L/5776, 7 February 1985.

GATT Panel, Spain — Tariff Treatment of Unroasted Coffee, L/5135-28S/102, 11 June 1981.

WTO Appellate Body, Argentina — Safeguard Measures on Imports of Footwear (EC), WT/DS121/AB/R, 14 December 1999.

WTO Appellate Body, Brazil — Measures Affecting Imports of Retreaded Tyres, WT/DS332/AB/R, 3 December 2007.

WTO Appellate Body, European Communities — Regime for the Importation, Sale and Distribution of Bananas Second Recourse to Article 21.5 of the DSU by Ecuador, WT/DS27/AB/RW2/ECU; WT/DS27/AB/RW/USA, 26 November 2008.

WTO Appellate Body, Mexico — Tax Measures on Soft Drinks and Other Beverages, WT/DS308/AB/R, 6 March 2006.

WTO Appellate Body, Peru — Additional Duty on Imports of Certain Agricultural Products, WT/DS457/AB/R, 20 July 2015.

WTO Appellate Body, Turkey — Restrictions on Imports of Textile and Clothing Products, WT/DS34/AB/R, 22 October 1999.

WTO Appellate Body, United States — Definitive Safeguard Measures on Imports of Certain Steel Products, WT/DS166/AB/R, 22 December 2000.

WTO Appellate Body, United States — Definitive Safeguard Measures on Imports of Circular Welded Carbon Quality Line Pipe from Korea, WT/DS202/AB/R, 15 February 2002.

WTO Panel, Argentina — Definitive Anti-Dumping Duties on Poultry from Brazil, WT/DS241/R, 22 April 2003.

WTO Panel, Argentina — Safeguard Measures on Imports of Footwear (EC), WT/DS121R, 25 June 1999.

WTO Panel, Brazil — Measures Affecting Imports of Retreaded Tyres, WT/DS332/R, 12 June 2007.

WTO Panel, Canada — Certain Measures Affecting the Automotive Industry, WT/DS139/R WT/DS142/R, 11 February 2000.

WTO Panel, Colombia — Indicative Prices and Restrictions on Ports of Entry (Panel), WT/DS366, 27 April 2009.

WTO Panel, European Communities — Conditions for the Granting of Tariff Preferences to Developing Countries, WT/DS246/R, 1 December 2003.

WTO Panel, European Communities — Measures Affecting the Approval and Marketing of Biotech Products (Panel), WT/DS291, 29 September 2006.

WTO Panel, European Communities — Measures Concerning Meat and Meat Products (Hormones) Complaint by Canada, WT/DS26/R/CAN, 18 August 1997.

WTO Panel, Indonesia — Safeguard on Certain Iron or Steel Products, WT/DS490/R; WT/DS496/R, 18 August 2017.

WTO Panel, Turkey — Restrictions on Imports of Textile and Clothing Products, WT/DS34/R, 31 May 1999.

WTO Panel, United States — Definitive Safeguard Measures on Imports of Certain Steel Products, WT/DS166/R, 31 July 2000.

WTO Panel, United States — Definitive Safeguard Measures on Imports of Circular Welded Carbon Quality Line Pipe from Korea, WT/DS202/R, 29 October 2001.

WTO Panel, United States — Sections 301–310 of the Trade Act of 1974, WT/DS152/R, 22 December 1999.

Correction to: Annex

Correction to:
Chapter 8 in: P. Wasilczyk, *Fragmentation of International Trade Law Reassessed*, EYIEL Monographs - Studies in European and International Economic Law 32, https://doi.org/10.1007/978-3-031-40601-0_8

The original version of the book was inadvertently published with wrong date format in sections 8.2.1.1 and 8.2.1.3 of chapter 8. The date format has now been corrected.

The updated version of this chapter can be found at
https://doi.org/10.1007/978-3-031-40601-0_8

Printed by Printforce, the Netherlands